Keynes and the Trogoautoegocrat

Second Edition

A Discussion of Macroeconomics for the Student of the Gurdjieff Work*

By Daniel Bright M.D.

*The Gurdjieff Work, also known as "The Fourth Way", was introduced by G.I. Gurdjieff in the first half of the 1900's. It is a teaching and practice of a way of self-development taught to a small group of students and still practiced today by various groups. There are a number of books available, that describe the teachings, both written by Gurdjieff himself, as well as some students of the work, who may outline their own understanding as well as personal experiences. This book is intended for people with familiarity with the teachings and terminology of Gurdjieff.

Keynes and the Trogoautoegocrat
A Discussion of Macroeconomics for the Student of the Gurdjieff Work*
Second Edition
All Rights Reserved.
Copyright © 2021 Daniel Bright M.D.
v2.0

The opinions expressed in this manuscript are solely the opinions of the author and do not represent the opinions or thoughts of the publisher. The author has represented and warranted full ownership and/or legal right to publish all the materials in this book.

This book may not be reproduced, transmitted, or stored in whole or in part by any means, including graphic, electronic, or mechanical without the express written consent of the publisher except in the case of brief quotations embodied in critical articles and reviews.

ISBN: 978-1-7328348-5-9

Library of Congress Control Number: 2020924953

Cover Photo © 2021 Daniel Bright M.D. All rights reserved - used with permission.

Daniel Bright

PRINTED IN THE UNITED STATES OF AMERICA

2nd Edition

The Work, often called "The Gurdjieff Work", is a form of work on oneself that has much in common with other forms of work on oneself such as esoteric branches of major religions including Judaism, Christianity (Gurdjieff, in fact, called his work "esoteric Christianity"), Islam (usually thought of as Sufism), Taoism, Buddhism, and so on. It also has much in common with philosophy (such as Hindu-Yoga philosophy, Taoist philosophy, Buddhist philosophy, and others). This is not to say that the Gurdjieff Work is not also unique, just as are all the forms of work on oneself. They are uniquely themselves and, at the same time, have much in common with one another. This is all by way of saying that the perspective offered in Dan Bright's book, which demonstrates an essential relationship between the Gurdjieff Work and Dan's understanding of the work of Keynes, is relevant in a similar way to these other forms of work on oneself as well as the system taught by Gurdjieff. I say this as a person who has been utilizing and teaching the Gurdjieff Work as well as many aspects of each of the others mentioned here for over 50 years. May you who go as far as to "cut these pages, and actually read them," as Gurdjieff might say, gain the benefit of the knowledge and wisdom they contain.

Dr. David M Brahinsky

Table of Contents

Introduction		i
Chapter 1	Supply and Demand in a Barter Economy	1
Chapter 2	Some Fundamental Definitions	6
Chapter 3	What is The Money Supply and How Does Money Move Through the Banking System?	22
Chapter 4	The Money Multiplier	42
Chapter 5	What Are the Essential Functions of Banks?	50
Chapter 6	Permanently Increasing the Money Supply	55
Chapter 7	Going from Barter to Monetary Economies	63
Chapter 8	How Spending and Income Relates to Inflation, Production and the Money Supply	69
Chapter 9	Can an Economy with Deflation Maintain Its Level of Growth?	78
Chapter 10	A Look at How to Avoid an Inadequate Money Supply with Precious Metal Coins, Representative Money, or Fiat Money	83
Chapter 11	Atypical Types of Currencies	89
Chapter 12	Effective Demand	99
Chapter 13	Wealth, Savings, and "Net Income"	107
Chapter 14	The Forms of Wealth	116
Chapter 15	More discussion on how wealth and income are not the same thing	125
Chapter 16	Influencing the Level of Effective Demand	128
Chapter 17	Measuring Output	146

Chapter 18	More on Using the Expression "Net Production"	148
Chapter 19	The Investment Multiplier	150
Chapter 20	Illustration of How Investment is Preserved as Savings	155
Chapter 21	Is Buying Current Production Consumption or Investment?	162
Chapter 22	Keynes, Phillips, and NAIRU	166
Chapter 23	More Discussion of the Ingredients of Excessive Inflation and the Explanation of Stagflation	178
Chapter 24	Marginal Efficiency of Capital	199
Chapter 25	Interest	204
Chapter 26	Does Investment Equal Savings?	208
Chapter 27	Monetary Policy	211
Chapter 28	Capital Goods	219
Chapter 29	GDP – The Production Approach	224
Chapter 30	GDP – The Income Approach	227
Chapter 31	GDP – The Expenditure Approach	232
Chapter 32	Calculating Different Multipliers Using Various Inputs Looking at the Effect of a Change from a Baseline	250
Chapter 33	The Multiplier Effect is Really About the Velocity of Money	254
Chapter 34	This Changes Everything	256
Chapter 35	Direct Spending	258
Chapter 36	Keynes' Multiplier Modified to Include the Effect of Loans and the Concept of Direct Spending	267
Chapter 37	Grow Like Crazy or Have a Depression?	285
Chapter 38	Choice of Units	294
Chapter 39	Flexible Wage vs Flexible Money Policy	296
Chapter 40	National Savings	307
Chapter 41	Uses of Savings	315
Chapter 42	Combining Private and Government into 'One Economy'	321
Chapter 43	Ricardian Equivalence and Debt Financed Government Spending	323
Chapter 44	Where You Spend Affects Total Income	332

Chapter 45	The Capital/Labor Split	336
Chapter 46	The Capital/Labor Split and The Solow Growth Model	341
Chapter 47	The Capital/Labor Split - Piketty Modified	361
Chapter 48	Zero Lower Bound	374
Chapter 49	Trade - Balance of Payments	381
Chapter 50	Trade - Currency Exchange	409
Chapter 51	Trade – an overview	417
Epilogue		445
Appendix A	The Employment Multiplier	446
Appendix B	Spending Directed at Causing Income for an Entity Versus Causing Income for a Human	451
Appendix C	Should the Expression for Savings Be:	452
Appendix D		454
Appendix E		456

Introduction

"This sacred 'antkooano' can take place only on those planets on which all cosmic truths have become known to all the beings there. And all cosmic truths become known to everyone on those planets because those beings, who by their conscious efforts learn some truth or other, share it with others, and in this way, little by little, all cosmic truths become known to all the beings of that planet, whatever may be their aspirations and degree of self-perfecting."[1]. This book started out as an attempt to understand the work of John Maynard Keynes (1883-1946), a famous and influential economist. I was originally attracted to Keynes' writings because his concepts reminded me of the concept of the trogoautoegocrat, as taught by Gurdjieff. I was also deeply moved by the hope that Keynes' theories inspired in me. Keynes' writings, however, are notoriously difficult to read, so my intention was not only to fully understand his concepts myself, but also to provide a study guide to make Keynes' ideas more accessible to others. This process was more difficult than I originally anticipated. Keynes was an explorer in a new land of economic concepts, and as such he was not able to fully develop every idea. Some of the ideas were not as fully generalized as they could be, while others were only partially correct. I believe that I have found ways to improve on the ideas, and so my study guide has become more than that. Additionally, I incorporate more recent economic theories that often have been presented as antithetical to or disproving Keynes' ideas. I attempt to show both how they do not disprove Keynes' work, and how they can be integrated with Keynes' discoveries.

What is the Trogoautoegocrat? Here is Gurdjieff's explanation: "This system, which maintains everything that arises and exists, was established by our Endless Creator to permit the 'exchange of substances,' or 'reciprocal feeding' of everything existing, to proceed in the Universe, so that the merciless Heropass would no longer have its maleficent effect on the Sun Absolute. This most great

---

1 Gurdjieff, G. I. Beelzebub's Tales to His Grandson (p. 515). Bookmasters. Kindle Edition.)

common-cosmic trogoautoegocratic process is actualized, always and in everything, on the basis of the two fundamental cosmic laws, the first of which is called 'the fundamental first-order sacred Heptaparaparshinokh,' and the second 'the fundamental first-order sacred Triamazikamno."[2] This quote states that the trogoautoegocrat is manifest through the law of 7 and the law of 3. The trogoautoegocrat, the law of reciprocal feeding, is described as a process whereby the interaction of various "cosmic" processes lead to constant creation and renewal. I contrast that to the concept of entropy. Entropy is considered a relentless, irreversible process whereby the universe becomes more and more disorganized, with a continuous loss of potential for accomplishing useful work.

As a trained psychiatrist I know that, in the mental health field, we are taught that people are born with a strong genetic predisposition, or that traits are developed early on in life, and that very little can be done to change. Whereas in the Gurdjieff Work we are taught that through conscious labors and intentional sufferings, personal transformation is possible. This process is presented as operating through the manifestations and understanding of the law of 7 and law of 3. Two concepts, the description of entropy as an inevitable irreversible process, and, on the personal level, that we are mostly stuck with ourselves the way we are, that is, the prevailing notion that, for people, only limited, mostly behavioral change is possible, and that deep characterological change is not a practical or realistic goal, engender in me feelings of helplessness and despair. It doesn't even make sense to me. Regarding entropy, if the only thing the universe is doing is slowly dying, how does it exist in the first place? And I cannot accept the idea that we have little to no possibility of personal growth and change. Thus, my attraction to the Gurdjieff Work.

This brings us to economics. Too much of what is commonly taught in Macroeconomics courses at the college level create in me a similar emotional reaction. Things are the way they are, we can't change them, if we try to implement policy to change the economic situation, we will only make it worse. "Nature" must take its course, we are stuck with what we got. Not according to Keynes. Keynes believed that through the proper understanding of financial interactions and the flow of money through the economy, we can effect positive change. This process, according to Keynes, requires much directed effort and understanding and involves the interaction of individuals and systems in a process of reciprocal feeding where, as Gurdjieff sometimes puts it, "one hand washes the other." Reciprocal feeding (the trogoautoegocratic process) is Central to every economic

---

2 Gurdjieff, G. I.. Beelzebub's Tales to His Grandson (p. 129). Bookmasters. Kindle Edition.

transaction. Overcoming challenges and resistances and obstacles is essential in achieving business goals and financial success. Being able to complete tasks, completing the octave, is essential. This means, as I will attempt to explain below, that a certain mastery of the law of three and the law of seven are needed to implement Keynes' discoveries successfully. To me, Keynes really discovered the manifestation of the trogoautoegocrat in Macroeconomic theory and practice.

I will occasionally use Gurdjieff's terminology in this book, when I feel it is applicable, but since my understanding of macroeconomics comes from studying John Maynard Keynes and other standard macroeconomics texts, I will be using mostly their terminology. However, I have found that some of the terms used by economists are not clearly or consistently defined or used. Therefore, I have needed to modify how some of the terms are defined and used. The definitions I give are precise and I will attempt to use them consistently throughout the text. I believe that the material in this book is accessible, with sufficient effort, to anyone who can do some very simple algebra. It is presented in a way that the concepts build upon one another, so it is recommended that one master the material in the order it is presented. The simpler concepts are presented earlier. The ideas become more complex towards the end of the book. My goal is to make the material straight forward and understandable to the interested reader.

Daniel Bright M.D.

If at any time while reading this book, you have questions, comments or criticisms or if you simply want to engage in a dialogue, please contact me at this email: Danbrightec@gmail.com

I will aspire to respond to the extent life circumstances allow.

Please note that this book is basically just a version of the book "Enlightened Capitalism: A Keynes Primer", modified and expanded for students of the Gurdjieff Work. The main difference in this second edition is an expanded treatment of International Trade.

CHAPTER 1
Supply and Demand in a Barter Economy

CONSIDER A SMALL community with a barter economy:

Everyone would contribute by producing some essential or desired commodity. They would then use what they produced to barter, to acquire other items to satisfy their needs or wants. If an individual produced more than they needed for that purpose, this would be comparable to building up savings, a reserve of items they could use for barter in the future.

In a monetary economy, building up wealth by increasing the holding of assets also occurs. But since, in the barter economy, the product, i.e., the assets, are in essence, the money, this is analogous to having the ability to print more money. In the barter system, when that extra supply decays, deteriorates, becomes obsolete or otherwise loses value in trade, it is equivalent to destroying money. If something no one wanted is produced, it is equivalent to producing zero money.

In the barter system, all the goods and services that are produced is 'the money supply.' It will either be "spent" (bartered) or "saved." If it is not used up, destroyed, deteriorates or becomes obsolete, the stored 'savings' makes society richer overall and also increases the money supply. This is different than a monetary economy, where having more goods stored up does make the society richer overall but does **not** increase the money supply. In a barter economy, we have a situation where all the product existing is considered as **both** the wealth and the "money supply", i.e., as the currency.

The "currency" or "money" in a barter economy is always being created and destroyed. Also, the currency in a barter economy has a 100 percent correlation to the product because it is the product. By this I mean, anyone who has wealth has

Supply and Demand in a Barter Economy

it in the form of product, which can be bartered.

"Demand"[3] in any economy means the amount which a society spends to purchase product. In a barter economy, demand is how much product people use in trade to obtain the products they desire. In a barter society all parties involved in the trade are producing demand. Each bartered item is payment for some item in return. However, in a barter, not only is each item payment, it is also the desired product the other party is paying for, and vice versa.

If Person One trades Item A to Person Two in return for Item B, then Item A is the demand, the spending Person One does in order to be supplied with desired Item B. Item A is how much Person One pays to be supplied with Item B. From Person Two's perspective, Item B is the demand, the spending Person Two does in order to be supplied with Item A. Item B then becomes the income for Person One and Item A becomes the income for Person Two. To put it another way, "demand" can be thought as what people are paying, and income is what the people are receiving in return.

If you look at the whole economy, demand will always equal income. Each item traded counts as both demand and income. That which they give is demand, and that which they are supplied in return is income.

To sum up: in a barter economy, everything is 100 percent paid for by production, and all the "money" is 100 percent correlated to "product" because it is the product. For a monetary economy it is a little different. What that means, from a macroeconomic perspective will be explored in detail as we go along.

Obviously, an economy based on a barter system is very coarse. It is an inefficient way to conduct transactions and requires people meeting one another and determining if what they have to trade is exactly what is wanted. It is also possible that people would have to go through multiple trades before being satisfied with the transaction. Further, all sorts of issues with transportation, storage and maintenance of the commodities would prevail that would slow the process and increase the expense of these transactions. Through the use of money, a lot of these complications are eliminated. Money has properties that allow it to be utilized more

---

3 In economics, usually when the word **demand** is used it is referring to the **actual spending** that pays for the purchase of the acquired items. That is the definition for demand I am using in this book. Many people will think of demand as the **desire** to do the spending to purchase the items. For macroeconomics, in the model I am presenting, demand is the actual spending, not the desire to acquire the items in question.

rapidly and efficiently and with less effort and expense. Since everyone accepts its value, it can be used to trade for any desired product or outcome, alleviating many of the complications of barter.

⌘

Barter appears to be a clear example, using Gurdjieff's terminology, of "living under more laws", meaning life is more complicated, more is required to accomplish what is desired or needed. In a monetary economy, on the other hand, we are living under fewer laws.

Gurdjieff introduced the idea of the centers, the physical or moving center, the emotional center and the intellectual center. He taught that each of these centers has its proper function and that people run into trouble when they try to force one center to take over or interfere with the work of another center. In addition, he taught that the centers themselves are divided by function into three parts. They also have a moving or automatic part, an emotional part, and an intellectual part. Gurdjieff also described higher being bodies like the emotional body and the intellectual body, that can develop in man on the basis of conscious labors and intentional sufferings, but I am not referring to those at this point.

Focusing in on the intellectual center, Gurdjieff refers to the automatic part of the intellectual center as the formatory apparatus. This part is expressed by automatic continuous thoughts that run through our heads more or less continuously and participate in many automatic functions that occur as a result of input from our other centers or from other parts of the intellectual center. The formatory apparatus functions in verbal expression, automatic habitual behaviors and automatic reactions to external stimuli, including human interactions. If the contribution by the intellectual center to our functioning came entirely from the formatory apparatus we would be, in Gurdjieff's terms, in "waking sleep", a form of consciousness below a level that he considers to be truly awake.

We also have, as part of the intellectual center, an emotional part and an intellectual part. I understand the emotional part of the intellectual center as the part that allows us to "feel around" the concept, try to make connections, try to understand relative relationships between different parts of the idea. The intellectual part of the intellectual center I understand to be that part of the intellectual center that can see the big picture and understand how everything fits together. To the extent that the intellectual part of intellectual center is utilized or able to be utilized by the individual, the intellectual part of the intellectual center can direct the emotional part of the intellectual center through exploring the connection between different parts of ideas or concepts and can also participate, along with the emotional part of the intellectual center in influencing and directing the functioning of the formatory apparatus and the other centers.

My understanding of this is that the more participation we have of these higher parts of the intellectual center, the more conscious and less mechanical we are. By less mechanical I mean that our actions, reactions and thoughts are influenced by being in contact with and aware of whatever process is currently occurring, both inside ourselves, including our thoughts and feelings, and outside ourselves, in the world.

More conscious and aware thinking requires more effort, but it puts us more in touch with reality. It allows us to adapt our strategies and plans to deal more intelligently with the obstacles or challenges we face. Gurdjieff speaks of our desires as "first force," and the obstacles to achieving them as "second force," thus more conscious and aware thinking enables us better to reconcile these two forces (bring in what he calls "third force").

A person who was putting more constant being effort into maintaining the level of awareness described above would not need to rely so much on rules and regulations to guide every reaction. For such an individual too many rules and regulations could become a hindrance to accomplishing essential tasks or achieving desired outcomes. That is how I understand Gurdjieff's idea of living under more laws and fewer laws.

Ouspensky quoting Gurdjieff:

"The fewer laws there are in a given world, the nearer it is to the will of the Absolute; the more laws there are in a given world, the greater the mechanicalness, the further it is from the will of the Absolute."[4]

In contrasting a monetary system to a barter system, I believe the monetary system represents an example of "living under fewer laws". I also believe that it requires some functioning of the higher parts of the intellectual center to understand **symbolism**, the idea that something can "represent" something other than itself. For example, for money to be useful, we must all have the capacity to understand that it represents the value of anything we are negotiating to purchase. We understand it as having value only because we have the capacity to make that connection. Now although, in our normal everyday function, this is something

---

4   Ouspensky, P.D.. In Search of the Miraculous (Kindle Locations 1872-1873). Kindle Edition.

that occurs quite automatically without much need for conscious effort, the actual development of and establishment of a monetary system was quite another story.

It is beyond the scope of this book to understand the history and development of our monetary system as it exists today, but it is my understanding that the development, understanding and establishment of monetary systems did not occur quickly, it took most of humanity's history to develop. It was a gradual transition. As trade became more common and especially as it began to occur over longer distances, traders, obviously limited by how much and what they could transport, would find certain items that were more favorable to transport and had more value in trade. Over time, what those items were, changed, but eventually became metal coins, often made of so called precious metals, and at some point paper IOU's became paper currency and gradually it progressed to become the system we have today.

Even though there was, and remains, much cruelty, conflict and misunderstanding in the evolution of the economic systems from pure barter to a monetary economy as we know it today, it could never have existed if not for the existence of integrity, trust, and the more noble human qualities that require a more conscious effort on our part.

This web site gives an interesting short history on the evolution of trade and the evolution of currencies from commodities to coins.[5]

As far as the development of our economic system goes, any knowledge, any technology, any scientific endeavor or field of study developed by humans is always in evolution. It is the people who study, master and utilize the knowledge that determine the results of the applications of such knowledge. The participants in the process can help it to evolve to a more conscious process or can cause it to involve or devolve (so to speak) into a more mechanical, less conscious process. Money and monetary systems are simply tools, and economics is a field of study. The direction the application of this tool and this knowledge takes us, is determined by the efforts of its students and practitioners. Keynes died in 1946, thus we have had the opportunity to study how this struggle has played out over a period of many decades since his death, a struggle in which we are all participants.

---

5   Https://www.quantinsti.com/blog/evolution-trading-barter-system-algo-trading

CHAPTER 2
Some Fundamental Definitions

This is one of the most important chapters in the book. To understand the rest of the book it is essential to understand this material. I recommend you go slowly through each section until the concepts are mastered. You may find it helpful to read through this chapter several times because, in order to be able to completely understand the material in the earlier part of the chapter you will have to understand the material in the later part of the chapter and vice versa.

IN CHAPTER ONE we saw that, in a barter economy there is no difference between money and product. The product **is** the money, and whenever new product is created more money is created. And when product is depleted, destroyed, or decays, then money is destroyed. Things are different in a monetary economy. **A barter economy could be described as a monetary economy with unlimited different currencies all of which are constantly interacting to determine their exchange rate.**

In a monetary economy we have one currency, that which we call money. We could, of course, have a few currencies but with exchange rates it amounts to a single currency. For simplicity sake as I develop my thesis I will initially focus on a monetary economy with one currency, examples of which would be dollars and cents, euros, rubles, etc. My study of a single currency monetary economy will be examining how that money moves through the economy and the effect it has.

Spending and **income** are equal, that is, income is the result of spending. In a monetary economy, spending is accomplished by money changing ownership.

Money is given by the spender, to the income earner, who is the recipient of the spending. A necessary and sufficient condition for income to occur is for spending to have occurred for a purpose. Spending and income are looking at the same process from two different perspectives.

Here it must be understood that spending for a purpose means that the person spending is attempting to purchase something of value, a product. The word "product" is here used in a very general way and includes any desired outcome that one is paying for. This includes paying for goods or services, but also includes paying for labor or for any other desired outcome. The desired outcome is "the product", at least to the extent that the desired outcome is achieved. Whether the desired outcome is achieved or not the spending still occurs, and income equals the amount of spending. For some spending, achieving the desired outcome is likely, such as buying something at the store. For other spending, achieving the desired outcome is more uncertain, such as donating for research to find a treatment for a disease. Both are spending, and both create income for the recipients.

Money is defined and quantified in terms of the specified currencies, therefore the terms **money** and **currency** will be used interchangeably. I will refer to money or currency or in certain examples I will use the name of the specific currency, such as dollars.

In this discussion of macroeconomics when I speak of "the economy" I am referring to the whole economy, which usually means the economy of a given country; the country that utilizes and maintains the money supply of one specific currency. Although economies from different countries do interact, I am not including that in the analysis at this point.

When we do accounting, in macroeconomics, it is always done for a given specified time period. I will frequently use the term "for a given time period" to remind us that everything is defined only in reference to the start and end points of that time period.

Let us start with a thought exercise:

Over a certain period of time, the output that is produced by the whole economy leads to sales producing a certain revenue. Now let us suppose the revenue gained from the sales goes into paying the income of everyone involved in the

Some Fundamental Definitions

economy. Let us further suppose that there is NO other income, that this is the only income people get for that time period.

Then let us also suppose that the sales must be totally paid for by the current income. I am describing a situation where income is totally generated by the sales and all the sales are paid for by the income from the sales. This means that current income must be less than or equal to current sales if the sales are going to be sufficient to pay for the income. and that current sales must be less than or equal to current income if income is going to be sufficient to pay for the sales. In other words:

current income <= current sales,

and

current income >= current sales

This means the only possible solution is

current income = current sales.

That is, the only possible way such an economy could work is if the income earners spend **all** their income paying for the sales.

Would this be a basis for a viable economy? The answer is NO! It will not work. The income would be **inadequate** to pay for all the sales. Why? Because in a monetary economy, **people do not spend the entirety of their income**, they spend some and save some. If the current income comes entirely from the current sales, there will not be enough income to pay for the sales. This is because you will need ALL of your income to pay for all of the sales, there will be nothing left over for saving.

The only possible conclusion then, is that current income will not be adequate to pay for current sales if the spending is paid for solely by revenue gained from current sales. In order to have current spending be enough to pay for all of the current sales, we need the spending to be increased by some spending that is not paid for out of current income gained from current sales

In order for this concept to be valid in general, in macroeconomic theory, when we talk about sales we must think of it in very general terms. What is "sold" in the macroeconomy is everything that spending pays for. This includes goods, services, labor and any other desired outcome. The sales revenue I am referring to, is caused by the spending done for the purpose of attempting to acquire all of those things.

Some Fundamental Definitions

You will notice that I have made these categories broad enough so that those things I consider being sold include any possible result that a person or entity is trying to achieve by spending, i.e., by transferring ownership of an amount of money from one person or entity to another.

In this model, in the macroeconomy, all the income results from all the spending, which is done to pay for all the sales. Or to put it a different way, every bit of transfer of ownership of money for a purpose (every bit of spending) is paying for sales; is paying for some good, service, labor or some other desired outcome. And every amount of spending creates income, in the same amount, for the recipient of that spending. The amount of spending, and therefore income, is always going to equal the sales.

FIGURE 2.1

In a viable economy, while it is true that total income is always going to equal total sales, it is not true that all the sales will be paid for completely out of current income. Because people do not spend all of their income, if the economy is going to be viable, some spending will have to be funded by money already owned, by money acquired in a previous time period, money previously saved. Spending paid for with that money subsidizes the spending paid for out of the current income to make the total spending sufficient to pay for all the sales. This is the only way that current income earners will have some money left over out of their income to save. This extra spending, paid for by money **other than** money acquired as income in the current time period, is what Keynes called '**Investment**.'

This is not the usual definition of Investment. However, I am alleging that it is only by using this definition of Investment that I will be able to develop a model that allows us to properly understand what Keynes discovered.

In "The General Theory of Employment, Interest and Money" Keynes calls any spending that is paid for out of current income '**Consumption**.' He coined a term, the "propensity to consume", by which he meant the fraction of current income that is used for spending. Using this terminology means that consumption pays for only part of the sales, while investment pays for the rest. This is because only a fraction of income is used for (consumption) spending and the other fraction is saved. Usually the larger fraction of income is spent, and a smaller fraction is saved.

This is not the usual definition of Consumption that economists or lay people use, however, as with the term Investment, I am alleging that only this definition of Consumption will allow us to properly understand what Keynes discovered.

The amount of the current income that income earners will NOT have to spend, i.e., the amount they will not be using to pay for sales, will be the amount of money they have left over, which is also the amount they save. The amount of current income the income earners do not use to pay for current sales, is the amount of spending that will need to be paid for by sources other than current income, i.e., that paid for by investment (aka "investment spending"). This means the amount current income earners will have left over to save is exactly equal to the amount of investment.

Savings equals Investment.

This is where the "Savings equals Investment Identity", commonly taught in economics, comes from. I present that pictorially below.

FIGURE 2.2

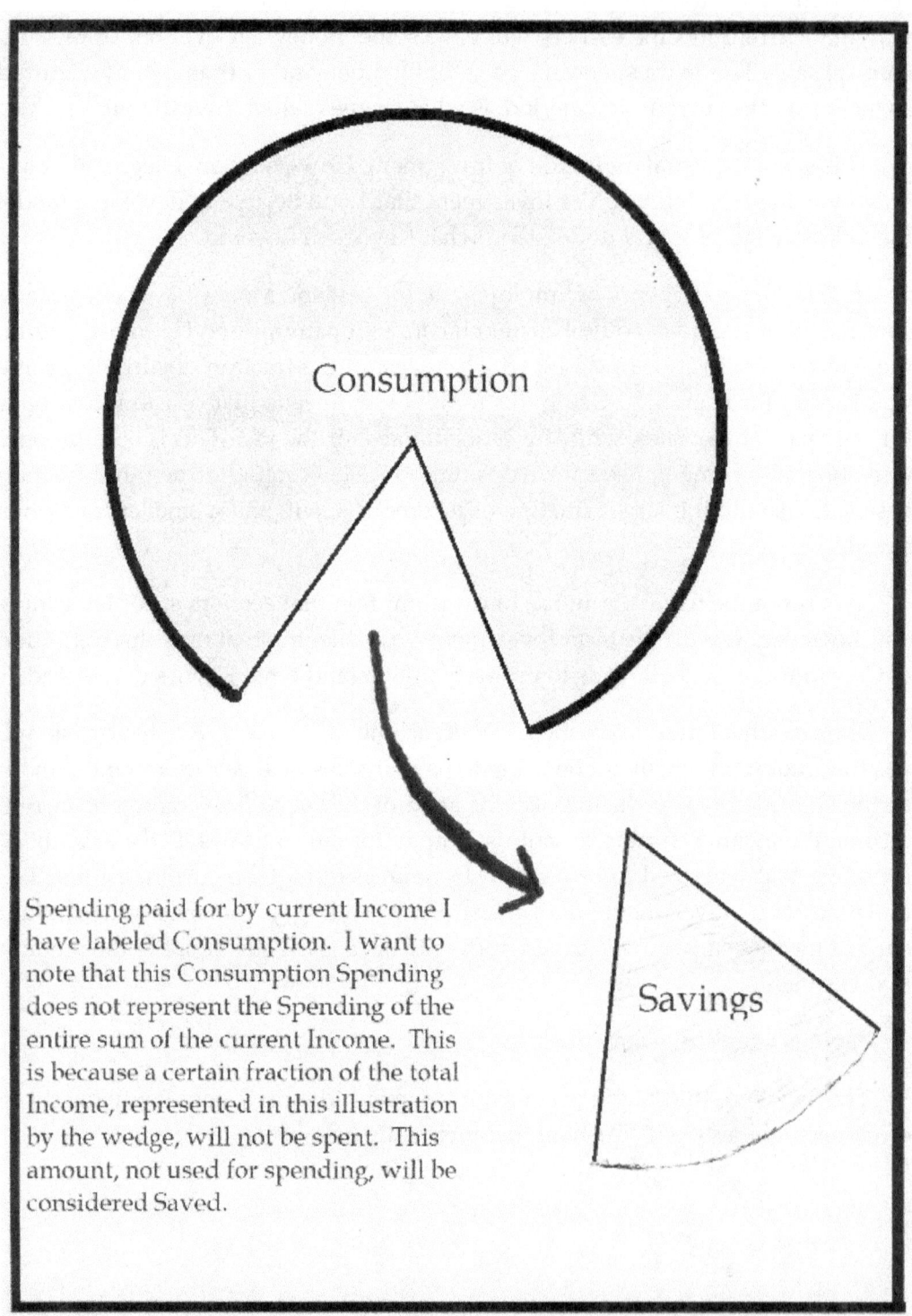

Spending paid for by current Income I have labeled Consumption. I want to note that this Consumption Spending does not represent the Spending of the entire sum of the current Income. This is because a certain fraction of the total Income, represented in this illustration by the wedge, will not be spent. This amount, not used for spending, will be considered Saved.

FIGURE 2.3

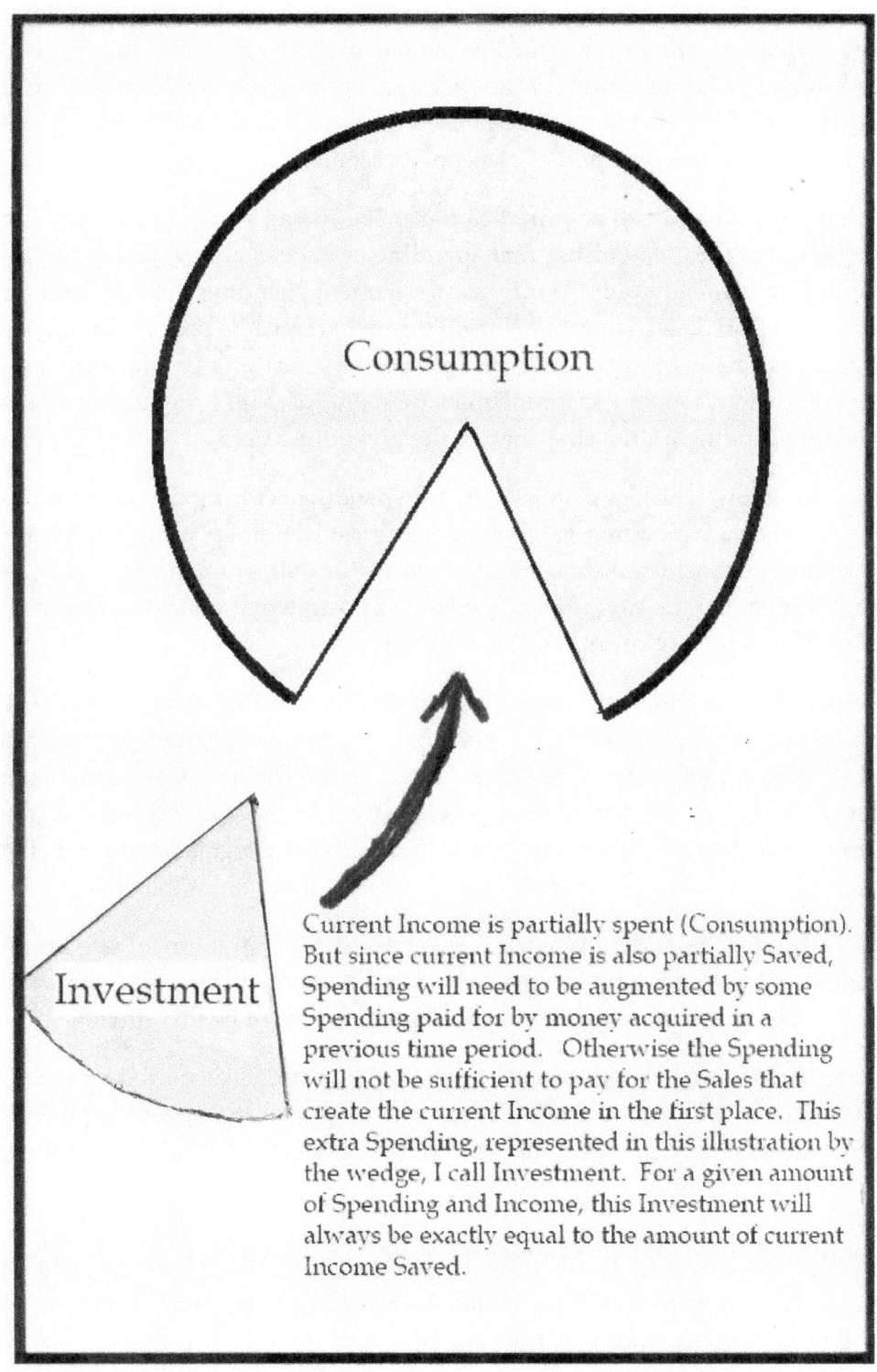

Current Income is partially spent (Consumption). But since current Income is also partially Saved, Spending will need to be augmented by some Spending paid for by money acquired in a previous time period. Otherwise the Spending will not be sufficient to pay for the Sales that create the current Income in the first place. This extra Spending, represented in this illustration by the wedge, I call Investment. For a given amount of Spending and Income, this Investment will always be exactly equal to the amount of current Income Saved.

Some Fundamental Definitions

I would like to point out that the investment spending must be paid for with money being used for spending for the first time in the given time period. This is because if that money had already been used for spending in that time period, it would have already become part of someone's income.

If that money had been acquired as part of someone's current income, and is then used again for spending, that spending counts as <u>consumption</u> not investment. I have already pointed out that investment spending must be paid for by money **NOT** obtained as part of current income. It must be paid for by money acquired in a previous time period, paid for out of someone's previous savings. This means, that investment spending must be spending paid for with money being used for spending for the **first time in the given time period**.

Since we know that if a person pays for spending with money acquired as current income that spending is classified as consumption spending, this leads us to the logical conclusion that money used for investment can only count as investment spending the **first time** it is spent in that time periods, because **any re-spending of that money counts as consumption**.

Further, if money **is** being used for spending for the first time it **CANNOT** count as consumption. Consumption spending requires using money that is acquired as someone's income in the current time period. The only way money contributes to income in the current time period is by it being spent. Therefore, any spending paid for out of money acquired as income, will mean that money is being spent for the second time at a minimum and possibly more times than that.

The operations I am identifying as 'consumption' and 'investment' are mutually exclusive. If the spending is classifiable as investment, it cannot be consumption. If the spending is classifiable as consumption, it cannot be investment.

Money being spent for the second or more times, is money acquired by spending in the current time period and counts as consumption. Any spending paid for using that same money, however many times that money is re-used for spending, counts as consumption.

This gives us these formal definitions:

For the given time period, if the money being used for spending is being used for the first time, that spending is **investment**.

Some Fundamental Definitions

If, in the specified time period, the money is being used for spending for the 2nd time or any time thereafter, each and every time it is re-used, it is added to the total for **consumption.**

Investment spending can only occur once with the same money. Consumption spending can occur repeatedly using the same money. To count as investment, it does not matter when, in the given time period, the investment spending occurs, as long as it is money being used for spending for the first time. To count as consumption spending, it does not matter when, in the given time period, the spending occurs, as long as it is paid for out of current income.

Notice the interesting fact that consumption spending does not introduce any new money into the spending. The only money that gets used in consumption spending is the money originally introduced into income as investment spending. More generally, the only money used for ANY spending, investment or consumption, is money introduced into income as investment spending.

The total of consumption spending can be greater than the amount of money actually used for the spending, because of the fact that the same money can be re-used for spending and each and every time it is re-spent the amount of that transaction gets added to the total for the consumption spending.

The same is not true of investment spending. The money used to pay for an investment spending transaction can only be used for investment spending once, and still count as investment. Every time, in the given time period, that money, first used for investment is re-used for spending, it counts as consumption spending. This gives the fact that the total amount of the investment **spending** is exactly equal to the total amount of **money** used for the investment spending. The **amount of investment spending** is equal to the amount of **money** used to pay for that spending. That then becomes the only money used for any and all the spending, in the current time period, including all the consumption spending.

At the end of the given time period, those individuals or entities, in possession of some portion of the money, are the ones who last received that amount of money as income. Since they did not re-spend that money again before the end of the given time period then that money qualifies as income that has not been spent and therefore is income that has been saved.

Since any of the money used for spending will still exist, and since any of the money used for spending has become income for at least one person or entity, then we can be certain that, for each quantity of money, someone received it **last** as income, in the given time period. Anyone who received that money last, did not re-use it for spending (because they were the last ones to receive it in that time period) so they still possess it, as savings.

This is the same thing as saying that **all** the money that was put into spending as investment continues to exist at the end of the time period as savings owned by some person or entity who received it as income.

This savings is also the total amount of savings generated from current income in the given time period. No other savings will occur, because it is only those income earners who have retained ownership of some of their money received as income, who have saved anything. If they have not retained ownership of any of the money received as income it is because they have spent it all.

This means, that when I say that the amount of savings equals the amount of investment spending, I am also saying that the amount of savings equals the amount of the **money** used for investment spending. The money that is put into investment spending will be the only money used in any spending, it will be the only money used in transactions that pay for the sales and creates income. At the end of the given time period, each quantity of that money will still exist and be owned by one of the people or entities who received it as part of their income. That is the only savings that will occur. The total of that savings will equal the total amount of money put into spending as investment.

In fact, the reason that the money being saved will be equal to the amount of investment money, is because it is actually the **same money.** The investment money put into spending, circulates through all the rounds of spending and still exists at the end of the given time period, "in someone's pocket", if you will, as savings.

The expression savings equals investment is basically acknowledging that the money used for investment spending is neither created nor destroyed as a result of commerce. That same money, which was put into spending, continues to exist at the end of the specified time period, at which point it is called savings.

The savings that equals investment is really just the **preservation** of the investment money. Money is not used up in the process of economic activity, it is just passed on from spender to recipient, over and over again, and still exists at the end of the given time period, designated as savings, owned by someone who received it as income in this time period.

Some Fundamental Definitions

"The Same Money"

One might wonder how it could be said that when some money gets used for re-spending it is the "same money". How can I say that the spending I am calling consumption is really re-spending of the same money that was used for investment? How can I know that some recipient of spending did not just switch out some of the money they just got paid with, with some other money they already had?

The simple answer is that just switching out one dollar for another dollar does not count as spending, because it is not done for the purpose of obtaining a good, a service, some labor or some other outcome -- it is not really a change in ownership of money for a purpose. An equal trade of the exact amount of money without the parties obtaining something or some result in return, cannot be considered spending.

When I am talking about the same money, it is not the ownership of the same exact dollar bills that counts, it is the ownership of the actual amount of money that is the important thing. I have described some examples below of what does and does not count as spending.

Even though that money might have been "switched out" and is not the same exact dollar bills or coins it can still be the same money. For our purposes, the fact that it exists in the place it exists in the quantity it exists is the main thing. How it got to that place in that amount is what matters. It is the chain of spending starting with investment that caused it to be there that defines it as the same money.

For any given time period, for any money used for current spending, the chain of spending of that money can be traced back to the first time it was spent (i.e., traced back to some investment spending). The chain could be short, i.e., only the investment spending, or long, i.e., the money could have been used for spending multiple times. The important thing is, if we had good enough records, one could always trace the chain of spending of any money back to the first time, in the given time period, it was spent.

Let me give a couple examples of situations to help us better understand when something should count as spending or not:

You and I keep passing a 20-dollar bill back and forth a number of times where nothing is provided in return and the person to whom that 20 dollar bill originally belonged ends up with it. The movement of the money was for no purpose. That is not spending. On the other hand, if I gave you 20 dollars for a basketball and you gave me the 20 dollars back for a tennis racquet, that is spending. It is 40 dollars' worth of spending.

Suppose I needed change to buy something. I gave you a dollar and you gave me 4 quarters, that is not spending. I then bought a soda for 75 cents, that is spending.

My dollar bills were looking pretty worn out. I gave them to the bank, and they gave me new crisp bills. That is not spending.

Two people are on a trip, they keep all the money in the glove compartment, one person takes 20 dollars out but accidently takes it from the pile of the other person's money. He notices what he did later and replaces it with some other money he had before the other person noticed. Even though 20 dollars changed hands twice, it never really changed ownership. When it was in the possession of the person who accidently took the money from the same pile, it did not influence their further spending in any way, and it did not influence the spending of the person who originally owned that money and got it back before they noticed. It does not affect things in any significant way. That is not spending.

Spending is the change of ownership of a quantity of money done for a purpose, not just an exchange of the same amount of money with no consequence. Outcomes that could justify the change of ownership of money being called 'spending' can include something as simple as making the people involved leave the situation owning different amounts of money than what they came in with. Since having different amounts of money could affect future spending decisions, that counts as spending. Although the purpose of that spending may not even be known to those involved in that transfer of money, it does end up affecting the mindsets of those involved and possibly the future spending decisions and therefore ended up having a purpose. The change could end up being just decreasing the stress level of the recipient of the extra money. Or the purpose could be that it starts a chain of spending that causes other results.

Spending can be initiated by the recipient and not necessarily for a good reason, or not necessarily with the awareness or consent of the spender. An example is when someone steals someone else's money. In my definitions that counts as spending even if it was not intended by the spender. The person was the passive participant in their own spending, without their consent. Still that counts as spending.

Some Fundamental Definitions

Of course, spending is usually done with the awareness of the spender for the purpose of obtaining a desired result, typically to obtain a good or service, or to pay for someone's labor. But transferring ownership of money for the purposes of effecting many other outcomes allows us to classify it as spending as well, in this model. (I should note that when I am talking about income I am talking about gross income, not net. I will explain the significance of this later.)

I am making this point to portray the concept of the same money, money that exists, in the given place, at the given time, in the given amount, because of the chain of spending that got it there. If we included things such as giving a 20-dollar bill back and forth between people as spending or exchanging a dollar for 4 quarters as spending, then the concept loses all meaning and purpose. So, one has to use judgement. For example, if I go to the store and buy something for 17 dollars and pay with a 20 getting 3 dollars in change, I would count that as spending 17 dollars. I would not count it as me spending 20 dollars and the store spending 3 dollars when it gives me back my change.

There are reasons to carefully distinguish between what I call investment and what I call consumption, and this will become more apparent as we go on, but I should mention, for many of the scenarios I will be analyzing, it is the total spending that matters, not whether any of that spending is classified as investment or as consumption.

In this section I have described how spending, whether it is consumption spending or investment spending, creates income. You will also note that ALL spending, all transferring of ownership of money for a purpose, during the given time period, must be categorizable as EITHER investment or consumption. That means that total income equals the sum of investment and consumption. The letter Y is commonly used to designate total income, the letter I is commonly used to designate investment and the letter C is commonly used to designate consumption. I will follow that convention and that gives us this equation for total income:

$Y = I + C$

This is not the only way to define income. Here is another way:

In terms of the total money supply, the expression for total income $Y = I + C$ accounts for all the actual spending in the given time period. All the money being used for spending gets put into income first as investment and then that same money is used again for any spending counting as consumption. That money used will be the total amount of money actually used for spending in the given time period.

But there may be other money that exists. Money that is part of the money supply but was not used in the spending. If you were to consider the entire money supply including that being used for spending and that which was not being used for spending, you can still take an overall average for how many times each unit of currency was spent. That is, for every dollar in the money supply, whether it was used for spending or not, we can get an average for how many times each dollar was spent in a given time period.

For example, if 50 percent of the money was put into investment and all the money put into investment was spent one more time (consumption), then 50 percent of the total money supply would have been spent twice, once for the first time in the given time period and one more time when re-spent. The other 50% would have been spent zero times. The average number of times each unit of money in the entire money supply would have been spent, is one time. Therefore, the total amount of spending would be 1 times the value of the total money supply.

Now that is a simple example, but if we define **V** as the **average** amount of times **each unit of currency** in the **total money supply** is spent, during the given time period, we know that the **total amount of spending**, the total income, is equal to **V** times the total amount of money in the money supply. If we designate the total amount of money, i.e., the whole money supply as **M**, we would know that **total spending** is the value of the total number of units of money in the entire money supply, (**M**) (for example the total value of the money supply in dollars) times the average number of times each unit of money (each dollar) is spent (**V**). **V** is referred to as the **"velocity of money"**. Since **Y** is the total spending then **Y = M∗V**, where the "∗" means "multiplied by."

Thus, we have **Y = I + C** which is where all the money actively being spent is accounted for. And if one wanted to include the whole money supply one would use **Y = M∗V** to calculate the total spending, i.e., to calculate the total income. In both cases you are describing the same quantity, total spending, i.e., total income:

Y = I + C = M∗V

There is a third way total income can be defined. If I define every time a quantity of money changes ownership for a purposed as "a transaction," then the

Some Fundamental Definitions

income caused by one transaction is the amount of that transaction. One could call the amount of the transaction, "the price of the transaction."

Let us designate **P** to mean the **average price** of all transactions during a given time period (that is, the average amount of money changing ownership in each transaction). That would mean total income would be the average amount of each transaction, **P**, times the number of transactions. Let **T** equal the total number of transactions then the total income (**Y**) generated would be the average price of each transaction (**P**) times the number of transactions (**T**). **Y** = average price **P** times number of transactions **T**, that is: **Y = P∗T**.

We have shown three ways to calculate income **Y** and they are all equivalent to each other:

Y = I + C = M∗V = P∗T

CHAPTER 3
What is The Money Supply and How Does Money Move Through the Banking System?

The purpose of this chapter is to share my insights into how the banking system functions but not to give a comprehensive overview of the entire system. My goal is to give a basic overview of what the money supply is and to encourage an understanding of how transactions can take place with or without the actual movement of paper currency or coins. Since more and more transactions are done electronically, I do not believe it is possible to understand the money supply, nor understand how money moves through the economy, without having a basic understanding of these concepts.

BEFORE I TALK about coins and dollar bills and all that, I want to explain how we can have spending, that is, a change of ownership of money, without money moving anywhere. I will go even further and say that spending can occur without the money even existing in a physical form, such as coins or paper notes etc. I will develop these concepts by introducing several scenarios.

First Scenario:

Everyone in the local economy gives their paper money and coins to "Guy" to hold. Guy keeps track of how much each person gave him, as if they all had an account with Guy. Whenever someone pays someone else, they do not give the other person money, they just tell Guy to transfer the money from their account to the other person's account. Guy changes his records to update who owns that particular money, he does not have to physically move the money anywhere. That is how spending can occur without money moving anywhere.

Second Scenario:

None of the people in the local economy, including Guy, have any physical money. What Guy does have is a ledger stating how much money each person has in an account with him. Other than that, there is no money, the only form in which it exists is entries in a ledger book. When someone pays someone else, they just tell Guy and he adjusts the amount in each person's account. No physical money ever existed and no physical money changes hands, but money does change ownership. How much money each person owns is kept track of by Guy who adjusts the amounts in each of their accounts.

Third Scenario:

People have some paper money and coins. They give all that money to Guy to hold and he keeps track of how much paper money and coins each person gave him. But the total in each person's account also includes some money for which paper currency or coins do not exist. The only way that particular part of those people's money exists is because it shows on Guys ledger as existing. In other words, stored with Guy is a mixture of actual physical money, paper and/or coins plus that money we only know exists because Guy has an accounting of it on a ledger. Spending is still accomplished the same way as the first two scenarios. In all three scenarios Guy knows exactly how much total money each person in the local economy owns. In all three scenarios described, spending occurs because when directed, Guy will adjust the balance in people's accounts by subtracting the amount of the purchase from the buyers account and adding it to the sellers account, which is to say that ownership of that money will move from the buyers account to the sellers account. In all three scenarios, spending occurs without physical money moving anywhere.

Of course, the type of spending that we are all familiar and comfortable with, where someone pulls out some cash and gives it to another person in return for some goods or service, also occurs. In our usual economy both types of spending occur; spending that is a result of paper currency or coins being exchanged, or spending that occurs without any physical money moving anywhere.

The above scenarios would give one a reasonable handle on how the banking system worked if we did not have to account for LOANS. If we have an economy where loans occur, one must make some modifications to account for them.

Let us say that Guy is not just a keeper of people's balances and a safe guarder of their money. Let us say he also is a lender of money. Now Guy does not just want to lend his own money. Guy really is in business to make a profit by loaning out his depositor's money. Let us explore what changes I need to make in our model to accommodate that.

If Guy lends depositors' money out, then he will owe the depositors. This means that **before** Guy can lend out any money, he must borrow it from the depositor. If he borrows it from the depositor that means he takes ownership of the money. What does the depositor get? The depositor gets an asset. They are no longer owners of the money, but they do get a promise from Guy that he owes them that amount of money. That promise, that "being owed the money", is the asset. The records are adjusted to show how much Guy owes the depositor. By agreeing to owe the depositor, Guy has not only acquired ownership of the money, but he also has acquired a debt obligation of an equivalent amount.

At this point, if you look into Guy's ledger you see that the depositor has listed in his account all the money he has not loaned to Guy, as well as that asset just described. The total worth of the money plus the asset in the depositors account after Guy borrowed from the depositor, would equal the total worth of the money in the depositor's account before Guy borrowed some of it. Guy will have a record that he **owns** the money he just borrowed, and that he owes the depositor he borrowed it from in the same amount.

It is risky for the depositor to let Guy borrow his money. What if he does not pay it back? As a result, the depositors probably would not want to lend Guy their money just out of the goodness of their hearts. They would want some sort of compensation in return. Perhaps for some people the compensation of just having their wealth safeguarded by Guy is enough, or just being able to do those transactions without always carrying cash around would be enough, but usually in addition to those benefits, people want a little bit extra, i.e., those depositors would like to earn some interest on that loan they gave to Guy. That interest would give extra value to that asset they essentially purchased from Guy by lending him the money.

We know that Guy intends to loan the money he has just borrowed to someone else, a borrower from him. After all, the whole reason Guy is borrowing that money from the depositor is so that he can get something in return for his efforts. And when he loans the money, for him to earn a return, Guy will have to charge his borrower interest. And the amount of interest he charges will need to be greater than the amount of interest he pays the depositor.

Let us say someone borrows the money from Guy. When Guy gives the money to a borrower, Guy is purchasing an asset from the borrower. a debt obligation from the borrower. That borrower will then own the money. The asset called the "loan," this debt obligation owed to Guy, now shows up on the books, as an asset owned by Guy, who no longer owns the money. The money loaned, spending for Guy, has become income for the borrower, who acquires that debt obligation in the same amount.

This is all consistent with our description of income being a measure of movement of money through the economy, that is, it is consistent with our description of income as being the transfer of ownership of money from one person or entity to another. (Remember, when talking about income here, I am talking about gross income).

Ownership of the money moves from the depositor (who purchases an asset from Guy) to Guy. This money becomes income for Guy who spends to purchase an asset from the borrower. This money becomes owned by, and income for, the borrower. In the first transaction, Guy gets ownership of both the money and a debt obligation, and in the second transaction the borrower gets ownership of both the money and a debt obligation.

But the lending scenario as described so far is not really how it works. When you deposit money in a bank account, the bank does not just wait until it wants to loan money to somebody, then asks a depositor to lend them SOME of their deposit money in return for an interest-bearing asset of that exact amount. The bank does not ask the depositor at all. As soon as they get the depositor's money the bankers just lend it, whenever they want and whenever they can.

How can one describe this in terms of my model? I describe it by saying that as soon as you deposit money in the bank the bank has acquired ownership of the money and the depositor has acquired an asset worth the amount of the deposit, plus whatever other benefits may come with it. One of the benefits is the bank starts paying the depositor the agreed upon interest rate starting immediately and on the entire amount of the deposit. The bank, being owner of all the money, can, without getting permission from anybody, loan out that money.

This means that the act of depositing your money in the bank is the act of lending your deposit money to the bank, alternatively described as the depositor purchasing an asset called a "bank deposit" from the bank. As soon as you deposit your money in the bank, you are no longer the owner of that money. The bank is. This means that your bank account is not a pile of cash sitting there waiting for you to use anytime you want. It is not money, it is an asset that is

What is The Money Supply and How Does Money Move

valued in terms of money, but it is not money. Putting money into a bank account is not saving, it is spending, spending to purchase an asset.

When you withdraw money from your account, what you are really doing is asking the bank to pay back some of the debt it owes you. This will simultaneously decrease the value of your asset and decrease the value of the debt obligation the bank has to you. At that point, you become owner of the money the bank used to buy back part of its debt obligation to you.

Additionally, when the bank loans out the money to the borrower the bank is spending to acquire an asset called "the loan" from the borrower. The act of depositing money is spending by the depositor, and is income for the bank, and the act of lending that money to the borrower is spending by the bank and becomes income for the borrower. Ownership of money goes from the depositor to the bank to the borrower. Assets and debt obligations are created in the process.

I have just expanded the description of our scenario to include loans. I have previously described how Guy can facilitate spending without money physically moving any place, and I have described how Guy can facilitate spending without the money existing in physical form except that it is kept track of on a ledger. But how would one describe this spending without the money moving, if one looks at Guy as being the owner of all the money in the bank, and the depositors only being owners of assets held there?

Here is an example of how to do that accounting: Let us say Bob and George both have accounts with Guy. Bob desires to buy something from George and requests the money for the transaction from Guy. Guy then must give Bob ownership of that amount of money. In so doing Guy simultaneously decreases the amount of debt he owes Bob and decreases the balance in Bob's account, i.e., decreases the value of Bob's asset, called a bank deposit. But before he can arrange to give Bob the cash, Bob asks Guy to give it directly to George since that is what Bob was going to do with the cash anyway. So far in this scenario the money was owned by Guy but becomes briefly owned by Bob who then causes it to be immediately given to George who now owns it. But George never wanted to keep the money as cash, so he tells Guy that he just wants to put the money into his bank account. This causes ownership of the money to go back to Guy. In return the value of George's asset, i.e., the value of his account, increases by that amount. In addition to re-acquiring ownership of the money, Guy also acquires back a debt in the same amount, but this time owing it to George instead of Bob. The money never actually moves yet the spending occurs, and the transaction is accomplished. In this scenario, spending occurs three times; Spending by Guy giving money to Bob to decrease Guys debt to Bob; spending by Bob giving money to George to purchase the good or service; and spending by George who gives money to Guy to purchase an increase in the value of his account.

In this new scenario, the one where assets and debits are continually being created, (or increased and decreased in value), whenever we have one "virtual transaction," where money does not physically move, the transaction is really a combination of three transactions. The end result of the described transaction is that Bob purchased what he wanted from George, George's account increased in value by the amount of the purchase price and Bob's account decreased in value by the same amount. The only thing that changed were the numbers on the ledger and Bob acquired the good or service from George.

Of course, Guy could have physically handed the money to Bob and Bob could have physically given it to George who could have decided to put it in the bank, which sequence would also be 3 transactions. The extra 2 transactions involve understanding that putting money in a deposit account is purchasing an asset from the bank. And withdrawing money from a bank account is the bank purchasing back some of a depositor's asset and decreasing its debt to a depositor.

This is a more accurate description of the banking system as it actually operates. There is a constant process of assets being created, added to, or subtracted from, which are always matched by debts created, subtracted from, or added to, in the same amounts. There is also the constant process of interest being paid to the asset owners by the debt owners. Whenever the value of an asset and a debt is changing, money is spent, i.e., money is changing ownership.

What is a person purchasing when they acquire an asset by lending? All the benefits of the asset including the ability to get a return, i.e., interest payments, plus the value of the asset itself.

What is a person purchasing when they pay interest on a debt? They are paying in the current period for the purchase of having had the ability to own that money in the first place, which would give them the ability to purchase something with it whenever they want or need to. When the bank agrees to pay interest to the depositor it is done to entice the depositor to put that money in their bank, so they can loan it out and make a profit. This is all a form of spending, as it is done for a purpose.

What is The Money Supply and How Does Money Move

So far, I believe this chapter has gone a long way in explaining how the banking system works and how spending can occur without money physically moving about. But there are still some important issues I have not yet discussed. I have not discussed how that money comes into existence in the first place, or how it gets into anyone's account. That is, more generally, how does money get put into circulation? And how do we keep track of how much money there is? How do we keep Guy, who only has to show that he has the money by showing us his ledger, from falsifying his books and claiming he has a lot more money than he actually does?

The answer to all these questions is "Janet". You see, although Guy is physically holding the money that he possesses as paper currency and coins, he is not actually holding the money he alleges exists but whose only physical presence is an entry on a ledger. Somebody else is holding that money. "Janet" is the one holding that money. And Guy is only allowed to say he has ownership of that money if Janet agrees that he is the legitimate owner. And Janet keeps great records, so she always knows when Guy is owner of any part of the money she is holding.

Janet has a unique position in the economy. She is the one in charge of the money supply. Janet has the ability to create new money any time she wants. She is the one who can put that money into the money supply, or she can take money out of the money supply. Janet can create money in two ways. She can order it to be printed or minted, or she can simply declare it as existing. When she declares it to exist, she has to keep track of it on a ledger. Janet is ultimately the source of all the money Guy has.

Janet ordering paper currency to be created or declaring money as existing and keeping it on a ledger does not make it in the money supply. Any money "owned by Janet" is not in the money supply. It is only when that money becomes owned by some person or entity other than Janet that it becomes part of the money supply. I will discuss my use of this definition of the money supply in more detail later.

In order to create paper currency, Janet orders the Treasury to print it up, which is then given to Janet for distribution. Janet does pay for the expenses incurred in the printing of this paper currency, but that is a very small fraction of the face value of the currency. Janet does distribute coins too. When the Treasury Department mints them Janet pays the Treasury for them, with paper currency or virtual money, but, unlike with paper currency where she just pays the production expenses, for coins she pays face value of the newly minted coins. Janet uses money she owns, and possibly just created, to purchase them, at which point the coins switch from being owned by the Treasury, to being owned by Janet. This is how it works in the United States since 1996. Prior to that time coins were treated the same as paper currency, only the expense of production was paid to the Treasury, but since then, Janet pays face value for the coins.

I do not fully understand why this was done. I think the rationale had something to do with sparing the expense of creating coins since they cost a greater percentage of their face value to produce than paper currency does, and this was a way to have the treasury expenses in effect be paid for by the actual minting of the coins, since the treasury either owns the coins until they sell it to Janet or they own the exact same amount of money when Janet pays them face value for the coins. At any rate, that means as soon as the Treasury mints the coins, they own that much more money, and they will own that much money after Janet pays for the coins. And that means there is more money in the money supply because when the money is owned by the treasury is it owned by an entity other than Janet, hence it is in the money supply. Printing paper currency does not increase the money except to the small fraction of face value Janet reimburses the treasury for newly printed paper currency.

However, it is also true that most paper currency put into the money supply does not end up increasing the total money supply because it is just being exchanged for worn out bills that will be destroyed, or it is being traded for virtual money which already existed and will no longer exist after it is replaced by paper currency.

Coins tend to last longer than bills but they too can be taken out of circulation when determined to be to worn out, presumably for new coins, but that exchanging of old coins for new coins does not affect the money supply either, since the old coins will be destroyed. In such a case institutions like Guy will hand over to Janet old worn out coins that are intended for destruction, and Janet will replace them with newly minted coins.

Now, just to confuse you further, I need to confess that the information I just gave is not totally accurate. Janet paying face value to the Treasury for coins and production expenses to the Treasury for paper currency DOES NOT, in the end, increase the money supply. This is because when Janet pays for physical money, the payments are considered part of operating expenses for Janet. And Janet's operating expenses, as we shall see later, are paid for out of interest payments

Janet has received, mostly from the Treasury. The money received as interest payments by Janet are used for operating expenses, but then any of that money left over, after paying for operating expenses, gets returned to the Treasury. So any money paid to the Treasury for coins or paper money, would have gone to the Treasury anyway, if it had not been used to pay for the bills or coins. That money was in the money supply when the Treasury owned it. Then it was given, as interest payments, to the Central Bank where it is temporarily out of the money supply. Then part of it is used for operating expenses, including paying for coins and bills. The operating expenses become income for those entities who get paid as part of the operating expenses, including the money that goes to Treasury to pay for the physical money. This operating expense money thus becomes once again owned by entities other than Janet and is back in the money supply. Then any remaining "interest money" paid to Janet by the Treasury, gets sent back to the Treasury general fund, where it also becomes, once again, IN the money supply. Either way, in this whole process, there is no overall increase in the money supply.

But this law in the US from 1996 that made Janet pay face value for coins, did allow for the interesting theoretical considerations. All the bills and coins made by the Treasury are, to my understanding, at the behest of the Janet, and are given to Janet for distribution after Janet pays some money to the Treasury. Theoretically, if the Treasury was able to keep that money, then it would be the Treasury who controls the money supply, not Janet. Fortunately, this does not happen.

I have just explained how, all production of paper currency and coins is basically, in the end, paid for by the Treasury, since it is paid for out of money given to Janet by the Treasury as interest payments. Since any money left over is going to be returned to the treasury, then in essence, production expenses for coins and bills is footed by the Treasury.

What if it was decided that the Treasury should mint an extremely large denomination coin, so large that interest payments collected by Janet were not sufficient to cover the cost of paying face value for that coin. Then when Janet reimburses the Treasury at face value for that large denomination coin, she would have to use other money, money she either already owned or newly created, to pay the Treasury for the face value of the coin.

All that extra money over and above that total she has available from interest payments, becomes new money added to the money supply and in fact goes directly to the Treasury. The spending of money by the Treasury is ultimately controlled by the politicians. One thing that holds politicians spending in check is the need to tax or borrow to obtain funds for spending.

After the creation of a large denomination coin Janet could purchase it with new money and replaces it in the money supply with any combination of virtual money, paper currency or normal denomination coins, allowing that money to be partitioned and used for any spending desired by the politicians who control Treasury spending. The spending of this money would not be subject to the normal restraints on government spending provided by the need to tax or borrow to obtain funds for spending. This, in my opinion, could, and once the politicians got a taste for it, would lead to disastrous consequences. In my opinion, the availability of unlimited spending to those in power would completely corrupt the democratic process, to the point where we would end up with authoritarian regimes, but it would also create situation where hyperinflation becomes a strong possibility, and that would completely destroy the given country's economy. Even if hyperinflation did not occur, loss of a true democratic government would have severe negative consequences for a country's citizens. This is because free, democratic societies have always proven superior to autocratic societies in terms of wealth production, standard of living and quality of life.

In order to understand the connection between Janet and Guy and Guy's customers, one must examine the way money goes from creation to being put into circulation. The answer is quite simple. The way the money that Janet creates gets into the money supply is that Janet buys something with it. To get money into circulation Janet must spend it. Theoretically, Janet could buy anything with the money, and that would get it into circulation, but even Janet, as powerful as she is, has restrictions put on her by the government. When she buys things, she cannot just buy anything. As I understand it, she is generally restricted to buying assets, and the assets she can buy are assets created by loans. The ways Janet gets money into the money supply include:

Lending the money to commercial banks of which Guy would be an example. This is the same as using the money she wants to get into the money supply to purchase an asset, the asset being the debt that Guy would owe her for the money she lends him. According to the banking rules set up by the government Guy is supposed to try to get money for loans from depositors first, or from other institutions like Guy, rather than borrowing it from Janet. Guy is only supposed to get the money from her as a last resort, when people want loans and he cannot otherwise get the money to lend. For this reason, it is my understanding that direct borrowing by Guy is very limited usually only for very short term loans. That money becomes part of the money supply as soon as Guy becomes owner of it, that is, as soon as Janet loans it to him. The main way Janet puts money into circulation is she buys bonds. Bonds are nothing more than loans. In America, the bonds Janet buys are, in the majority, bonds issued by the Treasury department. Not newly released bonds, meaning that is she is not the one who just loans money directly to the treasury. She buys already sold treasury bonds owned by people or entities in the private sector. Apparently, she does not buy privately issued bonds, like corporate bonds (although in England, she might since they have started to do that in limited fashion). When Janet buys the bond, she acquires an asset, the asset being the debt obligation of the bond issuer (the Treasury). But the bond seller gets the money which they can spend on other stuff and that is how buying bonds gets the money into circulation. Note that all this money usually is paid directly to someone's bank account or ends up in the bank eventually. This increases the cash available to banks for lending and is one reason why if banks need cash for lending and end up having to borrow directly from the Central Bank it is, usually, only for a short time.

After assets are purchased by Janet they become owned by Janet and are added to what is called Janet's "Balance Sheet". Buying Treasury Bonds (Treasuries) is a way to grow the money supply, and increase the balance sheet. This process can be reversed. If Janet decided to sell bonds, the money she received would become owned by her and then be out of the money supply. That would shrink the money supply, and shrink the balance sheet as well. Overall, if Janet is buying more bonds (in terms of total value) than she is selling, the money supply is increasing. If she is selling more bonds than she is buying, then the money supply is shrinking. When she owns those assets, that are described as being on her balance sheet, she is owed a debt obligation. The bond issuer (mostly the Treasury) makes payments to her. The portion of those payments that was applied to reducing the principle owed on those debt obligations reduces the money supply. If the principle paid off, on the bonds owned by Janet, is greater than the total value of newly purchased bonds, then the money supply is shrinking.

Just FYI, bond holders, including when Janet is the holder of the bond, earn interest. Regarding interest paid to Janet by the Treasury, that interest amount is used to pay for the operating expenses of the Central Bank. Any excess after those expenses are met gets transferred back to the Treasury General Fund. This, in effect, means that interest money will remain in the money supply, because it will come from the Treasury where it is in the money supply, becomes temporarily owned by Janet, then when used to pay for operating expenses, it becomes income for entities other than Janet, so goes back into the money supply. The remaining interest collected is also sent back to the Treasury General fund, which means it also is back in the money supply.

Notice, also that when Janet buys treasury bonds, she is NOT paying off any Treasury debt. The Treasury debt remains, it is just that the debt is now owed to Janet. It is simply a shifting of who the Treasury owes. From the former bond holder to Janet.

Now there will, at this point, be readers familiar with economics who will allege that I have no idea what I am talking about. That money owned by the Treasury is NOT considered to be in what is called the "base" money supply. And they would be correct. As normally taught, money owned by the Treasury is not considered to be in the "base" money supply. My definition of the money supply, which is essentially a description of what I think the base money supply should be, differs in that I insist that money owned by the Treasury MUST be considered in the money supply, and that it is this definition that allows us the most clear and consistent definition of the base money supply and to determine the actual size of it.

I differ with many who believe that it is not really possible to get a handle on the what the money supply is, or the size of it, that it is always changing, appearing and disappearing, being created and destroyed by economic activity. I believe it is absolutely possible for us to make clear definitions of what the money supply is, in terms of a given country's currency. The key concept in defining the money, in my opinion, is that money should be considered to be in the money supply when it is available to be used for spending by a persons or entities other than Janet. Janet does not need to have any money for her to have money available for spending. If she wants any money for spending she can just create some. That is why having money being owned by Janet is different than having money being owned by the Treasury (or any entity other than Janet). It is because the Treasury (or any entity other than Janet) needs to obtain money already in the money supply in order to have money for spending. They need to first obtain that money as income, that is they need to be recipients of some other entities spending (taxes are spending), to have money they themselves can spend. ...... unlike Janet, who can just create it.

Let us say that a certain amount of money was spent by Janet, but she never actually transferred physical possession of it to the recipient of the spending. Either because the money was never actually produced in physical form, being just an entry on a ledger, or because even though Janet was holding physical money, paper currency or coins, it was just more convenient for her to keep possession of it, and mark her books to show who actually owned it. Let us say that ownership of the money passed to Guy when it was put into a bank account. That is the type of money that Guy owns and keeps track of on a ledger, and that Janet would also keep track of in her records showing that it belongs to Guy. This could be money that only exists because Janet declared it as existing and keeps track of on a ledger, which I refer to as "virtual money". But whether Janet is holding it for him as virtual money or physical money, Guy owns that money and Janet will confirm that he owns it, if anyone asks.

If Guy ever has a need for more paper currency or coins he can ask Janet to send him some, after which Guy will **possess and own** the physical money and Janet will make sure her records are adjusted to show that the amount of money she is holding for Guy is reduced. To get the physical money to Guy, Janet could send money already existing in physical form or she could convert some of her virtual money to physical money, send it to Guy and have her records reflect that she has less virtual money, and less virtual money owned by Guy. None of these maneuvers increases the money supply, because the money was already in the money supply, as it was already owned by someone other than Janet (Guy). In this scenario the only money Janet is sending Guy is money owned by him and already in the money supply or money traded for money already owned by him. Converting virtual money to physical money does not change the size of the money supply.

Janet can give Guy as much paper money or coins as he wants up until the point where her records show that she is no longer holding any money that Guy owns, virtual, coins or paper. The only way Janet could give Guy more physical currency at that point is by buying something from him, either a debt obligation by giving him a loan, or buying a bond from him. If Janet gives Guy any money to pay for those things, including paper money, that **does** increase the money supply. In that case, we have money not in the money supply, which only Janet owns, as either coins, existing paper currency or money she just printed, being given by Janet to Guy, at which point it becomes part of the money supply.

For Janet, since she can create money, if she is the sole owner of a given amount of money, she can destroy as much of it as she wants, or replace it or add to it at any time and in whatever amount she wants, by printing paper currency or declaring it existing all she wants. If it never becomes owned by someone other than her it has no effect on the economy (except for the cost of production which does create income for people or entities other than Janet).

When Janet buys treasuries, she can pay the bond sellers by transferring ownership and possession of physical money to the sellers, but usually she transfers ownership of the money to the sellers without transferring physical possession. The money used can be virtual or exist in physical form but would remain possessed by Janet even though it has become owned by someone else. Normally the sale is made by transferring money to the seller's financial institution, an institution like Guy. That is, Janet purchases a bank deposit from Guy for the seller and Guy becomes owner of the cash and has a debt obligation to the bond-seller. Guy owns the money, and Janet's records show that Guy owns the money.

The success of this system being described depends entirely on honesty, integrity and good record keeping. By the way, since Janet keeps such good records and since Janet can inspect Guy's ledger books any time she wants, then Guy had better be honest about his balances or he could be in trouble. That is part of how the integrity of the banking system is maintained, by bank inspections.

One more additional concept: even though there can be only one Janet, there can be multiple different entities like "Guy". If there is more than one Guy, say we have Sharon who operates just like Guy, what does one of these "virtual transactions" look like, where ownership of the money changes but no money is physically moved? Suppose that Bob has a bank account with Guy and George has a bank account with Sharon. Guy owns money stored with Janet but has a debt to Bob in the form of Bob's bank account. Bob tells Guy that he needs to withdraw some money from his bank account for a purchase. Guy gives ownership of that amount of money to Bob. This is spending by Guy to purchase back part of the asset that is Bob's bank account and reduces his debt to Bob. He could give paper money to Bob, but Bob wants the money to go right to George to pay for the item he is purchasing. Guy tries to oblige and give the money to George, but George asks Bob to tell Guy to just give it to Sharon, that is, give it to Sharon as payment for an increase in the value of George's bank deposit account. Sharon then becomes owner of the money and George becomes owner of a deposit account worth more money. In the process, George has been paid, the asset called his bank account, has a larger balance, and Bob has acquired the item he wished to purchase, while his bank account has a lower balance. The cash Guy owns is less but so is his debt obligation to Bob, and the cash Sharon owns is greater but so is her debt obligation to George.

That is 3 transactions, Guy buying back part of Bob's asset, Bob paying George for the item and George buying an increased value of his bank account from Sharon, and all that could have happened with money not physically moving, just through the process of record keeping. The ownership of the money changes from Guy, temporarily to Bob, then temporarily to George, then to Sharon. Sharon is now owner of the money. This is how electronic transfers would occur.

Now, it is also a possibility that money transferred is money Guy owned AND physically possessed as paper currency or coins, but that Guy did not actually give the physical money to Sharon during the transaction. If not, the only thing documenting that Sharon owns the money is Guy and Sharon's records. This is like money being stored with Janet but records showing it is owned by Guy or Sharon. So, in this case the money may physically remain with Guy, even though Sharon owns it. At some point in the future they will settle accounts, but at that point they will be able to settle accounts for multiple different transactions. This will probably save the labor of transferring cash back and forth between Guy and Sharon so much because there might be transactions where ownership of cash Sharon was holding was transferred to Guy, but Sharon is still holding the actual cash. So, if they wait and settle accounts after a while, they would just have to transfer the net of all those different transactions, in terms of how much Sharon owes Guy or Guy owes Sharon.

Now the transactions would probably also involve the transfer of money that Janet is holding for them, where neither Guy nor Sharon have physical possession. This could be virtual money, paper currency or coins. In that case, the settling of accounts would be informing Janet of any change in possession of those moneys so Janet could adjust her accounts to reflect how much money she is holding now belongs to Sharon, and how much to Guy. So, when Guy and Sharon settle accounts, this may involve the actual transfer of physical money, or it may just involve Guy and Sharon telling Janet to shift her records to change how much money she is holding for each of them (or both). If Guy and Sharon and Janet keep good records, there should not be a problem by waiting and periodically settling the accounts.

These are how the transactions could operate when more than one entity like Guy is involved in transactions where transfer of ownership of some or all of the money occurs without money physically changing its location. In such a case, the banks do all the work with the money, but Bob and George instruct the banks on what transactions they want to occur.

In the scenarios I have described **Guy** and **Sharon** represent **Commercial Banks**. **Janet**, on the other hand is the **Central Bank**, which in the United States is known as the Federal Reserve Bank.

Something I want to say about this 3-step process of spending by Bob to pay George using the banks to conduct the transaction. Two steps involve spending to purchase loans. When Bob withdraws his money from the bank, that is Guy buying back part the loan he got from Bob when he deposited the money. This buying back of part of the loan reduces Guy's debt obligation to Bob. And when George buys an increase in his deposit account, he is loaning the money to Sharon, in exchange for an asset called a larger deposit balance. Only when Bob gives the money to George is the spending not purchasing a debt obligation. This is the part of the spending I call "direct spending". Buying a debt obligation by loaning money is not direct spending. Paying down some of that debt obligation is not direct spending. This will become important in a later chapter. Another term I use for an asset whose value is based on the debt obligation the issuer of a loan acquires from the borrower is a "purely financial asset". Neither paying to obtain such an asset, nor paying to reduce the debt obligation upon which the value of that loan is based counts as direct spending.

Defining the Money Supply

Now I am ready to describe what contributes to the total money supply:

All coins valued in terms of the given countries chosen currency, like pennies, nickels, dimes and quarters etc. in America, where these are produced by the Treasury Department in their mints at the behest of the Central Bank.

All paper currency, also in America created by the Treasury at the behest of the Central Bank.

All money designated by the Central Bank as existing and kept track of on a ledger, which I am calling virtual money.

The Central Bank, i.e., in our scenarios, Janet, is the one who controls the money supply. The Central Bank can create more money. For example, the Central Bank has the option of just saying the money exists and keeping track of it on a ledger, or it can print the money on paper. The Central Bank can convert the two types of money back and forth. It can convert the money that only exists because "Janet" (the Central Bank) said it does, i.e., "virtual money" into paper money and it can adjust the ledger to reflect less virtual money. The Central Bank could also destroy the paper money but say the money still exists by adding the amount destroyed to a ledger, that is, it could convert paper money into virtual money.

When the money is stored at the Central Bank, either as paper currency, coins or as money kept on a ledger, it may or may not be considered part of the money supply. I consider money to be in the money supply if it is available for spending by entities other than the Central Bank. That means money is in the money supply when it is owned by persons or entities other than the Central Bank. When the money is stored at the Central Bank but not OWNED by the Central Bank -- when it is owned by concerns outside the Central Bank -- it is part of the money supply; it is available to be spent.

Again, any money **owned by the** Central Bank is NOT in the money supply. If money is owned by the Central Bank, the Central Bank could change the form of it back and forth from paper to virtual all it wants. It could create as much money as it wants by ordering it printed or by just saying it exists, or it could reduce the amount of money by saying it does not exist or destroying the paper money. None of that matters, if the money is **not** owned by some person or entity outside of the Central Bank, the money is **not** in the money supply, and it has no effect on the economy. Only when the money becomes owned by someone outside the Central Bank does it become part of the money supply. Only at that point does it become consequential, because at that point it becomes available for spending by entities other than the Central Bank. **The money supply therefore consists of:**

1. Paper money, coins or virtual money (declared as existing and kept track of on a ledger) that is **stored** at the central bank but **owned** by an entity other than the central bank

2. Coins and paper money owned AND possessed by entities other than the central bank.

The probable reason that virtual transactions and virtual money exists is because financial types realized if we just kept good records and everything was done honestly, we could do everything quicker and easier and avoid having to transport physical cash all over the place and that we can even avoid having to create physical money to a certain extent. In modern society, where we have electronic virtual money, it is important to again emphasize how record keeping is so important, and that honesty, integrity and reliability are vital, or the economic systems will break down. Without those human factors in operation the advantages of our current monetary system that come from convenience and speed of commerce could be negated. Those human qualities, those human efforts are of central importance.

Standard economic teaching describes different types of money supplies. My definition of the money supply most closely matches what is called the "base money supply".

Investopedia says, "A monetary base is the total amount of a currency that is either in general circulation in the hands of the public or in the commercial bank deposits held in the central bank's reserves."[6]

In my definition, currency in general circulation is the coins and paper currency possessed and owned by entities other the Central Bank. The "commercial bank deposits held in the Central Bank's reserves" correspond to money stored at the Central Bank but "owned" by the Commercial Bank.

As mentioned, what I call the money supply also includes any money owned by the Treasury, physical or virtual, where virtual money owned by the Treasury is money "stored at the Central Bank but owned by the Treasury". The definition of the money supply I use in in this book differs from what is generally called the base money supply, in that the standard definition does not include money "owned" by the Treasury. Since money owned by the Treasury is money owned by an entity other than the Central Bank, money owned by the Treasury is part of the money supply in my model.

Reserves of Commercial banks stored at the Central Bank is money "owned by the Commercial Bank but stored the Central Bank" and we could also call "money owned by the Treasury but stored at the Central Bank" as **reserves** of the Treasury stored at the Central Bank.

In both cases the description of virtual money means that the money is stored as records on the Central Bank's ledgers, which records also show who owns each piece of that virtual money.

---

6   https://www.investopedia.com/terms/m/monetarybase.asp#ixzz5A1UGgoTj

Other definitions of the money supply all consist of the base money supply and/or some other asset or assets. All these other assets I count as being just assets, not a part of the money supply. All those assets that are claimed to increase the money supply are, to my understanding, based on loans. Money that is part of the base money supply is itself an asset, but not all assets are part of the base money supply. Assets that are completely based on loans I call "purely financial assets", not money.

The claim is that "banks create money" by lending, and creating these purely financial assets. The common teaching is these assets can be used for spending just like base money. If a purely financial asset could be used for spending, that is a barter. I believe that a more accurate description of how a purely financial asset may affect the level of spending is to say that the asset must first be liquidated, i.e., sold for base money, which can then be used for further spending. It is the base money supply that is used for any spending, not the other assets. A barter economy is different than a monetary economy because in a barter system all traded commodities are considered 'base' money. That means each item of wealth is currency and there are as many different types of currencies as there are different types of items of wealth. In a barter economy every item of wealth that can be bartered is part of the base money supply of that economy.

Typically, labels are assigned to what are described as the different types of money supplies. Base money is usually designated $\mathbf{M_B}$. They label other so-called money supplies as M_0, M_1, M_2 and the like. I will not go into any detail on the definitions, except to say they are combinations of base money and loans. It is standard teaching that our system of loans "multiplies the money supply". I do not agree. I will describe what I think is a better way to understand this "money multiplier money" in the next Chapter.

Some people might like to claim that when spending has occurred with virtual money that the actual bank deposit was acting as the money, that the spending is done with all or part of a bank deposit, because it is the bank deposit that has changed ownership. Now, because, by definition of virtual money, the Central Bank has to keep track of who owns the money, it is not practical for it to follow that money to individual owners. What happens in reality is the Central Bank only follows the ownership of the money to the level of the Commercial Bank. The way the Commercial Bank gets to own the money someone has deposited, is by agreeing to owe the bank depositor a debt obligation in the amount of the deposit. However, the spending of that amount of money is still directed by the bank depositor, and the transaction does require spending of money to purchase an asset, i.e., to purchase a debt obligation, or to buy back part of and reduce a debt obligation or to actually purchase the desired item. All of that is spending. But even though the end result is just a shifting in the value of two bank accounts, the ownership, or the nature of the ownership of the money used for spending in that transaction has changed. Either the ownership of the money has shifted from the buyer's Commercial Bank to the seller's Commercial Bank, a change in ownership of that amount of money. Or if the buyer and seller had the same Commercial Bank, the ownership of the money is shifted from that amount of total deposits deemed acquired as a result of having a debt obligation to the buyer to that amount of the deposits deemed as acquired as a result of a debt obligation to the seller. The spending has occurred due to the transfer of ownership of money that is "stored at the Central Bank (on a ledger) but owned by the Commercial Bank". The spending occurs in this fashion due to the nature of virtual money.

CHAPTER 4
The Money Multiplier

The reason this chapter is important is because it is standard macroeconomic teaching that due to something called the money multiplier, Commercial Banks, via lending, create most of our money. In this way money and the money supply is represented as some ephemeral thing, something that is "not based on anything" and could quickly disappear. I counter that view and show that the money supply is on much firmer ground, and that it is only the Central Bank that creates money, and it is the Central Bank that controls the size of the money supply.

FIRST I WILL explain how the money multiplier is typically presented, then I will show what I believe is a better way to understand the concept.

The money multiplier concept is based on loans. The standardly taught explanation is as follows:

Economists say banks create money by loaning out a fraction of deposit money, up to 90%. The fraction they are not allowed to loan out (typically 10%) is called the reserve requirement. The reserve requirement is the amount of deposit money that banks must keep ownership of, they are not allowed to loan that money out. The reserve requirement affects the money multiplier.

The money multiplier starts with an original deposit. An account is created in the amount of the deposit, or the value of a preexisting account is increased by that amount. Let us say it is 100 dollars. Then the bank makes loans from that money. Let us say it was able to loan out all 90% allowed. It loans out 90 dollars out of the

100. The borrowers use the money for spending. The money cycles through the economy being spent and re-spent until eventually those that end up as "the owners" of that 90 dollars decide to put that money back into the banks. This means that now there would be an account with a balance of 100 dollars at the original bank, plus other accounts totaling 90 dollars for a grand total of 190 dollars of deposits.

No more of that 100 dollars from the initial deposit account can be loaned out, since in our scenario, they have already loaned out the maximum 90% allowed. However, there are also new deposits of 90 dollars and 90% of that money is allowed to be loaned out up to a total of 81 dollars. This is done and that creates another round of spending and re-spending after which the people who end up with the money put it back into deposit accounts in the banks. Now we have total deposits of 100 plus 90 plus 81 dollars, a total of 271 dollars.

The bank cannot loan any more of the original 100 dollars, having already loaned 90% of it, and it cannot loan out any more of the 90 dollars, having already loaned 90% of that, but it can loan out 90% of the 81 dollars, and so on.

Little by little, round upon round of lending and spending and re-depositing of the money occurs. In each succeeding round the total amount of deposits increases. The increments in the total amount of bank deposits gets smaller and smaller but the total of deposits keeps growing until all the money that would have been available for lending gets tied up into those 10% required reserves, so that no more can be loaned out.

Mathematically we can show that if we repeat this process, loaning out the maximum possible each round, the total amount of deposits created will be the original deposit amount times 1 divided by the fractional reserve requirement, or in this case, 100 dollars times the amount (1/0.10) which equals 1000 dollars [100*(1/0.10)]. (This is based on the formula for an infinite geometric series for those who are interested). This means, that if in every round all the money gets re-deposited and the banks were able to lend out 90% of the re-deposited money, the total amount of bank deposits would have increased from 100 dollars to 1000 dollars. The system of lending and redepositing would have created additional bank deposits of 900 dollars.

It is true if some of the money did not make it back into bank deposits that would lower the maximum possible deposit account balance and matching debt. For example, if 10 dollars did not make it back into the bank accounts, and people in the community kept it, then the total amount of base money the banks would own would be 90 dollars. This means deposit account totals could not surpass 900 dollars because that is the maximum deposits the banks could have with only 90 dollars actual cash or "base money" owned by the banks. This is because they must keep at least 10% of total deposits in cash. In such a case, with 10 dollars not returning to bank deposits, the banks would have 90 dollars cash and would be able to lend 810 dollars for total deposits of 900 dollars, 90 being 10 % of 900.

If all the deposit money loaned out returns to bank deposits, then the only thing that limits the maximum amount of deposits is the fractional reserve requirement. If it were 20 percent, the most deposit account totals could reach would be 500 dollars (100*(1/0.20) = 500 dollars). If the reserve requirement were 5% the maximum the deposit amount could reach would be 2000 dollars (100*(1/0.05) = 2000 dollars).

The standard teaching is that for all intents and purposes this money functions like any other money. This would be true unless people attempt to withdraw too much money out of their accounts all at once. Because even though the banks show total deposits of $1000, the actual amount of money in the banks is $100. If the depositors tried to withdraw more than $100 the banking system would not be able to pay. This would create a panic as more and more people begin to worry that they could not get their money out of the banks and people would attempt to withdraw it all. This is an illustration of what happens when there is a "run on the banks".

Nowadays, we prevent the need for runs on the banks because we have deposit insurance. In such a case the government would have to provide money to the bank depositors, so they would not lose their deposit money up to whatever limit the government insures (currently around $250,000 per deposit account). In the United States this is called FDIC deposit insurance.

Why the Money Multiplier is Not an Increase in the Money Supply

Why it is Really Just an Increase in the Velocity of Money

This is my explanation of the phenomenon known as the money multiplier. I try to show how the multiplier is really caused by an increase in the velocity of money, that is, it is an increase in the re-spending of that original deposit money.

The Money Multiplier

Let us say that at the beginning of a given time period a depositor puts money in the bank. That depositor just purchased something. He or she purchased an asset called a bank deposit. They have in the process given over ownership of the money they just deposited to the bank. In return the bank acquires a matching debt obligation to the depositor.

Let us say that 100 dollars is put into a bank account. That purchases a 100 dollar asset for the depositor. But the bank obtains, and now owns the actual 100 dollars of money and in return for that, has acquired a debt obligation of 100 dollars.

The bank is now allowed to loan 90 of that 100 dollars out. After the bank approves the loan it gives ownership of the 90 dollars to the borrower. By law, the bank has to keep ownership of 10 dollars in case the original depositor wants to withdraw some money(fractional reserve requirement). But despite the bank only having 10 dollars, the depositor's asset, his bank deposit, is still worth 100 dollars. The bank still has a debt obligation to the depositor of 100 dollars. However, the bank also has an asset, a 90 dollar debt obligation of the borrower to the bank.

Let us say that the 90 dollars given the borrower is spent, goes through the economy as spending and re-spending and eventually the final owners of the money, the ones who end up with it, put the 90 dollars into their bank accounts. That 90 dollars then becomes owned again by the banks. Those that deposited the 90 dollars have purchased assets, i.e., bank deposits worth 90 dollars, but the banks own the money at that point. The money the banks own is the real money, the base money, like coins, currency, or virtual money, not just an asset. At that point, the banks become owners of that 90 dollars and now there is 10 dollars base money still owned by the bank of the original depositor, and 90 dollars base money owned by the banks of the second round of depositors. At this point the amount of base money is 10 + 90 = 100 dollars still, but total value of the deposit accounts and the banks total debt obligations to the depositors are 100 dollars plus 90 dollars = 190 dollars.

At this point there has been created two deposit accounts showing values of 100 dollars and 90 dollars for a total value of 190 dollars, yet the total amount of cash amounts to the 10 dollars saved out of the original deposit at the original bank, plus the 90 dollars which was redeposited, for a total of 100 dollars.

The amount of cash still totals 100 dollars because in the process of depositing and lending and spending and redepositing, no actual new money was created. What were created were ASSETS called bank deposits of 190 dollars. There are also matching debt obligations of the banks for the value of bank deposits, and matching debt obligation of the borrower to the bank.

Banks don't want to sit on that 90 dollars since they make their profits by lending. The bank of the original depositor can't loan out the 10 dollars they have. They have already loaned out the maximum, but the banks that got the 90 dollars as deposits can lend up to 90 percent of that 90. That means they can lend out an additional 81 dollars of the cash they are owners of. They of course are obligated to continue to hold 10% of that 90 dollars as a reserve requirement, i.e., they must keep and not lend out 9 dollars in case those depositors want to withdraw some money.

Let us say that in the second round banks loan out 81 dollars. This means that they purchase assets called **loans** from the borrowers and they give over ownership of the 81 dollars to the borrowers who can then spend it, leading to a cycle of re-spending until those who end up with the money again put that 81 dollars into their bank accounts, i.e., they purchase assets called bank deposits from their banks. Those banks then have another debt obligation to the depositors of 81 dollars, but the 81 dollars become "owned" again by the banks.

At this point the assets the depositors have, called bank deposits, which are paired to the debt obligations of the banks, have increased in value to 100 + 90 + 81 = 271 dollars. The amount of cash, all of which is again owned by the banks is 10 + 9 + 81 = 100 dollars.

The borrowers, at this point, have a debt obligation to the banks of 90 plus 81 dollars, 171 dollars, i.e., the banks own purely financial assets of 171 dollars, but the banks also own all the cash, i.e., the banks also have ownership of 100 dollars. That is, the assets the banks have plus the cash the banks have total 271 dollars. And the debt obligations the banks have to depositors also totals 271 dollars. Despite deposits increasing to 271 dollars, the base money, the actual money, remains 100 dollars.

The cycle continues with the same results as described in the standardly taught explanation. The 100 dollar value of the original bank deposit can turn into a maximum of 1000 dollars value total in all the deposit account assets. Yet despite that, there is still only 100 dollars actual base money. The rest of the 900 dollars are just assets based on the 900 dollar debt obligations the borrowers owe the banks. This 900 dollars the banks, in turn, owe to the depositors, plus the 100 dollars they owe to the original depositor. Presumably, the banks don't mind being owed because the borrowers will also have to pay interest, and the depositors don't mind being owed because the banks have to pay them interest, though in a lesser amount.

In every transaction in this scenario involving the banks, spending is always accomplished by the change in ownership of the actual cash, that is by change in ownership of the base money, not the transfer of other assets. By the "actual" cash or money, I mean it is part of the base money supply, part of what I called the money supply in a previous chapter. When this money is spent purchasing a loan, that is, a purely financial asset, both an asset and a matching debt obligation are created. When someone puts money into a deposit account, an asset to the depositor is created, sold by the bank to the depositor, in return for the cash and a new debt obligation the bank owes to the depositor. When a bank lends money, the loan is an asset to the bank, sold to the bank by the borrower in return for the cash and a matching debt obligation of the borrower to the bank. The assets and debt obligations are purchased by, and created by, the change in ownership of actual money, i.e., base money, not by the change in ownership of the assets. The assets which are based on loan obligations are purchased using base money when they are created. When the debt obligations are paid off, in part or in full, it is spending by the debt holder to "purchase back" the asset and reduce or eliminate the debt. This spending, to buy back part of the asset and reduce the loan obligation, is accomplished by the transfer of ownership of base money. At no time in the process was any "asset" being used for spending. It was always the base money being used for the spending.

I am not saying that assets of any type cannot be bartered. I am saying that in the system of lending by the banks that creates the money multiplier, all of the spending is accomplished by the change of ownership of money, and not the change of ownership of assets.

The rationalization that this system of loans has created new money, is predicated on the implication that the value of the assets called bank deposits is the same as money. They are not money, they are assets.

We will cover the difference between income and wealth later, but for now I will just mention that while the assets are not money, they are, however, wealth. Although these assets may increase in value they are not used for spending and therefore do not create income, with income defined as being caused by the transfer of ownership of money from one person or entity to another. One way the assets increase in value is when the entity with the debt obligation pays interest. This is spending and is caused by the transfer of ownership of money. The borrower

The Money Multiplier

not only has to spend to pay down his debt's principle, but they also have to spend to pay interest accrued. Paying for both is spending.

It is important to note that even though, when these banks deposit assets are created, they add to wealth on the positive side, since they are all matched with an equal amount of debt obligation on the negative side, the overall level of total wealth is not increased. It is possible that the spending facilitated by these loans will lead to some production that increases wealth, but the loans, in and of themselves, do not.

What the system of loans does to deposit money is to increase the number of times it gets spent. This means that what the system of lending does is to increase the **velocity** of the deposit money. It does not increase the money supply. It does create a lot of assets, and all the matching debt obligations, but it does not create money. All the actual spending uses base money, that is, in this description of the money multiplier phenomenon, any spending that occurs is accomplished by the transfer of ownership of actual money, coins, paper or virtual, from one person or entity to another. In our example, all of the spending occurs using "the same money"; money that was part of the 100-dollar original deposit.

Yes, some money may have been switched out with other money, but by the same money, I mean money that is in the position it is in the amount it is because of the chain of spending that caused it to be there, (see Chapter 2 for the explanation of "the same money").

Remember how in the standard explanation of the money multiplier I said this:

"The standard teaching is that for all intents and purposes this money functions like any other money. This would be true unless people attempt to withdraw too much money out of their accounts all at once."

Well, in the case where banks were able to loan out the maximum possible, **"too much"** would be any attempt to take more than 10% of the deposits. That is because in this example, the only money existing and being used for spending is the base money, not the "money multiplier money". If depositors tried to take more than 10% of the deposits, the money wouldn't be there, and the bank would be in default. That 100 dollars, in our example, is the only actual money that can be used for spending even though, in our example, there could be deposits valued at 1000 dollars (and do not forget 900 dollars in offsetting debt).

So actually, the statement is not true, money multiplier does not, "for all intents and purposes", act like base money. In our example, if that 900 dollars functioned like base money, depositors would be able to withdraw and spend all of it, which as mentioned they cannot, because all the banks would have available to give them is the 100 dollars originally deposited. In the normal course of banking, none of the "money multiplier money' is used for spending, only the base money is used for spending.

Now, whether they know it or not, anyone who uses the banking system to store their wealth has agreed to certain conditions. One central condition is they have agreed to participate in the system of lending. They have agreed to allow the bank to use a certain amount of the money they deposit, say 90%, to buy debt obligations from the bank's borrowers. This means that, if the banks successfully make those loans, that not all the money depositors have put in the bank will be available for immediate withdrawal. With 10% fractional reserve requirement, only 10% of that deposit money will be available to be withdrawn.

But this condition is not simply a one person one bank agreement. The agreement really applies to all the depositors of that bank combined. The agreement is that all the depositors of that bank agree to the condition that combined, they will not be able to withdraw more than, in this example, 10% of their money. Some can withdraw more, some can withdraw less, but if all the customers combined tried to withdraw more than 10% of the total deposits, they would not be able to. This implicit agreement allows the system of lending to function and still gives the flexibility to individual depositors to be able to make cash withdrawals in excess of that 10% at times. Via loans, and this implicit agreement just mentioned, the fractional reserve system of banking serves as a way to get money to people and entities who want to use it for spending, at the time they have the need or desire to do so.

CHAPTER 5
WHAT ARE THE ESSENTIAL FUNCTIONS OF BANKS?

What essential service do banks provide to a society other than the aforementioned increase in the velocity of money lending provides? What other service do they render that justifiably supports them earning income?

A BANK'S SERVICES include processing transactions and safeguarding people's monetary wealth. However, in my opinion, the most important service they provide is administering the loans they dispense. This refers to the entire process from the person's application for the loan, to checking credit, to the dispensing of the loan, to tracking loan payments, to the collections process.

Properly administering a loan requires the banks to loan responsibly and this requires ensuring that the borrowers have the ability to pay back the loans. It also requires providing the structure for payment and the monitoring and maintenance of that structure. The design and implementation of that structure needs to motivate borrowers to be responsible in paying back the loans. In other words, the banks do the hard work of setting up and administering an entire behavioral modification system that ensures the lending system works the way it is supposed to. It ensures that borrowers are rewarded for acting responsibly and have consequences when they do not.

Acting responsibly includes making sure you have an income and that becomes a motivator for people to be functional and continue to work and contribute to society, to make sure that they have the means to pay back the loan. For the banks to be able to accomplish these functions requires the whole structure of the banking system we are used to dealing with. The banks must keep track of credit histories, manage records of accounts and account details, communicate

What Are the Essential Functions of Banks?

and interact with borrowers on a regular basis via statements and being available for customer service issues, do the hard work of dealing with late or delinquent borrowers, etc.

In real life, either a person is going to try to find ways to function without ever having to take a loan, which for most people will require a lot of hard work to accomplish, or will require them to sacrifice taking advantage of a lot of opportunities in life. For most of us, in order to achieve the standard of living we hope for, we will have to obtain loans of various types and manage making the payments. Most people require accessing credit and managing debt as a part of their normal existence.

Having to make regular loan payments can have a positive influence, it can serve as a motivating force for people to keep working and producing at the level they currently do. I suspect that without that motivation it would be more difficult to get people to perform a lot of the tasks that are required to keep our economy and our society functioning at the level to which we have become accustomed. I suspect that a lot of people need that motivation. If so, then the system of lending becomes an essential ingredient to maintaining our standard of living. The banks are integral to keeping that process running smoothly and in an intelligent fashion.

The way things are set up, with a competitive banking sector, that is, as long as our government prevents overriding monopoly power in the banking sector, the banks will need to treat their customers well to keep getting their business. If the banks want to be the "lender of choice", then they need to keep their customers satisfied. In administrating the loans, the banks will need to work with their borrowers in humane and compassionate ways. All of this is hard work, a lot of labor, and those providing the labor are providing an essential service which justifies being paid.

These are the essential contributions of the banking system to our society. I think the motivation that being in debt provides people is probably a necessary ingredient of our economy at the present time. I suspect if we suddenly tried to eliminate all debt we would have serious adverse consequences.

Some in the Gurdjieff work interpret his expression, that one should follow the "way of the sly man" to mean putting oneself in a position where one must work or face consequences. I believe that the banking system and the system of loans works kind of like that. Not that everyone getting loans is practicing the Gurdjieff work, but owing money does motivate people to work and perform essential tasks.

Administering these loans is hard work, so banks do provide legitimate services for which they and their employees should be compensated. This is the "fair profit of able dealing" as Lao Tzu puts it in the Tao Te Ching (Witter Bynner translation). So, the fair profit of able dealing can apply to banks too, as they do provide a real service and benefit to society.

There are dangers with the banking system of course. If there are not enough banks to keep the market for loans and deposits competitive then those banks that have acquired a degree of monopoly power would be able to overcharge and underserve their customers, even for the above mentioned legitimate services. The utilization of virtual money in transactions, i.e., the idea that money exists only on a ledger and is not ever put into the form of physical currency or coin, suggests the possibility of misuse or abuse by unscrupulous bankers. For these reasons, banks probably more than any other business need government oversight and regulation and strong anti-trust laws. Further, it is possible that a tyrannical government could come to power and misuse our financial records as a way to control its citizens or to punish dissent. The electronic accounting of our assets would make this task more easily and rapidly accomplished. No doubt all these things will occur, and probably already have in different places at different times.

Some people wonder why banks should not be allowed to be "investment houses" in addition to institutions that make all their money from loans. This, I submit, is a no brainer. Banks absolutely should not be allowed to be "investment houses".

Why? Because banks would use the money they own, for which they have debt obligations to their depositor, to acquire financial interests in things other than loans. If they lost money on those ventures they could be put in a position where they no longer have the required reserve, and this could lead to bank failures.

Any resulting bank collapse would obligate the FDIC to pay the banks to replenish those reserves, with real money, not money multiplier money. Actually, they would only have to replenish the reserves enough to support individuals' deposit accounts of up to $250,000 (at this time in the U.S.) meaning some peoples' savings would be at risk.

I have mentioned how much hard work it is for banks to administer loans. The motivation for banks and their employees and officers to provide that labor, in an ethical and efficient manner, comes not only from the profit motive but also from regulations and regulators. If banks could put their money anywhere other than loans, the ability to regulate such spending would be infinitely more complicated. This puts bank deposits at higher risk and makes bank failures more likely. More frequent bank failures increase the need for more frequent and more expensive FDIC intervention, all of which must be paid for somehow and diverts money away from other uses.

Our economy cannot function without a stable banking system. If an individual private investor goes belly up due to a private venture failing, then too bad for those invested in the venture, but they will unfortunately have to suffer the consequences. But if a bank acquires risky assets and they lose significant value, the consequences are borne by everyone. The situation where if a bank loses significant money from risky assets, they will be bailed out by the FDIC shelters the banks somewhat from the consequences and makes it more likely that the scenario would be repeated. If a gambler got their funds replenished every time they lose, what incentive would they have to stop gambling.

Commercial Banks are generally expected to get their money for lending from depositors, but if circumstances are such that the commercial banks find themselves with inadequate deposits to fund more lending, the Central Bank can provide loans of money to the Commercial Banks for lending, at rates lower than the Commercial Banks will charge for the loans. The Central Bank will create the money and dispense it to the Commercial Banks. This would be done so banks have enough money to satisfy the desire for loans by qualified borrowers. If the bank diverted that money to risky ventures, instead of loaned it, or if the bank is short on deposit money because, instead of providing loans, they already put the money into other types of riskier assets, then the Central bank providing those wholesale loans to Commercial banks would, in essence, be funding those riskier investments with wholesale loans. That would give the banks a competitive advantage on their investments, as compared to those of us who would have to fund their investments with higher interest rate retail loans. The Central Bank providing loans to commercial banks is supposed to be for the socially beneficial purpose of making sure there is an adequate liquidity for essential lending, not to give bankers a competitive advantage over the rest of us.

What Are the Essential Functions of Banks?

Banks are essential to the functioning of our economy and our society, but they should never be allowed to function as "investment houses". Other than paying for operating expenses needed to exist and provide their normal services, the only spending Commercial Banks should be doing is paying to acquire assets whose value is based on the debt obligations of the borrowers.

CHAPTER 6
Permanently Increasing the Money Supply

I have already covered how the money supply is increased or decreased on a temporary basis. In this chapter, I explain why it is necessary to have the money supply gradually increase over time, to prevent economic hardship. I consider different ways this can be done.

TO REVIEW: IN order to increase the money supply the Central Bank takes money that is not in the money supply including new money it has just created, and purchases assets with it. That makes that money available for spending by people and institutions in the economy. It has then become part of the money supply. To decrease the money supply, the Central Bank sells assets. When someone gives money to the Central Bank for the asset being sold, the money paid becomes owned by the Central Bank. At that point it is now out of the money supply.

Any money owned by the Central Bank and being out of the money supply has no effect on the economy. Whatever internal accounting the Central Bank does of that money is meaningless. It can keep saying it exists on some ledger and is owned solely by the Central Bank, or it can just say it does not exist on that ledger anymore, either way it doesn't matter. If it is paper money owned by the Central Bank, the Central Bank can destroy it or store it, or print up brand new money, it doesn't matter (except to the extent that money is paid for production costs of printing money, which amounts leave the Central Banks ownership and become part of the money supply). It does not matter because when the only one who owns it is the Central Bank, meaning it cannot be used by anyone else for spending, it is out of the money supply.

Permanently Increasing the Money Supply

The money supply is always in flux, and if the buying of assets by the Central Bank is greater than the selling of assets, the money supply increases, whereas if the selling of assets by the Central Bank is greater than the buying of assets, the money supply decreases. One way we get a decrease in the money supply is when the bond issuer (The Treasury) is paying off their debt, making payments to the Central Bank on a bond to decrease their debt obligation (bonds are a loan, and issuers of bonds are borrowers). That is because those transactions are equivalent to the Central Bank selling back all or part of those assets. Each time a payment is made, that money becomes owned by the Central Bank and the money supply gets reduced by that amount. As mentioned in a previous chapter, in America, any interest payment on a bond or loan paid to the Central Bank will stay part of the money supply, because that money will be used to pay for Central Bank operations, with any remainder being returned to the general fund of the Treasury, both of which return that money to the money supply, according to my definitions.

The amount of loan or bond assets owned by the Central Bank, for which the Central Bank is owed a debt obligation is what is called the Central Bank's "**BALANCE SHEET**". Every time the Central Bank buys an asset it increases the balance sheet and every time the Central Bank sells an asset it decreases the balance sheet. If the Central Bank holds a lot of assets, then the Central Bank is said to have a "large balance sheet".

All those discussions so far about how to increase or decrease the money supply are about interventions which are reversible.

How does one permanently increase the money supply? Is it even necessary? If so why?

If the money supply does need to increase gradually over time, the reason for this would be the amount of spending (**M∗V**) in nominal terms keeps increasing. By nominal terms, I mean the total amount of spending in terms of the face value of the money, for example, the worth of the money in terms of the actual dollar amount (as compared to the buying power of a given amount of money which is how much product that amount of money will buy). This increase in nominal spending occurs in part because of inflation and in part because of increased production.

In the modern economy it is generally a normal feature for there to be a baseline inflation. As prices go up, nominal spending must increase by as much or the spending will end up purchasing less. That is, if nominal spending does not increase as much as prices, real, inflation adjusted spending will decrease. Since spending equals income this means real income goes down as well.

In addition to needing to have nominal spending (which equals income) increase to keep pace with prices, an additional amount of spending will be needed to pay for any increase in total sales caused by increased production. The increased production could result from an increase in the amount of production per worker (increased productivity), or an increase in the population and the number of workers making the product.

Generally, if an economy produces more product it is because there is a market for it, meaning we are only going to produce more if it is going to sell. If the amount of spending, in nominal terms, is kept constant but the amount of product sold increases, that means prices have decreased. When prices decrease, we call that deflation. Deflation means the buying power of that amount of spending has increased. If the buying power of a certain amount of spending (income) increases, we say that the real income has increased.

I have already mentioned that, normally, there is a baseline inflation. This means that if we are maintaining that rate of inflation and selling the same amount of product, nominal spending must be increasing at the same rate as inflation. However, if we were producing and selling more product, the only way we could be maintaining the same inflation rate is if nominal spending is increasing faster than prices, i.e., faster than the rate of inflation. We need a spending increase to keep pace with inflation, and we need a further spending increase to pay for the increased production.

We know that we can increase spending and income by either an increase in the money supply or an increase in the velocity of money, because spending equals **M∗V**.

If the velocity of money had no limits on how high it could go, then there would never be a need to increase the money supply. You could support whatever amount of spending you wanted to with just an increase in **V** and you would never have to increase **M**.

In today's world of electronic transactions **V** can get pretty high. but there are always things that put a practical limit on **V**. Even in electronic transactions there is the human factor slowing velocity. No matter how fast the computers process transactions humans will still be involved in reviewing transactions and in spending decisions. So, at certain points in the process even transactions done electronically with virtual money will be slowed. There are, also, parts of the money supply that do not get spent at all, in a given time period, because people and institutions and even foreign countries hold that money as cash, as a store of wealth. That part of the money supply will have a zero velocity.

Whatever the causes, it is reasonable to assume that the velocity of money cannot increase infinitely. When the limits on velocity of money are approached, spending and income increases may begin to slow. Historical situations where lack of adequate money supply slowed the economy are not uncommon. The reason they put a Mint in San Francisco, California in the 1850s was because lack of money was hurting trade. In the civil war they created Greenbacks to increase the money supply to fund the war effort. In the late 1800s the people fought to have money backed by silver be issued as the supply of money backed by gold was inadequate to meet their needs. In 1935 the government increased the price of gold from 20 dollars an ounce, to 35 dollars an ounce, so they could print more money.

If one accepts that the velocity of money has practical limitations then one can reason that there will come a time when the total money supply **M** will need to be increased, and held at an increased level, that is, there comes a time when the money supply needs to be increased permanently. To do otherwise can cause a situation where spending is inadequate to pay for new production and keep pace with inflation. Eventually this would lead to a deflation, but not a deflation caused by making things cheaper by producing more, so ones money will buy more. That would be a supply caused deflation. Instead what I am talking about here is an inadequate demand caused deflation. A decreased ability for people or entities to be able to spend to buy the product that could otherwise be available for sale, simply because the current money supply is inadequate to support the desired level of spending, i.e., that level of spending that could occur, if the money supply were larger. This can have significant adverse consequences. (See Chapter 9). To have that occur simply due to a lack of an adequate money supply should be completely avoidable.

How is the money supply increased permanently? There is actually a very simple answer, but it requires complicated explanations of how it is done. The simple answer is that we permanently increase the money supply when, over a sufficiently long period of time, we have increased the money supply more than we have decreased it. Restated, this says that we have permanently increased the money supply when over a sufficiently long period of time the Central Bank has paid more for purchasing assets than the Central Bank has earned by selling assets.

Those two statements express the easy answer. Let us try to explore some ways to make that actually happen.

One way to keep growing the money supply is to have the Central Bank's "balance sheet" keep growing. The balance sheet of the Central Bank is how much it is owed for bonds it purchased or loans it dispensed. If the Central Bank is buying more bonds than it is selling, then it is increasing the balance sheet, and increasing the money supply. But the bigger the balance sheet, the more assets the Central Bank needs to buy just to prevent the balance sheet from shrinking. This is because those who owe debt, mostly the Treasury, will be making required payments. As they pay off some of what is owed on the bonds or loans, the balance sheet shrinks, and so does the money supply. The bigger the balance sheet, the faster those payments will be coming in, and the faster the balance sheet will be shrinking. This will require the Central Bank to increase the rate of bond purchases to keep the balance sheet and money supply growing or even to just keep the balance sheet and money supply from shrinking. We would have to be constantly fighting the tendency for the money supply to shrink. That would mean, in the long run, constantly increasing the purchase of debt to maintain an increasing money supply. Perhaps not the ideal way to keep the money supply stable or increasing.

What other ways might the money supply be increased permanently? Some have proposed increasing the money supply by having the Central Bank forgive debt, that is, retire Treasury bonds. Simply tell the Treasury, they do not owe the money anymore. But in the United States, the Central Bank is not currently authorized to do so. That type of intervention could permanently increase the money supply and directly benefit the poor and the middle class because it would then directly fund government programs. But it is outlawed. The concern here would be that irresponsible politicians and officials would misuse this for political purposes leading to market inefficiencies and supply shortages.

If it were legal the Central Bank could simply print money and give a small amount to everyone, or to everyone whose net worth is below a certain amount. That would permanently increase the money supply, but the concerns here are that this tactic would be inappropriately and unscrupulously utilized for political reasons. If that were the case, it could cause market distortions that reward inefficiency and adversely affect production and productivity. That could lead to very real supply problems and reduce wealth production and standard of living. In extreme cases it can lead to hyperinflation and humanitarian disasters such as has occurred in Venezuela and Zimbabwe in recent times. That is probably why this also is not allowed under current U.S. law.

Is there a way, to legally permanently increase the money supply without increasing the balance sheet? Yes. One way this can occur is by having the Central Bank "Buy high and Sell low". The Central Bank could pay more for the assets than it gets back when it later sells them. It is reasonable to expect that this occurs, because when demand for bonds is higher, it causes the prices to increase. When demand is lower, it causes the prices to decrease. Therefore, the fact of the Central Bank buying bonds will drive the prices up compared to a baseline value (especially during times when they are purchasing a lot of bonds). Whereas the fact of the Central Bank selling bonds, especially if selling in high volume, will drive the prices down. The difference between the higher price they pay for the bonds and the lower price they sell the bonds for will become the amount of money that is unrecovered by the Central Bank, that stays in circulation and becomes a permanent part of the money supply. This maneuver, buying an asset for a high price and selling it later for a lower price, does not increase the balance sheet either; it does not increase the amount the Central Bank is owed, but it does increase the money supply.

In the previous section I was just sharing my understanding of the basic principles involved in permanently increasing the money supply. I do not represent myself as an expert on the subject. The bottom line is the Central Bank puts money in the money supply by spending, and it takes money out of the money supply by selling, and permanently increasing the money supply requires one to find a way for the Central Bank to buy more than it sells over time.

The Effect of Increasing the Money Supply as Understood by Proponents of the Quantity of Money Theory

There are those who are proponents of something called the Quantity of Money Theory, who believe that increasing the money supply by a certain proportion, is equivalent to increasing prices by the same proportion. That is, they believe that doubling the money supply will double prices. They believe that the sole cause of inflation is increasing the money supply.

I disagree with this claim. First off it is not the money supply that puts pressure on prices, it is the amount of spending. Spending equals income but income is not equal to **M**, the money supply. Income equals the value of the money supply in nominal terms (face value), **M**, times the velocity of money, **V**.

The other thing that affects prices is the amount of availability of opportunities to purchase product, the amount of goods, services, labor, or other outcomes available to be purchased.

If we increase spending by 10% and the amount of product available for purchase stayed the same, then one might expect prices to go up around 10%.

One of the ways the Quantity of Money theorists justify their belief is that they state that the velocity of money **V** remains constant. That way, doubling the money supply **M** would cause spending to double because with **V** constant and **M** doubled, **V∗M** would also be doubled. If the amount of product sold remained the same, then prices would have to double.

I believe their theory goes awry because their assumption that the velocity of money is constant is wrong. For example, if I had the authority to do so, I could double the money supply, give all the newly created money to myself and not spend any of it. That would be a situation where the money supply doubled but the velocity of money was cut in half, leaving the product **M∗V** unchanged, i.e., spending and income would not be affected at all. In that case, if production were constant, prices would not increase at all. That is an extreme example but illustrates the point.

Our current way of increasing the money supply mostly gives the money to richer people. The Central Bank buys bonds from people who own bonds and that means the recipients of that spending are skewed towards being wealthier people. That being the case, it is reasonable to assume that, even if the economy were at full employment, i.e., even if production could not be increased, prices will likely **not** increase proportionally to the amount of money received by the bond sellers. Why? Because the wealthier someone is, the lower the percentage of their income they will spend on goods and services, so extra income to them means less pressure on prices. Giving them all the new money will not increase prices as much as if you gave it all to poorer people. The poorer people will spend a greater percentage of it on goods and services, so giving the money to poorer people will put more pressure on prices. Giving it to the already wealthy will not necessarily increase spending that much, because the overall velocity of money will probably be reduced. A larger money supply, without a proportional increase in spending, means the velocity of money must have been reduced.

Another reason I believe the Quantity of Money advocates are wrong is that they ignore the possibility that if the economy is at less than full employment, and if increasing the money supply led to an increase in spending, that could lead to increased employment and increased production. If production was increased, then prices may not go up or may not go up as much. Even if the rest of the Quantity of Money theory were correct, in the situation where production increased, prices would not go up as much as the money supply.

It is my belief that the error made by Quantity of Money theorists is their assumption that increasing the money supply will have no effect on either production or velocity of money.

Conclusion:

The money supply does need to be increased to some extent over time, or we can end up with a money supply that is inadequate to allow the spending necessary to keep the economy growing, or at least continuing to function at the established level. Lack of adequate money will artificially slow economic activity.

I say artificially because once one understands the advantages of having FIAT money (F-I-A-T money), instead of "representative money", (such as gold standard money), one realizes there is really no reason to allow ourselves to be in such a situation. I can think of no justification for allowing commerce to be slowed simply because our society has an inadequate available money supply. The next chapter begins a discussion of this issue in more detail.

CHAPTER 7
Going from Barter to Monetary Economies

I briefly address my understanding of how economies have progressed from barter to monetary economies. Then I look at properties that make something a good currency, and describe some examples.

IN HISTORY, AS time progressed, barter transitioned to monetary economies. The change was gradual in that barter trade began to favor some items in trade over others. Items became favored due to certain properties. The properties that were favored certainly had something to do with their usefulness in terms of specific applications for surviving life's challenges or enhancing standard of living. But also considered were properties that made them useful as a currency.

Currencies are useful because they can be used as a store of value and because they can be used as a medium of exchange. If something is going to be useful as a store of value, that means people know those items will keep, that they can store them, and they will maintain their value in trade. If something is going to be useful as a medium of exchange, it means that people will accept the item for payment, but it also means that the process is sufficiently convenient to make its use practical.

Over time store of value and medium of exchange became so important for certain commodities that people began to value those properties more than their other uses. It became primarily their use as currency that caused people to value certain commodities, not their use in other applications. Such things as coins of precious metal are an example.

Eventually IOU's and receipts recorded on paper came to be used for trade as well. IOU's would be issued by one person to another and then these same IOU's would be passed from person to person as if they were money. The only reason people accepted these IOU's as money is because they trusted that the holder of the IOU could request and receive payment from the original IOU issuer at any time, if they chose. Upon payment the IOU would no longer have value and would be destroyed or be marked as no longer having value. Another form of paper which became used as currency would be receipts for stored wealth. The only reason these receipts were accepted as money is because the holder of the receipt trusted they could go to the place storing the item and acquire it upon presentation of the receipt. After the item is acquired the receipt would be destroyed or marked in some way to indicate it no longer had value. Obviously, in both those examples, the trust that those papers were backed by something of value, which could be redeemed if the holder of the paper wished, was paramount. The level of integrity of people living in that society was the essential ingredient in determining how successful these receipts would be in serving as currency, or even if such systems could work at all.

Governments began doing a similar thing by issuing something called "representative" money. The paper money they issue presumably represents the value of items the governments possess and keep in storage, which the holder of the paper note can acquire by presentation of the note to the government. After the note holder gets possession of the item of wealth the note would be removed from circulation. Mostly when governments issued representative money, its value was based on gold or other precious metals.

Another option governments have is to create money, including paper money, declaring its worth without saying it is backed by any other commodity, that it has value in and of itself. This is called **fiat** money. It is the type of money that we are studying in this book, for the most part. Fiat money is not only in the form of coins or paper money, but it can also be virtual money, existing only as an entry on a ledger at the Central Bank.

From Wikipedia:

"The first use of fiat money was recorded in China around 1000 AD. Since then, it has been used by various countries, usually concurrently with commodity currencies. Fiat money started to dominate in the 20th century. Since the **decoupling of the US dollar from gold by Richard Nixon in 1971**, a system of national fiat currencies has been used globally, with freely floating exchange rates between the national currencies."[7]

---

7   https://en.wikipedia.org/wiki/Fiat_money

What we call gold standard currency is a form of representative money. If all the money in the money supply was gold standard currency, the value of all the money in the money supply could not be greater than the value of the gold the government has in storage. The gold itself is tied in value to the currency, such as each ounce is worth so many dollars. This changes only when the government decides to change it.

Currency has evolved from favored barter items, to precious metal coins, to representative money, and finally to fiat money. Fiat money is created by the government and has value because the government says so. For example, the government empowers the use of this money by stating it is legal tender and must be accepted as payment for "all debts, public and private". This gives the Central Bank extra flexibility in managing the economy. This allows it greater flexibility in keeping the permanent money supply slowly increasing, so as to prevent the adverse consequences of having an inadequate money supply. It also allows the Central Bank to temporarily increase or decrease the money supply. Temporarily increasing or decreasing the money supply is part of what is known as Monetary Policy. Monetary Policy, which is discussed later in this book, is a way for the Central Bank to intervene when demand is considered to be too low, causing a recession or is considered too high, causing excess inflation.

Properties that Make for a Good Currency

Keynes, in The General Theory, analyzed how certain properties of commodities made them useful or not useful as a currency. I review this briefly, then talk more about these properties as they apply to certain currencies, specifically precious metal coins, representative money (such as gold standard currency), and fiat money.

According to Keynes, when analyzing a commodity's usefulness as a currency we need to consider 3 properties.

1. Can the value of or quantity of the item be changed by the holder of the commodity. Keynes called this value q, which I assume is the initial for quantity. If anyone can increase the amount of the commodity they have, then that would be as if anyone could just print more money. If no one values your chosen currency because anyone could just make more, then it does not hold its value. If the amount of the commodity decreases due to spoilage or obsolescence, this means after one takes it in trade its worth could decrease, making it less attractive to accept as compensation for the

item one is selling. If the quantity of your item decreases because it is spoiling or becoming obsolete, then it is also not maintaining its value. The important thing we are talking about with this property q, is store of value. If for whatever reason the value of a commodity in trade varied widely and unpredictably this would make it a poor choice for currency.

2. Does the item cost anything to keep it, i.e., are there costs inherent in holding onto it? Does it have maintenance cost, does it have storage costs etc.? Keynes calls this value c for carrying cost. The costs of storage and maintenance are expenses incurred to the holder of the commodity and would decrease its attractiveness in trade compared to any form of currency that does not have those costs. If the commodity is not used in a timely way one could imagine having the entire value of the commodity being eaten up by maintenance and storage costs. This is also a store of value issue.

3. How liquid is it? That is, how easy is it to use as currency? He calls this l for liquidity. One can imagine significant transportation and handling difficulties and costs attached to attempts to use certain commodities as currency. Extra expense would be incurred by the buyer or seller or both and would adversely affect the return on the transaction. Plus, the clumsiness of handling could slow commerce. These are issues that affect the commodity's desirability for use as a medium of exchange.

By these standards, qualifying as good choices for currency are 1) coins made of precious metals such as gold and silver, 2) representative money, which could exist as physical money, paper currency or coins, or as virtual currency, in either case backed by something of value, usually precious metals, and 3) fiat money, which could include coins, paper money or virtual money.

In a previous chapter I discussed how money could exist only because the central bank said it exists and keeps track of it on a ledger. This I am calling virtual money. The central bank can print or create virtual money if it is fiat money, or it can print or create virtual money with gold standard currency. The difference is that with representative money, such as gold standard money, the central bank is limited as to how much money it can create, by how much gold the government has in storage whereas with fiat money, the central bank is not subject to that limitation. With representative money the money is only considered to have value because there exists something of value that you could theoretically obtain by presenting the note. With fiat money, the money has value independently.

Each of these three currencies does pretty well with regard to l, liquidity. All three currencies would be convenient to use as a medium of exchange with minimal or no extra expense incurred by the buyer and seller just from using the currency to make payment.

What about q, quantity? One assumes that with gold and gold standard currency the supply cannot be easily increased. Gold is limited in quantity unless more gold is found. Gold standard currency is also limited in quantity unless other ways are devised to increase the money supply, like the government ruling to change the price of gold, or adding currency based on silver to the money supply.

With fiat money, only the Central Bank can increase the quantity. If the Central Bank acts responsibly in controlling the money supply, fiat money can satisfy the q standard of a good currency.

Representative money and fiat money would have minimal carrying costs, c. Coins made of precious metals would probably require a lot of security costs to protect them in today's world, and so perhaps they would not be so practical in today's day and age. The security costs would count as carrying costs.

Some Concerns About the Different Types of Currency

Some might assume that gold and gold standard representative money are superior to fiat money because they seem more solid, reliable, and will not lose value. However, there are some troublesome issues with gold or gold standard money as a currency.

Having gold or other precious metal coins being the main currency creates the motivation to acquire gold or precious metals in whatever way one can. It does not matter that, for the most part, the gold will not be used for any application other than as a currency, i.e., as a store of wealth and a medium of exchange. The acquisition of gold simply to acquire it as currency has led to all sorts of negative consequences. Wars have been fought over it, for example. Genocide has been committed. Plunder of other people's or other country's gold supplies, so that one's country could be richer than others, may have seemed rational to rulers at one time, but once one understands how to manage fiat money as a currency, it all just seems so incredibly tragic and unnecessary.

Columbus' travels to the new world were said to have been motivated in large part to seek gold. According to Howard Zinn in "The People's History of the United States" Columbus' discovery of the "New World" resulted in the genocide of native peoples.[8] The later conquering of Central and South America and destruction of the indigenous people's civilizations was in large part motivated by desire for gold, no doubt at least in part, because of gold's use as a store of wealth and a medium of exchange.

I realize that getting rid of these motivations to "acquire gold in whatever way possible", just to "get the currency needed for trade" does not end the battle for control of wealth and power, but it is definitely one of the advantages of fiat money. Fiat money can be increased if need arises no matter what the supply of gold. If we have an inadequate money supply slowing commerce, we do not need wars to acquire more gold in order to be able to address the shortage. In such a case the Central Bank has the ability to address the money shortage by creating more.

One concern some people have about fiat money is that if it is too easy to increase our money supply, then governments will just print money whenever they want to pay for something and this will cause the value of existing money to decrease, harming its value as a store of wealth. They have the concern that this would cause inflation. While, as previously discussed, there is not such a straight line between creating money and inflation as a lot of people think, this does not mean they are entirely unrelated. We do know, for example, that the existence of inflation does require a periodic and or steady increase in the money supply due to limitations on the velocity of money. But inflation, at reasonable levels, can be a good thing, which is discussed later. Although concerns about irresponsible management of the money supply are valid, the reality is that most of the time Central Banks do an excellent job with managing the money supply.

---

8   Zinn, Howard. A People's History of the United States . HarperCollins. Kindle Edition.

CHAPTER 8
How Spending and Income Relates to Inflation, Production and the Money Supply

I discuss how in a stable economy it is not enough for incomes to just keep pace with inflation but that total income must keep pace with inflation plus the real rate of increase in the value of production. In addition, I show how an inadequate money supply can lead to deflation.

PRICES CAN CHANGE based on the relationship between **spending** and production. This is a simple supply and demand phenomenon. If the products people desire are in shorter supply, then prices will go up, the same amount of spending will buy less product than if products are not in short supply. In the macroeconomy, since **income** is equal to spending, prices can also be seen to change based on the relationship between **income** and production sold.

At the present time we are used to having nominal incomes steadily increasing just because society has gotten used to the fact that it will need to keep increasing. Having spending and incomes keep increasing, for the same amount of production, causes prices to keep increasing. If the spending increase goes into paying for the same things (i.e., the same amount of labor, goods, services or desired outcomes) in the same proportions, then that spending increase has nothing to do with any increase in production or change in standard of living. This spending increase is the result of inflation, where more nominal spending is required to pay for the same amount and types of products.

It is possible however for some of the increased spending to go into paying for more products, either more of the same items or new items not previously being purchased, or it could just be paying for items that are more expensive presumably because they are of higher quality. If that is the case then the increased spending is related to **increased production**, not inflation.

Or it could be more confusing. We could have a mixed bag of spending where we would have a hard time figuring out what's inflation and what is paying for extra product. In other words, we could have changes in the pattern of spending where that change might be more of some items are bought and less of others, and/or lower priced items being substituted for some higher priced items, and/or purchases of totally new items, and/or having some other lower priced items getting replaced by higher priced items, and/or spending to just acquire a larger amount of production items in general, etc.

Whatever the case, **if** it has been determined that increased production has occurred, by increasing the amount, quality, and variety of production items, that increased production could have two types of causes. It can be caused by more people working to produce things, that is, **population increase**, or it could be related to increased production per worker, also known as **increased productivity**.

If we look at the equation income equals price times transaction (**Y=P∗T**), changes in spending and income could be caused either by changes in average price or change in the number of transactions, but likely it is contributed to by both. The change in the amount of spending could be a result of inflation or it could result from an increase in the quantity, quality and variety of product purchased, that is, increased production.

It is hard to attribute all the specifics as to what part of increased spending is related to inflation and what part is related to increased production. While that may be true I think it is an accurate comment to say that our current economy exhibits both a baseline inflation and a steady increase in production.

I would further say that it is reasonable to assume that increased production results from a combination of both increased population and increased productivity.

If Production Has Increased, then the Rate of Spending Increase Must Exceed Inflation

If we are in a situation where we have a baseline inflation, that means that prices are increasing regularly on the same items. That means, if the same type and quantity of product is being purchased, spending and income are increasing at the same rate as inflation. If additional product is going to be purchased, in terms of increased quantity, quality and variety, the increase in spending and income must not just match the inflation rate, it must exceed the inflation rate.

This must be true, or one of two things will happen, **either** the rate of inflation will be decreased, or extra production will not be able to be sold, or some combination of the two. If extra product is not sold, its continued creation will not be supported.

For just inflation, without an increase in production, average price **P** increases but the amount of transactions **T** stays the same. In that case, increased spending goes totally into **P**, i.e., increased prices, which is inflation. If the spending increase has to pay for increased prices on transactions to purchase the same quantity and type of items, and it also has to pay for purchases of extra stuff as well, then both **P** and **T** increase. If that is the case, all the spending increase cannot go solely into **P**, it also goes into **T**. Therefore, if the same spending increase is paying for increases in both **P** and **T**, **P** cannot increase as much, meaning the rate of increase in prices, inflation, is decreased. That is why I say, if inflation rate is going to remain at a given baseline rate, we must increase spending, (and therefore income), by the rate of inflation **plus** the rate of production increase.

Production can increase due to increases in the number of workers caused by population increases, in which case though total spending will increase more than inflation, spending per person may not. If production goes up solely because more people are involved in the economy, average income per person may not go up, or it could even go down, relative to inflation. Production can also increase due to increase in productivity. Productivity is the amount of production per worker. If increased productivity is the cause of increased production, the amount of spending per person would be expected to increase relative to inflation. If total spending goes up, to pay for extra production due to productivity increases, the average per capita income will go up as well, relative to inflation.

Productivity has been going up pretty steady for a long time in the United States. See this productivity graph from the Federal Reserve Bank website:

FIGURE 8.1

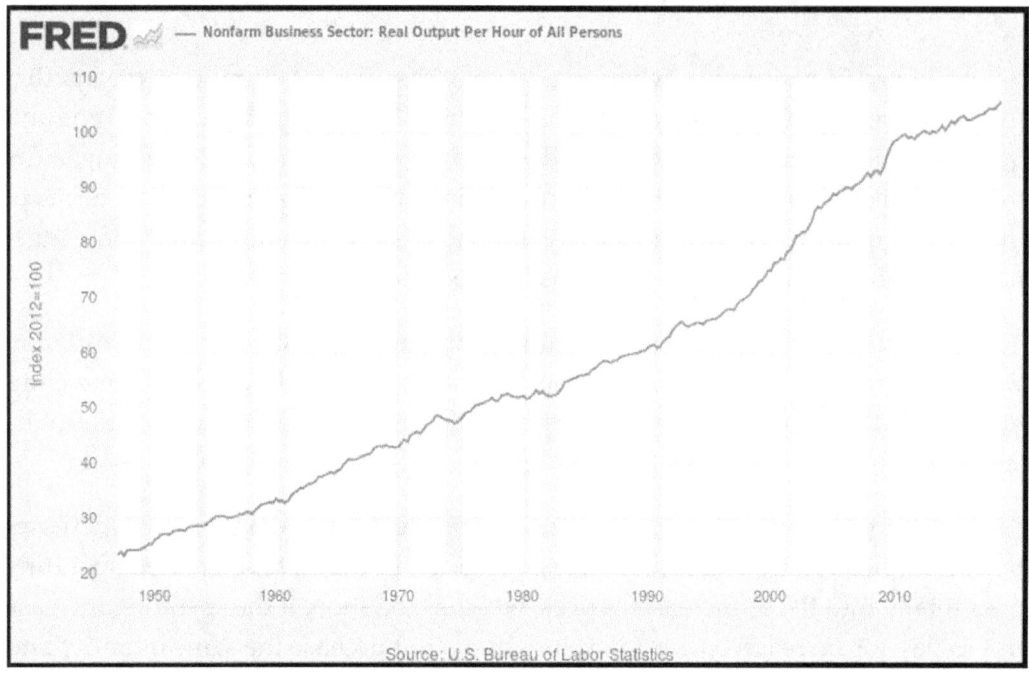

Change in productivity from 1947 to 2018

U.S. Bureau of Labor Statistics, Nonfarm Business Sector: Real Output Per Hour of All Persons [OPHNFB], retrieved from FRED, Federal Reserve Bank of St. Louis; https://fred.stlouisfed.org/series/OPHNFB, November 25, 2018

FRED® Graphs ©Federal Reserve Bank of St. Louis. 2018. All rights reserved. All FRED® Graphs appear courtesy of Federal Reserve Bank of St. Louis. https://fred.stlouisfed.org/

The chart refers to real output. Real output is inflation adjusted value of the output. Therefore, the increases shown in this chart have inflation factored out and only show us productivity gains over time. As this chart shows the productivity per worker, the effect of increased population is also factored out.

Increased productivity affects not only our standard of living and quality of life, but also the amount of spending required to pay for the extra production. Although not all of the extra production will need to be, or is expected to be sold, certainly a good portion of the extra output will need to be sold or it will not be produced.

I am trying to drive home the point that in our economy where inflation and increased production and productivity are normal features, it is not possible to support this if nominal spending, the actual amount of spending in dollars, just keeps pace with inflation. The rate of spending and income increase must exceed inflation. Due to the fact that a lot of increased production occurs as a result of productivity increases, that means the average spending and income **per person** must increase faster than inflation. If we are going to have an economy where a baseline inflation is a normal feature and productivity increases are a normal feature, this requires **average** per capita income increases greater than inflation to also be a normal feature.

Rationale for saying if we have productivity increases, real median income must increase faster than inflation

By median income earners, I mean all those workers whose average income tends be about the same as the median income. I do that because **average** income will be skewed upward by the very wealthy and average income does not accurately represent the average income of middle class or poorer people. Median income would more closely represent the average income of regular people.

Although generally over time one can expect changes in the patterns of spending and income (what gets bought, how much gets bought, who gets paid, how much, etc.) this is a gradual process, so generally we will only notice slow changes. In the short run spending patterns tend to be fairly stable, unless there is some sort of sudden major disruption to the economy such as a war or a natural disaster.

Now if average per capita spending and income needs to be increasing as productivity increases, and if spending patterns are relatively consistent then that means that spending and income **distribution** should be similar even as total income increases. That would mean since total income has to be increasing at a rate **greater than** inflation that all income levels would be expected to be increasing at a pace greater than inflation, specifically, the **MEDIAN** spending and income will also be increasing at a pace greater than inflation.

And that is what I was trying to get to. What I am saying is that in an economy where we have a regular increase in productivity, we would expect that the **median income** would increase, not at the same rate as inflation, but at a rate greater than inflation. The stable situation in the modern economy is **not** that the rate of increase in the **median income earner's** pay **keeps pace** with inflation but that it **exceeds** inflation. In fact, the stable situation is more likely to be when median income rises at the rate of inflation **plus** the rate of productivity increases.

To put it another way, inflation adjusted (real) median wages do not need to stay constant, they need to increase at the same rate as productivity does.

It is theoretically possible that we could have a radical change in spending such that even though the **average** income went up with productivity plus inflation, that it was accounted for by massive increases in the income of a few very rich people and income for everyone else only keeps pace with inflation. That would need to include a very radical change in what is produced and sold, and a radical increase in the total spending by the very rich few. That is unlikely. What is more likely is that the spending of the median income earner goes up faster than inflation.

Income, as defined in this book, is the transfer of ownership of money from one person or entity to another. Included in income, in my model, is the amount of loans dispersed. This amount gets added to the (gross) income of the recipient. Whether you accept this or not, you must certainly accept that receiving a loan increases the buying power of the recipient. This becomes a way to get that extra income needed to buy the extra production. If total gross income, including loans, keeps pace with the inflation plus production increases, mainly as a result of increased lending, the extra production and increasing standard of living will be supported, for a while…… eventually however, that spending will be altered because as the debt increases more and more money will be diverted away from the direct spending on goods, services, labor or desired outcomes, and into spending to pay back the loan obligations. It is the spending on goods, services, labor and other outcomes (besides loans) that is the type of spending that leads to increasing the standard of living. I will discuss more of this in future chapters.

Reinforcing Some of these Concepts

Inflation as measured by official government statistics is based on the price of what is called a "basket of goods". They take the price of that basket of goods at one moment in time and then compare the price of that same basket of goods, the same goods in the same quantity, at a different moment in time. The percent change over that time is the inflation rate for that time period.

When talking about increased spending due to **increased production** I am **not** talking about inflation. I am not talking about things being more expensive, I am instead talking about the increased spending needed to pay for increased amount of production, probably from a combination of increase in quality and selection as well as volume of transactions. I am talking about either buying more of the same goods we usually do or buying a different distribution of items or buying items of higher quality or entirely new items not previously part of the purchases.

How Spending and Income Relates to Inflation, Production

Bottom line is when increased production is the cause of increased spending, that is **not** increased spending that supports inflation, this is spending over and above inflation.

Buying power of income, or inflation adjusted income, is how much product a certain amount of income will buy. Inflation adjusted income is also called real income, i.e., the real buying power of that income. If in a previous year, the economy had 100 dollars of income and that paid for Y amount of product, and this year the economy had 150 dollars of income, but it paid for the same amount of product, then the real amount of spending power, the real income for both those years was the same. The buying power of 150 dollars this year would be equal to the buying power of 100 dollars in that previous year. That increased spending is inflation. If we had to pay for increased production in the later year then that would require additional spending. The nominal spending (= nominal income) required to pay the additional amount due to the inflated prices would be only part of the additional spending. More nominal spending (creating more nominal income) will have to be occurring to pay for the extra production.

Let us say that we have a 2 percent inflation rate, and the year before income was 100 dollars. This year the total spending needed to pay for the same items would increase to 102 dollars. This is the scenario that would play out if production stayed the same and we had a baseline inflation of 2 percent. The income that pays for the same amount of product would go from 100 dollars in the previous year to 102 dollars from this year. That means the inflation adjusted income also known as the real income, has stayed the same.

But what if we continued with the same rate of inflation but production increased and that increased the amount of product sold by another 2 percent? Then if the income only increases to 102 dollars that would not be sufficient to pay for the original amount of stuff plus the additional production. To pay for all the original stuff plus the extra production, income would have to go up by approximately an additional 2 percent. In that scenario, total spending and income would have to increase to 104 dollars.

Formally Analyzing the Relationship Between Money Supply and Inflation

Income is defined as **M∗V**. If income is increasing steadily and if **M** is held fixed, then **V** will have to keep going up. From a previous chapter we remember that there are limitations to how high **V** can go, and if we approach that level, spending increases will slow and eventually stop.

Income (spending) also equals **P∗T**. **T** represents the amount of transactions, i.e., each piece of production that is sold. Let us say, for simplicity sake, we break up all the production into units of equal value, **so that each transaction is selling an equal amount of product in terms of value**. **T** is the total number of these units sold. For example, if our original total production in one year is broken up so we have 100 units of the same value to be sold, then **T** equals 100. But if in a later year we double the amount of production to be sold, then **T** would equal 200. The value of **T** correlates to the inflation adjusted buying power of a given amount of spending and income. Defining **T** this way simplifies our analysis.

From the expression **P∗T** if **T** stays constant and spending keeps increasing then the average price **P** of transactions will have to increase. That is inflation. As the limitations on **V** are reached spending and income increases slow and eventually stop. Since spending equals **P∗T**, and since **T** is constant, price **P** increases will also have to slow and eventually stop. What this shows is that for a given money supply **M**, and a constant amount of product being sold, eventually, when the economy approaches the limit on velocity **V** we reach a point where inflation slows and eventually stops.

That is what happens when production and number of transactions remains unchanged. What happens if **M** continues to remain constant, but production does not stay constant, that is production keeps increasing. Remember in a successful economy we expect productivity and production to keep increasing. That would mean there would be more pieces of production sold and **T** would increase. If we were not at the limit of velocity of money **V**, then average price **P** could continue to rise even as **T** increases. Eventually when the velocity of money **V** reached its limit, for a constant money supply, **M∗V** could not increase further, and *the product* **P∗T** also would not be able to increase further, because total spending **Y** = **M∗V** = **P∗T**. In that situation if **T** kept increasing due to production increases, the average price **P** not only would have to stop increasing, it would **actually have to start decreasing**. That is deflation. In an economy with increasing productivity, if we never increased the money supply **M**, we would eventually reach a point where we would have deflation.

The discussion of limitations in the size of the money supply as it relates to inflation and deflation is pertinent to our analysis of the three different types of currency, precious metal coins, representative money, and fiat money. I discuss this more in the upcoming chapters.

I will first say that if we could live with deflation and have a successful economy, then there would be no problem. Some people even think that would be a good thing. By successful economy I mean one where we have a continuous steady increase in productivity and standard of living over time.

COMMENT

Increasing production does not just mean we have to be depleting natural resources and polluting the earth. Production means all manner of things that can improve our lives on earth. This includes technology to save our resources and stop polluting, preserving our wealth in that way. It includes emotional and spiritual development, education, arts and sciences, academic achievements, peace and security, infrastructure, good health, anything and everything you can think of. In a monetary economy, the way society values those people who provide all these different things, is they get paid, so they can survive, and be healthy and be able to produce those things mentioned. All of these things mentioned are indeed part of the monetary economy and part of what we should be considering when we calculate the total value of production.

CHAPTER 9
CAN AN ECONOMY WITH DEFLATION MAINTAIN ITS LEVEL OF GROWTH?

This Chapter discusses the effects of deflation on an economy.

I WANT TO analyze if it is possible to have a successful economy when we also have deflation. I define "successful" as an economy that has a continuous and steady increase in production, productivity and standard of living over time. Having that occur has a requirement that we have a steady increase in the amount of sales, i.e., a steady increase in the units of wealth sold; a steady increase in **T**.

Assume we are in an economy where dollars are the currency. When we have deflation, it means that the value of everything, in terms of dollars, decreases. The exception would be that the value of **dollars in terms of dollars** would not decrease. In addition, **purely financial assets** that are valued in terms of dollars, would **maintain their value**, in terms of dollars. With deflation, money or purely financial monetary assets will **increase in value relative to other items or assets**. With deflation, those people or entities who own more of these purely financial assets would have their spending power increase compared to those who have less purely financial assets.

Additionally, with deflation, the value of **debt obligations increase** relative to the value of other forms of wealth, besides money and purely financial assets). Deflation increases debt burdens. A person or entity with less debt will see their buying power reduced less than a person or entity with more debt.

A person with more purely financial assets and with less debt is going to see their relative wealth, and relative spending power go up more as compared to a person with more debt and less purely financial assets. I think it fair to say that this describes the difference between wealthy people who are more likely to be net lenders as compared to poorer people who are more likely to be net borrowers.

Wealthier people tend to put less into direct spending on goods, services, labor and desired outcomes (other than the outcome of acquiring purely financial assets). That is, they spend a smaller fraction of their income on the type of spending that increases employment and production the most. They also tend to purchase more purely financial assets. Poorer people tend to spend more on that direct spending, meaning their spending, on a dollar for dollar basis, stimulates employment and production more. From this factor, it is reasonable to assume that deflation will have an adverse effect on the level of employment and production.

The only way we could avoid some of this would be if we could somehow reduce the value of purely financial assets to match the reduction in the value of everything else. This would mean the balance in everyone's bank account would decrease at the rate of deflation, and the total principal owed on loans would also decrease at the rate of deflation.

Can you imagine the total debt you owed going up with inflation, and down with deflation?

Actually, there is a way this is handled. It is called interest. What I am talking about here is the economy would need positive interest rates when we have inflation, which we have of course. But we would also need negative interest rates if deflation got bad enough, which is problematic. (keep reading to find out why).

If inflation turns to deflation and the deflation rate gets big enough, we will need interest rates to also become negative or fewer people will be able to afford or qualify for loans. That is because if the interest rates do not become negative, the inflation adjusted cost of loans will keep increasing (interest rate minus inflation rate). This will lead to a serious reduction in the amount of borrowing able to be afforded. With less lending there will be less spending and that will adversely affect the level of employment and production.

But what would a negative interest rate on a loan mean? Here is an example to illustrate what would happen with a negative interest rate:

Let us say the bank gives a one year, one payment, loan of 100 dollars at a negative 5 percent interest rate. This means the bank gives the borrower 100 dollars today and in one year gets paid back 95 dollars. Now ask yourself, why would the bank do that? The bank could just keep the 100 dollars, not lend it out, and at the end of the year the bank would have 100 dollars not 95. And that 100 dollars, due to deflation, is worth more in terms of purchasing power, than it was a year previous. Banks would have no incentive to lend at negative interest rates.

If the only way people would be able to afford to borrow is if nominal interest rates are negative, lending will not happen because the bank could just hold the cash.

Further, if the banks were charging negative interest rates, or even extremely low positive interest rates on loans, in order to make any profit, they would have to pay negative interest rates to their depositors. If that happened then people would not deposit money in the bank. Why would someone put money in the bank if the bank kept reducing their balance without that person withdrawing any money? If they just held the cash they would be better off.

If all the banks were giving negative interest on deposits, then no one would deposit any money and in fact everyone would start withdrawing their money. This, in essence, would be a run on the banks. An economy that has a system of lending would definitely be negatively impacted by deflation.

Deflation might possibly be workable if there were no loans. But we have also previously pointed out the beneficial effects of loans on motivating people. And loans also have a way of allowing money to be best positioned for the desired spending to occur. Loans are a way to increase the velocity of money.

Loans in the model presented in this book are considered (gross) income to the recipient and spending by the bank (to acquire an asset call a loan). Eliminating loans, in and of itself, negatively impacts overall income and spending. And I don't know how, realistically, most people would ever be in a position to purchase big ticket items like cars or houses, or college educations etc. without obtaining loans to pay for it.

Even if some of that could be replaced with leasing instead of borrowing to purchase something, we would lose the extra motivation that comes from owning your own stuff. People tend to take better care of those things they own than those things they rent. Changing our society to one without loans, would totally change everything. I suspect if we could create such a society, losing the positive impact that loans have on motivation would severely negatively impact production and standard of living.

And, aside from those other factors, deflation encourages "not spending" because of hoarding. It discourages spending to acquire purely financial assets,

Can an Economy with Deflation Maintain Its Level of Growth?

like bank's lending and people putting money in deposit accounts, because of the negative interest rates. Deflation also discourages direct spending to purchase goods, services, labor, and other desired outcomes, because, anytime you can delay spending, your money will have increased purchasing power in the future. If you can put off buying the desired item and hoard the money, you will need to use less money when you finally do buy the item.

Deflation would have such a powerful adverse effect on spending, especially spending to acquire things that lead to the need to increase employment and production, that it is unreasonable to expect such an economy to continue to maintain the same increasing rate of production and standard of living. That is, deflation won't just decrease nominal spending, but it will be expected to decrease real spending as well, meaning it will decrease the amount of product purchased and therefore the amount of product produced. It is more probable that an economy with deflation would see a decrease in production and standard of living. **T** would have its increase slowed or stopped and more likely, **T** would be reduced. Eventually **T** may be lowered enough that prices will begin to rise again, and the economy may stabilize, but at that point the standard of living could be expected to be much lower than it otherwise would have been.

If you had a situation where production was not increasing, where it was staying the same, you might be able to keep the money supply the same, as long as things did not happen to slow the maximum velocity of money, like increased hoarding. That would be a situation of zero inflation and zero growth. But even with zero inflation, if you were in a situation where you had regular growth in production, due to productivity increases and/or population increases, you could then expect to eventually need the money supply to increase, or economic activity will be adversely affected.

I hope I am painting a good picture of the types of adverse consequences we can suffer due to an inadequate money supply. By inadequate money supply, I mean a money supply that is too small to allow income (**M∗V**) to keep pace with the rate of inflation plus the rate of increase in production. A money supply of a given size **M**, becomes inadequate when money moves through the economy too slowly to allow all the desired and possible transactions to occur at the time the parties wish for them to occur. The decreased spending will result in decreased prices, which will eventually cause deflation and all those demand decreases that causes. But also, prices being sticky, (by which I mean people delay lowering prices in a depression, until they cannot avoid it any more), will cause a decrease in the amount of product sold before deflation even occurs. All this will limit the amount of inflation adjusted spending that occurs in a given time period, and since it is spending that spurs production, the amount of production that occurs in a given time period would be expected to be reduced. If the amount of production occurring in a given time period is reduced, then the amount of product available to be possessed and used, in the given time period will also be reduced, meaning our standard of living will be reduced, all because of an inadequate money supply.

CHAPTER 10
A Look at How to Avoid an Inadequate Money Supply with Precious Metal Coins, Representative Money, or Fiat Money

IF GOVERNMENTS COULD find a way to increase the money supply, they could avoid this situation where limits on velocity of money cause deflation. But where would the government get the money?

They could tax people whose money is being hoarded, and spend that on various programs, or transfer payments. That would increase the amount of money being used for spending. This would increase the velocity of money, since that hoarded money was not being spent at all and had a zero velocity. Eventually, however, even if they get all the hoarded money back into circulation, the money supply is still limited, and one could assume there would still come a day when **M** needs to be increased.

Let us look at how one could create more money with the three things I identified as good choices for currency.

Creating more money in the form of gold coins requires more gold, which is often in limited supply. That is why at times governments have allowed coins to be made out of silver, or at other times they decreased the quantity of gold or silver in coins of given denomination, allowing more coins to be created. But if population kept increasing, and if productivity kept increasing, and if the economy had a baseline inflation, then one would have to continue finding ways to keep increasing the amount of coins that contain precious metals.

For representative money, one could just print more money, but the amount one could print would be limited by the amount of gold the government had in storage. In this case when all the "allowed" money is created, that is all you get.

The United States officially came off the gold standard in 1971, after which money was no longer representative money, but fiat money. This does not mean that prior to 1971 the U.S. government did not have a need to increase the maximum allowed money supply periodically. Prior to 1971 strategies were needed to increase the money supply. They had to resort to other means, such as increasing the price of gold from 20 dollars to 35 dollars like they did in 1935 allowing them to create more money. Prior to 1935, the maximum money they could create was 20 dollars for every ounce of gold they held, and after the price increase they could create an additional 15 dollars for every ounce of gold. This was accomplished just by having the government "adjust the value" of gold.

For some years after the price of gold was increased, the base money supply did increase at a more rapid rate as shown in this graph.

FIGURE 10.1

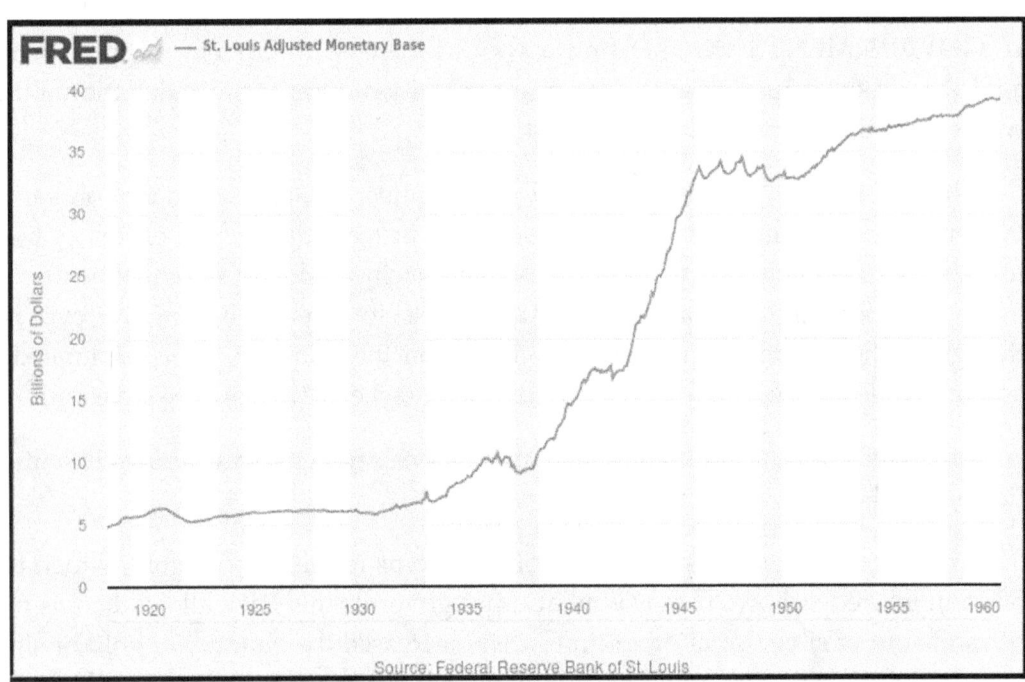

1918 to 1960, Units: Billions of Dollars Seasonally adjusted monetary base

Federal Reserve Bank of St. Louis, St. Louis Adjusted Monetary Base [AMBSL], retrieved from FRED, Federal Reserve Economic Data, Federal Reserve Bank of St. Louis; https://fred.stlouisfed.org/series/AMBSL, November 25, 2018.

FRED® Graphs ©Federal *Reserve Bank of St. Louis. 2018. All rights reserved. All FRED® Graphs appear courtesy of Federal Reserve Bank of St. Louis. https://fred.stlouisfed.org/*

Another strategy used to increase the money supply was issuing representative money based on silver and adding that to the total amount of dollars in the money supply.

For both gold coins and representative money, it is possible for a government to increase their countries money supplies, but this can require different interventions or manipulations, that often leads to controversy, unrest and even war. If we have the same people, infrastructure, technology and natural resources, it should only be the hard work and creativity of those people utilizing those resources that keeps our economy thriving and growing. It is those things that should determine our quality of life, not the amount of gold and silver we have in storage. Having a currency shortage is no longer necessary, even with limited supplies of precious metals, with properly managed fiat money.

With fiat money the Central Bank can adjust the money supply to economic conditions. The Central Bank will be able to make sure an inadequate money supply does not become a cause of inadequate spending. Further, fiat money is integral to allowing the Central Bank to implement something called Monetary Policy, as a tool to help alleviate demand deficiencies caused by factors other than an inadequate money supply. Monetary policy is discussed later.

If having fiat money allows us to maintain an adequate money supply which, along with Monetary Policy helps facilitate a slow gradual **inflation**, that will discourage hoarding.

Those who tend to hoard would be more likely to do so if the economy were experiencing a deflation , and perhaps even if we had zero inflation. But if we had a reasonable level of inflation, they would be less motivated to hoard. With inflation, the buying power of a given amount of dollars will decrease over time. Hoarding that money would cause the value of the hoarder's cash holdings to shrink, in terms of buying power. In order to maintain or grow their wealth, it would be better for them to seek to spend that money on an asset whose value would increase to keep pace with or exceed inflation. Also, even for people who intend to spend the money on goods and services that are necessary to maintain their quality of life, depriving themselves of those items now is less intelligent, because, due to inflation, it is less likely waiting will get one a better deal. With inflation, prices go up on the average not down, and this encourages more spending now, just as deflation encourages less spending now.

A Look at How to Avoid an Inadequate Money Supply

Gold standard representative money and the gold it is backed by are not more secure than fiat money in safeguarding wealth.

People are attracted to the idea of acquiring wealth, storing it and having their financial concerns solved, once and for all. To most people this seems more possible if our money is gold or "backed by gold". But remember, we can still have inflation up to a point even with the gold standard currency, because it is spending, $(M*V)$, that affects inflation, not just the size of the money supply M. If velocity of money V has not reached its maximum, even if the gold supply will not allow any more money to be created we can still increase spending further and support more inflation for a time.

Even though you would be able to turn a given amount of representative currency in and receive the designated amount of gold, and even though the amount of gold you can receive for turning the paper note in doesn't change over time, it doesn't mean the gold holds its value, in terms of buying power, any more than the paper note would. If the buying power of your gold representative note went down, then so would the buying power of the amount of gold that note "represents".

And if having the gold standard money results in an inadequate money supply, then, total wealth and standard of living for all can suffer.

If an economy had a gold standard currency, and people hoarded the notes, that would lower the amount of money being used for spending and could adversely affect total spending by decreasing the velocity of money. And, if people turned in their representative money in order to obtain the gold it was based on, that would decrease the money supply and that could adversely affect the amount of spending. Both of those strategies being used in attempts to "preserve wealth" could result in slowing of the economy and decreased production, as well as decreased standard of living.

This is how it should be because you cannot eat gold, you can't make clothes out of it very easily, you can't use it to heat your house or run your car. You get the idea. It is the things one can buy with money that have the real value. It is those things that we buy with money, not the money in and of itself, that determines our standard of living. Having an adequate money supply will prevent that factor from slowing the economy. Fiat money is the type of money that will allow us to avoid an inadequate money supply.

Nowadays, since gold is not used as a currency, people buy it as an asset. It is one of those things people consider having value and they buy. It does have some value because people enjoy things made out of it. In the main, however, people buy it, in whole or in part, as an asset they think has a store of value. It is not used as a currency, it is really just treated as a commodity. And it is a commodity whose value swings widely. Its value is influenced by all sorts of advertising. As a commodity that is sold on exchanges, it may hold its value, or it may decrease its value. As a commodity it could be currently underpriced where one might get a positive return if they purchased some, or it might be overvalued where one could suffer a loss if they bought gold.

If you are thinking of "investing in gold" as a way to preserve your wealth, I would recommend you try to answer one question before doing so. Why are so many proponents of purchasing gold for its "store of value" advertising all the time to try to get you to buy gold? Is it possible that they are just trying to drive the price up, so they can sell their own supply to acquire more fiat money? Are they trying to manipulate people, so they can sell gold at a higher price and then wait for the price to fall so they can purchase more at a lower price, and then advertise again to drive the price up, selling it again at a profit?

In the Gurdjieff work, the idea is to continue to practice conscious labor and intentional suffering. The idea of attempting to get to a position where you have solved all your problems "once and for all" can be considered a way of self-calming and can lead one to putting efforts into goals that are contrary to the teachings. A person in the Gurdjieff work, might sometimes even take on debt or make promises or acquire obligations so as to put themselves in a position where they have to put efforts into working on themselves.

Still, just a reminder, that whatever the advantages or disadvantages of the various forms of money are, and no matter what form of currency we have, in the Gurdjieff work, we are always challenged to turn adversity into opportunity, that is, no matter what the situation, there is always an opportunity to work on oneself.

Fiat money, which is the form of money mostly being discussed in this book, has many advantages over the other forms of currency. If properly administered by the government and the Central Bank, it can be used to keep economies maximizing production and help us preserve or improve our standard of living without having to deal with the drawbacks and complications the other types of currency cause. That is why fiat money has become the standard across the world.

Keynes and the Gold Standard

Keynes was against the gold standard. He did not like the idea of keeping money scarce. He knew that in keeping money scarce, those who had it could use their position to gain unearned profits from all sorts of economic activities. That is, they could put little or no effort into a venture and come away with profits just because they have the money other people need to conduct transactions. So, for example, in such a situation, scarce money would imply there would be a limited number of lenders, and the borrowers would have to compete for the loans, rather than the banks having to compete for the borrowers. This means they can charge higher interest rates.

Keynes was not talking about the contribution to the process of funding by "educated investors" who study and learn and have a good idea what ventures are likely to do well and what are not. That is labor and deserves some return for it, although perhaps not as much return as they get either. He was talking about profits earned simply due to people having too much monopoly power over the agent of spending, i.e., the money supply.

Keynes believed that these unearned excess profits, supported because of the lack of money, hurt the economy. He believed it slowed spending, income, employment levels and production, and kept the economy from functioning at its maximum. Keynes actually believed that, ultimately, society would realize this and the idea of paying excess "rent" (i.e., unearned or excess profits) to these "rentiers" as he called them, would gradually fade away, if money became less "scarce". Unfortunately, this has not yet happened, because, as we have found out, even with an adequate money supply, there are other ways to control economic activity and strengthen monopoly power.

CHAPTER 11
ATYPICAL TYPES OF CURRENCIES

CRYPTOCURRENCY

SHOULD I MENTION cryptocurrencies? An example of a cryptocurrency is something called BitCoin. A cryptocurrency lives totally in computers. It is some sort of a code. A computer program exists that determines which codes qualifies as a unit of that cryptocurrency. If someone discovers a code that qualifies they get registered as the owner of that unit of cryptocurrency. The person who finds that code is said to have "mined" that unit of cryptocurrency

Apparently, the programming monitors and registers who owns a given amount of cryptocurrency. And information about transactions is not just stored in one place but stored multiple times in multiple computers. Here is how I understand cryptocurrency to work:

Information about transactions with cryptocurrency is stored some on your computer in what is called the wallet file, and some is stored in what is called the public blockchain.

What is stored in the wallet file are accounts that the individual controls and a 'secret key'. This secret key is needed to be able to spend coins that are stored in those accounts. The public blockchain is stored on every computer using "bitcoin client" and is a record of "every transaction ever made" including transactions of that person.

To spend one's coins, one apparently "checks the blockchain" to locate bitcoins the spender has acquired in the past and currently owns. They then specify what coins they want to spend and what account to send them to. The spender uses the secret key to authorize the transfer.

Then, apparently, the spender sends the proposed transaction to what are called 'miners'. These miners then confirm everything is valid and cause to be entered into the public record the code applicable to the particular bit coin, the chain of spending done with it and the new owner of that bit coin. This is how I understand bitcoin to work. Most of my understanding is thanks to this excellent blog post.[9]

Proponents of cryptocurrencies have a fantasy that they will take over for government-controlled money as the standard currency. They allege it will be superior because there are only a limited number of codes that are allowed, and that it will keep its value because no one will be able "debase its value" by "printing extra money" and increasing the money supply. And they allege that no one is needed or able to "control it" like governments. I wonder about this last point, because to exist and function it seems there would be a need for at least some centralized administrative control.

Anyway, how does cryptocurrency rate on those measures of being a good currency?

Well, their supply cannot be increased by those who possess it. So theoretically, from that perspective, at first look, it would qualify as having a stable quantity, i.e., a stable **q**. Except that now what is happening is people are creating all sorts of competing cryptocurrencies. So maybe **q** is a concern. Plus, if the value, in terms of dollars, changes quickly and frequently, as is the case in the real world, then the quantity of cryptocurrency in terms of its VALUE is changing all the time. I would conclude that **q** is a major concern, both because of the ability of people to create competing currencies, and the high variability in the value of the cryptocurrency in terms of dollars.

Since this asset, this commodity called cryptocurrency, is such an ephemeral thing, one could imagine its value would be easily manipulated by rumor, innuendo and salesmanship. I do not know how one is going to prevent that.

Most commodities that are held as assets, have some inherent value regardless of the price. Cryptocurrency has very little if any inherent value, making it worrisome that there is no limit to how low its value might go. If something does not

---

9   See blog entry at this site by David Schwartz https://bitcoin.stackexchange.com/questions/1600/where-are-the-users-bitcoins-actually-stored

reliably maintain its value, people will be uncomfortable accepting it for payment. I believe cryptocurrency fails the **q** test

For the other properties it does not have much in carrying costs **c** except perhaps the labor involved in keeping track of what is happening to its price in terms of fiat dollars. It also takes up a lot of digital memory since records of the transactions are "distributed" over an apparently limitless number of computers. Liquidity, I assume, is not a problem because it is electronically traded. It is pretty easily exchanged if you are trading with people who accept it as a currency

Overall, based on its unreliability in maintaining its value, I rate cryptocurrency as a very poor choice for use as a currency. What a cryptocurrency really is, is a commodity whose ownership can be electronically traded. This means, that when it is used for transactions, it is really a barter.

It is a commodity that some people claim is very secure for transaction purposes, because of how records of all the transactions are stored on every computer (Although who would mediate any conflicts if they occurred?). Some claim it is that particular property, secure transactions, which makes it superior as a medium of exchange. But if people are going to use something as a medium of exchange they have to have faith that it will keep its value. And I do not see this as a realistic expectation. If people lose faith that cryptocurrency will keep its value, then it is hard to see how it will survive as a commodity, much less a currency. If its value collapses, as I expect it will, a lot of people will lose.

A lot of people made a lot of money off the whole cryptocurrency thing, when they converted their holdings to fiat money. I have heard of the strategy called "pump and dump" being used with cryptocurrencies. This is where individuals or groups buy large amounts of the cryptocurrency to drive up the price, and then carefully divest themselves of their "coins" after the price has gone up. The profit these crypto traders obtain with this strategy is gained by convincing others to buy when the value of the cryptocurrency is high, and sell when it is low.

More or less it seems like high prices of cryptocurrency can be looked at as a "bubble", an investment whose price increase is not necessarily supported by the fundamentals. You could have an oil price bubble or a real estate bubble, but at least after the prices fell to a more appropriate level you would still have an interest in something of worth, i.e., you would have an interest in oil or houses or whatever. There would be a bottom to how low the value of those assets would go. As a commodity cryptocurrency has no intrinsic value. With cryptocurrency there is no bottom. Its value could and most likely would go all the way to zero.

Like most commodities, cryptocurrencies can be traded for and valued in terms of standard fiat currencies, like dollars, and can be traded on exchanges set up for that purpose. In recent times there have been wild swings in its value.

That one property that may make cryptocurrency better, security of its transactions, (because records are spread out on so many computers), will not be enough to save it, in my opinion, as a currency. Most financial transactions are pretty secure already. And if the only advantage it has is that it handles transactions more securely, then that same technology could probably be easily adapted and used for transactions with standard currency. In fact, some banks are already looking at doing that for some types of transactions.

It is possible, since cryptocurrencies are easily electronically traded private commodities, they could be used as a way to hide transactions, avoid taxes or even hide illegal activities, but in terms of it substituting for government currency, I do not see how it could work. I do think a lot people looking for an easy fortune will be hurt by it ultimately. If I had to guess, I would think that in the long run it is likely to end up losing all it is worth and being relegated to the history books.

I expect governments will eventually crack down on its use for illicit purposes and that the government will probably even figure out ways to track and tax cryptocurrency transactions. I suspect that due to the fact that transactions are recorded on every computer that deals in bitcoins, it would be easy for government to track and recover information on the transactions. If so, then eventually it should prove easier to tax cryptocurrency transactions than it is for other types of barter. And for people trying to use bitcoin for illicit purposes or to avoid tax liability this feature may make bitcoin unattractive for those uses as well.

Interesting Thought

Let us say the money supply is too small, or at least if a significant portion of the money supply was being hoarded, slowing the velocity of money, such that maximum possible **M∗V**, the maximum possible spending is adversely affecting commerce. It would be at times like that we would expect the amount of barter trade in the economy to increase. It is at times like that, that alternative currencies may find a place.

If a poor understanding of economics, or greed is preventing the money supply from being increased to an adequate level, or if hoarding of the money supply is slowing the velocity of money, then those responsible may inadvertently be supporting the wider adoption and use of alternative currencies. At any rate, whenever currency is in short supply we can expect barter or alternative currencies are to be utilized more.

Cell Phone Minutes as Currency

Here is an interesting situation where barter has helped make up for a lack of trustworthy currency. In some African countries people are using cell phone minutes in trade for items. Some people have said that this means the cell phone minutes have become money. Let us look at how this works.

For simplicity suppose a country does not have their own currency, but instead utilizes the euro. A cell phone customer pays the cell phone company in acceptable currency, i.e., euros, for calling minutes. The minutes are an asset which the cell phone company must provide them when requested. But let us say the cell phone company allows customers to give their minutes to other customers, to trade them.

Let us say that customers often find themselves SHORT OF MONEY to be used for spending. One reason they are short on cash is because they had to pay for the cell phone minutes. But then some enterprising individuals amongst them figures out that since they can transfer their cell phone minutes, they can use their cell phone minutes in barter instead of paying cash. After a time, the vendors realize they too can use those cell phone minutes in barter, so they have value to them. They begin accepting the cell phone minutes as payment.

And then (THIS IS THE MOST IMPORTANT STEP!) since the customer does not have cash to pay for the products the vendor is selling, the vendors realize, if they don't accept the cell phone minutes, THEY DONT MAKE THE SALE AT ALL! Without accepting the cell phone minutes in barter, the number of transactions is reduced, the economy slows, the income of the vendors is reduced and the standard of living of the citizens of that country is reduced.

Even though using cell phone minutes can be considered a barter, that is you are trading assets, those who utilize the cell phone minutes have found they are pretty reliable in holding their value in trade. In fact, for some of them, where their country has its own poorly administered currency, they find the cell phone minutes are superior to their own currency, in respect of holding their value. This being true because there are valued in terms of a more stable currency, the euro. They also carry no extra expenses to store and are easy to use in transfer with minimal effort and cost. These properties, in essence, make cell phone minutes a good currency. They are a form of "representative money". In this case what is being described is a representative currency backed by a form of wealth called cell phone minutes.

Here is a website describing cell phone minutes being used as a currency[10]

In the situation described above a second currency, a representative currency, has been added to the already existing money supply, in effect increasing the total money supply.

I have just described a situation where the lack of adequate reliable currency for spending led to the use of barter where one item was so convenient for barter that it became, in fact, a currency. The second currency, the representative currency known as cell phone minutes, is added to the fiat currency, euros, to have a bigger money supply. The two currencies have an exchange rate determined, in part, by how many cell phone minutes you get per euro. You use the exchange rate to calculate the total money supply in terms of euros. You have actual euros and the cell phone minutes valued in terms of euros.

As with any representative money, you cannot create it without having the wealth that backs it exist in the first place in some form. The only reason representative money has value in trade is because of the wealth backing it, and the fact that the person holding that representative money can redeem it for the item of wealth. Turn it in, get the item of wealth and then the representative money must be destroyed. That is what happens, in effect, when someone, instead of using their cell phone minutes for spending, makes a phone call.

It is also possible that, for some, the cell phone minutes were just more convenient, once they became commonly accepted, than using cash. And this led to more widespread use of this representative money, making it responsible for a larger fraction of the spending. In other words, it is possible that having the government "print" (or declare as existing) more fiat money, is not the only way to have enough currency around to facilitate all the desired spending. This is another way to ensure that commerce is not constrained.

---

10 https://www.economist.com/news/finance-and-economics/21569744-use-pre-paid-mobile-phone-minutes-currency-airtime-money

ATYPICAL TYPES OF CURRENCIES

SOME CAUTIONS REGARDING FIAT MONEY

Fiat money is different from representative money in that it does have value in trade in and of itself. In that sense fiat money does "increase wealth" which is why it must be carefully and responsibly managed. Too little money constrains the economy, but too much new fiat money can have adverse effects as well.

With fiat money, if, when an economy is doing poorly, Central Banks or government leaders decided to print fiat money and gave it out directly as income, with no consideration for what that will do to production, that could exacerbate any supply problems. Generally, most functional countries do not do that, they use Open Market Operations to increase the supply of money. But even with that, buying bonds, and having this decrease the cost of government borrowing, could lead to increased borrowing and spending by the Government. This could be completely appropriate at times of recession, but if this is done at times when things are going well, perhaps for political reasons, it could lead to excess inflation. Government spending, done irresponsibly and for the wrong reasons, such as to benefit special interests rather than the general welfare, could harm the economy, reduce incentives, distort the market and lead to supply shortages. These types of things have occurred, even to the point where in some noteworthy cases it has destroyed whole economies and led to hyperinflation.

There are adverse consequences to too small a money supply and adverse consequences to too large a money supply. In either case the guiding factor would be what is happening to the level of net production and why.

ONE LAST WORD ABOUT CRYPTOCURRENCY

The cell phone minutes could only be considered representative money because they could be traded in for something of value, i.e., calling minutes, and once they are used for calling minutes they disappear, no longer exist.

Cryptocurrency is not backed by anything of value, so it is not a representative currency. Cryptocurrency is in and of itself the thing of value. Its value is totally based on people believing it has worth. It is kind of like a fiat money produced by private concerns. The proponents believe that if they design it so as keep the supply limited, that will mean it keeps its value, that no one can "debase its value". Of course, that is not true since you see people keep coming up with competitor cryptocurrencies, by different names, so it would be impossible to control how much cryptocurrency there is out there. If someone had the hope that cryptocurrency will be the ultimate currency because it "holds its value" because it is "limited in quantity" then that person will likely be disappointed.

Cell phone minutes became a representative currency because they were in the economy and had a purpose and an intention other than its use as a currency. Then people found out they could be used as a currency also. It was more natural for their use as a currency to develop that way. The cell phone minutes would exist whether they were a currency or not. Of course, the cell phone companies could put a stop to it in an instant if they stopped allowing transfer of cell phone minutes, or if they charged fees that people found excessive for those transfers. At any rate it was a somewhat natural progression for the cell phone minutes to become a currency.

Cryptocurrency is trying to make its way directly into being used as a fiat currency, created by its inventor instead of the government. The tactics to try to get this to happen involves using various forms of overt or covert advertisements, and for this purpose they appear to be utilizing and stoking people's paranoia that government money will "lose its value", because the government "prints too much money" and is "debasing the dollar". Or having people believe that they could use cryptocurrency to avoid taxes. Or believing that they would be "free" of government interference, that the government would not be able to keep track of what they are doing. I have serious doubts that any of those reasons is valid or that establishment of cryptocurrency as a reliable and widely accepted currency will be achievable.

More Thoughts on Atypical Currencies

Some people think that checks, like from a checking account, should be considered money. A check would be considered a representative money whose value is backed by the debt obligation the bank has to the checking account depositor where the checking account is held. The check would have the unusual property of losing all its value when cashed in, and so would the asset (the debt obligation), and this would require an equivalent amount of fiat money to change ownership, going from being owned by the bank of the check writer, to the bank of the check casher (spending occurring without money physically moving). That means the only thing that occurred as a result of the check being used is spending of fiat money. In such a case, to the extent that checks facilitate increased spending, it is probably better to look at its function as being to increase the velocity of money rather than being an increase in the money supply.

Meanwhile, these checks may, from time to time, be traded for items of wealth without being cashed, traded as uncashed checks. In such a case it should be considered a barter. But if that became common practice, if checks were being passed from person to person, being used for purchases without being cashed, then we may have to consider it as being established as a representative currency. If that were the case, then for the time those uncashed checks existed, and were being traded, they can be considered as added to the money supply. Their contribution to the economy would be measured by their total spending. That is, by the average number of transactions paid for with uncashed checks, times the average value of each transaction.

A debit card functions in a similar way to a check, but presumably electronic communications have advanced so much that each transaction can be directly communicated to all the banks involved and so all the transactions would be equivalent to transactions that occurred with a check that is cashed right away. That is, debit cards can help speed the velocity of money, but are not functioning as a currency.

Any sort of paper or credit whose value is based on some underlying asset that has value could possibly end up being considered a representative money, if the trading of it is accepted as payment. If it only happens a few times then it is probably better considered a barter, but if it occurs that this practice becomes more wide spread then that asset may better be considered a currency. In that case, its contribution to the economy can be determine by the total amount of spending that occurs as a result of the transfer of ownership of that paper or credit. The average value or price of each transaction times the number of transactions. It one wanted to put the value of the transactions in terms of a fiat money, one would probably have to use an exchange rate. So, if people or entities in an economy, or multiple economies, learn to trust that any of these papers or credits will maintain their value in trade, and they are in such common use they may be considered a currency, the total value of those papers or credits has been added to the money supply, like those cell phone minutes mentioned earlier in this chapter.

Credit cards, on the other hand, in my opinion, are better understood as loans, the design of which may allow for more convenience and faster dispensing of loan money than other types of loans. The effect credit cards have in increasing the amount of spending would be, like other loans, to increase the velocity of money.

There has been mention recently of certain large companies wanting to create their own currency. This would be sort of like allowing coupons or the equivalent of gift cards to be created and given nominal values in terms of their "currency". These would be like some sort of credit kept in a customer's account. These credits can then be used for spending. What might make these credits less attractive to the average consumer is that their use for spending would likely be controlled by the corporation, and limited to being used for purchases that maximizes the profits of that corporation (in the short or long run). To entice use of these credits, and as such, to gain more of a share of a customer's spending, one would expect these corporations would have to offer some sort of incentives.

Presumably, the way people collect these credits would vary, for example getting credits for prior purchases, or, if possible, such a corporation would love to get to a situation where customers actually use fiat money to purchase such credits. If the number of corporations got small enough, and monopoly power increased enough, then such credits could possibly become a larger and larger share the money supply in use, perhaps even becoming considered a significant portion of the money supply.

But given enough competition, it may not be so easy for such a corporation's "currency" to become established the way these companies may envision. We all remember and may still utilize store cards issued by certain retail chains. In the past it was common for some retail chains to issue such store cards and then limit spending in their stores to either cash purchases or the use of these store cards. Eventually this practice of only allowing their own store cards to be used for credit purchases ended because customers preferred to be able to shop at stores that accepted other forms of credit payment such as credit cards issued by banks. (Another factor was the very high interest rates store cards charged). I suspect a similar dynamic will make it more difficult for corporate issued "credits" to become established as dominant currencies, or, if any of them were actually able to attain that status, to maintain it.

CHAPTER 12
Effective Demand

A look at Keynes' model for determining how the amount of spending affects employment levels.

ANOTHER WORD FOR income or spending is demand. Demand is the amount that will be spent to acquire that labor or that outcome or those goods and services.

Now I am going to move into the microeconomic sphere for a bit, but I am doing this as a foundation that will let me describe a macroeconomic concept. This concept is something Keynes introduced in his book, "The General Theory of Employment Interest and Money"

If an entrepreneur wants to hire people for a certain venture, he, in his mind, **needs** to make a certain **total income** on the project to hire that amount of people.

Total income, i.e., total revenue from selling the product, has to be enough to pay for all the costs. The costs include rental costs, raw materials, employees' wages and benefits, investor profits, taxes, training expenses, costs associated with labor laws and union demands, subcontractors, minimally acceptable profit to entrepreneur himself. Anything and everything you can think of that the entrepreneur will want or need to pay for to have that level of employment, and the associated level of output production.

That amount just described, is the amount he **needs** to make for that that level of employment. Keynes defines that amount as the **supply price.** This is also referred to as the Supply Function when plotted against the employment level or simply the **supply curve** and this is illustrated in the graph below. The supply price is the total minimum amount the entrepreneur needs to make to be able to sustain the given level of employment.

Supply price is the amount the entrepreneur needs to make to hire that many workers, but he may expect to actually make more than that minimum required amount. The amount the entrepreneur **actually expects to make**, the amount he actually expects to gross, the amount he expects customers to spend buying his product, for that level of employment, is called the **demand**, or demand function, or when plotted against the number of employees, the **demand curve**.

The next important point to discuss here is what happens as the number of employees is increased, in other words, what happens to the **demand curve** and to the **supply curve** as the employment level continues to increase. Keynes believed that the productivity for each new worker eventually starts to go down as you hire more and more workers. Here he is talking about productivity in current conditions, not productivity over time as new technologies and improved techniques may increase productivity.

Why did he believe production per worker goes down as employment levels increase? The law of diminishing returns is a commonly accepted principle in economics and reasons for it can include: best workers hired first; less skilled workers hired last; best equipment used first, worst last; crowding out on current equipment; competition from competitors putting a squeeze on prices one is able to charge. A search on diminishing returns on the internet will find numerous references and explanations of these phenomenon. Now, it is not true that diminishing returns would occur at every level of employment. In fact at certain levels, due to economies of scale you can have increasing returns per employee as you hire more people. Eventually however we get to a level of employment where diminishing returns do occur. This model can be applied to a more complex situation where at some levels of employment there is not diminishing returns but our graphs really only look at the part of the curve where diminishing returns do apply.

Diminishing returns means that the extra amount of sales the entrepreneur generates by hiring one more worker become less and less as each new worker is hired. On the graph this shows as the demand curve **curving down** (see the graph below).

In this model of Keynes, the idea is that while the increase in sales the entrepreneur generates for each worker hired decreases as more workers are hired, the minimum amount by which the entrepreneur needs his sales revenue to increase, for each extra hired worker, **does not**. That is, while the **demand curve curves down**, the **supply curve** does not. Possibly the minimum amount the entrepreneur needs to make to hire another new worker could even increase (possibly the supply curve would curve up some). That is, at the part of the curve where diminishing returns are occurring, as we near the limit of viable employment, this model expects that the entrepreneur's total cost, as he hires each additional worker, tends to increase at the same pace or possibly even a faster pace.

On the graph, the distance between the demand and supply curves for a given level of employment is the profit margin for hiring an extra worker. Since the demand curve is curving down and the supply curve is not, then eventually the profit margin shrinks until it becomes zero. At that point hiring an extra worker will not bring any extra profit. On the graph this is the point where the demand curve and the supply curve intersect. That point is significant because **if you go beyond that level of employment,** the entrepreneur will no longer increase his profits by hiring extra workers and may even start to lose money, so he will stop hiring new workers.

He might hire more people if he knew he was going to make more money in the **future** and that is true, but he accounts for this in his supply price. His supply price is what he determines he needs to make, and if he knows he will be making more money in the future then he will need, in his estimation, to make less money now.

Keynes describes the point of intersection of the demand curve and the supply curve as the point of **Effective Demand.** The number of employees at the point of effective demand will be the equilibrium point, that is, it will be the level of employment that one can expect to **actually exist**. This graph shows the aggregate demand and aggregate supply curves and illustrates the point.

FIGURE 12.1

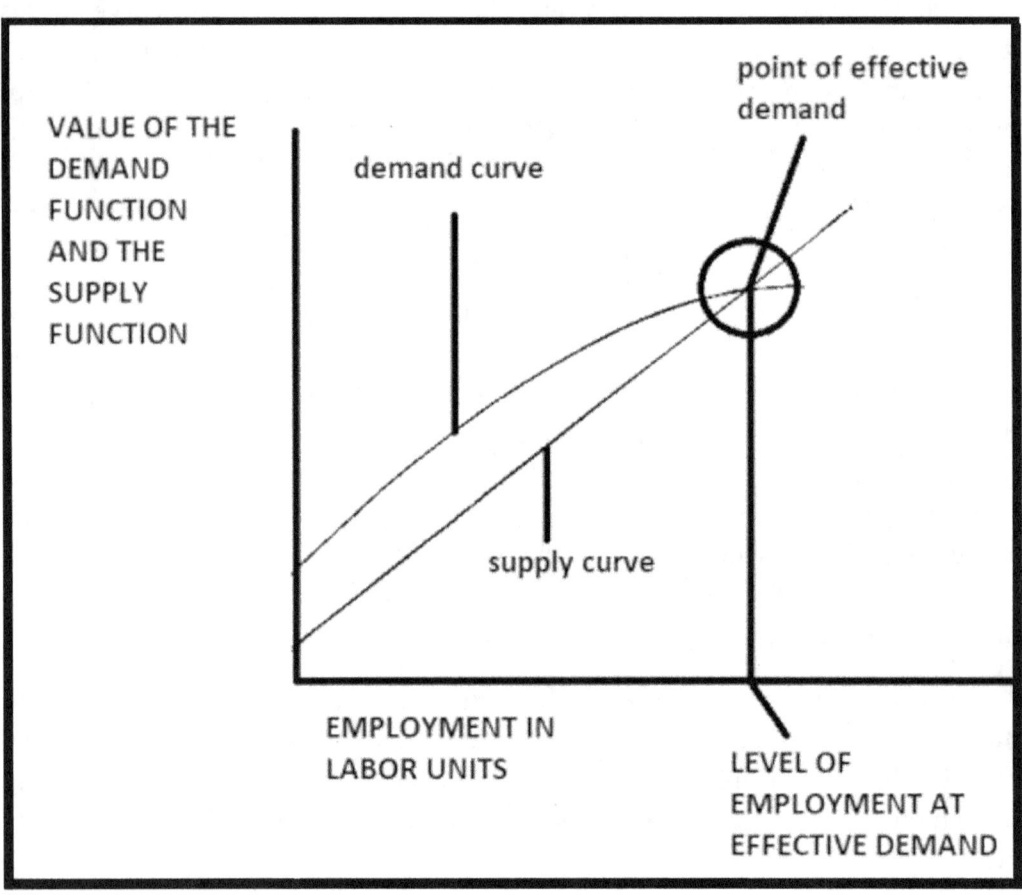

This is a simplistic model and kept so for the purposes of elucidation. As mentioned, it is very probable that the demand curve would not be a nice curve with gradually decreasing slope throughout. It is very possible that the supply curve is not a nice line of constant slope. Particularly at lower levels of employment it is possible that the difference between the demand curve and the supply curve may increase, or vacillate and would not be steadily decreasing throughout. But what Keynes believed is that due to diminishing returns eventually a point is reached where the curves intersect. Eventually, a point of effective demand is reached.

The model does not account for **where the demand comes from.** That is, where do the people who are buying the entrepreneur's product get their money from? For that reason it is not a fully macroeconomic model.

Effective Demand

The demand, i.e., the spending to purchase the entrepreneur's product cannot be totally paid for by the income paid to the wage earners, because the entrepreneur will not just give all the proceeds from the sales to the laborers.

Demand could come from all of the people getting income from the venture, like the suppliers, the subcontractors, the entrepreneurs, the investors and the laborers. In other words, the amount of spending to buy the product becomes income for everyone involved in the venture. If everyone who got that income from the sales used the entirety of it to pay for the sales, (that would be equivalent to agreeing to take the product in lieu of payment), then in that case, there would be enough income to pay for all the sales. Of course, that is a scenario that would only be viable if everyone spent the entirety of their current income on buying that product. But people do not spend all of their current income purchasing current production. They spend some of their income and save some. For now, I will just leave it that total demand, the total spending must be subsidized by some source of funding, not specified in this model, other than the current income paid to those involved in the described venture.

The demand curve represents the estimate of the entrepreneur of how much customers are willing to pay for their product, in the aggregate. Due to diminishing returns, there is a limit as to how much production will be induced by that level of demand.

The most important concept that Keynes was trying to introduce with this model, is that if one could increase the amount of demand, that is, increase that amount customers were able and willing to pay for the production, then based on the simple supply and demand principle, for a given level of employment, it is reasonable to expect the entrepreneur to sell his product for a higher price. This increasing of the total level of demand would show on the graph as shifting the entire demand curve up.

FIGURE 12.2

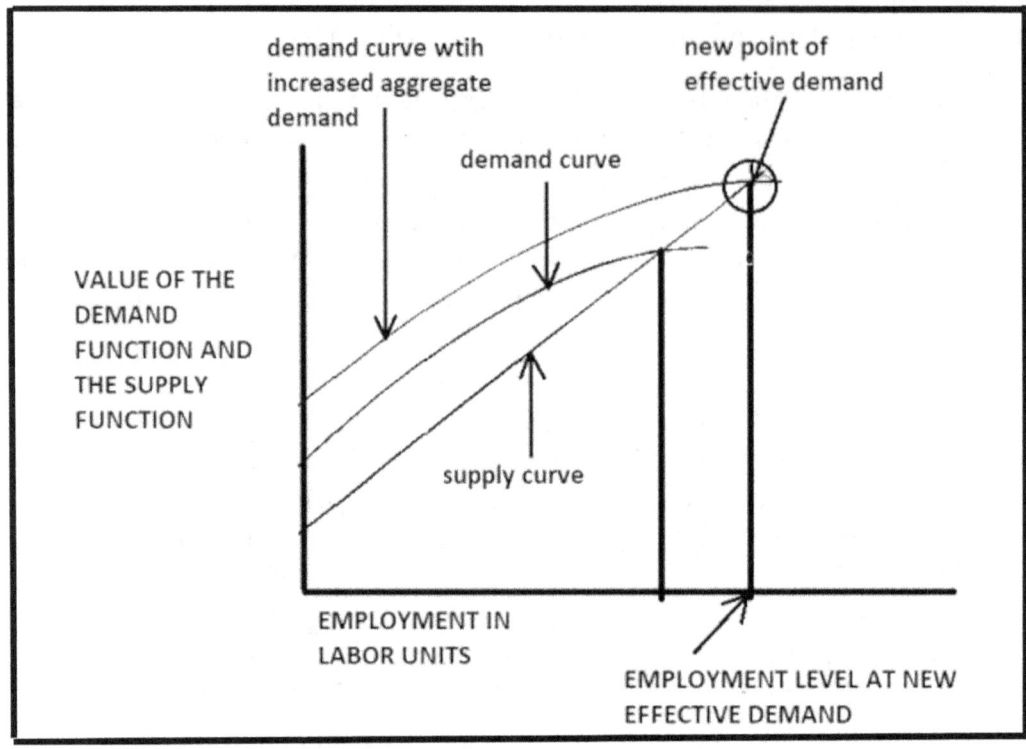

This will cause the point of effective demand to shift to the right, that is, equilibrium will occur at a higher level of employment.

So far, I have imagined what would happen with one entrepreneur. Let us expand our scenario to include all the entrepreneurs in the whole economy. If we consider all the entrepreneurs en masse, what would be the limit to how high the employment level could go? That is, how high could the employment level go if demand could keep being increased? Increasing demand could cause the employment level to increase up to the point where there is no one left to hire. This point, Keynes referred to as **full employment**.

The total demand that exists in the whole economy, for a given time period, Keynes called **Aggregate Demand**. One of the central concepts in Keynes' work is that if you are at less than full employment, if you increase aggregate demand, all else being equal, you will increase employment.

In terms of the Gurdjieff work we see at play here both the law of 3 and the law of 7. The entrepreneur and the workers have to know what needs to be accomplished in order to reach one's goal. They need the **knowledge**. In addition, they need to have the ability to perform the duties required, i.e., they need the **being**. They cannot truly **understand** and implement the business plan without both elements. Their being efforts will have to be such that they are able to keep the goal in mind and provide reminders to themselves at the right time, both individually and as a group, in order to keep the process (**octave**) going. If those involved in the venture are not able to keep in mind their goals and focus on continuing the work needed to accomplish them, then all the planning, all the intellectual understanding of what should be done, will not bear fruit. So, we have just described the role of knowledge and being in allowing understanding, and how knowledge is able to be implemented over time by being and being effort.

The law of three involves an active, a passive and a reconciling force. We can view the demand for product as the active force, first force. The passive force, 2nd force is the factors you need to "get moving" to accomplish the production goals. The spending of the money used to buy the product, i.e., the demand, is the expression of the desire for the product, the expression of the active, or first force. The reconciling, or 3rd force is the way that this process is put into action, the strategy. We can imagine more conscious and less conscious approaches to the forces affecting the process and thus the ultimate outcome, the result. Is the result a quality product? Did the process of producing it damage the environment or waste resources? Or did it minimize damage and efficiently use resources? Did the process harm worker's health, mental or physical? Or did it foster a sense of accomplishment and self- esteem and not damage physical health?

Many of the elements that make up the 3rd force or reconciling force, if applied more consciously, can result in increasing our total wealth. Or if those controlling the reconciling process are less conscious perhaps the process would decrease the wealth or at least increase wealth less. Now, when I speak of "overall wealth," I include the product or service produced, but also **what effect the process has on our natural resources and environment, and what effect it has on the people involved**. As an example of the reconciling influence coming from a less conscious source, think of businesses administered by leaders who give minimal or no consideration to environmental destruction and depletion of natural resources in their planning and implementation.

Effective Demand

The process of completing the task, any task, involves attention to the process but also periodic reminders of the goal in order to complete the task. At times it is useful to have several pathways to completing the work going on at the same time as they can interact, and the interaction can sometimes function as shocks, as reminders to the various pathways (or octaves) that keeps one or the other of the tasks moving towards completion. That is the **law of 7, of the octave,** in operation.

CHAPTER 13
Wealth, Savings, and "Net Income"

How to define wealth and savings and an explanation of why "net income" is not a useful concept in macroeconomic theory.

I HAVE TALKED about income. Now the next term I want to define is **wealth**. Wealth is anything that has value. For now, just know that it includes the money supply and everything else that can be said to have value. Over the span of a given time period the total value of wealth ordinarily does not stay still, it could decrease or increase. As an alternative term, I also call wealth "**capital**". These are completely equivalent terms, in my definitions. Also, an equivalent term is **total savings**. The term **savings** is slightly different from total savings, because total savings is all the wealth, but I define **savings** as the amount of wealth that results from a period of economic activity.

The wealth we call savings that results from a period of economic activity will include two parts:

The money used for spending in the given period is part of the wealth. This money will continue to exist at the end of the period. Think of this money as disappearing into the economic activity when it first enters the spending and then if one takes a snap shot of the wealth at the end of the economic activity, there it is, still existing in the same amount.

This part of savings is not NEW wealth. It is preservation of preexisting wealth, the investment money. It causes no change in the level of wealth. This is the famous **Savings = Investment Identity** which is supposed to be true "always and everywhere" according to standard economic teaching.

Wealth, Savings, and "Net Income"

What is not generally recognized, in standard economics teaching, is that this is only part of savings. To account for any change in the level of wealth one needs the second part of savings.

The second part of savings is the amount of new wealth produced, minus the amount of wealth used up or depleted. I call this **net production**.

The total amount of wealth that comes out of that given period of economic activity is the preserved money which is equal to **Investment** plus the **net production**

The famous identity is incorrect and should be corrected to:

"Savings equals investment plus net production"

Spending creates and is equal to the demand which equals the amount of income, **Y**

Which equals investment plus consumption, **I+C**

Which equals money times the velocity of money, **M∗V**

Which equals the average price of transactions times the number of transactions. **P∗T**

Every time money changes ownership from one person or entity to another, it gets added to the total for income for the given time period. Income is not net, income is **gross**, income is every transaction. Income accounts for all the movement of money through the economy.

Income is one of the things people look at when examining the macroeconomy, and the second part of what gets looked at is something that income can affect. Something that can be affected by the movement of money through the economy. This is where wealth enters the discussion.

Income and wealth are NOT the same thing. Income and wealth are related and affect each other but are independent variables. Income and wealth must be accounted for on different axes, the income axis and the wealth axis. Savings is part of wealth, and it is accounted for on the wealth axis. It is not part of income.

In this model I do not consider **net** income, just gross income. But I do consider **net changes in wealth**. Wealth is a measure of the value of everything that exists. Income is a measure of the movement of money.

Wealth, Savings, and "Net Income"

The money used in spending is wealth, but the spending of that money, the movement of ownership of that money from one person or entity to another is what we measure when we measure income.

Capital a.k.a. wealth a.k.a. total savings is measured on the wealth axis, and income is measured on the income axis.

Here is putting the whole thing together:

Income, the movement of money, results from and is equal to **Spending**.... spending to pay for labor to create goods and services, or to pay for items of wealth already created, or to create some outcome. The actual goods, services or outcomes are the **wealth** that is created by the economic activity, but the spending is the demand for, and therefore, ultimately, the cause of the creation of that wealth.

Income leads to production of wealth. On the other hand, it is the existence of wealth or the possibility of acquiring wealth that causes people to spend in the first place. That is the relationship between income and wealth.

People in the economy want to acquire wealth. It is the goal of purchasing wealth and increasing the standard of living that people or entities seek when they spend. They seek this improvement in standard of living in both the short run and the long run.

Some of the wealth is just temporary wealth, which serves a purpose and is gone. More often than not, that temporary wealth helps preserve other more durable wealth, including wealth known as human capital. (The temporary wealth might be food).

Some of the wealth is durable and outlasts the current time period.

If we take the wealth existing at the end of the given time period and subtract the wealth existing at the beginning of the time period, the difference is the net amount of wealth created during that time period.

It does not matter if we put a money value on all wealth, both that wealth created or destroyed. But if we were able to, that would give a single value, so one could say wealth increased or decreased by a certain amount of dollars. Or we could just make an inventory of all the different forms of wealth, keep track of how much we have of each item at the end of the given time period and subtract off all the wealth that was depleted to give us our net change.

Wealth, Savings, and "Net Income"

In other words, we could give all the different forms of wealth a dollar value and add or subtract the value of what is produced or what is depleted, to give us a total value in dollar terms, or we could just list everything we have, like an inventory, and add any new production to our inventory and subtract off any depleted wealth. We could then include the value of all or any part of that wealth in our accounting in dollar terms, depending on how we decide to analyze the data.

But no matter how the value of the total wealth or the change in the value of that wealth is calculated, the important thing here is that all this accounting occurs on the wealth axis, not the income axis.

As I previously mentioned, when I am talking about income in this document, I am talking about Gross income.

Net income is really not something that makes any sense in a completely macroeconomic model. Net income is the total income minus the total spending in an economic period. Every time someone spends, this amount of spending is subtracted off the spender's net income, and that exact same amount of money gets added to the recipient's net income, so the total net income for everyone in the economy, all added together, will be zero.

In our viable economy where we have investment spending and consumption spending, first, some person or entity puts money into spending as investment. For that person or entity their **net income is negative the amount of the investment spending.** The people who get income from that spending add that to their net income but when they "re-spend" the money the amount they spend gets subtracted off and their net income is only what they saved. When all the consumption spending is done, the total **net income for all the income earners** is the **total of what they saved**. The amount they save in total just so happens to be equal to the amount of original investment spending, because that is the savings that is the preservation of investment.

That makes the net income: Savings minus the original investment amount equals zero. **Net income equals S - I = 0.** In a purely macroeconomic where all spending and all income is accounted for, **net income** always equals zero.

Defining income as the transfer of ownership of money from one person or entity to another will always result in having net income equal zero, if one calculates net income for the whole macroeconomy.

The reason this model uses gross income is because gross income is a measure of all the spending. Gross income is the income that results for all the spending, all the movement of money through the economy. It is **gross income** that equals **Y** in these equations:

Y = I + C

Y = M∗V

Y = P∗T

In Keynes famous formula, **Y = I + C**, Income equals investment plus consumption, the income he is measuring is gross income. That equation does not measure wealth or the change in level of wealth. I believe that interpreting **Y** to be a measure of both spending and the change in the level of wealth has created all sorts of confusion in macroeconomics. I propose that the most useful way to model macroeconomic theory is to keep income and wealth on separate axes. Define income as a measure of the movement of money when used in spending and define wealth on its own axis as a measure of everything that can be assigned a value.

The fact is that assigning a dollar value to everything one considers to have value and be part of total wealth is not always easy to do and is often subjective. But that is not the most important thing. The most important thing to understand is that the accounting of wealth occurs on the wealth axis, it is a measure of wealth, not a measure of spending, which is what income is.

In macroeconomics, studying **net** changes in **wealth** is absolutely essential,......... but **net income** is not a fully macroeconomic concept.

Studies of net income are useful in **MICROECONOMICS**. For the individual person or firm net income makes sense. In microeconomics, everyone knows that individuals can subtract expenses from gross pay to get a net, but even there one will have to decide where does one stop subtracting off. Does one only count all the deductions that shows on our paycheck stub, or does one deduct expenses paid after our check is deposited, such as life expenses, like rent or car payments or food? In any case, in this microeconomic scenario, one can calculate a "net income".

Let me illustrate with a concrete example how in the macroeconomy, net income, unlike net wealth, is always going to equal zero:

Wealth, Savings, and "Net Income"

I am going to describe a scenario where everyone who gets income, saves 10 dollars out of it and spends the rest.

Let us say there are 11 people involved in the economy, the first person spends, no income to him, he just spends creating income for the person he gives the money to.

He gives 100 dollars to purchase something from the second person.

That is money spent for the first time in the given time period and counts as investment totaling 100 dollars.

The second person being the recipient of that spending, gets 100 dollars income.

(Total gross income now is 100)

The second person saves 10 dollars and buys something from the 3rd person for 90 dollars

(total gross income now 100 +90 = 190, total saved is 10)

3rd person takes their 90 income and saves 10 and buys something from 4th person for 80 dollars

(total gross income 190 + 80 = 270, total saved is 20)

4th person gets 80 income and saves 10 and buys something from 5th person for 70 dollars

(total gross income 270 + 70 = 340, total saved is 30)

5th person takes their 70 income and saves 10 and buys something from 6th person for 60 dollars

(total gross income 340 + 60 = 400, total saved is 40)

6th person takes their 60 income and saves 10 and buys something from 7th person for 50 dollars

((total gross income 400 + 50 = 450, total saved is 50)

Notice that at each step for each person the net income is the income minus they amount of the income they spent, that is the net income is the amount saved by that person, so that the running count for total net income is the total amount saved

Wealth, Savings, and "Net Income"

7th person saves 10 and buys something from 8th person for 40 dollars

(total gross income 450 + 40 = 490, total saved is 60)

8th person saves 10 and buys something from 9th person for 30 dollars (total gross income 490 + 30 = 520, total saved is 70)

9th person saves 10 and buys something from 10th person for 20 dollars (total gross income 520 + 20 = 540, total saved is 80)

10th person saves 10 and buys something from 11th person for 10 dollars

(total gross income 540 + 10 = 550, total saved is 90) 11th person saves 10 and buys nothing

Total gross income is 550 dollars of which 100 was investment spending and 450 was consumption spending. And the total saved is 100 dollars. If one is thinking of net income then the net income of the investor would be **minus 100 dollars**, and the net income of everyone else is **plus 100 dollars.**

That is, the net income of everyone is the amount saved….plus 100 dollars…. minus the amount originally invested, that is minus 100 dollars. The net income is 100 – 100 = 0. Gross income is $550. Net income is zero.

⁓⁕⁕⁕⁓

The total net income will always be zero in the macroeconomy*, it is only on the wealth axis that one is able to calculate net changes. Most economist would count net changes in wealth as income. I do not because I am defining income solely as the movement of ownership of money from one person or entity to another. Even though income encourages production of wealth, it is not a measure of that wealth.

⁓⁕⁕⁕⁓

*Note that net income will always be zero in a closed, private economy where we do not consider interactions with the government or foreign economies. Net income in the private domestic economy can be different from zero if one considers transactions occurring between the government and or foreign countries. For example, government spending targeted at the private economy would cause positive net income to the private economy, of course it would cause negative net income to the government. Spending by the private sector aimed at the government

would cause negative net income to private sector but positive net income to the government. Similarly, with the foreign entity, spending from foreign entity to the private domestic entity is negative net income for foreign entity and positive net income for the private domestic entity. Spending from the private domestic entity to the foreign entity is negative net income for the private domestic economy but positive net income for the foreign economy.

This apparent contradiction is resolved if one were to combine private domestic, government and foreign. That is when adding together the government income, trade partners income and private domestic income, **NET INCOME WILL ALWAYS EQUAL ZERO.**

The concept of net income not being zero when considering spending back and forth between the government, foreign countries and the private domestic economy, also affects our discussion of GDP later in this book.

My point here is simple, in a purely macroeconomic analysis, when we measure spending (=income) it is a measure of GROSS spending (=GROSS income). And the spending in and of itself is **NOT** a measurement of the change in the level of overall wealth in the world. Spending is simply the transfer of ownership of money. Whether that transaction which is a transfer of ownership of money is between a private domestic entity and another private domestic entity, or private domestic entity and the government, or private domestic and foreign entities, or the government and foreign entities, or two foreign entities. None of that transfer of ownership of money, none of that spending, is a measurement of the change in the total level of wealth in the world. It may affect production which can cause a change in the level of wealth, it may contribute to the increasing or decreasing the amount of pre-existing wealth depleted or destroyed, but it is not, in and of itself a change in the level of wealth.

Comment on nomenclature:

I could, perhaps, change up the whole terminology and call the change in the level of wealth "income", and the change in ownership of money something else. But I believe that Keynes **Y = I + C** is most accurately described as a measure of spending and, that the expression is commonly understood to be a measure of spending. I don't want to lose that connection to how economists currently understand these terms, even if, in fact, there is some variation in how exactly such terms are understood by different economists. So for me, **Y** and the expressions that define **Y** will remain purely measurements of the change in ownership of money for a purpose, that is, it will remain a measurement of spending and income measured on the income axis. Wealth, a measure of things that have value, will be accounted for on the wealth axis.

CHAPTER 14
The Forms of Wealth

These categories of wealth may seem atypical, but they are defined as they are for a reason and will be needed as I develop my model.

WEALTH BASICALLY TAKES three forms:

1. **Money**

2. **Purely financial assets**
   all purely financial assets are **based on loans** in one way or another

3. **Other assets**
   this category, which accounts for all other forms of wealth includes anything and everything you can think of that has value, except loans and money.

Money is self-explanatory and is the amount of money which exists as paper currency, coins or virtual money. When a certain amount of Money changes ownership, that creates income, but the money itself is wealth. I would add that the type of money I am talking about here is fiat money. Representative money is not wealth in and of itself but is dependent on the existence of the item of wealth it "represents" which is accounted for in the "other assets" category.

Purely financial assets' values are based on the debt obligation that is created when a loan is created. These loans include things like:

1) loans banks make to individuals or firms, these loans are assets to the banks and therefore a form of wealth.

2) buying bonds is a loan to the bond issuer and an asset to the bond purchaser, and

3) putting money into a bank deposit account is a loan to the bank by the depositor and becomes an asset for the depositor.

4) Savings bonds are a loan to the government, and an asset for the bond holder, and so on.

Whenever a purely financial asset is created, the purchaser then owns the asset while the seller, in addition to becoming owner of the cash paid for the asset also becomes owner of a matching debt obligation. Every time a purely financial asset is created, so is a debt of the same value. Therefore, the creation of purely financial assets does not increase the total combined wealth of the economy.

The category of **other assets** is comprised of everything else that has value that is not based on a loan. Enumerating them would result in a very long list. Typically, when we think of people or entities owning such wealth we think of ownership of tangible items, of any type. This could include things personally owned, or things co-owned, including such things as an interest in a business. It could be things owned by private concerns or it could be publicly owned assets like infrastructure. It could be what is called human capital, the worth of a human being and all the qualities and knowledge and abilities they possess. It could be those human's capacity for labor, both in terms of quality and quantity. It could be knowledge stored in books, it could be other things people value like nature that has been preserved, or good will amongst our neighbors, or the good feeling in our hearts that we didn't let our neighbors starve to death or the feeling of safety and security we have because of law enforcement efforts, and so on. I would just mention that the value of these assets could be added to by the lasting effects of services provided. At any rate, as long as the form of wealth is not accounted for in the other two categories, it belongs in this category.

The commonly used concept in economics called utility is really a measure of wealth and is often incorporated into models as representing the value of a given amount of wealth. This term tends to emphasize the subjective nature of wealth, how individuals might rate its value differently. In this book I just stick to the terms wealth, capital and total savings. I do acknowledge that any valuation of wealth is, in part, a subjective thing, and the valuation of an amount of wealth given by different people may differ.

Accounting for total wealth is done simply by combining everything that has any value. Even when it is not easy to assign a money value to some wealth it still counts as part of the total wealth. One should not dismiss or diminish the significance of spending that creates wealth solely because that particular wealth is not easy to value in money terms. If people dismiss things solely because they are hard to value in money terms, then people may not want to spend to acquire them, even if they are vital to our economy, and our standard of living and quality of life. It is hard to value education. It is hard to value peace and security. It is hard to value health. It is hard to value free speech. Does that mean spending that pays to help these things exist is wasteful?

Wealth is produced by humans or by nature, on purpose or by accident, or as a natural process. Wealth is also regularly depleted, destroyed, decays, or depreciates, caused by the actions or inactions of man or by nature. Wealth can be a stable thing or rapidly fall or increase in value, depending on its type and the current situation. Assets formerly of little value can increase in value when new technologies are discovered. The worth of certain things can increase or decrease based on advertising, education, rumor, innuendo, manipulations of news, prejudice, changing fashion or tastes, politics, religion and many other influences.

Wealth can be more stable and based on durable more lasting factors or it can be more ephemeral, temporary, based on easily changed and subjective valuations. Wealth can be a tangible physical item, or it could be embodied in human qualities, such as higher levels of knowledge, and skills. Even integrity, and how much it is embedded in the lives of the people living in society has value and can be considered as wealth, and perhaps one of the more durable and valuable types of wealth.

Wealth interacts, that is, increasing some forms of wealth can increase or decrease the value of other forms of wealth. For example, new scientific knowledge, a form of wealth, may make some natural resource more valuable. Or tastes may change, and society may increase its desire for and spending to acquire a certain item of wealth, increasing its value, and that may increase the value of commodities needed for its manufacture. At the same time, the switching tastes may decrease the desire for, spending to acquire, and value of some other items. Or new inventions and discoveries may replace old technologies, with commodities associated with the new technology increasing in value and items associated with the old technology decreasing in value.

Income is **not** the production of wealth, income promotes and facilitates the production of wealth, but income is not a measure of the change of wealth. Income **is** a measure of the demand for production of wealth, demand for any goods, services, labor, or outcomes. Spending of a given amount creates income for the recipient of the spending in the same amount. This can result in wealth increasing, or wealth being preserved, or it can result in services being rendered. Spending can result in all kinds of outcomes being achieved. Any goods produced as a result do count as part of the wealth until they are used up. Any of the effects of services rendered that persist, as a result of the services, can count as wealth.

The wealth that comes out of the economic activity of a given period of time is anything that is left over at the end of the given time period. It includes the money that was being used for spending. Savings is defined by that money plus any net production of wealth occurring during that time period.

I define total wealth, total capital and total savings as equivalent terms for all the wealth in existence in the economy at the given time. Even though savings can be negative, I would venture to say it is impossible for total savings to ever be negative. It is impossible for total wealth, total capital and total savings to be negative since that would imply that not only does nothing exist, but less than nothing. However, savings defined as investment plus net production can be negative since it is possible for more wealth to be depleted or destroyed in a given time period than is newly created. It is even possible to have periods of high investment spending and high income but negative savings. This is true because it is possible to have net production be negative. Think war or natural disasters. If a hurricane comes through there are going to be a lot of new jobs created to recover and rebuild, causing a large increase in spending and incomes, but the value of the destruction could far outweigh the value of the new production, in a given time period, and cause negative net production and negative savings.

The valuation of wealth will always be, at least partially, a relative or subjective thing, and the valuation will often change over time. It is possible that people may agree that a certain outcome is desirable but disagree on how much it should cost. It is not always easy to determine what the value should be. Two groups of people might both value having housing for the homeless, but one group might think the government or charities should pay X for it, whereas others might think they should pay Y for it.

One of the greatest misunderstandings that occurs today is the belief that, in macroeconomics and macroeconomic policy, spending is the same thing as the depletion of wealth. When we consider the economy as a whole, while spending may decrease the spenders supply of money, it increases the recipients supply of money by the same amount. Spending is simply the movement of money, the change of ownership of the money as it goes from one person or entity to another. In the macroeconomy, i.e., in the overall economy, spending, more often than not, leads to **increased**, not decreased, production of wealth.

A period of economic activity where spending occurs can be associated with increased wealth, or decreased wealth, or no significant change in wealth. Spending can lead to a mixture of increasing wealth and decreasing wealth. Think of producing something but depleting natural resources in the process. But spending itself is not a depletion of wealth.

Income is not wealth, but it can buy wealth. One might think that one can increase the overall amount of money by putting money into a bank account. One might think that when one purchases an asset, i.e., the bank deposit, and when due to interest payments, the value of that asset grows and then, since one could withdraw more money than they deposited that means money has been created. It is true that if the value of the asset called a bank deposit grows, the personal wealth of the owners of that asset has increased, and their access to money should they need or desire it for spending, has increased. But that does not mean the overall money supply in the whole economy has increased.

In the macroeconomy, that is not a valid description of what has happened. What has happened is that when one deposits money they have purchased an asset called a bank deposit from the bank, and the bank has acquired ownership of that money, along with a debt obligation to the depositor. No new total wealth was created, and no additional money was created. From that initial transaction one's wealth stayed the same, all they did was change the value of their wealth from cash to an asset called a bank deposit of equal money value. The bank as a result acquired a debt obligation of the same amount and the cash has become owned by the bank. The asset called the bank deposit is a form of wealth, but in terms of total wealth it is offset by the debt obligation the bank has. No change in level of wealth there. The debt obligation of the bank is balanced by the cash they acquired. No change in level of wealth there either. The money given to the bank was wealth that existed prior to the transaction and that money continues to exist. As with the creation of any purely financial asset, no increase or decrease in total wealth has resulted.

The bank now owns that money and can lend it to a person or entity. This creates an asset for the bank called a loan. That borrower would acquire the cash but also acquires a debt obligation. Still no increase in wealth has occurred. In the macroeconomy, the asset called a loan is a form of wealth, but the value of that asset is offset by the debt obligation the borrower has acquired. The money's ownership changes from the bank to the borrower, but that is not new wealth, as that wealth already existed.

Later, when paying back the loan, the borrower buys back part of the asset called a loan he sold to the bank and reduces part of his debt obligation. This step does not account for any new wealth being created. In addition, however, interest on the loan must be paid. It is here, with the payment of interest that a form of wealth creation is involved. This spending is payment by the borrower to the bank for the purpose of having been able to have that money available for spending at the time of the loan. This interest money paid to the bank is what pays for the entire structure of the banking system. It pays for that which makes it possible for loans to be dispensed and serviced, that which allows for the safeguarding of our wealth, and that which facilitates banking transactions. The structure of the banking system is a form of wealth, and that is paid for by interest payments. The borrower is also paying for the ability to have money to spend when they want to spend it. The bank pays the depositor so they can have money available to dispense loans when they need or want to. In that sense, having the money to spend when needed is another form of wealth that interest pays for.

Still, if one just looks at the banking transactions and does not consider those factors mentioned, just the movement of money through the banking system, paying that interest on loans, the overall wealth of the borrower decreases while the net wealth of the bank and the depositors increase by the same amount. And although the infrastructure of the bank system is a form of wealth, it would have no purpose if wealth were not created somewhere else in the economy. And just moving money around is not the actual creating of wealth.

To analyze where this other production of wealth occurs, that which allows borrowers to pay interest to banks, and that allows banks to pay interest to depositors, and which allows the bank depositors wealth to grow, one must look further.

I have still not accounted for where the borrower gets the money needed to pay off the loan debt obligation including any interest charges incurred. Somehow the borrower needs to come up with enough money to do that, either from money he already had or from money he newly acquires.

How does the borrower acquire money to be able to make his loan payments? A number of different ways. When the borrower gets loan money he can then spend it to purchase labor that can produce a product for him to sell at a price that allows him to profit, after he pays for labor and other expenses. Or he can buy things previously produced and sell it at a higher price. Or he can sell his own labor for money. Or he can sell something he produced with his own labor, making sure it is priced to recoup his expenses and get a profit. Or he could take the money and buy an interest in a "for-profit" venture that someone else is administrating, getting a return on the purchase of that venture asset.

In all of those described options, the common theme is that borrower participates in and profits from the sale of some sort of production, leading to the borrower acquiring money as income. The sale could have been of a good or service, or the sale of the borrower's own labor, or it could have been the borrower acquiring income due to the desire of the purchaser to acquire some other outcome. The point is, as long as the other outcome is not a loan, it is production that provides the impetus for spending that leads to the borrower acquiring money as income that he can freely spend, i.e., receiving that money does not cause them to be encumbered by another debt obligation. That money can be used by the borrower to reduce or pay off his debt, not just cause him to substitute one debt for another of equal value.

That is how the borrower can pay back the loan plus interest. It does not matter when the wealth he is selling is produced, past, present or even future production can all be sold in the current time period. As long as the sales occur in the given time period, they create income for the borrow in the current time period. The borrower acquires ownership of some of the money in the money supply because people who desire to purchase some of the things he has to offer for sale, will trade the money for those items. He then can use that same money to pay for items he wishes to acquire or he can use that money to pay his debts, including interest payments.

That is how the new wealth is created that allows the value of the depositors account to grow. Ultimately, money a borrower acquires to pay back a loan with interest comes from the result of that individual providing, in exchange for payment, some good, service labor or some other desired outcomes. It does not come from any increase in the money supply, instead it comes from selling any of those things to people or entities who already have money. Wealth is not increased by creating assets that are completely offset by a debt obligation. Creation of new wealth does not occur from the creation of purely financial assets.

Generally, total wealth is not increasing as a result of an increase in the money supply **M,** especially since most of the increase in the money supply done at one time is balanced by that the money supply being decreased at a different time period. Only very slowly, over a very long period of time is the money supply increased on a permanent basis, and this is not generally what allows the paying of interest to bank depositors. We are describing a situation where income is increasing, and income is increasing because the economic activity is leading to an increase in spending, done to acquire those items of wealth. We are really talking about having economic activity increase the velocity of spending of money, **V**, to cause that increased income needed to pay back the loans with interest.

It is outside of the banking system where the wealth production occurs. It is the spending that pays for goods, services, labor, other desired outcomes (other than paying for a purely financial asset) that allows the loans to be paid with interest, which then allows banks to pay interest to depositors. It is this economic activity that occurs outside banks that allows banks and depositors to earn interest payments and increase the wealth they hold within the banking system. When the bank depositor withdraws all his or her money from the bank account and the amount withdrawn is more than the original deposit, extra money was not magically created, extra money was not created at all. Extra goods were created, services provided, labor provided, other outcomes paid for and hopefully achieved. It is the movement of ownership of money in paying for all of these which allowed the bank depositor and the bank to increase the value of their purely financial assets.

The money itself can keep circulating, for example those depositors will probably withdraw some of that money out of their deposits (request the bank to buy back some of its debt obligation to the depositor) and purchase things with it. In fact, it is possible that some of the spending they do with withdrawn deposit money will be to acquire non-monetary products that contribute to the income of the borrowers of money from the very same bank. That can help the borrower pay back the bank with interest allowing the bank to add interest to the value of that depositor's savings asset. In that way, the depositors spending contributes to the increased value of their own bank account. Of course, the spending of the depositor was motivated by wanting to acquire those non-monetary products, increasing their wealth and standard of living that way.

Also, the spending of those who make their income from the bank's operation, paid for by those interest payments, may also directly or indirectly contribute to their borrower's income, helping the borrower be able to pay back the loan and the loan interest to that bank. The cycle of economic activity that is caused by money changing ownership can have us all playing different roles at different times as the money from the same money supply keeps getting spent and re-spent on different transactions.

Putting it as simply as possible the point I am trying to make is that while money is a form of wealth, that is, the actual money itself is an asset, one does do not grow wealth by increasing the supply of that particular asset, i.e., one does not grow wealth by increasing the money supply*. And wealth does not increase simply by increasing the amount of purely financial assets, i.e., loans. Wealth is increased only by the net production of non-financial forms of wealth. Wealth only increases by production of the 3rd type of asset mentioned in the beginning of this chapter, labeled "other assets". And, of course, one should also note that spending is the change of ownership of that first type of asset listed in this chapter, the asset called money, from the buyer to the seller.

*Strictly speaking, when the Central Bank increases the money supply it increases total wealth a little. But that is only done by the Central Bank, when appropriate, for the purpose of keeping employment and production of non-monetary wealth maximized. It is not, and never should be, the purpose of the Central Bank to replace production of non-monetary wealth with the creation of fiat money. In fact, it is for that very reason that the Federal Reserve Bank in America was created in such a way that it has a degree of independence from the government. That was done to reduce the likelihood that political leaders would, for short term political gain, be able to misuse the authority of the Central Bank to create money in such a way that it harms the economy.

CHAPTER 15
MORE DISCUSSION ON HOW WEALTH AND INCOME ARE NOT THE SAME THING

IN MY MODEL, total spending equals total gross income. In the macroeconomy gross income is a measure of the total amount of exchanges of ownership of money from one person or entity to another for a purpose that occurs in a given time period. I have shown in Chapter 13 how, in macroeconomics, if spending is defined in that way, in a fully macroeconomic model net income is not a useful concept because it always equals zero.

In the way I have defined spending, income, investment and consumption, I have shown Keynes' **Y** is a measure of gross income. Given these definitions, I have also shown how production of wealth, and gross income are not the same. Someone might say "Of course, if you are using 'Gross income', that would not equal wealth production", but I have also shown that net income equals zero and so wealth production cannot equal net income either. So, neither gross income nor net income is a measure of wealth production.

When an economist assigns value to a product this normally is construed to mean they are stating what the product is worth, that is, what it would or should sell for. People sometimes try to say that if someone buys an item by transferring a certain amount of money to the seller, that transaction proves the equivalency of the income earned by the seller to the value of that item of wealth. This results in some concluding that wealth and income are the same thing.

Even though it might seem stupid because "of course gross income does not equal wealth", I will run through a few examples to drive home the point and get us in the mindset of thinking of income as gross income and showing that, in

MORE DISCUSSION ON HOW WEALTH AND INCOME ARE NOT THE SAME THING

macroeconomics, income and wealth are not the same thing.

It is possible to have income paid for producing nothing that people would generally describe as wealth, no equivalency between income and wealth there. Examples might be social security, welfare, food stamps or charity. Of course, I have pointed how these transactions are purchasing things we can refer to as wealth, although the wealth these transfers of money are purchasing is not necessarily easy to value. If you do produce something that is difficult to value, whereas the money paid to produce it, i.e., the income associated with that production, is clearly defined, then you have no clear equivalency of wealth and income there. Other examples of things not necessarily so easy to value would be infrastructure, or education, or a safe and secure environment created by law enforcement. You may be able to calculate how much spending was done to pay for these things, but to calculate what value they have to society is a different and often subjective thing. And your dollar value of what they are considered worth can certainly differ from what is paid for them.

You can have identical amounts of income paid for producing something, by two different firms, and even if the items, the final products, were identical, one firm may be very efficient and productive, and produce more product and another firm may produce less product despite workers getting the same pay. You have a mismatch between production and (gross) income there.

Also, the value of a product can vary widely in different circumstances and over time, after the workers were already paid. That would mean there is not a clear relationship between (gross) income and wealth there either.

Or an employer could have paid workers to produce items. Spending for their labor created income for the workers. Later when the employer sold those items, it created income for the employer. This means that the same item of wealth resulted in (gross) income twice. Once when the workers produced it and once again when the employer sold it. Furthermore, the item might be something the buyer could use for a while, and then resell it, causing income again, all from the same item. Each time it is sold the amount it sells for gets added to the total gross income.

Y, i.e., income, in macroeconomics refers to gross income. Y equals average price P times the number of transactions T, ($Y = P*T$). In this scenario each time someone is paid for their labor, that is a transaction, and each time an item is sold that is a transaction, and each time the item gets sold again, that is another transaction. The price paid for each and every transaction gets added to gross income Y, but since items could get sold more than once, or items could be used up, or items could change value, then **Y** will not represent the total value of all the items involved in transactions during that time period. **Y** is, however, a measure of all the total amount of spending, the total amount of change in ownership of money during the current time period. **Y** does equal gross income, but it does not equal wealth.

⚜

Here is another example to strengthen the understanding of this concept:

Suppose I pay workers 100 dollars to produce something. That is 100 dollars income for the workers.

Then I sell it for 150 dollars, that is 150 dollars income for me. Then after using it for a while, the person who bought it from me sells it again, this time for 75 dollars. Let us assume at that point the value of the item is 75 dollars. But income for the whole period is 100 + 150 + 75 = 325 dollars.

Thus, **Y** = 325 dollars, but the value of the product is 75 dollars. Depreciation you say? Well, even when first produced the value of the product was at most 150 dollars, not 325 dollars. This is a concrete example of how income varies from the value of the product.

An item of wealth, at a given time, may be valued in terms of how much money would purchase it, but the income associated with the production, selling and reselling of that item can be different than the currently assessed value. In macroeconomics defining spending and income as I do, net income always equals zero and cannot equal wealth, and gross income, as I have shown, also is not the same thing as wealth.

CHAPTER 16

INFLUENCING THE LEVEL OF EFFECTIVE DEMAND

Demand is increased by increasing spending. This chapter looks at ways to do that and how increasing total demand can increase total employment.

AS MENTIONED ABOVE, in a barter system, demand is how much is traded to acquire certain goods or services, and income is what goods and services are received in exchange.

If the first party trades 10 of the widgets they made for 23 thingamajigs from a second party, then the first party is spending 10 widgets and gets 23 thingamajigs in return.

The 10 widgets are the spending of the first party and the demand for the 23 thingamajigs and the 10 widgets the first party pays (for those 23 thingamajigs) become the income for the second party.

From the perspective of the second party the 23 thingamajigs is their spending and the demand for 10 widgets they are getting from the first party. The 23 thingamajigs becomes the income of the first party, who hands over the 10 widgets in return.

The total spending in this transaction includes the spending of 10 widgets by the first party, and 23 thingamajigs by the second party, and thus the total spending is 10 widgets and 23 thingamajigs.

The total income is 23 thingamajigs for the first party and 10 widgets for the second party. The total spending and the total income are both 10 widgets and

Influencing the Level of Effective Demand

23 thingamajigs. Spending causes income in an equal amount. Spending equals income equals demand.

But notice here, the income is really calculated in two different types of wealth. That is like saying transactions are occurring in two different types of currency, widgets and thingamajigs. If the entire economy were based on barter then this type of accounting would lead to having to calculate our income in an almost limitless number of products or "currencies".

In transactions occurring in a monetary economy, we also have an exchange of items of wealth. The difference is, one of the items of wealth is money.

Let us say person A paid 50 dollars to person B for 10 widgets. Then from the perspective of person B, the 50 dollars was the demand for, and the spending to, purchase his 10 widgets. This 50 dollars becomes the income for person B, who hands over the widgets in return.

For person A the 10 widgets was the spending to acquire, and the demand for, his 50 dollars. Those 10 widgets become the income for person A, who hands over the 50 dollars in return.

The total spending is 50 dollars by person A and 10 widgets by person B, and this generates a total income of 50 dollars for person B and 10 widgets for person A. Both total spending and total income equal 50 dollars plus 10 widgets. And again, income is calculated in two different currencies, widgets and dollars.

The essential difference between a barter economy and a monetary economy is how one calculates income. In a monetary economy there is only one currency, and income is calculated in terms of that currency. The one currency is referred to as money. So, for example, in the latter scenario, the total income is 50 dollars, NOT 10 widgets and 50 dollars. One does not include the **items** purchased by spending of money as income. The value of the items purchased are accounted for on the wealth axis, but only the exchange of ownership of **money** counts as income, the accounting of which is done on the income axis.

Macroeconomists often use demand and spending interchangeably. I mostly agree with that usage. Which would also mean that demand equals income as well. Later in the book (Chapter 35), I will introduce a different way to look at spending, income and demand.

Influencing the Level of Effective Demand

Keynes describes something called the "propensity to consume," by which he means the fraction of the total spending that qualifies as consumption. It is described by the following formula: Propensity to consume equals [consumption]/[total income] which equals [consumption]/[investment + consumption].

Keynes says that in the current conditions, that is, with a given **propensity to consume** of the community as a whole, for a given level of **investment,** we can determine the total income. Those two variables will be enough to make that calculation. Or to put it another way, those two variables will be enough to determine the total demand. And if one goes back to the concept of effective demand, the conclusion of Keynes is that those two variables could determine the level of employment.

Investment is money being spent for the first time in the given time period and **consumption** is any re-spending of that investment money in that time period. Consumption is also identically described as the amount of current income for that time period that gets spent.

The **fraction** of **current income** used for spending, another way to describe the **propensity to consume,** could be a large fraction like 0.9 or whatever, but is still a fraction. In other words, it will never be greater than 1.0 since the amount of spending that qualifies as consumption can never exceed total income.

Aside

Since I expect people will find fault with that last statement: "the amount of spending that qualifies as consumption can never exceed total income."

I will address the anticipated criticisms immediately:

What about borrowing money and using that for consumption, wouldn't that cause consumption to be greater than total income?

No! Borrowing, and then using that money for spending, will not cause the propensity to consume to be greater than 1. The definition of income in this model is the change of ownership of money from one person or entity to another. Loans are income to the borrower. The borrower gets this income by agreeing to a debt obligation, that is, by selling his agreement to pay back the loan with interest. This means if someone is given a loan, their total income is increased by the amount of that loan. Even if the money used for the loan by the bank and given to the borrower was money that had previously been spent in the given time period, meaning, even if the money dispensed as the loan was counted as part of consumption spending instead of investment spending, consumption spending would not increase more than the total income. The most that could happen, if all the loan money were considered consumption spending, is that income and consumption would increase by the same amount. Lending could not cause consumption to increase more than total income, so consumption spending could not surpass total income from lending.

What about people spending out of their savings, wouldn't that cause consumption to be greater than income?

If people tried to make consumption greater than income by spending money saved in a previous time period that would NOT cause consumption to be greater than total income. When money acquired in a previous time period is used for spending, it is being used for spending for the first time in the given time period. Therefore, that spending counts as investment and adds to total income. Further, it does not count as consumption spending. Increasing investment income if consumption stayed the same would cause propensity to consume to go down. Generally, when you increase investment you also increase consumption, but since they both get added to total income, then increasing either will not cause consumption to increase more than total income. Again, consumption spending could never surpass total spending, and using savings for spending would not cause propensity to consume to be greater than one.

What if people sold some assets they owned, then used that money for consumption, couldn't that cause consumption to surpass total income? If people sold some assets to acquire money for spending, this selling of the assets itself counts as spending and income. The purchaser of their asset would be transferring ownership of money to the asset seller in exchange for the asset. This counts as income to the asset seller. Whether the payment to those asset sellers counted as consumption (paid for out of money already received as income in the current time period) or investment (paid for out of money being used for spending for the first time in the given time period) the act of selling the asset increases total income by the amount of the purchase price paid.

Just the selling of the asset will not cause propensity to consume to be greater than 1. If the asset seller then took the income he received from selling his asset, and spent it, that would count as consumption. That consumption spending also

Influencing the Level of Effective Demand

would have to be added to total income. The maximum consumption spending could possibly increase would be if we assume the selling of the asset is all counted as consumption spending. In that case, then all new income would be added to consumption spending, but you guessed it, all that extra consumption spending counts as income and would get added to the total income too. Once again, consumption could not go up greater than total income, and propensity to consume could not become greater than one.

I have talked about loans, but where does charity fit?

Charitable giving is also considered spending. It is money changing ownership for a purpose. It is considered investment spending if the money being given as charity was money being used for spending for the first time in the given time period. It is considered consumption spending if the money is paid for out of current income, that is, if it is paid for with money that was already spent and already caused income in the current time period. (see the explanation for what is considered the same money in Chapter 2). Either way, charitable spending is also added to total income so that spending could not cause propensity to consume to be greater than one.

If the charitable spending is money changing ownership for a purpose, what is the purpose? What is the desired outcome?

The product that a charitable giver is buying is to improve the charitable recipient's financial position. That outcome alone is enough for that charitable giving to count as spending and income. There are, however, many other outcomes that charitable spending can cause or contribute to causing, such as having a good feeling in your heart, or social stability, or goodwill of your fellow man, or a decreased crime rate. It could be said to be purchasing many different outcomes, perhaps even some of them bad, like supporting the recipient's laziness, but the point is, it is spending, and it gets added to total income.

Somebody just gifting some money to another person is treated like charity. The act of gifting counts as income to the recipient and will not cause the propensity to consume to be greater than one.

What about government transfers like welfare and social security? First off, the entity that is buying something does not have to be an individual and it doesn't even have to be a private entity to count as spending and get added to total income. Government transfers are spending* which gets added to total income.

No matter how someone might try to make it happen, in our model, the propensity to consume can never be greater than one.

Influencing the Level of Effective Demand

*Social security payments could be viewed as purchasing all the past efforts by individuals who worked and paid into social security. And it could be said to be purchasing all the continuing efforts of current workers to contribute and allow for future payments. I cannot imagine there would be much support for those social security taxes if the government stopped meeting its obligation to give payments to retired and disabled people. The government making good on those payments motivates the continued work effort and paying of taxes, and the continued support of the existence of the program. Such transfers by the government are also a way for us, as a community to purchase the knowledge and reassurance that our elderly and disabled will have some basic needs provided for and some comfort and "utility" in life. This is helping purchase social stability. And one can probably think of a lot of other outcomes this spending might be causing or contributing to causing.

Welfare helps pay for the reassurance that our fellow man is not starving to death or exposed to the elements and that if we ever find ourselves in such difficulties we also will not starve to death, and it may be paying to decrease the crime rate and increase our safety. By preserving any human life, being preserved is all of what they are and all of what they know and all of what they have to offer us. Welfare helps purchase that too.

So, our government spending helps produce those desired outcomes. In fact, it is important to realize that a lot of spending, private or public, is not necessarily done for the purpose of producing new wealth, but to preserve existing wealth. I have shown how propensity to consume can never be greater than 1. In fact, it can never really equal 1. For the propensity to consume to equal 1, all spending would have to be consumption spending, and in the model presented here, this is an impossibility. In a monetary economy, if all spending is consumption, there would be no spending at all.

Why? Because our definition of spending is having the ownership of a quantity of money changing hands. By definition, in this model, consumption spending requires the use of money that has been used for spending at least once already. It is from spending that income occurs, and if there has been no initial spending, no investment spending, then there is no income. If there is no income to start with then there cannot be any "spending out of current income", that is, there can be no consumption spending. So really, there will have to be at least a little investment spending. And if there is any investment spending, the consumption spending cannot cause all of the income and therefore the propensity consume can never actually be equal to one. It will always have to be at least a little less than one, that is, the ratio of consumption spending to total spending will always be less than 1. Propensity to consume cannot be greater than one, and it can never equal 1, propensity to consume is always less than 1.

How we classify a specified amount of spending as investment spending or consumption spending can be open to interpretation. This has to do with how we decide something is the same money or if it money being used for spending for the first time in the given time period (see chapter 2 on the same money). Theoretically one could have a situation where one decides more of the spending is investment and less is consumption giving a lower propensity to consume, or you could decide less of the spending is investment spending and more is consumption giving a larger propensity to consume, with either of these interpretations being able to be justifiable and considered valid. This could even change simply by changing the starting and ending points of "the given time period." At the start of the given time period, no spending has yet occurred in that time period, so the initial spending is all going to qualify as investment spending, according to my definitions for investment and consumption. But as long as one accounts for all the spending, however one decides to classify each piece of the spending, counting it as either investment or consumption, one ends up with the same total spending = total income = total demand.

There will be times during our study of macroeconomics when specifying whether some spending is investment or consumption is not important, just the fact that spending has occurred and the total magnitude of the spending. There are other times of course, when making the distinction is important to understanding the concept.

As seen previously, for a given total demand, there is an equilibrium point, called "effective demand." Let us assume an economy is at less than full employment. Less than full employment means there are people willing to work who cannot find jobs. If total demand increased, then we can expect the employment to increase, i.e., the equilibrium point will move to the right on our graph:

FIGURE 16.1

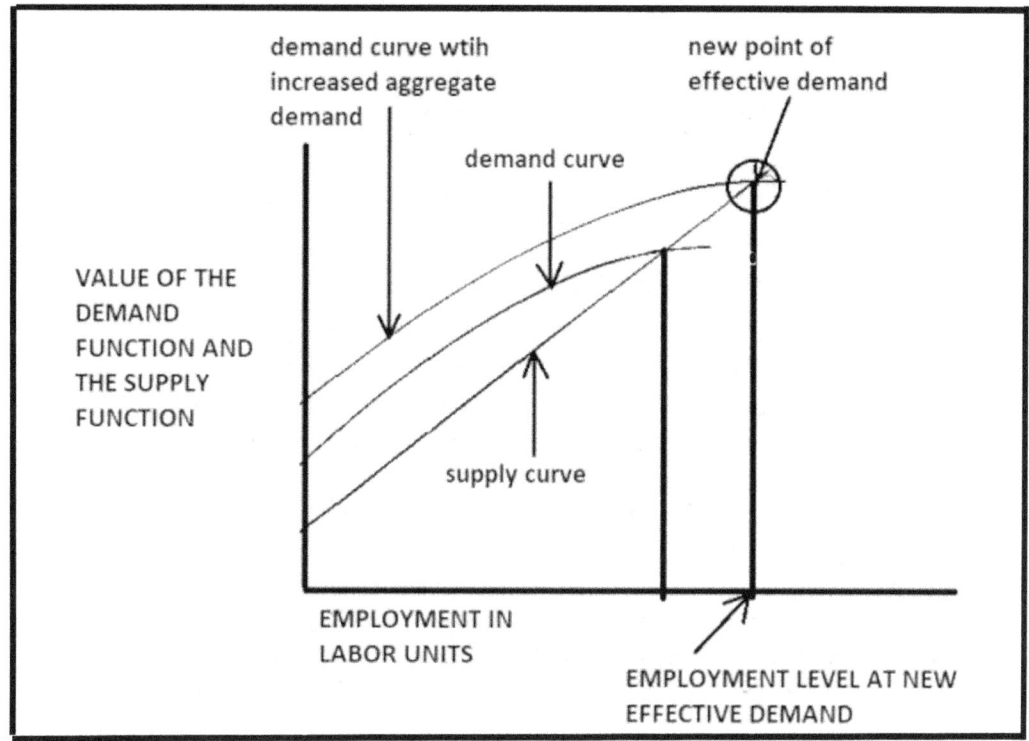

Let us say the aim is to increase employment. This can be done by increasing demand, which means it can be done by increasing spending. I have shown how our income is partly spending designated as investment and partly spending designated as consumption.

Y is equal to income, and income is equal to demand. Consumption spending is C and investment spending is I. Total income = total spending = Total demand equals **Y = I + C**.

In order to increase demand **Y**, we must either increase **C** which is consumption, or **I** which is investment, or both. If we hold I constant and increase C, the fraction of total spending that is consumption would increase... **C/Y = C/(I + C)** would increase, meaning the propensity to consume would increase.

That is one way to increase demand, for a given level of investment spending, increase consumption spending. But this is not always possible or easily done, that is, getting people to spend more of what they make is not so easy.

Influencing the Level of Effective Demand

On the other hand, assuming the propensity to consume is relatively constant, if I (investment) were increased, which is easier to do, then an increase in C and Y will follow.

It probably will not hurt your understanding of the material if you skip this section. I am just formalizing some of the concepts mathematically. I will mark the end of this section, so you will know where to skip to.

Here I will do some simple math to show that if propensity to consume is constant that an increase in **I** will increase C and Y in the same proportion. My purpose for showing this is to show that, if at less than full employment, you can increase demand by increasing investment.

Mathematically:

Assume that fraction known as propensity to consume does not change, that is, I designate that fraction to be a constant, call it **F**. Then by definition we have:

F = C/Y = C/(I + C)

Rearranging we get **F∗(I + C) = C**

Where **F** is a fraction such that **0<=F<1**

The recipients of the spending, i.e., the income earners can choose to spend none of their income, in which case **F** would equal zero, but they cannot spend less than none of it. The most they could save is their total income. If one tried to disprove this by saying someone gave them money and said don't spend it, making it so that by adding that amount to their savings, their savings was greater than their total income, then guess what, that extra money they were given and told not to spend, counts as spending and is add to total (gross) income. This means that propensity to consume can be equal to zero but not less than zero. I have also previously shown that the propensity to consume must always be less than 1, that it can never equal 1. That is how one shows that **F** the propensity to consume must meet this requirement:

0<=F<1

Solving **F∗(I + C) = C** for **I** we get:

Influencing the Level of Effective Demand

F∗I + F∗C = C --> F∗I = C - F∗C = (1-F)∗C ->

I = [(1-F)/F]∗C or C = [F/(1-F)]∗I

Since F is a constant then [F/(1-F)] is a constant, meaning if propensity to consume is constant, C equals a constant times I, meaning increase I and C increases proportionally.

since Y = C + I = [F/(1-F)] ∗I + I Rearranging :

Y = [F/(1-F) +1]∗I = [F/(1-F) +(1-F)/(1-F)]∗I Y = [1/(1-F)]∗I

Call 1/(1-F) = k so Y = k∗I..................in this equation k is known as the multiplier, and this equation is valid IF propensity to consume can be considered constant for all levels of investment. This describes a situation where total income goes up proportional to investment I. Total income Y is also equal to demand.

This gives us the result that if, for a given extra amount of investment spending, <u>propensity to consume is constant</u>, then increase in investment will cause both the consumption and the total income to increase proportionally.

We can also see from this Y = [1/(1-F)]∗I, that if we increase F to get it closer to 1 we increase Y. So that equation confirms what we said above, one can increase Y by increasing propensity to consume or increasing investment.

This is the end of the section I said you could skip, without missing much

We conclude that there are two ways to increase demand, increase the propensity to consume or increase investment (or both). <u>In reality, it is much easier for a small group of investors or the government to control the amount of investment, than it is to change the overall propensity to consume.</u>

In other words, the rational for favoring increasing investment versus increasing propensity to consume is a practical one, it is much easier to increase total income and demand by increasing investment spending, than it is to increase demand by trying to get people to spend a larger percentage of their current income. That is why increasing investment will often be considered the main intervention needed to stimulate economic activity, either paid for by private sources or government. Keynes strongly supported the need for investment to be able to increase total demand. Keynes used the term **Aggregate**

Demand to describe the total spending, all the demand, occurring in the macroeconomy.

In practice the private investor will either sell some assets or borrow using the value of those assets as collateral to generate the investment spending. And the government would either tax or borrow to get the money needed for investment.

Again, this figure shows the effect of increasing total (aggregate) demand.

FIGURE 16.2

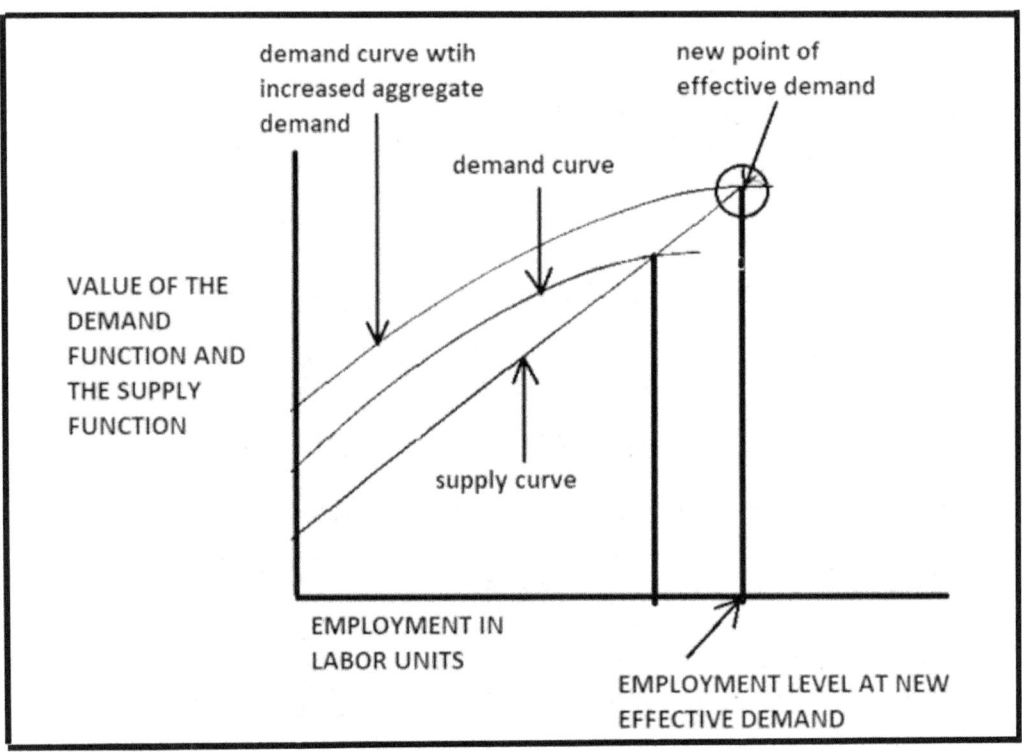

It is important to note that in this model of Keynes, the level of employment actually achieved can be any level, depending on the level of demand. There is no reason to expect that this equilibrium will occur at full employment, that being only a special case, when demand is at a certain level.

That is an important contribution by Keynes because, prior to that, most economic theory took as an a priori assumption that economies are always at full employment. The proponents of such theories did not acknowledge that people could be involuntarily unemployed. They did not acknowledge that people could be ready, willing, able, and qualified to work at jobs which would certainly exist,

Influencing the Level of Effective Demand

if only there was more income, if only there was more spending being done to purchase those products. It was a new thought that the economy could have a situation where the level of demand was too low to achieve full employment. It was a new thought, in economic theory, that inadequate amounts of spending caused unemployment, and economic depression.

In Keynes' model, increasing demand is able to continue to cause increased employment until the economy has reached full employment.

Just to point out, Keynes is talking about the short run, not about such a long period of time that technology and technique, and productivity could be appreciably different. He would phrase this by saying, "In a given situation of technique, resources and costs"[11]. Meaning he is acknowledging there are other things that can change over time, that can change the variables, such as what is the supply cost, how much demand is needed to attain full employment, what is the propensity to consume etc. In his model, he is assuming those factors do not change significantly during the time period under analysis.

When it comes to policy, the most crucial point being made in this chapter is you can **increase effective demand by increasing investment.**

Just to mention the following definition:

If your effective demand is not enough to produce full employment, then there will be a number of workers who are considered **involuntarily** unemployed. Those are the people who are willing and able to work, and willing to accept the available wages, but are unable to find jobs.

And the idea presented here is if demand had reached a level where enough workers were able to be hired so we could say the economy is at full employment, that is equivalent to saying that we are at a point where there is no involuntary unemployment. Repeating, Keynes' definition of full employment is when there is no longer any involuntary unemployment.

---

11   Keynes, John Maynard. The General Theory of Employment, Interest and Money (Illustrated) (p. 24). Green World Publication. Kindle Edition.

Influencing the Level of Effective Demand

Showing That Even in a Barter Economy We Still Must Calculate Income and Wealth on Different Axes.

Let us say we have an economy with the following items as the total wealth. They are all owned by different people.

15 whatchacallits

10 widgets

23 thingamajigs

7 hoosits

That means the total wealth is 15 whatchacallits + 10 widgets + 23 thingamajigs + 7 hoosits

Now we make the following barters

15 whatchacallits for 10 widgets

23 thingamajigs for 7 hoosits

Spending (and therefore income) equals 15 whatchacallits + 10 widgets + 23 thingamajigs + 7 hoosits

Well what do you know! In this example, so far, income is the same as wealth.

But then let us assume, **using the same items,** the following trades are made

7 hoosits for 15 whatchacallits

10 widgets for 23 thingamajigs

From those trades the income is 7 hoosits + 15 whatchacallits + 10 widgets + 23 thingamajigs

That means the total income for both trades is

15 whatchacallits + 10 widgets + 23 thingamajigs + 7 hoosits + 7 hoosits + 15 whatchacallits + 10 widgets + 23 thingamajigs

Which equals 30 whatchacallits + 20 widgets + 46 thingamajigs + 14 hoosits

And the total wealth remains 15 whatchacallits + 10 widgets + 23 thingamajigs + 7 hoosits

Due to the extra trades being done income is no longer equal to wealth Now suppose this barter is done next

15 whatchacallits for 23 thingamajigs

7 hoosits for 10 widgets

From those trades income is 15 whatchacallits + 23 thingamajigs + 7 hoosits + 10 widgets AND the total gross income would now be 45 whatchacallits + 30 widgets + 69 thingamajigs + 21 hoosits

Yet total wealth is 15 whatchacallits + 10 widgets + 23 thingamajigs

+ 7 hoosits

Again, total income is different from total wealth. **Even in a barter economy, income and wealth are not the same thing.** This model assumes that the items of wealth remain constant during the period of trade. If these items changed, depreciated in value or perhaps in quantity, that would make the relationship between income and wealth even less certain.

Income is a measure of spending in terms of the designated currency. If all items of trade are considered currency then any amount of changing ownership of any item is added to the total for gross income. The total wealth, however, remains a measure of the wealth existing, not a measure of the amount of changes in ownership of that wealth.

There may be a certain amount of barter in the economy. It is possible to convert barters into equivalent cash transactions in order to be able to include them in a one currency economy where all the spending and income are calculated in terms of that currency. Strictly speaking, doing that is not completely correct. This is because to include a barter as part of the spending of our money supply, one would have to recognize that at least one of the bartered item was functioning as money and had become part of the money supply. (The money supply would include all the fiat money, plus the supply of one of the bartered items).

But if for accounting purposes one wanted to include barters as part of the spending and income to make sure the barter "spending" showed up in the calculation of total demand, one would simply translate the barter into an equivalent cash transaction. Say Fred traded a hat to Sam in exchange for a shirt. Estimate they are each worth 20 dollars. This barter, in terms of how much it added to demand, would be able to be translated into equivalent transactions using money. This would be "as if" Fred gave Sam 20 dollars for the shirt and Sam gave 20 dollars back to Fred for the hat. For accounting purposes, one would say that 40 dollars of "gross" spending, and 40 dollars of "gross" income occurred.

What has really happened here is that we have added shirts and hats to the money supply. We could have added only shirts and then said that in that equivalent transaction only $20 dollars of spending has occurred. And so we are, in effect, dealing with a larger money supply with at least two different types of money, i.e., a commodity, and fiat money, for example. The fiat money would be the dominant currency being used in most of the transactions, and its dominance would show up in both the amount of money being used in spending, and the velocity of the spending of that currency. The supply of fiat money dwarfs the supply of shirts, and the velocity of spending of fiat money would be much larger as well. I mean how much could be added to total spending if shirts were used for barters only a few times. The velocity of spending of shirts would be so low that even if we had a big supply of shirts, the contribution of spending done with shirts would be infinitesimal and for all practical purposes able to be completely ignored.

In fact, since money is such a superior currency, and the accepted medium of exchange, then I think it is reasonable to assume that spending with the national currency (money) probably is so much greater than the total of all barter spending, that, for the purposes of elucidation, I can ignore that factor, and assume barter spending to be a relatively insignificant part of the economy. So in developing our model, we will, for the most part, be looking at economies that function using a single currency, where purchases occur as the result of change in ownership of that single currency.

When I am talking about a monetary economy, I am talking about an economy in which transactions are conducted by the transfer of ownership of money. No matter how many currencies are allowed, the spending is done with currency. Some economists have said that currency does not have any value in and of itself, that it just acts as an intermediary between things of value. In a way they are right, it does act as an intermediary. But, in a monetary economy, it does have established value, and that is why it is able be used in transactions. Anything that does get established as a good currency will established itself as having value. It will also have shown it has all those qualities that make it a good currency, discussed in a previous chapter.

Influencing the Level of Effective Demand

※

In the Gurdjieff terminology, demand for goods and services is the active force and it is expressed by money. The desire for the item is expressed by the spending of money to acquire it. This active force works to overcome the obstacles to satisfying that desire for the products. The spending activates the economy, causing the attempts to create that product or outcome, i.e., the result. In the process other people get income and they can spend that money to activate the economy as an attempt to satisfy their desires. The point is we move from active force to result and from another active force to another result, and on and on. The description of using money as an expression of the active force, and expression of one's desire, is a description of the function of spending.

In the opposite direction of spending to satisfy desires is hoarding. By hoarding I do not mean rational and necessary saving such as saving enough to pay bills, or to have some money saved for unexpected expenses, or saving for retirement. By hoarding I mean holding back from spending, even when one really desires to spend to acquire something and even though those desires are realistic, rational, and affordable to the hoarder. Hoarding is a holding back, a repression of one's desires. It is a way to avoid allowing involvement in, and interaction with, the world. Hoarding of money is an avoidance behavior. It is an attempt to avoid uncomfortable or difficult emotional states and avoid potentially challenging situations that will require being effort to deal with. Hoarding is a way of self-calming.

I bring up hoarding, i.e., not spending, as a concept with the realization that hoarding of money is a luxury. Only those who have their basic needs met can even consider it, everyone else will not have that choice. When the basic needs are met, that is when the person has the option to spend or not spend. The spending they are avoiding could be depriving themselves of desired goods or services or labor. Or it could be avoiding spending that could benefit others as well. For example, the person may forgo something that only they will benefit from, a new car, a meal, a vacation, etc. Or they may forego spending that could benefit others. Spending that may benefit others could be spending on a business venture that could create jobs and also earn the spender increased wealth. Or, spending that may benefit others may simply be charitable giving that gives the spender a good feeling in his heart because they have relieved someone's suffering.

In any case, the most likely explanation for hoarding is self-calming. The person hoards due to the desire to avoid having to make being efforts. Perhaps they are paranoid that they will not have enough money for future use even though they really do, and want to calm that associated feeling of anxiety. Perhaps they are worried that in the future they might have to put in more being efforts to replace money spent or wealth liquidated, and want to avoid even the worry that they might have to do some extra work. Perhaps they are paranoid that they need all their wealth to maintain their station in life and if they don't have it they will lose power and influence, and this will require new being efforts to either adjust to their new circumstances or regain their status. They want to avoid putting themselves in that situation and any being efforts it would entail. Perhaps the hoarders fear that improving the lives of others will cause the ones they helped to be a threat to their status, and if that happened, they would be required to make more being efforts to adjust.

I accept that there are situations where all is not as it seems, and what appears to be irrational hoarding may not be so and may actually be a necessary behavior that will ultimately have an overall beneficial effect. (I also suspect most hoarders would claim that is the case with any of their hoarding). Despite that I believe that the most common explanation for hoarding is self-calming.

In the practice of the Gurdjieff work one begins to become more aware of our desires and recognize the friction one feels when coming against the obstacles to satisfying those desires. When one practices the Gurdjieff work, it is possible for one to see how one's habitual laziness and self-calming can lead one to want to avoid even the recognition of those desires. We see how we learn to bury awareness of the desires and avoid the associated inner discomfort.

Gurdjieff's teaching would be that one should try, to the extent they are able, to deal with and suffer the difficulties having desires create. That to the extent we do not do so we are self-calming. The suffering created, by practicing self-observation and self-remembering can make us feel more alive and live a fuller existence. It will reduce our level of "waking sleep". He teaches that it is our psychological buffers that keeps us from fully feeling those difficult feelings and being fully awake, and struggling to reduce those buffers requires a continuing effort because there is always a tendency for people to maintain or revert back to more unconscious states.

In macroeconomics the expression of the first force that is expressed by intended spending will encounter obstacles in the achieving of the desired result. If the spending is for basic needs there will be strong motivation to overcome any obstacles, but if the would-be spender is not so strongly motivated then those obstacles may lead to the choice to not spend.

Influencing the Level of Effective Demand

Keynes clearly kept a strong awareness of the suffering of people who were unemployed and in poverty. As a result, he found it unacceptable to believe there was nothing one could do about it. It was in that setting that he developed theories that showed how spending can help pull us out of depressions and that hoarding, as defined here, will only make the situation worse.

The insight gained by working on one's self can help us understand the resistance to Keynes' work. Specifically, I am talking about the resistance to, and difficulties in, applying Keynes' understanding of economics to macroeconomic policy. Despite the fact that Keynes has shown that NOT spending does not increase wealth and in fact is likely to decrease it, theories persist and are regularly still taught that the way to get out of economic downturns in the macroeconomic setting is to decrease spending. With the psychological tendency of people in waking sleep to self-calm, it is not surprising that such theories gain support, especially by those power possessing beings who have the luxury to not spend.

In this setting then, perhaps it should not be surprising how common it is in standard macroeconomics textbooks and courses that students are taught that macroeconomic policy must focus on **increasing savings** by **reducing spending**. This teaching says that we must "save up" so we can "build up wealth", so we will be able to "spend later". Keynes knew that this wouldn't work because decreased spending decreases income, and likely decreases production. "Not spending" will likely reduce the savings that is net production, the only measure of change in the level of wealth. "Not spending" will not help us save up, it will more likely do the opposite, reduce savings. This is something Keynes called the *paradox of thrift*.

I believe that the resistance to understanding or accepting Keynes' model, and the apparent need to constantly marginalize his work, are understandable, in terms of the teaching of Gurdjieff. This phenomenon is understandable as occurring due to those crystalized consequences of the organ Kundabuffer. These theories are justifications of the behavior of hoarding, which is caused by self-calming.

Nevertheless, it has been self-calming that has slowed the acceptance of new knowledge and scientific discovery throughout history. And yet, eventually a lot of that knowledge became accepted. Keynes and others who have followed him have gone very far in having his work become known to and be accepted in some ways by mainstream economists. It is my hope that by some of the modifications and corrections of his model I am presenting in this book, I am helping this process. I am hoping that by putting the principles he discovered into a more generalizable form I am helping to put his work on a firmer footing

CHAPTER 17
Measuring Output

Keynes does talk about measuring output in "The General Theory" and I wanted to make some short comments about that. His definition of output as a function of employment level is not utilized in my model and I explain why.

I DEFINE SOMETHING as included in what counts as wealth if it can be said to have value. With that definition, there are a lot of things I call wealth that are hard to put an actual monetary value on. Some people tend to exclude things as wealth if they cannot find a definitive way to put a monetary value on it.

Keynes addressed the difficulties of calculating value, but he was more concerned with the idea that it was hard to figure out units of output because things that are produced are so different. How would we measure overall output?...... in terms of number of refrigerators or cars, or cooking oil, or number of miles of road built, or how many comedy shows, or amount of history lectures, or any other thing you can think of?

His solution was to look at output in terms of how many units of labor it takes to produce it, since he viewed the production of each of them as requiring labor.

$\Phi(N)$ was his function. Φ is the output in terms of money value, and N is a measure of the level of employment. This is an attempt to say that one can determine the value of output by the level of employment.

There are problems with this concept for both the input N and the output Φ. For example, a given level of N could be associated with different levels of spending that do not directly create employment, such as government transfers and charity. This can be expected, for the same level of N, to create various different values for Φ. In fact, as I have pointed out elsewhere, it is very easy to show how the same level of employment can be associated with many different levels of output. Even if it were possible to have a unique single value of output for a given employment level N, the value of the output Φ for the whole economy, in terms of money, is difficult to determine. When I talked about spending to purchase output, in Chapter 2, I was careful to allow output to mean any outcome people would spend money to acquire or cause to happen. And many of those things are difficult to assign a money value to.

From a macroeconomic perspective I think that concept of an output function whose value is based on the level of employment has limited application. Specifically, one would have to limit the study of the macroeconomy to jobs where the outputs were clearly able to be given a monetary value, and where each level of employment was associated with a unique output, to have a useful model. Such a model would not be inclusive of all the spending, all the transfers of ownership of money, occurring in the whole economy.

The attempt to define the value of output in terms of employment levels is a way to try to define output in terms of wages, that is, in terms of income. The real problem with that is income and wealth production are independent variables. An attempt to make an output function that is strictly a function of the employment level is an attempt to remove one degree of freedom. That is, to try to make a model of the macroeconomy where income and wealth are not independent variables. Such a model will never have the flexibility to describe the economy as it really exists.

CHAPTER 18
More on Using the Expression "Net Production"

In this chapter I discuss whether we should use the expression "net production" or "capital appreciation" for the change in the level of wealth

WHAT I CALL "net production" -- and the formula for net production -- is wealth created minus wealth depleted during the given time period. Net production is calculated by <u>adding</u> the amount of production and <u>subtracting</u> off wealth that has been used up, decayed, destroyed, depreciated in value, or is otherwise depleted. It is only from **net production** that total wealth can be increased or reduced.

An alternative term for net production might be "capital appreciation." The way I define net production is broad enough to allow it to be used interchangeably with the term capital appreciation. Here is my thinking on this:

Even with bubble wealth, if the value of an item has increased due to advertising, it can be said that the labor involved in the advertising produced more value in the item. If the value of any possession increases or decreases because of rumors or information or even disinformation it can be said that those efforts produced or reduced wealth. The value of some items can be increased by technological discoveries and advances. The effort of education and discovery and research can create new wealth by increasing the value of different products, if those discoveries increase the desire to acquire and use of those items. Those factors can also decrease the value of other items, if those factors reduce the desire to acquire and use them. Production as such can occur apart from the involvement of human effort, such as when things of value are produced by nature.

More on Using the Expression "Net Production"

Thus, net production needs to be defined in a broad sense. Or, perhaps, capital appreciation is the better term? I prefer net production because if reinforces the idea that wealth is increased by production of some result, implying it needs some sort of active force to get it all going. The bottom line is, whether you call the change in total wealth net production or capital appreciation or depreciation is not the important thing. The important thing is that wealth is calculated on the wealth axis not on the income axis.

CHAPTER 19
THE INVESTMENT MULTIPLIER

The essence of the investment multiplier is this: Some investment put into the economy leads to an even greater amount of total income and to all the consequent production. The interaction of the parts creates more income and wealth than existed previously. This chapter shows the derivation of the investment multiplier as Keynes understood it.

IF Y IS income, I is investment and C is consumption, the equation $Y = I + C$ shows Y being greater than I by the amount C.

Keynes really wanted to describe what would happen to the economy as a whole, if, given a certain baseline situation, the values of certain variables were altered.

Following Keynes, if income is increased by ΔY and consumption is increased by ΔC, then the ratio becomes: $\Delta C/\Delta Y$. This is called the **marginal propensity to consume,** the fraction of the new income that will be used on consumption.

Let us refer to marginal propensity to consume as **MPC**, that is $MPC = \Delta C/\Delta Y$. I will show that the significance of **MPC** is this:

With a change in investment spending we get a corresponding change in total income. The fraction of change in total income accounted for by the change in consumption spending, (which is what **MPC is**), will be the determining factor in how much total income changes, for a given change in investment.

If ΔI is the increase in investment **I**, then from $Y = I + C$ we also have $\Delta Y = \Delta I + \Delta C$.

The Investment Multiplier

Let $\Delta Y = k\Delta I$. k is called **the investment multiplier.**

Let us see what **k** has to equal for $\Delta Y = k \Delta I$ to be true.

Since $\Delta Y = \Delta I + \Delta C$, we divide both sides by ΔY and we get:

$1 = \Delta I/\Delta Y + \Delta C/\Delta Y$.

Next we take $\Delta Y = k\Delta I$ and rearranging to $\Delta Y/k = \Delta I$ or $1/k = \Delta I/\Delta Y$,

So $1 = MPC + \Delta I/\Delta Y = MPC + 1/k$,

which gives us $1/k = 1 - MPC$ or $k = 1/(1-MPC)$

$k = 1/(1-MPC)$ is the **investment multiplier.**

The closer the marginal propensity to consume gets to 1 the bigger the multiplier. If the marginal propensity to consume equaled 1 then that would mean any change in investment spending would lead to an infinite change in income, which is impossible, so **MPC** can never equal 1, but it can equal any value less than 1. This means that $0 <= MPC < 1$.

If the marginal propensity to consume is zero, the multiplier equals 1. With a marginal propensity to consume of zero, the only increased income comes from the investment money. And, in this case, none of that money gets spent on consumption, it is all just saved. There is no re-spending of the investment money.

If the marginal propensity to consume is ½, then half the additional income goes into consumption and ½ into savings. Thus, in this case, the multiplier is 2. The total income would then be 2 times the amount of investment. An increased investment of x thus creates an increased income for the whole economy of 2x.

If the **MPC** is 4/5 then the multiplier is 5. The increase in total income would be 5 times the increased amount of investment. And increased investment of x creates an increased income for the whole economy 5x. If the **MPC** is 9/10 then increased investment of x creates increased income of 10x, and so on.

The multiplier shows that because money can be spent over and over, an increase in the amount of spending can result in overall total spending being multiple

The Investment Multiplier

times that of the original increase. If you add more spending from money not currently being used for spending, the multiplier tells how much of a change that will cause in total spending.

As a practical application of the multiplier principle, Keynes would imply something like this: Of the money a poor or middle class person gets as income, a larger portion of it will be re-spent, i.e., be used for consumption spending. That means **MPC** is greater. If extra income is given to the poor and middle class, this will **make the multiplier larger.** Whereas the extra income is added to the income of richer people, a smaller percentage will be spent on consumption (MPC smaller). Thus, increased income to the richer would make **the multiplier smaller.**

Also, Keynes might imply that spending money on small businesses, where the middle-class owners or their employees reap a large percentage of the money spent, leads to an increase in the multiplier, whereas spending the money at large corporate enterprises where much less goes to the employees and a much greater percentage goes to extremely rich executives and investors leads to a shrinking of the multiplier.

We can apply this concept to government spending paid for by taxes.

We will look first at what happens when government spends. In other words, let the change in investment ΔI be called ΔG, and we will call the multiplier here the **government multiplier** k^G. The change in income ΔY from the change in government spending (ΔG) **equals** $k^G * \Delta G$.

k^G is dependent in the main on who receives the benefits of the spending, i.e., k^G is greater if poorer people get the benefits and smaller if richer people get the benefits. This is because poorer people will spend a greater percentage of their new income than richer people, the percentage of their new income used for spending, **MPC** is greater for poor/middle class people, and so the multiplier for income to poorer people would be larger, according to Keynes.

We will next look at what would happen if the government levies taxes. In other word, let the change in investment ΔI be called ΔT, and we will call the multiplier here the **tax multiplier** k^T. The change in income ΔY resulting from the taxes = $k^T * \Delta T$. Only this time the change in investment spending goes in the opposite direction. This would be what happens if we reduce the amount of investment because the money was unavailable due to taxes. $k^T * \Delta T$ gets subtracted from the total income change ΔY. k^T will be larger when poorer people are taxed and smaller when richer people are taxed because you are *reducing* total spending a lot more if you take money away from poorer people than if you take it away from richer people.

Now, the total change in income for this economy will equal that increase in income that comes from the government spending, $k^G \Delta G$, minus the reduction in income caused by taxes, $k^T \Delta T$.

$$\Delta Y = (k^G \Delta G) - (k^T \Delta T)$$

Let us assume for simplicity that the change in amount of government spending equals the change in the amount of taxes, that is, assume $\Delta G = \Delta T$. We can call that quantity ΔS.

$$\Delta S = \Delta G = \Delta T$$

Then $\Delta Y = (k^G - k^T) \Delta S$

This means that if the change in taxes equals the amount of change in government spending, then, from the expression $\Delta Y=(k^G-k^T)\Delta S$ we see that if $k^G > k^T$ then the taxing and spending will increase overall income. But if $k^G < k^T$ then the taxing and spending will decrease overall income.

If poorer people get more government spending than richer people and richer people get more taxes than poorer people, then we will have $k^G > k^T$ and taxing and spending will increase overall income. If richer people get more government spending than poorer people and poorer people get more taxes than richer people, then this means we have $k^G < k^T$ and taxing and spending will decrease overall income.

⚬⚬⚬⚬⚬

The multiplier effect only occurs at less than full employment, where increased spending, increased investment can lead to increased employment and production of wealth.

The concept of full employment assumes everyone is working and producing to the extent that society can reasonably expect. We are assumed to be at maximum production capacity, in accord with the lifestyle expectations of the citizens of that culture.

At full employment when we are presumably producing everything possible, increased investment spending leading to increased total spending will just cause

The Investment Multiplier

an increase in prices, because we would be having increased spending paying for the same amount of product. So, at full employment increasing investment is not likely to give us much, if any, benefit.

The idea of Full Employment is a theoretical concept. It would be defined by a society's social norms, which can be different in different cultures and change over time and circumstance. It is possible that some societies might believe full employment means more hours worked than others, and there might even be differences in who is expected to work, for example. What those differences do to total production however is not always clear in the long run.

The idea that at full employment, extra spending will go into price, not employment level, is not absolutely true, if for a time the extra spending supports increased production by the same workers. At that point one needs to consider changing the expectation of what value producing at maximum takes. Or one can assume this is a temporary thing and it will fall back to a baseline, in which case the approach might just be to do some kind of averaging to determine the expected value of maximum production.

It is not just current production that plays a role in prices. One could assume that, normally, some of the sales are of items produced in other time periods, usually in the past, but also, possibly, in the future. One could then assume this value tends to reach an equilibrium so that new production is always a relatively constant fraction of total sales. At that point let us assume that full employment, defined by the established expectations of what full employment means in terms of hours worked and who should work, is when production has reached its maximum. Let us assume the economy has reached that point and has reached a steady state as to the amount of product sold, both that produced in the current time period and other time periods. It is reasonable to assume, at that point, increased spending will go into increasing prices only, not production. This is the idea behind understanding how increased investment, after the economy has reached full employment does not create the multiplier effect that occurs prior to reaching full employment.

At full employment, the task becomes to gradually try to increase the efficient utilization of all resources, including workers, to maximize net production of wealth, so as to maximize overall standard of living. Included in this task is the incorporation of improvements in "technology and technique" as Keynes has put it.

CHAPTER 20
Illustration of How Investment is Preserved as Savings

Just to help get a visual representation of how it would look to have that first part of savings (not including net production) end up equaling investment after multiple rounds of spending. Additionally I give a visual representation of the extra income created by the multiplier effect after multiple rounds of spending.

THIS CHAPTER IS a graphical illustration of how investment gets preserved as savings but also how total income can be a multiple of investment. This is an illustration of the classical multiplier effect as defined by Keynes.

I wanted to show a couple graphs to illustrate what happens as a result of an additional amount of investment working its way through the economy, in a sort of round by round effect. In this example I assume that the propensity to consume is the same for each round of spending. I assume a ⅔ marginal propensity to consume, mainly to make the chart more readable.

Remember the multiplier effect only occurs at less than full employment.

Illustration of How Investment is Preserved as Savings

FIGURE 20.1

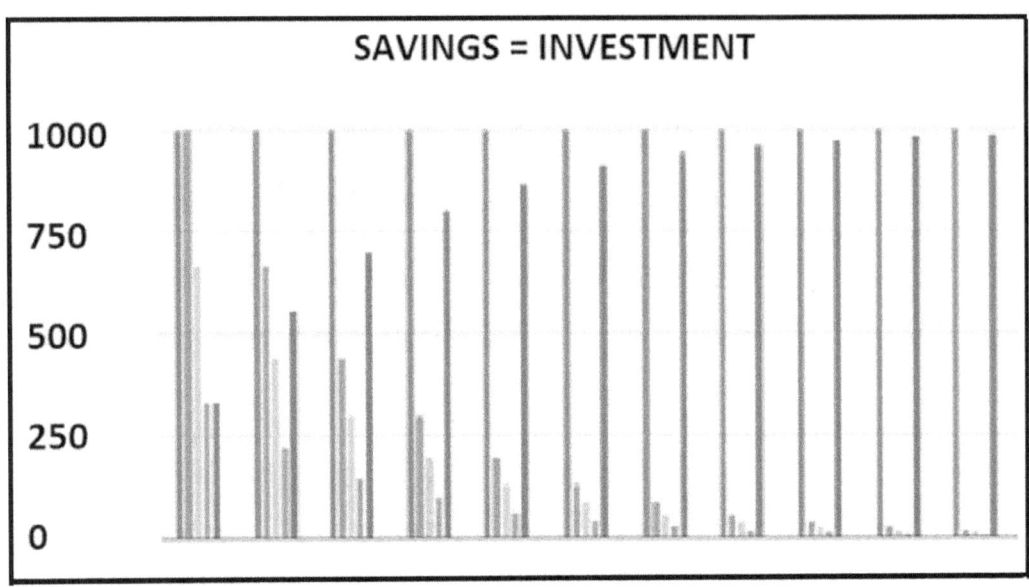

In each grouping, Far Left is the original investment.

Center Left is what is left over after ⅓ of the previous rounds income has been saved. The ⅔ of the previous rounds income that has not been saved has been spent and becomes income for the recipients of that spending. Those recipients now have that money available for further spending. They, in turn, will save ⅓ and spend ⅔, creating further income for the recipients of that spending. Each round, as more is saved, the amount left over and available for spending is reduced.

Center is what will be used for spending in the current round, which is two thirds of what was spent in a previous round.

Center Right is what is saved in each round. Far Right is cumulative savings.

If we had made the chart keep going to the right, more rounds of spending and saving, then eventually Far Right (Cumulative or total savings) would equal the Far Left (initial investment).

In each "round of spending" another chunk of the money being used for spending is saved, put "out of action", and no longer available for spending, and the cumulative amount of savings eventually will be equal to the original amount of money put into spending as investment. "Savings equals investment".

ILLUSTRATION OF HOW INVESTMENT IS PRESERVED AS SAVINGS

Let us look at what happens to total consumption, left out of above chart, and compare it to total savings.

FIGURE 20.2

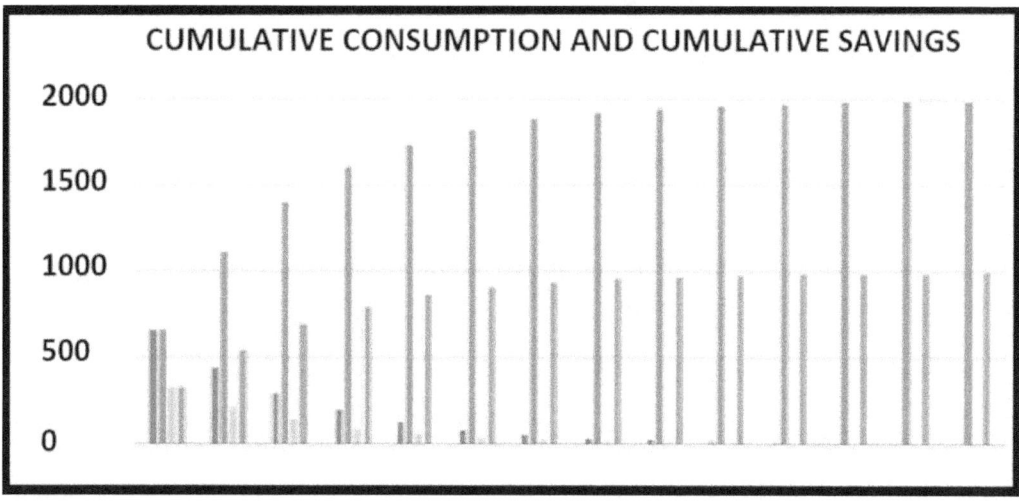

Far left is consumption for each "round". Center left is total cumulative consumption. Center right is savings for each "round".

Far right is total savings.

Total Savings being the preservation of the investment spending eventually equals the investment which in this case is 1000.

Total consumption, on the other hand can be multiple times the investment.........In this case total consumption, if we let all the "rounds" play out, would equal 2000.

So, we have savings = 1000 = investment spending, add cumulative consumption spending = 2000 for a total amount of spending (=income) of 3000.

Every time a dollar is put into income as investment the amount of times that dollar gets re-spent determines the total consumption generated by the dollar and allows us to determine the total income generated by that dollar and the propensity to consume of that money.

Illustration of How Investment is Preserved as Savings

If the money is spent one more time in the given time period the propensity to consume is 0.5

Example:

1 dollar investment = 1 dollar income

Add 1 dollar consumption you get 1 dollar investment and 1 dollar consumption = 2 dollars income

1 dollar consumption divided by 2 dollars income equals ½ = 0.5 propensity to consume

If the dollar is used to buy something two more times in the given time period the propensity to consume is 0.67,

Example:

1 dollar investment = 1 dollar income

Add 2 dollars consumption you get 1 dollar investment and 2 dollars consumption = 3 dollars income

2 dollars consumption divided by 3 dollars income equals 2/3=

0.67 propensity to consume

If used three more times in the given time period the propensity to consume is 0.75,

Example:

1 dollar investment = 1 dollar income

Add 3 dollars consumption you get 1 dollar investment and 3 dollars consumption = 4 dollars income

3 dollars consumption divided by 4 dollars income equals 3/4=

0.75 propensity to consume

For every dollar used in spending, the amount of income caused by that particular dollar is totally determined by how many times that dollar gets spent in the given time period.

Illustration of How Investment is Preserved as Savings

If we expand the length of the time period. If we decided to calculate the total income for 2 years instead of one year or 10 years or 100 years ..., this would give any money put into income more time to be spent again and again and again. This would mean for a longer period of time the propensity to consume would probably be higher just because there is more time and opportunity to spend and re-spend and re-spend again.

When looking at propensity to consume, economists usually do not count for 100 years, or 10 years, or 2 years, they generally count for 1 year. If the time period is 1 year, then there are two ways to increase income, increase the amount of money first put into income, that is, increase investment or.......increase the number of times money gets reused for spending in the given time period, that is, increase consumption.

Increasing the number of times the money supply gets re-spent in the given time period is also known as increasing the speed of re-spending, which is the same as saying the economy has an increased VELOCITY OF MONEY.

As long as we are still in the given time period, we could still add to the total income any amount by having the money be spent and re-spent over and over, until we have reached whatever income level we want, theoretically anyway.

What determines the total income, that is, what determines total demand, is not just how much money is put into spending as investment, but also how many times that same money gets spent and re-spent.

Now if we are unable to speed up the respending and demand was still too low, causing unemployment and production suffered, we are left with investment being the only way to increase demand.

We can increase income if we speed up the re-spending of investment money (increase consumption), or we can increase income if we add more investment.

The main point is, it is the spending, for labor or for goods and services, that counts, not whether it is investment or consumption. Anything that gets that money moving causes income. Having things to buy, i.e., products, goods and services, whether they will be owned privately or publicly is the prime motivator for the money to move. And, at the same time, the spending, i.e., the demand, encourages the production in the first place.

Illustration of How Investment is Preserved as Savings

Let us look at this from the perspective of the Gurdjieff Work.

Anything that encourages the spending and or re-spending of money increases income. What typically increases spending and re-spending? Desire does. Desire for goods and services, or other outcomes.

Spending that results from the desire for some result could occur in the beginning of the time period where it counts as investment, or it could be any spending of that money that is encouraged any time after, where it could be classified as either investment or consumption according to whether it meets the definition for investment or consumption. The important thing is that it is spending, and the spending is caused by desire for some result. As I mentioned in a previous chapter. To understand many macroeconomic concepts, it is often better just to look at how much total spending occurs, not whether the spending is investment or consumption.

Anything that gets the money moving causes income. Having things to buy, i.e., products, goods and services, whether they will be owned privately or publicly is the prime motivator for the money to move. And, at the same time, the spending, i.e., the demand, encourages the production in the first place.

This is a manifestation of the law of three in that it is desire for the product (first force, active force) that overcomes the obstacles to producing the product (second force, passive force) using the strategy devised (third force, i.e., reconciling force) to produce the desired outcome (result). Successfully implementing the strategy requires some mastery of the law of 7. Mastering the law of 7 is about completing the octave, completing the process. How and if one completes the process determines the result. The result, the successful implementation of the strategy, the quality and quantity of the product, even the chosen strategy itself, is strongly correlated to being effort and to the level of knowledge, being and understanding.

Reinforcing a previously made point:

In macroeconomics, spending does not reduce or deplete wealth. In fact, if the economy has unused production capacity, spending tends to do the opposite. In that case, it will, more often, lead to increased overall production of wealth. This is

Illustration of How Investment is Preserved as Savings

the opposite of what we would expect if we were talking about a microeconomic situation, such as an individual person's spending. Their spending could deplete their wealth, i.e., if they spend money, they will no longer have it. If what they bought gets used up or loses value they have less wealth. But in the macroeconomy, someone's spending becomes someone else's income. That money continues to exist and the transaction itself, the transfer of ownership of money, causes no decrease in the amount of money.

The spending will promote production of wealth, some of which will be used up, some of which will be used to preserve wealth and some of which will endure. The movement of money, the change in ownership of money, the spending itself, does not deplete anything. It is just the movement of ownership of money. And, as I showed graphically in this chapter, it is not just the effect of the first persons spending that can lead to production of wealth. The recipient of that spending will then use that money for more spending and that could also cause more wealth creation, and so on. That is the essence of the multiplier effect.

CHAPTER 21
Is Buying Current Production Consumption or Investment?

This is just a mention of some of the thought processes I was going through in figuring out the concepts elucidated in this book. I was, at the time, trying to look at money as all mixed up with wealth, as if production somehow increased the money supply. I think I was trying to do what I believe some economists do. I was thinking that production increases the buying power of the money supply, and that, as a result, perhaps we can consider the "real" money supply increased. Some economists consider money as just an intermediary and they always consider spending as equal to the value of product sold anyway, that is, they are always looking at spending as "real" spending. That may sound like it is a more objective way to look at spending, i.e., only considering "real spending", but Keynes knew that including the value of nominal spending is important to be able to fully understand macroeconomics.

THIS THOUGHT CAME to me because I was trying to figure out if, somehow, new product created in the current time period could be considered like new money and could be used to increase spending and the multiplier effect. I assume I was trying to think in terms of the "real", inflation adjusted spending, based on the buying power of a given amount of money. But I found this confounding for a long time. It was too difficult to make the transition from spending being the accounting of nominal spending, i.e., transfer of money, to adding in the effect of production to the calculation of the total "real" spending. It was difficult for me to even determine what we should call the money supply, and what role the size of the money supply, compared to the total amount of wealth in the economy, would play in this scenario. Does the money supply include both money and product? If so then would we not really be talking about a barter system? If the money supply is just currency, then should we be looking at the value of the money supply in terms of "buying power". If that is the case, then would we not be constantly adjusting the "real" value of both spending and the money supply as result of production? What happens if someone takes some of the production from the current time period and, in the current time period cashes it in and uses that money for more spending, still in the current time period. Is that investment or consumption? Or something else?

I was looking at the multiplier effect as something that is a calculation of the increase in wealth, not, as I do now, where I represent it as a calculation of the increase in spending. The problem I was having, was figuring out a way to add production into the calculation for spending and income. That is, I could not figure out how to add to income both the money received by the income earner, and the value of the product produced. I knew that money could be further used for spending, but how does the product itself get further used for spending, in a monetary economy. Do we add the value of the production to spending by saying the spending has increased, because with more product available to buy, the buying power of the money used for spending has increased? Meaning, if the same amount of money is spent, but that money has increased buying power, does that mean that more "real" spending and therefore more income has occurred?

Would that mean every time something happens that causes a change in the level of wealth, we have to adjust our calculation of the amount of spending that has occurred? What about the fact that, often, different amounts of spending are able to purchase the same quantity of identical items? In such a case, how would one know how to value the spending in "real" terms. One certainly could not get an exact measure. The person doing the calculation would have to start making a judgement or estimation of how they are going to value that item, which would make our estimate of the "real" value of our spending a subjective thing. In fact, due to the subjective nature of wealth valuation, and the constant shifting in the value of various forms of wealth, attempting to find an exact objective valuation of our spending in "real" terms will really represent a futile attempt. It will be a futile attempt because it will be an attempt to turn a system with two independent variables into a system with one independent variable. That, in essence, is what I finally realized. That wealth and income are independent variables, and therefore, when I construct a macroeconomic model, if that model is going to reflect reality, wealth and income must be treated as independent variables; their valuations must be calculated on different axes.

Is Buying Current Production Consumption or Investment?

Trying to combine these two variables into one, like trying to make the value of a given amount of spending always equal to a given amount of wealth, should serve to convince anyone that these are two different things; that, even though they do influence each other's valuation, they can, and mostly do, vary independently. Wealth can differ from spending because the value of any given item of wealth is always changing. Wealth can exist that is not involved in the spending, and may not become part of someone's calculation of "buying power". Total value of wealth can change unrelated to any spending occurring at all, in the given time period. This can be as a result of the actions or inactions of humans, or a result of nature.

So, I solved the dilemma of how to include income and wealth production in the same model by realizing they are two different things that must be accounted for separately. I defined spending as the transfer of ownership of money, which of and by itself, does not represent any change in the level of wealth. And I defined the value of wealth as being an accounting of anything that can be considered to have value, keeping the calculations of income and wealth on separate axes. Money, in this model, is part of wealth, and its value is added to the accounting of wealth on the wealth axis. However, it is the change of ownership of money that we measure when we calculate income on the income axis.

This does not mean that the concept of buying power, i.e., real or inflation adjusted spending and income has no use in economics. It is just that, if one ever wants to calculate buying power, you simply combine the two variables, spending and wealth, realizing that buying power is something that is both inexact and always changing based on the ratio between the value of wealth and the amount of spending occurring. And by the way, it is not the value of the money supply **M** that goes into the calculation of the buying power of income. It is the value of the spending. The value of spending and income is not **M**, it is **M∗V**, the Velocity of Money times the nominal value of the Money Supply.

So, back to the point that got me thinking about this topic in the first place. At one point I was considering that if production is like money, and if some new production occurred, and the owner of the new production added back the value of that production into the current spending, would that spending count as investment or consumption? I finally was able to solve this puzzle in my mind by explaining it this way:

If you want that new production to affect the level of spending, you have to cash it in, and use the cash obtained as a result for spending. Cashing it in means

Is Buying Current Production Consumption or Investment?

you are selling it. If the money acquired by selling it was paid for out of someone's current income it is consumption. If it is paid for out of money being used for spending for the first time in the current time period it is investment spending. Cashing in new production can either draw in money not already used for spending in the current time period, i.e., investment, or it can just be the re-spending of money that is already part of some person or entity's income in the current time period, i.e., consumption. The money earned from "cashing in" the new production can be further used for spending, which, if it occurs in the current time period counts as consumption spending, and if it occurs in a later time period will count as investment.

CHAPTER 22
Keynes, Phillips, and NAIRU

Attempts to use government spending to increase employment levels, lower unemployment, and reduce poverty were tried over several decades in the United States, but in the late 1960s and 1970s such policies became associated with some adverse outcomes. Economists who were, or had become opponents of Keynes' theories declared these developments to be a complete refutation of his work. This led to some new developments that I consider advancements in our understanding of economics, as well as to the adoption of some newer economic theories, (as well as some revival of old economic theories) that have, by influencing economic policy, in the composite, been associated with other kinds of adverse consequences. The next two chapters address these issues and give a new explanation for what happened that reconciles some of the newer concepts with Keynes' work. Hopefully, this will lead to a more correct understanding of events and better policy recommendations.

KEYNES WAS ADVOCATING increased spending when we suffer from a state of inadequate aggregate demand. It does not matter where that money for spending comes from, whether it comes from private sources or government sources. The money could come from loans or from private interests spending their resources or it could be government spending from funds previously collected from taxes, or it could come from bondholders who just sold bonds to the central bank in return for newly created money.

I have described Keynes' theories from the point where we are at less than full employment. I have shown how if aggregate demand is able to be increased enough, we can have effective demand occur when we are at full employment, that is, at the point where there are no longer any involuntarily unemployed people. We have described the process of increasing employment by increasing demand up to the point where we achieve full employment. But what happens at full employment?

What if, at full employment, demand continued to increase, that is, that income kept increasing due to more investment and consumption spending? We assume for this argument that by full employment the economy is maximally producing and cannot really produce anymore. At that point, then, if the income (demand) has increased, that means spending has increased, and we have increased spending for the same amount of product. With the extra demand for the same amount of products, we can expect the average price of transactions to increase.

A simplified version of Keynes' theories would be summarized as follows:

Up to full employment increased demand goes into increasing employment.

After full employment increased demand goes into increasing prices

If we graphed this the graph would look like an L

FIGURE 22.1

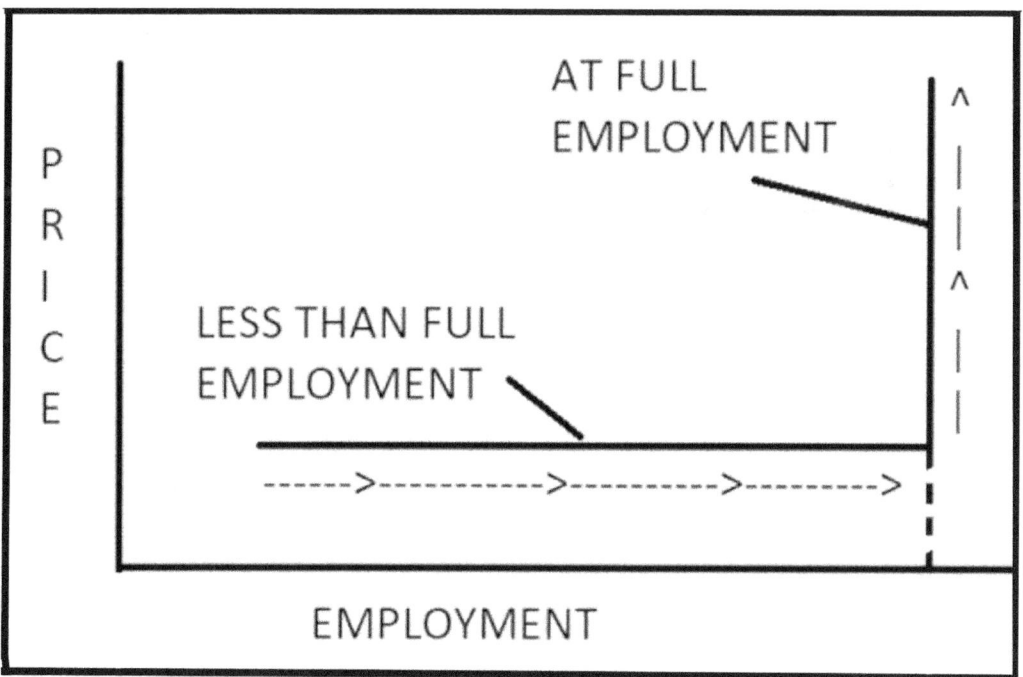

As time went on, economists began to notice that there is not a sharp transition between when an increase in demand causes an increase in employment and when it changes over to cause an increase in prices. They noticed that prices started to increase prior to full employment. Economist began to think this was a more gradual transition. Keynes recognized the influence of diminishing returns in his model about effective demand, so perhaps that was an influence into recognizing and accepting that this was happening. For whatever reason, there began a recognition that as we move closer to full employment, prices start to increase a little before full employment is actually achieved.

This understanding was portrayed in graph form as something called the Phillips curve, named after someone who wrote an article about this phenomenon. The Phillips curve looks something like this:

FIGURE 22.2

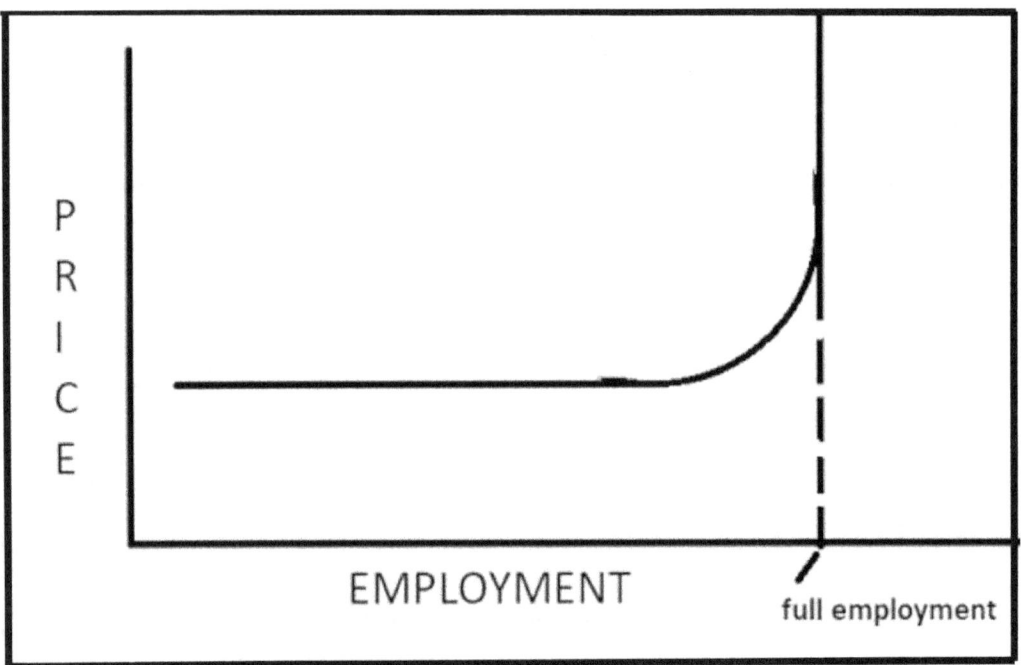

Both graphs show that continuing to increase aggregate demand after the economy has reached full employment will increase prices. The difference between the two graphs is that with the Phillips curve, by the time the economy has reached a state of full employment, there has already been some increase in prices. This gives us the shape of the Phillips curve graph. At any rate in both situations reaching full employment means that we have a situation where if the amount of spending done for a given time period increases it is still paying for the same amount of product . This means prices go up, not employment levels. That is inflation . It is important to note, that on both of these graphs it is assumed that having the economy reach true full employment is achievable provided aggregate demand is increased enough.

This understanding began to change after policymakers had been implementing Keynes' recommendations over several decades. Somewhere along the line, economists began to notice that inflation actually did not appear to occur or maximize at full employment, but seemed to occur in excess and runaway fashion prior to reaching full employment. They coined a new term called Non-Accelerating Inflation Rate of Unemployment, NAIRU, which defines the lowest the unemployment rate can go before you get accelerating or excessive inflation. This makes the Phillips curve look more like this:

FIGURE 22.3

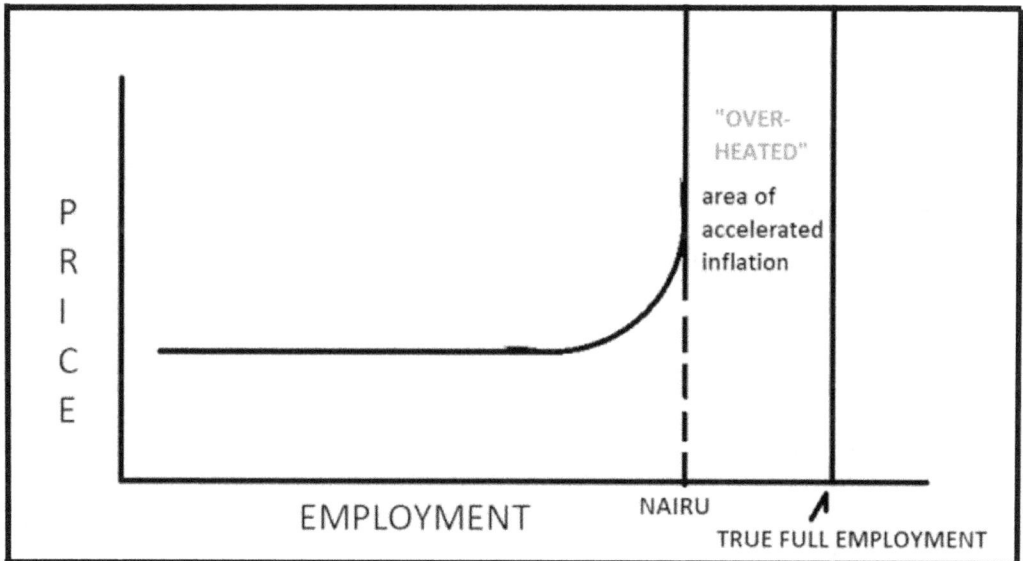

This is not a great chart in terms of expressing what I'm trying to express, but it presents the basic idea: When unemployment gets lower than NAIRU we are in a zone of excess inflation.

Excess inflation creates a situation that is essentially unsustainable and puts a block on achieving true full employment and would mean the lowest unemployment rate we could realistically achieve *and sustain* would be NAIRU.

Actually prior to economists settling on the term NAIRU that level of unemployment was called (and sometimes still is called) the "natural rate of unemployment." And some even call it "full employment." That is why I use the phrase TRUE full employment, to distinguish what Keynes meant by full employment from NAIRU. When you hear the Business News on the radio and you hear them say we are at full employment or close to full employment, they do not mean what I am calling true full employment, they mean the unemployment rate is equal to NAIRU.

The difference between Keynes' idea of full employment and NAIRU is that the unemployment that exists when the unemployment level is at NAIRU still includes some involuntarily unemployed people, whereas Keynes described full employment as being when you have NO involuntarily unemployed people.

Keynes described three types of unemployment:

1. Involuntary, when people are ready and able to work, qualified, and willing to accept the going wage, but cannot find work.

2. Frictional, which Keynes described this way:

"'frictional' unemployment. For a realistic interpretation of it legitimately allows for various inexactnesses of adjustment which stand in the way of continuous full employment: for example, unemployment due to a temporary want of balance between the relative quantities of specialized resources as a result of miscalculation or intermittent demand; or to time-lags consequent on unforeseen changes; or to the fact that the change-over from one employment to another cannot be effected without a certain delay, so that there will always exist in a non-static society a proportion of resources unemployed 'between jobs'."[12]

3. And the third type is voluntary unemployment which Keynes described this way:

"'voluntary' unemployment due to the refusal or inability of a unit of labour, as a result of legislation or social practices or of combination for collective bargaining or of slow response to change or of mere human obstinacy, to accept a

---

12 Keynes, John Maynard. The General Theory of Employment, Interest and Money (Illustrated) (pp. 5-6). Green World Publication. Kindle Edition

reward corresponding to the value of the product attributable to its marginal productivity"[13]

In other words, in this type, people are unwilling to work for what their labor would be worth, or at least the going rate.

Economists have also coined a term called "structural unemployment" which is closely related to frictional unemployment. In my opinion the two should be lumped together for the purposes of explaining the concept of NAIRU.

Here are some of the Wikipedia explanations of the concept of structural unemployment:

"from an individual perspective, structural unemployment can be due to:

Inability to afford or decision not to pursue further education or job training

Choice of a field of study which did not produce marketable job skills

Inability to afford relocation

Inability to sell a house (for example due to the collapse of a real estate bubble or of the local economy)

Decision not to relocate, in order to stay with a spouse, family, friends, etc."[14]

The Wikipedia article also mentions other causes of structural unemployment, like technology making certain job skills obsolete, requiring retraining for other jobs if possible. Or productivity increases, reducing the number of workers needed to produce the amount of product demanded, leading to layoffs (I would call this involuntary unemployment not structural). The mismatch between skills and work available at a given location, combined with people being unable or unwilling to work (I would call the 'unwilling to work' part voluntary unemployment). Political changes can disrupt a whole economy as happens so often. Even discrimination, not hiring people because of their race religion or ethnic heritage could be viewed as a form of structural unemployment, because it would be possible to change this if one could intervene to change the attitudes of the employers, but this too I would classify as involuntary unemployment.

Although there are grey areas on the boundaries of what we might assign to each different type of unemployment, from a conceptual framework, I believe that

---

[13] Keynes, John Maynard. The General Theory of Employment, Interest and Money (Illustrated) (pp. 5-6). Green World Publication. Kindle Edition.
[14] https://en.wikipedia.org/wiki/Structural_unemployment

we can accept, despite its imperfections, that it is reasonable to assume we have some voluntary unemployment, some unemployment that is best characterized as structural and/or frictional and some involuntary unemployment. As voluntary unemployment does not count as part of the unemployment rate and as those people are not considered to be in the workforce, we will consider unemployment rates as consisting of a portion of involuntary and a portion of structural and frictional.

For the purposes of simplicity in explanation I will consider structural and frictional as one category, and simply refer to the combination of them both as frictional. This means, that in our model, our unemployment rate is completely accounted for if we total the frictional and the involuntary unemployment rates.

But there is a key difference: involuntarily unemployed workers are ready willing and able to go to work. As soon as the employers are willing to spend to pay for their labor, the employment rate will increase. Demand for goods and services drives demand for labor to produce those goods and services. This means that involuntary unemployment is responsive to changes in demand. Frictional unemployment does not respond quickly to changes in demand.

According to Keynes, unemployment levels, in the short run, cannot fall below the unemployment level which occurs at full employment because full employment is defined as when there is no involuntary unemployment and all the unemployment is frictional. In other words, there always does continue to be an unemployment rate, but at true full employment all the unemployment is in the frictional category.

By our definitions, every time we describe an unemployment rate we are describing something that consists entirely of frictional and involuntary unemployment. When we say NAIRU, we are talking about an unemployment rate. It describes the unemployment rate, such that, if, in the short run, we have unemployment go any lower, we get accelerating or excess inflation. Therefore, although all unemployment rates likely have some component of frictional unemployment, NAIRU, in addition **must** have some component of involuntary unemployment.

Why is this so? Because NAIRU is the point where if the unemployment rate goes any lower, we get excessive inflation. The ascribed cause of unemployment being lower than NAIRU in that model is too much demand. Frictional unemployment does not respond in the short run to demand changes. The only type of unemployment that changes in the short run due to demand changes is the level of involuntary unemployment. Since the model for NAIRU assumes that unemployment level can get lower than NAIRU due to demand increases, even though this will cause excess inflation, then part of the unemployment that makes up the value of NAIRU **must be** involuntary unemployment.

I should take some time to explain the difference between the type of inflation that would theoretically occur if, after the economy reached true full employment and we increased aggregate demand further... and the type of inflation that occurs because increased demand causes the unemployment rate to be lower than NAIRU.

First, I describe the kind of inflation that the first two graphs describe, what would occur, according to those models, if the economy were at true full employment, and demand were increased further.

Assume an economy is at a state of short run equilibrium where there is a certain level of employment and the economy is producing a certain amount and mix of output items. Let us assume that the sales of all the output occurs with a specified number of transactions **T** which have an average price per transaction of **P**. The number of transactions is totally determined by the amount and mix of the output. Since it is the short run, and we have an established equilibrium, we assume that if we make small changes in demand, productivity remains constant and the mixture of items produced remains constant. This describes a situation where the only way to increase the amount of production is to increase employment.

Now let us assume the economy is at true full employment. At true full employment it is not possible to increase the employment level, in the short run, by increasing demand. We have already assumed that the mix of production will not change significantly with a change in demand. And at true full employment it is not possible to increase the amount of production, i.e., the number of transactions, by increasing spending, i.e., demand.

If demand is increased (which is the same as increasing spending and income) and the number and type of transactions **T** remains constant, then the only thing that can change is the average price **P** of the transactions. Income equals $Y = P*T$. If **Y** (total spending, i.e., total demand, i.e., total income) increases and **T** stays the same, then **P** must go up proportionally to **Y**. If demand increases by 5% then prices must increase by 5%. Notice that this is a one-time adjustment related to a one time increase in demand. That is how Keynes' model would describe inflation occurring at full employment. Every time you have an increase in demand it would affect prices only, proportional to the increase in demand, but it could not affect the employment or unemployment levels.

The type of inflation described when the unemployment level becomes less than NAIRU is quite different than the type of inflation that would theoretically occur at true full employment in Keynes' model.

First, I will point out, that IF the Non-Accelerating Inflation Rate of Unemployment does not contain any involuntary unemployment, then when the unemployment rate equals NAIRU, all the unemployment would be frictional. This is the same as saying the economy is at true full employment, so any description of inflation at that point would be equivalent to what I just described for Keynes' model. That means NAIRU must have a component of involuntary unemployment or the concept is meaningless. The NAIRU concept was specifically designed as a model of how, if demand were "too high" and the unemployment level got "too low", the result would be excess inflation.

In the NAIRU model, since NAIRU must have some component of involuntary unemployment, when the unemployment level is equal to NAIRU, it is possible for increased demand to push the unemployment level lower. Since demand can still cause total employment to increase, it can therefore also cause production to increase. So, at that point if prices begin to increase it is not caused by the inability to respond to the demand increase by increasing production, like what would happen at true full employment.

In the NAIRU model the cause of inflation is something different. The blame for inflation in the model with NAIRU is generally attributed to wage pressures. The theory is that if the unemployment level goes down, and the workers bargaining position improves, and they get wage increases, the employers need to raise prices to pay for the increased wages. The price increases reduce the buying power of the workers recent wage increase. This makes the workers negotiate for another wage increase. The employers respond in kind by raising prices again. Then the workers want another wage increase, causing the employers to raise prices again, etc.

This is not the same thing as the description of true full employment. In the NAIRU model, increasing demand to a certain point can set off a cycle of excessive or "runaway" inflation. As long as the workers continue to have bargaining power and are in a position to continue to negotiate raises then inflation can keep going up and up with no apparent limit. The only thing that eventually limits this runaway inflation is when this process causes such a disruption in the economy that it becomes unsustainable. The description given here, attributing the cause of excess inflation to workers bargaining power, is generally how this concept is taught. The idea being that too much demand in the economy leads to increased job growth until it gets us to the point where workers have that bargaining power.

Thus, when we have a situation where unemployment is below NAIRU economists will say such things as the economy is "over-heated", implying the economy is "producing too much". If these economist notice unemployment rates going down and wages going up they say we are "in danger of having inflation". The standard recommendation when that occurs is to do something to decrease demand. Typically, any intervention used to decrease demand has as its main goal to cause an increase in involuntary unemployment levels so as to decrease workers bargaining power, since that is the factor they consider to be the prime cause of excess inflation.

I have a different theory on the causes of accelerating inflation that occurs when unemployment is less than NAIRU. Workers' bargaining power is only one factor, and perhaps not even the most important. I will discuss this later.

I just wanted to mention that the economy generally has a regular and expected level of inflation, that is different than this excess inflation. The distinction between this regular inflation and excess inflation is that with regular inflation, the society has adjusted to it and all incomes and interest rates have adjusted to these expected, regular price increases. With excess inflation, inflation is too rapid, or unexpected, and causes portions of the society to be left behind. Not all incomes are able to keep pace, and people begin to find the buying power of their incomes to decrease. Investors find it harder to predict their returns and are afraid to put as much money into ventures, and factors such as these can begin to disrupt the economy. This too will be discussed later.

I should talk about "cyclical" unemployment. My understanding of cyclical unemployment is that it describes levels of involuntary unemployment. When the unemployment rate equals NAIRU, cyclical unemployment is considered zero. When the unemployment rate is less than NAIRU, cyclical unemployment level is negative, and when they unemployment rate is higher than NAIRU cyclical unemployment is positive. This means that the total amount of involuntary unemployment that exists at any time is the cyclical unemployment rate being added to whatever the involuntary unemployment rate is when the unemployment rate equals NAIRU.

We might consider seasonal jobs where people only work during certain parts of the year to be part of cyclical unemployment, for the part of the year they are not employed, but we could also categorize the unemployed period as being voluntarily unemployed.

The main idea behind the term cyclical unemployment is something called "business cycles." It is believed by most economists that the economy is always in a state of flux and so the job market is always adjusting to match, sometimes employment rates will be lower and other times they will be higher, sometimes the economy is more expansive and there are more jobs and sometimes it is more contracted and there are less jobs. Although there may be longer term causes of variations in employment rates that are best considered as frictional/structural, cyclical unemployment is something that changes more rapidly. Some would say that the definition of cyclical unemployment should also include frictional and structural but, in my opinion, that confounds the issue and makes the concept less useful. In "The General Theory of Employment Interest And Money" when Keynes discussed business cycles, he interpreted them in terms of variations in demand, and the type of employment that responds quickly to demand changes is involuntary unemployment. This describes cyclical unemployment, as I understand it. It is something that changes quickly with demand changes. It is a measure of the level of involuntary unemployment, specifically how much total involuntary unemployment differs from the value of involuntary unemployment at NAIRU.

The expression cyclical unemployment is in common use today, but I rarely see the expression involuntarily unemployed used. I find this unfortunate and somewhat misleading. To me the term cyclical unemployment is a way to normalize, and make more acceptable, the idea that there are people suffering from being out of work and unable to find a job, with all the consequences that a person in that position faces. It is an expression that implies that there is nothing to do about it, it is normal, just wait, everything will be fine. It is a term that implies we should just accept this "natural situation" and not try to make it a focus of our efforts to control or reduce it. Central to Keynes' work was the idea that it is possible that one could intervene in such a way as to reduce the adverse effects of business cycles on employment. That is, he wanted to reduce the frequency and magnitude of cyclical unemployment. I think just using the expression cyclical unemployment rather than involuntary unemployment is a way of minimizing the issue and deemphasizing the importance of reducing involuntary unemployment.

Monopoly Power and NAIRU

I mentioned that there is another factor that plays a role in the excess inflation that occurs when unemployment level is below NAIRU and cyclical unemployment is below zero. The first factor is workers bargaining power and the second one is the degree of monopoly power on the part of employers. It does not have to be absolute monopoly power, but the degree to which they have monopoly power will affect their confidence in raising prices.

It works as follows: workers get bargaining power and get increased wages, employers with some monopoly power are able to increase prices to preserve excess profits. Workers notice their buying power is lower due to increased prices, so workers negotiate and get higher wages, employers with some degree of monopoly power again raise prices to protect excess profits*. Workers notice their buying power is lower due to increased prices, so they again negotiate higher wages and so on.

* (also known as economic rents)

This will be discussed in more detail in the next chapter, but I wanted to introduce the general concepts here.

CHAPTER 23
MORE DISCUSSION OF THE INGREDIENTS OF EXCESSIVE INFLATION AND THE EXPLANATION OF STAGFLATION

In this chapter I introduce a model that than allows for an alternative explanation of the phenomenon known as Stagflation. This model integrates both Keynes' concept of Aggregate Demand and its influence on total employment, and the concepts of NAIRU and excess or accelerating inflation.

A COMMON PROPERTY that both structural and frictional unemployment have is that they both change slowly, and neither reacts quickly to demand changes. It is this common property that allows me to group them in the same category. I have elected to simply count structural unemployment as a component of frictional unemployment and add it to frictional unemployment's total. This leaves us with three types of unemployment: Voluntary Unemployment, which is not counted as part of the unemployment rate, Frictional Unemployment, and Involuntary Unemployment. This means that any unemployment rate is calculated by adding the amount of Frictional Unemployment with the amount of Involuntary Unemployment.

Total Unemployment = Frictional Unemployment + Involuntary Unemployment.

Of the two components of the Unemployment Rate, in the short run, only the Involuntary Unemployment Rate will change significantly as a result of Demand changes. This is because the Involuntarily Unemployed are ready, willing and able to work. They can be immediately hired, as soon as people have an increased desire for products, and the means to spend to acquire them. The same is not true of the Frictionally Unemployed. This is because, by definition, frictionally unemployed workers have obstacles to being able to be immediately employed.

NAIRU is an unemployment rate; therefore, NAIRU is made up of a component of frictional unemployment and a component of involuntary unemployment. It is because, and only because, there is some involuntary unemployment when the unemployment rate equals NAIRU, that the unemployment rate is able to fall lower than NAIRU. If NAIRU does not contain some amount of involuntary unemployment, then, when total unemployment equals NAIRU, all the unemployment would be frictional unemployment. If, when the unemployment rate equals NAIRU there is no involuntary unemployment, that means the economy is at the level of employment Keynes called full employment, and I call true full employment. This would mean that demand increases would not, in the short run, decrease the unemployment rate and the economy would never get into the zone of excess inflation. Having NAIRU occur at true full employment would make NAIRU a useless concept. Only when NAIRU consists of some involuntary unemployment is it possible for demand increases to push the unemployment rate lower and get into the zone of excess inflation.

Baseline Inflation

Inflation is a fact of life. People expect there to be inflation. The idea of a baseline inflation is that people expect the level of inflation to stay fairly consistent year to year. People, firms and institutions get used to that level. So, prices, wages, retirement incomes, interest rates etc. all tend to increase to keep pace with the expected inflation, or at least inflation values within a certain limited range. The concept of a **baseline inflation** I am describing, is one that is not excessive, and does not cause a problem since participants in the economy have adjusted to and compensated for it.

In the previous chapters that discussed effective demand and aggregate demand, the graphs did not include the baseline inflation as part of the analysis.

More Discussion of the Ingredients of Excessive Inflation

FIGURE 23.1

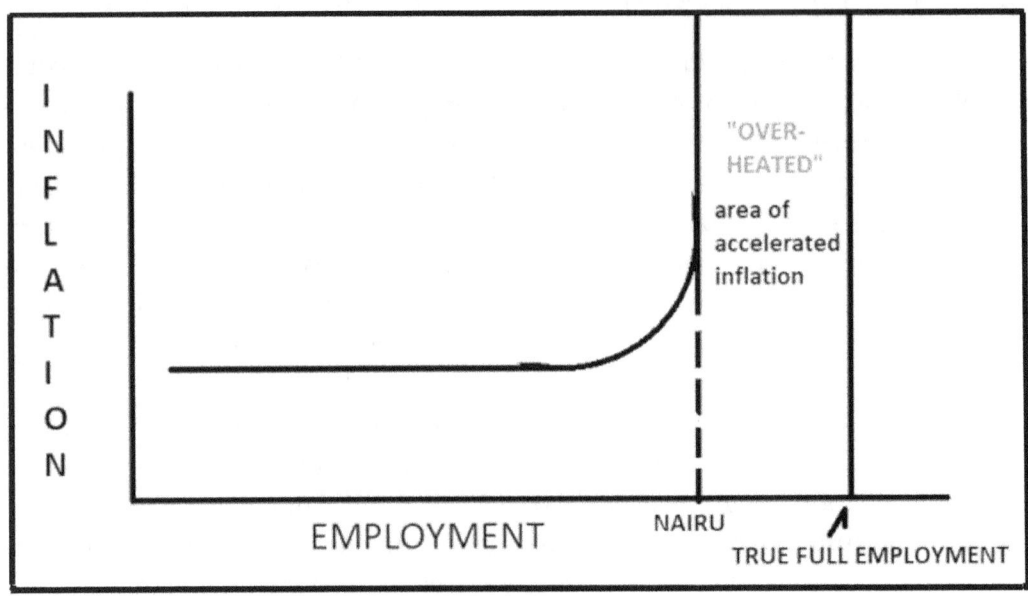

If one wishes to include inflation this is easily accomplished if we just put inflation on the Y axis instead of prices. When we are considering that we have a baseline inflation, instead of saying we have prices remaining the same, we say we have the rate of price increases being the same.

Excess inflation or accelerating inflation is inflation above and beyond the established level of inflation. Excess inflation can contribute, if persistent enough, to causing a new higher level of expected inflation to be established. If that occurred the horizontal line on the graph would move up.

In the NAIRU model when the unemployment level starts to get lower than NAIRU, inflation will begin to increase above expected inflation. If you **hold** the unemployment rate at less than NAIRU, the inflation level can **continue** to go up.

This excess inflation may not hurt the firms that can keep increasing their prices and it may not hurt the employees who remain in a position to keep negotiating increased wages. But the fact is, it may have adverse effects on others. For example, many people's incomes are tied to expected inflation, like retirement incomes. Those people's income may only keep up with the established expected inflation, not the excess inflation. If so, their buying power goes down, because prices will be increasing faster than their income.

More Discussion of the Ingredients of Excessive Inflation

Buying power is also known as inflation adjusted income or inflation adjusted demand. Inflation adjusted income is also known as real income, and inflation adjusted demand is known as real demand.

If the economy has excess inflation, because the unemployment rate is less than NAIRU, perhaps some of the worker's pay is keeping pace with the excess inflation, in industries where those workers are essential. Those people's **real** incomes will remain stable. But many other people in the economy will be losing ground, their pay will not keep pace with inflation, their real incomes will be decreasing. So, while some people's real incomes may stay the same, others real incomes will be falling. This can give us a situation where overall real income; overall real aggregate demand is declining. Think of that for a minute. Normally when we have a lower unemployment rate it is associated with a greater real (inflation adjusted) aggregate demand. But when the unemployment rate gets less than NAIRU and we get excess inflation that effect can be turned around, and what started as increased real demand can get turned into decreased real demand. Then, as we see in figure 23.2 (below), when REAL aggregate demand falls, so does the employment level, that is, the **un**employment level increases.

Having large segments of the population's real incomes go down even though their nominal incomes might have been going up, is one way real demand gets reduced. Another factor in this situation that reduces total demand is something called financial frictions. This is the effect of increased uncertainty on the part of investors, as to the future profitability of different venture assets. Excess inflation makes it more difficult to ascertain what future demand will be both overall and for certain items. Investors then will be more conservative and spend less on ventures, and this will contribute to a further reduction in real demand.

When discussing effective demand and aggregate demand in previous chapters, I did not consider inflation. Now, since I **am** considering inflation, I must explicitly state that on those charts, derived based on Keynes' work, when he introduced the concepts of effective demand and aggregate demand, the values of the demand and supply functions are really **inflation adjusted values.**

More Discussion of the Ingredients of Excessive Inflation

FIGURE 23.2

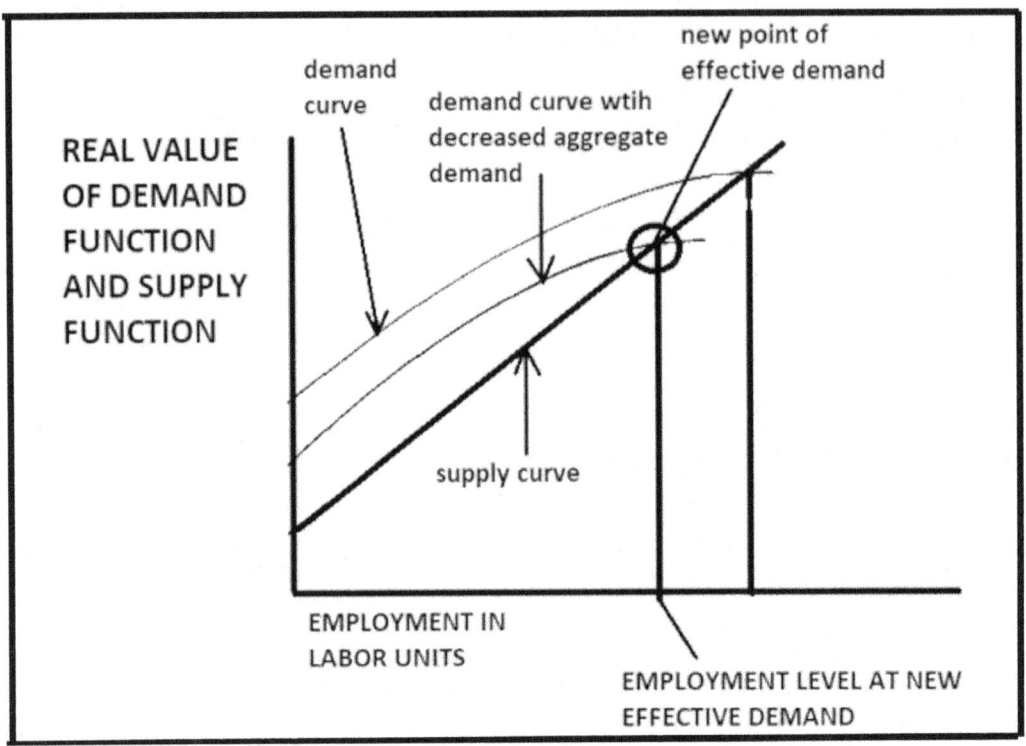

This chart exhibits what would happen to employment if real demand went down. Since I am saying that the values of the supply and demand curves refer to real inflation adjusted values, this chart shows that if real, inflation-adjusted demand decreases, the level of employment shifts to the left, employment levels will decrease, and unemployment will increase. This situation can be caused by excess or accelerating inflation. The United States in the late 1960s and 1970s exhibited excess inflation. It was during that time when the concept of NAIRU, first called the "natural rate of unemployment" was developed.

In that situation, even though it all started with attempts to decrease unemployment by increasing demand, if the increased demand causes the unemployment rate to fall to less than NAIRU, the result can be excess inflation. This excess inflation can, in turn, cause real demand to fall, which in turn will cause unemployment levels to rise. That would give a situation where the economy has both high unemployment and excess inflation.

Referring to the graphs below. Times when there were high unemployment and high inflation at the same time occurred in the 1970s in the United States. There were a couple peaks for the inflation and the unemployment during that time. It is interesting to note that the peak for inflation occurred first, and the peak for the unemployment a little later. While the unemployment was rising to its peak the inflation rate was coming down. This is consistent with a theory that says the excess inflation led to decreased real demand causing unemployment to rise. With the rise in unemployment one would expect a reduction in workers bargaining power and a reduction in wage increases. That in turn will reduce the rate of price increases that occur in response, decreasing the inflation rate.

FIGURE 23.3

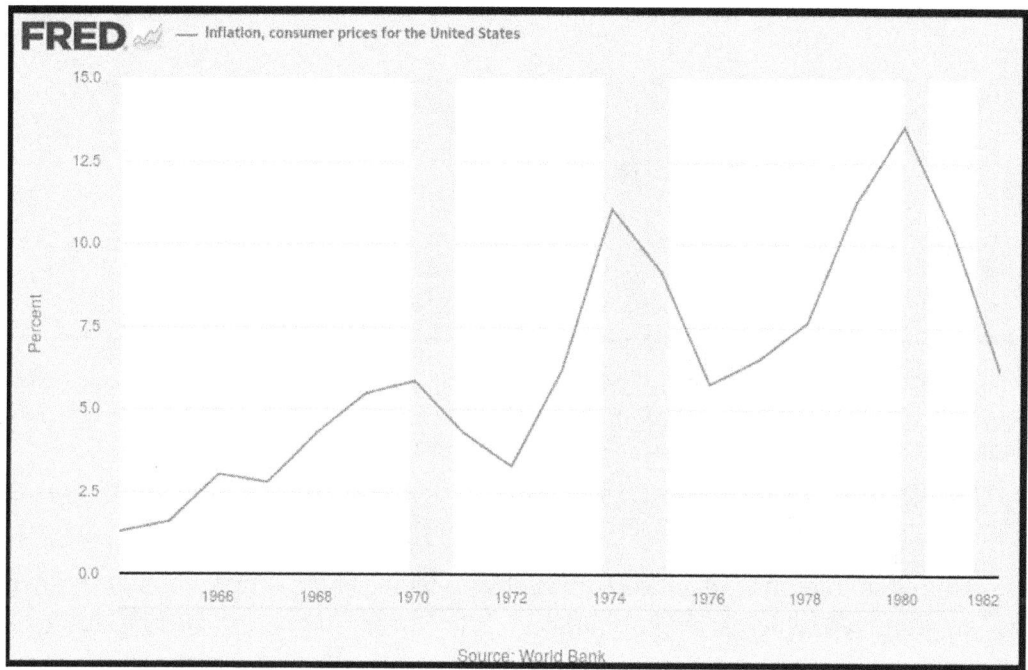

United States, Inflation, 1964 to 1982

World Bank, Inflation, consumer prices for the United States [FPCPITOTLZGUSA], retrieved from FRED, Federal Reserve Bank of St. Louis; https://fred.stlouisfed.org/series/FPCPITOTLZGUSA, November 25, 2018.

MORE DISCUSSION OF THE INGREDIENTS OF EXCESSIVE INFLATION

FIGURE 23.4

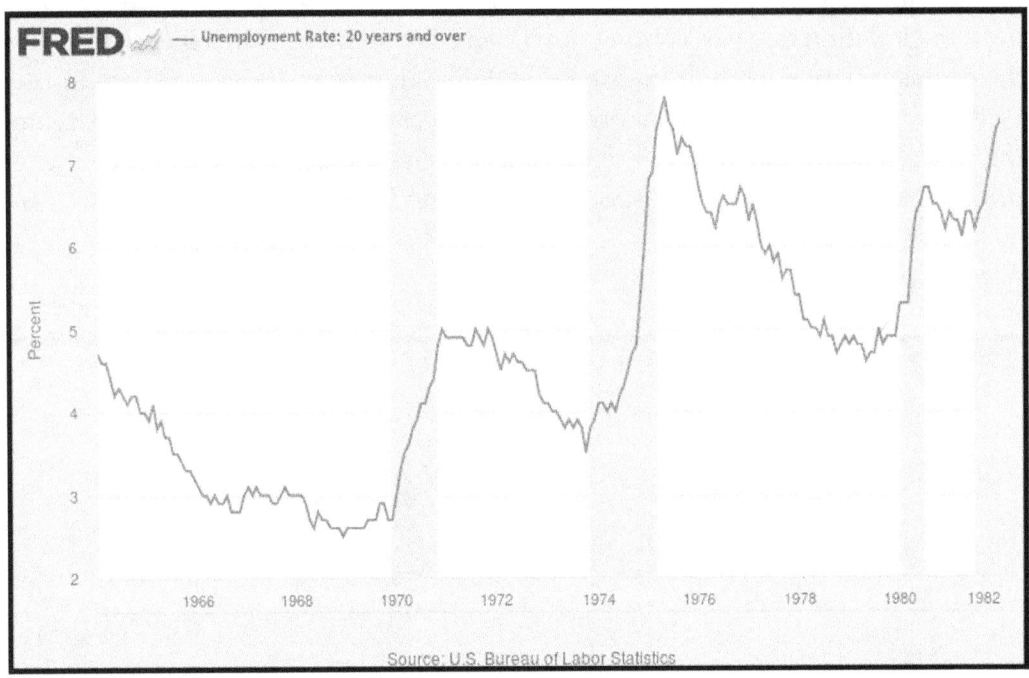

United States, Unemployment Rate, 1964 – 1982 U.S. Bureau of Labor Statistics, Unemployment Rate: 20 years and over [LNS14000024], retrieved from FRED, Federal Reserve Bank of St. Louis; https:// fred.stlouisfed.org/series/LNS14000024, November 25, 2018.

FRED® Graphs ©Federal Reserve Bank of St. Louis. 2018. All rights reserved. All FRED® Graphs appear courtesy of Federal Reserve Bank of St. Louis. https://fred.stlouisfed.org/

This combination of increased inflation and increased unemployment is known as "stagflation", which is a combination of the words, stagnation and inflation.

So, that is my model for explaining the occurrence of Stagflation, if attempts made to increase demand cause unemployment rates to fall below NAIRU.

Critics of Keynes implied that stagflation disproved his theory that one can increase employment and production by using government spending to increase income and demand. Most of the criticism was aimed at government programs intended to decrease poverty and give lower income people more money, by various means. Those critics would point out that this was a situation where having high inflation was associated with high unemployment, disproving the relationship between employment levels and demand. Those critics would say that this is an example where high demand was the **cause** of high unemployment.

More Discussion of the Ingredients of Excessive Inflation

To my understanding, what those critics are implying is that this stagflation phenomenon is caused by government programs that are inefficient and lead to decreased production. The decreased production would be because workers will not then want to work, or would not be available to work at jobs in the private sector. The decreased production leads to decreased supply and that is what causes prices to go up. The critics are implying that giving income to people, via government spending, will take away people's motivation to work as hard, and even cause them to not want to work at all, and that a good portion of that high unemployment is **voluntary unemployment**. Additionally, a criticism would be that decreased production leads to decreased sales, and that would reduce investment spending and employment as well. Additionally, increases in financial frictions due to uncertainty in the economy would further decrease investment. So even the hard working conscientious workers would have increased unemployment. That, as I understand it, would be the explanation for Stagflation given by those critics of government spending.

Keynes would only recommend increased government spending in a situation where there were involuntarily employed people, that is in a situation where people were ready willing and able to work, and would be working, except for a demand deficiency. He was advocating for increased government spending so as to increase spending overall, so that there is increased demand to purchase products, increasing the number of jobs needing to be filled to create those products, thus decreasing involuntary unemployment. Keynes certainly would prefer that government spending would go to create jobs for people who would otherwise be unemployed and producing nothing, so as to put them in a position where they ARE producing some good or service. But even if some of the money went to people who did not provide a tangible good or service, as long as there were involuntarily unemployed people **any** increased income created would lead, via the multiplier, to increased spending and increased employment and production in the private sector as well. In Keynes' model, it is not about taking people away from otherwise productive activities and causing them to be unproductive. In his model, government spending is for the purpose of increasing demand so as to activate un- or under-utilized resources, especially involuntarily unemployed people, both directly through government employment, but also, by the multiplier effect, to jobs increase in the private sector; all of this causing an increase in total employment and production, helping to make it so that **more**, not less people are able to contribute and cause an increase, not a decrease, in wealth production.

More Discussion of the Ingredients of Excessive Inflation

I want to point out how, in the previous Chapter, both Keynes' model and the Phillips Curve model allow us to get to true full employment. In the NAIRU model the complication of excess inflation causing decreased real demand, and decreased employment levels, essentially serves as a block to ever attaining true full employment, i.e., from ever attaining the outcome of having an economy with no involuntary unemployment.

∽∞∞∽

It is not irrational to think that there are dangers to government spending, if it is done irresponsibly. Responsible government spending has the goal of maximizing employment and production in the long run. If government spending is done for corrupt reasons, such as to strengthen political power, without regard to its effect on the economy, this can lead to severe consequences, including supply shortages, and economic depression caused by decreased buying power, i.e., decreased real incomes.

One of the things critics of government intervention and spending put a lot of focus on is regulations and laws. While it is true that sometimes laws and regulation can be harmful, in many, if not most cases they are essential. The idea of externalities, positive and negative speaks to this issue. For example, without any regulation, businesses could mistreat and endanger their employees and customers, unlawfully collude and use other anticompetitive practices including criminal activities to increase monopoly power, pollute the environment, and do other harmful things. Although the firm in question may be gaining a large income from their venture and increasing their wealth, they may also be creating consequences that are costly to the rest of society. Consequences that the rest of us have to pay for to deal with or to reverse, if reversing those consequence is even possible. Government laws, regulations and enforcement that prevent these practices are essential in these cases and will in the long run increase net wealth production, not decrease it.

By presenting this model, I am attempting show that the phenomenon of stagflation can have a demand side explanation caused by excess inflation leading to a fall in real demand. **I am saying that Stagflation CAN still occur even if government spending is extremely efficient, and even if it makes nobody lazy, even if there is NO increase in voluntary unemployment and even if all the spending is targeted at useful and necessary projects**. If what I am saying is correct, this changes the discussion.

More Discussion of the Ingredients of Excessive Inflation

The discussion regarding government spending will always be to make it as efficient and useful as possible, but now the question becomes, if stagflation can occur even when government spending is completely efficient, is there a way to address and solve the problem of stagflation. Is it possible for society to implement efficient government programs, so that we can do a better job of eliminating poverty, improving our infrastructure, and paying for essential government services, with the result of maximizing standard of living for all citizens and NOT cause excess inflation?

The answer to this, I believe, lies in understanding the causes of excess inflation. As I have stated, the two main ingredients are workers bargaining power and monopoly power. In general techniques to prevent excess inflation have focused mainly on reducing workers bargaining power by **decreasing demand.** We have all heard on the radio, how "economists are worried that wages are rising, and we are in danger of having inflation" so the Central Bank raises interest rates, to decrease demand. Unfortunately, when poverty exists in an economy there are people without adequate incomes. Decreasing demand means decreasing spending and income, hardly the solution for inadequate income.

Ultimately then, the only solution to allowing us to get closer to true full employment and increase wages, i.e., increase workers share of income, is to focus on increasing competition and decreasing monopoly power, which I discuss in more detail later in this chapter.

Just wanted to mention that if you held **un**employment below NAIRU for long enough, this might establish a higher level for **baseline** inflation. Since people would expect higher inflation they would try to get their income, or the prices they charged for their products, to increase at the higher rate, so as not to lose buying power. Theoretically, if you held the **un**employment level greater than NAIRU, that is if you kept employment levels low this will reverse the pressures on wages and prices and cause inflation levels to go down, even below expected inflation. And if you continued to **hold** the unemployment rate higher than NAIRU, this could lead to the establishment of a new lower level of baseline inflation, though this effect may not be totally symmetric. In other words, it might be more difficult to lower inflation expectations than to raise them.

Can NAIRU be reduced? Are we able to reduce the level of unemployment that we can attain without having excess inflation become a problem? How close can the economy realistically get to true full employment? If we could reduce the level of NAIRU, then perhaps we could be more aggressive with spending on programs that can benefit the poor, pay for infrastructure and essential government services. Is it possible to provide for more of these things before excess inflation becomes a problem?

First, we will need to consider in more detail the question: What are the factors that affect the value of NAIRU?

I already mentioned the two main factors:

1. The first ingredient is workers bargaining power. Increased bargaining power leads to increased wages.

2. The second ingredient is the requirement of some degree of monopoly power to allow firms to keep raising prices in response to wage increases.

Perfectly Competitive Market

In order to analyze the effect of monopoly power on excess inflation we first need to understand something called a "perfectly competitive market." A perfectly competitive market is one where the firms are price takers, not price makers. By this I mean, there is so much competition out there that each firm is required to keep their prices as low as possible in order to be able to compete on the market. That requires all expenses be as low as possible including the income of all those involved in the process of creating the product. It includes the workers and it includes the executives, owners, and investors of the firm...everyone.

If the workers were able to force being paid more than they were worth the firm would have to charge higher prices and would not be able to compete and would go out of business. If the executives, owners, and investors were to take more profits out of the business than is their true contribution, then their prices would be too high, they would not be competitive, and they would go out of business.

If there are involuntarily unemployed workers, then they could be offered lower wages and one firm will figure that out and be able to produce more product for the same labor cost, charge less for their product and threaten to put the other firms out of business. Thus, all the firms will compete for those workers, causing every worker who is ready willing and able to work to be hired and get paid their true worth according their level of their productivity.

In a perfectly competitive market, everyone ends up getting paid their true worth and there is no involuntary unemployment. All the firms would adjust their prices to charge the lowest price possible or go out of business.

The bottom line is this: in a perfectly competitive market, there is true full employment, and everyone gets paid what they are worth, and prices are as low as they can go, and anyone who wants to produce and sell something has to charge that price, no more. In such a situation, excessive inflation is NOT possible. But the reality is, that for many reasons, we do not have a perfectly competitive market.

Excess Profits

Excess profits are also known as "economic rent." This, I believe, comes from the time period when we were mostly an agrarian society and it was the landowners who got paid the rent for doing very little or nothing at all, while everyone else did all the work. It later came to signify any group of individuals who were in a position to profit in excess of their contribution, and these people are known as rentiers.

I would define the concept of "excess profits" as only being applicable when those profits are beyond the investor's, entrepreneur's and executive's true worth which is not always something easy to determine. The reason I say this, is because normally, motivating people to work hard, innovate, take risks, and work to improve the efficiency and productivity of their labors, requires some financial rewards. One reward is that a firm or person may be able to have an increased market share for a time. That is, due to their hard work, innovation and risk taking they are able to produce product more cheaply, or produce a superior product, or even produce a totally new product, giving them an advantage in the market for a time. Along those lines, if may be necessary for society to offer temporary copyright or patent protection, to prevent competition for a certain amount of time, to encourage such risk taking and efforts needed to produce new or improved products, that otherwise may never be developed. All of these things I do not consider excess profits and they all help society grow in wealth and increase standard of living.

Economies of Scale is another factor in determining market share. This is the idea that larger, better funded ventures can by enlarging the scale of their operations develop efficiencies that allow them to produce and sell things more cheaply than smaller firms. This could have them dominate market share for a time. As long as this was causing increased net production and productivity, one could

More Discussion of the Ingredients of Excessive Inflation

make a case that this situation is leading to increased overall wealth and increased overall standard of living in the economy. This situation, however. does introduce the possibility that these large firms could resort to anticompetitive practices to keep out competition and this could lead to a slowing, or even reversal of productivity increases preventing the standard of living from achieving what it may otherwise achieve. And even during the time when such a firm is able to produce its products so much more efficiently and cheaply, and able to dominate market share for that reason, it does have an advantage in bargaining power with workers in that industry. This means that during that time it can either use strategies to suppress wage increases, or, if need be, increase prices to maintain profits if workers are able to manage wage increases.

In my view, excess profits that we should be concerned about is the amount of pay that investors, firms, executives, entrepreneurs are getting which is not contributing to overall increased wealth and standard of living. All of this is hard to determine, but what I am alleging is that there comes a point where more profits to the few are not contributing to producing more results, i.e., more overall production of wealth.

As I have shown, excess profits could not exist in a perfectly competitive market. So, there must be things that reduce competition in the market to allow excess profits. Examples of ways that excess profits are supported include things like influence peddling, which can cause inappropriate regulation favorable only to certain people or firms. Or things like copyright and patent laws that are too broad or of excessive duration. It could include inappropriate government subsidies or tax deductions or credits that favor one group over others, or collusion preventing true competition, etc.

There are also things referred to as natural monopolies, where it is not practical or reasonable to have more than one or a few entities producing and delivering that product. Here, even though the products they produce may be essential to the economy, there exists the possibility of abuse of the privilege, i.e., to prices being set higher than is necessary to support their mission. Where such natural monopolies exist, people will need to be vigilant to the possibility of this abuse, by which I mean, from a practical standpoint, to the degree that these products are essential to the economy, these natural monopolies need to be monitored and regulated by government.

I have described a perfectly competitive market where excess inflation is not possible. I have stated that we do not in reality have a perfectly competitive market. I reviewed the idea that increasing market share can, for a while, be a

More Discussion of the Ingredients of Excessive Inflation

desirable, even essential, thing, as it can be promoting increased efficiencies, innovation, hard work, and risk taking. I have stated how this can have a beneficial effect on the economy, leading to increased wealth and standards of living. And I have described how one should only consider market share "excessive" when it no longer has those beneficial effects and begins to have a negative effect. I have discussed certain things that can support excessive market share or monopoly power even when it is having an adverse effect on the economy.

Accepting the reality that a certain degree of monopoly power and excess profits exists, I return to the analysis of excess inflation and stagflation.

Here is what I feel is the best explanation of excess inflation occurring due to demand increases:

Demand increases cause employment to increase, i.e., causing unemployment to decrease. When unemployment gets low enough workers start to feel more confident about bargaining for higher wages, and employers compete more for their services, all of which leads to higher wages.

Firms that have monopoly power may grant those higher wages, but their excessive market share makes them worry less about the competition, so they have the ability to protect their profit level from falling by raising prices.

The workers see prices going up and the buying power of their wages going down, so they again bargain for higher wages. The employers grant the higher wage but then again raise their prices to preserve their profits, etc.

The amount of confidence the employers have about being able to raise their prices, which no doubt is related to their degree of monopoly power, will affect how fast and by how much they will raise their prices. In other words, for a given level of demand, the amount prices are going to be increased is related to the degree of monopoly power that exists in the market.

If one accepts that these are the two main ingredients going into "demand caused" excess inflation, and one wanted to control excess inflation then it is reasonable to conclude that you might be able reduce excess inflation by affecting either or both of them.

That would mean that you could reduce excess inflation by reducing workers bargaining power or you could reduce excess inflation by reducing firms' monopoly power. Since around 1980 one of the main goals of the US government and their Central Bank has been to control inflation and since that time, we have not had any problem with excess inflation. The technique for controlling excess inflation has been focused on controlling the level of demand. The effect of this would be to increase unemployment and suppress workers bargaining power.

An argument can be made that inflation has also been controlled somewhat by reductions in monopoly power caused by enacting free trade agreements supporting globalization so as to increase competition.

If one focuses solely on controlling wages as a way to control inflation, while not controlling monopoly power, that could be expected to cause an increase in inequality. Controlling excess inflation by reducing monopoly power instead would likely have an effect of reducing inequality. Controlling inflation by reducing monopoly power and increasing competition in the market would also have the effect of simultaneously controlling wages, since employers would not be able to raise prices OR wages as fast, due to concern about being competitive.

The rise in inequality we have seen since around 1980 suggests society has done a better job of controlling workers bargaining power than reducing monopoly power. Some would argue that the rise in inequality is not a result of excess profits from excess market share. That profits that may appear to be excessive profits are driving the economy to new heights and that not only are we all experiencing a higher standard of living but that this would not be occurring if not for those "rewards" that some call excessive. This is a rather hard to believe assertion.

It is common knowledge that CEO pay has increased dramatically over the decades to the point where some CEO's pay is 400 times as much as a regular worker. To justify that this pay is not excessive we would have to believe 1) that the CEO is just so rare and talented that he is one of the few that could manage his job and 2) people with that level of ability would not come forth and exercise those talents without being paid 400 times as much as the average worker. I suspect that would be a hard case to prove and that such inflated salaries are, in fact a result of excess profits.

My conclusion on this subject is that policy makers are focusing mostly on suppressing workers wage increases to control inflation and not doing enough to control monopoly power. This has resulted in dramatic increases in inequality.[15] Extreme inequality can have adverse effects on total spending, support the development of oligarchies, propagate poverty, and even foment social unrest.

---
15 http://gabriel-zucman.eu/files/SaezZucman2015.pdf

More Discussion of the Ingredients of Excessive Inflation

In the past, this whole conversation of stagflation and its cause centered, in part, on the controversy over whether increased government spending in response to a depression was good or bad. I believe that Keynes' views of the situation are much more nuanced than that, and more nuanced than how they are normally represented by his critics.

When Keynes devised his theories, he was witness to terrible poverty and the crumbling and decay of private and public infrastructure and decay and loss of our industrial capacity all for want of income and demand. He believed that, at times, interventions were needed to keep us functioning at maximum capacity or even sometimes at a minimal standard. He was a capitalist. His recommended interventions depended on private enterprise to respond to increased demand by increasing employment and production. His recommendations for increasing demand were intended for times of inadequate aggregate demand, when the economy is **not** at full employment. Any government actions that would affect demand would be expected to change with conditions, and adjust to the need. The intended goals of any policy recommendations, coming from his theories, were to reduce unemployment and poverty and prevent degradation of our capital equipment and infrastructure. In modern times his idea would be that interventions like food stamps, welfare, and unemployment insurance, may only be needed in the short run.

Even in the short run, when this extra government spending is necessary to increase aggregate demand, it is better if the recipients are required, and able, to provide some useful service, or are able to produce things that enhance our standard of living. Programs could be designed in such a way as to effect that. At any rate, Keynes believed there will be times when the extra subsidies are needed and times when they are not.

As pointed out in a previous chapter, wages keeping up with inflation is not the stable situation. The stable situation is wages keeping up with inflation plus productivity. In the 1960s and 1970s attempts were made to increase employment by increasing demand. This worked, but it led to the unemployment level getting lower than NAIRU, and this eventually led to the situation previously discussed known as stagflation. Then for the next 40 years the Central bank did a great job of controlling inflation, using monetary policy to control demand and keep unemployment rates from getting less than NAIRU, suppressing workers bargaining power and wage growth. The Central bank did this by raising interest rates when inflation and wage growth started to rise. There did not appear to be much effort on the part of the government to control monopoly power, the other component necessary to have accelerating inflation.

FIGURE 23.5

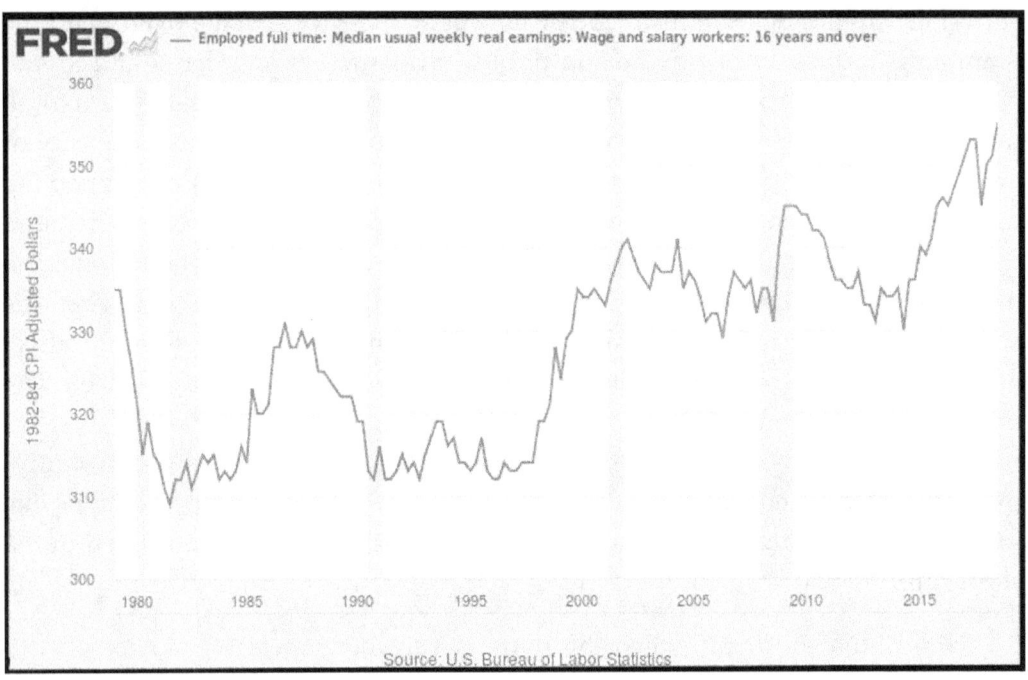

FRED, Federal Reserve Economic Database

Employed full time: Median usual weekly real earnings: Wage and salary workers: 16 years and over, 1979 to 2018

U.S. Bureau of Labor Statistics, Employed full time: Median usual weekly real earnings: Wage and salary workers: 16 years and over [LES1252881600Q], retrieved from FRED, Federal Reserve Bank of St. Louis; https://fred.stlouisfed. org/series/LES1252881600Q, November 25, 2018.

FRED® Graphs ©Federal Reserve Bank of St. Louis. 2018. All rights reserved. All FRED® Graphs appear courtesy of Federal Reserve Bank of St. Louis. https://fred.stlouisfed.org/

The effect of this was, for the most part, to keep wage growth rising at the same rate as inflation. Or to put it another way, to keep real wages, inflation adjusted wages from changing. This chart (Figure 23.5) shows median real wage going up no faster than 5% in 40 years. About 0.13% a year. Even if you took the extreme points in the graph it went up no faster than 13% in 40 years, about 0.3% per year. This would have been a stable situation if productivity stayed the same, but it did not. Productivity in the U.S. has been increasing steadily since that time. The

More Discussion of the Ingredients of Excessive Inflation

following chart (Figure 23.6) shows productivity going up by 100% over 40 years, about 2.5% a year.

FIGURE 23.6

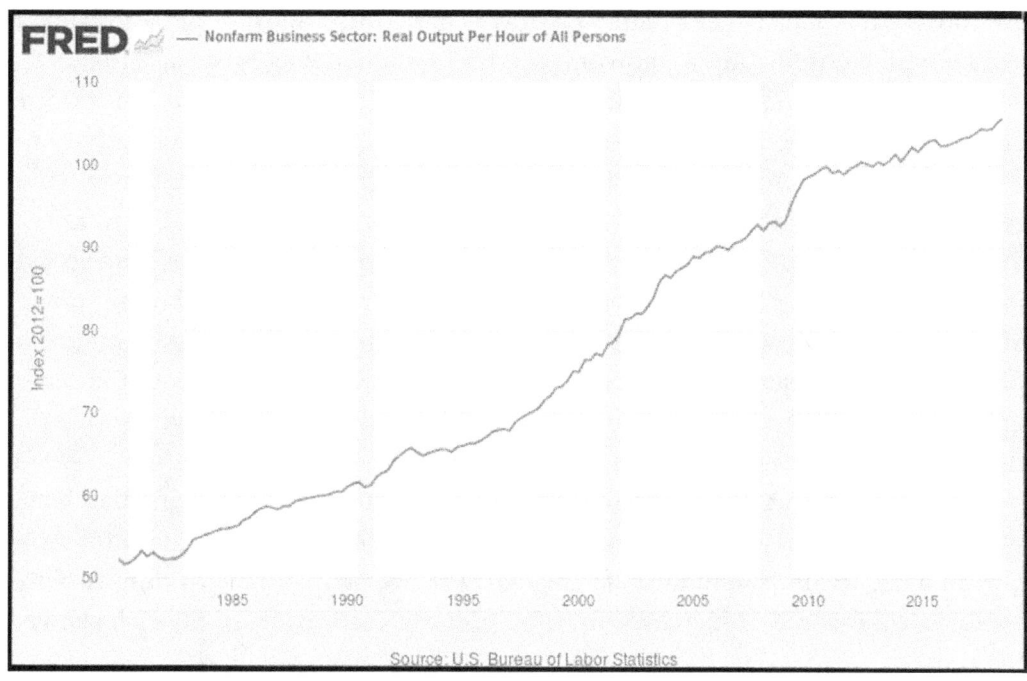

NonFarm Business Sector: Real Output Per Hour For All Persons 1980-2018,

U.S. Bureau of Labor Statistics, Nonfarm Business Sector: Real Output Per Hour of All Persons [OPHNFB], retrieved from FRED, Federal Reserve Bank of St. Louis; https://fred.stlouisfed.org/series/OPHNFB, November 25, 2018.

FRED® Graphs ©Federal Reserve Bank of St. Louis. 2018. All rights reserved. All FRED® Graphs appear courtesy of Federal Reserve Bank of St. Louis. https://fred.stlouisfed.org/

Real median wages being the same, means that the median wage workers will earn just as much in terms of the total sales as they did previously. This will be true even though the amount of sales in real inflation adjusted terms will be much greater because much more product is being sold. This means more and more of the sales proceeds will go in the pockets of the employers and their financial backers. Or to put it another way, the gains in income from increased productivity will not be shared with the workers but instead will be going into the pockets of the richer factions. Unless you believe that all of the extra production was directly a result of the labor of the employers, executives, investors, i.e., the highest income earners, then one must conclude that the extra income represents, at least in part, an increase in economic rents.

More Discussion of the Ingredients of Excessive Inflation

The next question that must be answered is, if the median wage earners could not possibly purchase the extra product out of the wages they earned at work, how did it get paid for? And that is what I try to analyze here:

By median wage earners I mean those whose average income tends to cluster around the median wage. I refer to real wages because here we need to be concerned with what the buying power is. I refer to median wages because that is the best measure of what is happening to most people, it is not skewed by income going to a small group of very wealthy people. We know that if productivity increases, and more product is produced leading to increased amount of production being sold, including all or part of the increased production, that the total real income, the total buying power would have increased. This is because the spending bought a greater amount of product. The real demand, the real buying power of a certain amount of spending is how much product it buys. If the amount of product sold is greater, then buying power of the spending that bought it is also greater. Such is the case here. So, we know total real spending (buying power of the spending) increased and the real income that spending created also increased, by the same amount. But if the real, inflation adjusted, pay of the median wage worker did not increase, that means all the extra buying power, all the extra inflation adjusted income went into the pockets of richer people. This would cause the average real income to increase, but only because the income of the rich skewed the average.

Suppose, as is apparently the case since 1980, that we have average real pay go up only due to the increased pay of the higher income earners, the employers, executives, investors, suppliers etc. It is theoretically possible, although unlikely, that as time went on, each year more of the steadily increasing product sales get paid for by steadily increasing spending by the richer income earners. If this continued enough years, one would assume the richer people's spending would begin to dwarf median wage workers spending. If that happened then it would be highly likely that the character of what is produced would have to change, meaning there would be more of a luxury market. And as productivity continues to go up, if the increased real income continues to go mainly to the very wealthy, the type and quantity of products would become even more skewed towards luxury items. One would expect there are limits to how far this process could go, so I would not really call that a stable situation. There may have been an increase in luxury spending to some extent, but I do not think it is sufficient to account for the total amount of sales of the extra production, especially since many of the products are targeted at regular people and of such volume that if would be unreasonable to think that a few rich people would have need of, or be able to use, all those products.

More Discussion of the Ingredients of Excessive Inflation

Median wage workers could help pay for more of the increasing amount of product by saving less or using up savings. This could help pay for extra sales for a while, but eventually the savings would be depleted, and with median real wage staying the same, spending more out of their income would become insignificant compared to the amount of extra spending needed to pay for all the extra production. So that would not help much in providing for the amount of funds necessary to keep paying for all that extra production, in the long run.

Next to consider is having median wage workers taking out loans to pay for the extra production. This extra lending would be funded from the ever growing accounts of the higher income earners whose real earnings have steadily increased due to extra income they garnered from the sales of that extra production. Which, to put it simply, is saying that **instead of paying higher wages** to give median wage workers more money to help buy all the extra product, the wealthier income earners would be **loaning those workers extra money to spend.** In general, however, paying for extra production with loans would be unsustainable, because the debt burden would divert more and more of the median wage earners income to paying off loans, decreasing the amount of money that could be used to purchase the extra production.

Another way to help keep spending adequate to buy all the production, one that would be, in theory, sustainable, even if in practice it has no chance of ever occurring, is if the government could tax the wealthier people and redistribute the income so that overall median **incomes** kept pace with both inflation and productivity increases, even if **wages** did not. This, no doubt, to some extent already occurs. If real median wages continued to stay flat and did not increase to match the productivity increases, and if the solution were to tax the rich and use government subsidies to increase median income, the amount of redistribution that would have to occur, in order to be able to pay for all the increased production, would need to grow and grow each year, until it became an enormous program. Politics aside, even if this were possible, there would be all sorts of problems with this. Perhaps the most important one is losing the connection between an individual's contribution to production and their level of pay, which is the most essential ingredient of a successful capitalistic economy. One could imagine all sorts of inefficiencies and corruption dominating such a system.

Suppose the employers just keep all the extra production and do not sell it? Then we would not need extra income because there are no extra sales to pay for. I am not sure hoarding larger and larger piles of product one is never going to sell is the kind of economy that would motivate all the effort to make that extra product. More than likely, if there is no demand for the product it will not be produced.

We could improve our trade balance, i.e., increase exports and decrease imports. Meaning we could be selling our extra production to foreign countries, but again, as time goes on, our trade balance would have to become a larger and larger surplus over time and it is not reasonable to assume that would be possible. Since our trade deficit has not decreased, this has not been a factor in paying for that extra production.

The best solution, for maintaining a viable economy in the long run, with a steadily increasing productivity, one that is also sustainable, is to **increase real median incomes to keep pace with productivity gains**. This is the only legitimate way, in a capitalistic economy, to have a stable economy over the long run. In fact, prior to 1980, for decades, real median wages went steadily up and did keep pace with productivity, but since 1980 real median wages have stayed flat, they have not gone up, even though productivity and production has gone steadily up.

Given that being the case, that since 1980 the buying power of the median wage worker has not increased significantly while productivity has almost doubled, where is the extra demand coming from to pay for all that extra product?

I suggest that the above mention factors have been playing a role in providing that extra real demand needed to buy the extra production. I further suggest that all of those solutions but one will prove unsustainable, and that ultimately the best, and perhaps the only solution that would allow us to have a successful capitalistic economy, (which I consider a prerequisite to a strong democracy), **is to raise the wages of the median wage worker to keep pace with both inflation plus the rate of productivity growth.**

CHAPTER 24
Marginal Efficiency of Capital

In this chapter, I start to discuss a point in Keynes' book, (chapter 11 of The General Theory), where he begins to introduce new concepts. In so doing he uses some similar terms, specifically investment and savings, but gives them different meanings. I do not know if he realized that he had done that, nor have I seen where this was noticed by anyone else, but the fact is that they cannot continue to mean the same thing in the new application. This chapter, and the following one, look at the new concepts he was presenting. However, to give these concepts proper treatment, what Keynes calls savings and investment (starting in chapter 11 of "The General Theory") will need to be given new names.

THE DEFINITION OF investment used in this book, which I will continue to use, says investment is any spending paid for with money put into income for the first time in a given time period. Savings will continue to mean wealth which comes out of a given period of economic activity, consisting of two parts, the preservation of the money put into investment spending, plus net production.

The new application of Keynes that we begin studying in this chapter is an analysis of what causes "for-profit investors" to put their money into ventures versus interest bearing accounts. While the subject matter under discussion will be an analysis of a large part of the economy, we should bear in mind that it does not describe the whole economy.

In discussing this new topic, when Keynes used the term "investment" he was talking about when the "investors" purchase interests in for-profit ventures. That spending could meet the definition of investment from chapter 2 of this book, but it could also be spending paid for out of current income, in which case, it would meet the definition in chapter 2 for consumption. So, it is a different usage. For that reason, I will refer to that which Keynes called investment starting in chapter 11 of his book as "spending to acquire venture assets." or "purchasing venture assets".

In this new application when Keynes is talking about savings he actually means spending. He means spending to acquire an asset. The asset the spender is purchasing is a deposit in an interest-bearing account. When they put money in the bank ownership of the money is being transferred to the bank in exchange for the interest-bearing asset. The bank gets the money and a debt obligation to the depositor. But here is the important thing, the money could then still be used again for spending in the given time period. It does not have to remain inactive till the end of the given time period. That is different than the preservation of the investment money that I have shown is part of savings. That money only becomes savings that is the preservation of investment money after it has been spent for the last time in the given time period. To distinguish the two definitions, I will continue call the savings that is the preservation of investment "savings" but I will call putting money into an interest bearing account "purchasing a savings asset".

So, in this new application, what Keynes refers to as investment, I call purchasing a venture asset, and what Keynes calls savings, I re-define as purchasing a savings asset. Notice that in both cases the investor is spending not saving. The spending, in either case, could be paid for by money being put in to spending for the first time in the given time period, in which case it is investment, or it could be paid for out of current income in which case it counts as consumption. But when the "for profit investor" purchases a savings asset, or a venture asset, it is spending, not savings. That "investor" will have the option of purchasing a venture asset or a savings asset or Keynes' third option, which is to just hold the money as cash.

Purchasing a Venture Asset and the Marginal Efficiency of Capital

When a "for-profit investor" decides to purchase a venture asset the price he pays is referred to as the supply price. He will only make that purchase if he expects to earn a return on that asset. The price he expects to be able to sell the asset for after a specified period of time is called the prospective yield. The expected percent or fractional increase in the value of the asset is what Keynes called the

Marginal Efficiency of Capital. The formula for the Marginal Efficiency of Capital is **[(prospective yield - supply price)/supply price]**. The Marginal Efficiency of Capital is the rate of return on that venture purchase.

In the scenario described here the "for profit investor" seeks to maximize his return on investment. They will attempt to purchase the assets which are likely to have the biggest percent increase in value over time. When many purchases of assets are occurring, the return on venture assets tends to equalize with the return of savings assets. The economy tends towards an equilibrium point where the "for profit investor" is just as likely to purchase a savings asset as a venture asset, because the interest be would be paid on a savings asset is the same as the return they will get from purchasing a venture asset, that is, the interest will be equal to the marginal efficiency of capital.

This occurs because as more and more money is spent on venture assets the marginal efficiency of capital gets smaller. Similarly, as more savings assets are purchased the interest rates tend to go down. That is the reason that the amount of spending into each asset can reach an equilibrium point. If the marginal efficiency of capital is greater one will buy more venture assets bringing the return on venture assets down until eventually it equals the interest rate or vice versa.

To explain why the marginal efficiency of capital gets smaller as more venture assets are purchased, I follow Keynes' explanation. He used a concept called "the schedule of marginal efficiency of capital:"

When an investor is deciding to purchase a venture asset, they will have multiple different assets to choose from. All of these opportunities will have their own marginal efficiency of capital. A listing of all these assets and their marginal efficiencies he called "the schedule of the marginal efficiency of capital".

Generally speaking, the investor will try to obtain the most profitable venture asset available, the one with the largest marginal efficiency. And after this opportunity is no longer available or giving the highest return, he will switch to purchasing the venture asset that gives the next best return, until that asset is no longer available or no longer giving the highest return. and then on to the next most profitable. As this process continues, as more and more of the venture assets are purchased, as the assets with better returns have been sold and are no longer available we can expect the return on investment will gradually be decreasing. So, the marginal efficiency of capital on the remaining assets will become smaller and smaller.

Marginal Efficiency of Capital

The largest return on an asset available for purchase at a specific moment in time Keynes called the "marginal efficiency of capital in general". When one is talking about the overall marginal efficiency of capital equilibrating with the interest rate one is talking about the marginal efficiency of capital in general. I will drop the "in general" and when I use the term marginal efficiency of capital I will be referring to the asset with the best return currently available.

I should mention that marginal efficiency of capital is not an absolute and certain number. It is a judgement call, an estimate; the investors best guess as to what will happen in the future, not just the present. And as we know in real life people will weigh the certainty or uncertainty of a return. In other words, people might take a more certain lesser return over a less certain greater return. So one would have to consider, for example, whether to purchase a venture asset with a higher, less certain return or a savings asset with a lower, more certain return, or perhaps just decide to hold their cash. The investor would probably be more conservative in his estimate of the prospective yield for an asset with a less certain return, causing that asset to be rated as having a lower marginal efficiency of capital than it would have if it had a more certain return. This is saying that the equilibration point, where one is just as likely to purchase a certain venture asset as to purchase a savings asset, incorporates the influence of uncertainty into the decision. The valuation a "for profit investor" gives to the marginal efficiency of capital of a given venture asset purchase factors in the certainty or uncertainty of the actual expected return from purchasing that asset.

Anything that affects the individual "for profit investors" estimate of the what the prospective yield will be, is incorporated in the value that investor gives to the marginal efficiency of capital. The prospective yield, and therefore, the marginal efficiency of capital, are all influenced by many factors. The "for profit investors" attitude regarding risk and uncertainty, their individual tastes, beliefs, or moral code, their opinion about the veracity of information about an asset, how they rate the reliability of other's opinions about the future return of a given asset, etc.

All of those things and more affect decisions to invest, including things like investment style and preference where some like to invest and hold the investment, i.e., invest for long term. Some prefer to constantly trade and change investments. There are many different "investment philosophies". All these factors are involved in forming an individual "for-profit investor's" decision on how to value the prospective yield of an asset. But, at any rate, the "marginal efficiency of capital in general" refers to the investor's judgement as to how to value the top yielding investment opportunity available at that particular time.

In order to get some idea of what the overall marginal efficiency of capital is in a given economy one would have to do some sort of averaging, to the best of one's ability, of all the investors' valuations of marginal efficiency of capital across the economy.

CHAPTER 25

Interest

IF MARGINAL EFFICIENCY of Capital is considered the inducement to purchase venture assets, then the **interest rate** is considered the inducement to purchase savings assets. The marginal efficiency of capital gets reduced as more and more spending occurs to purchase venture assets. Similarly, interest rates get reduced as more and more money gets put into interest bearing bank accounts, i.e., as more money is spent on purchasing savings assets. The reason for that is if more money is being put into banks, the banks do not have to compete as hard for the money, so they can offer less interest. Further since the banks have more money to lend, then this will drive down interest rates they can charge on loans, another reason they will not give depositors as much interest on bank deposits.

With the "for-profit investors" seeking to maximize return, equilibrium will occur when the marginal efficiency of capital equals the interest rate, because if those two were unequal spending would shift until they did equalize.

As conceived by the prevailing economic theories prior to Keynes, which Keynes referred to as the Classical School, equilibrium looks something like this:

Classical School of Economics:

Interest <---> Marg. Eff. Of Capital

But Keynes realized there is an intermediary, i.e., "liquid money," meaning money held as cash or at least money that is easily accessible and not generating as much, if any, income where it is.

Keynes saw it like this:

Interest <---> Cash <---> Marg. Eff. Of Capital

⁂

Keynes liked to divide the desire for holding cash into three categories:

i. **The transactions-motive**, need cash for current use... Personal or business

ii. **The precautionary-motive**, unexpected needs

iii. **The speculative-motive**, wanting money on hand for "investment" opportunities

The transactions motive and precautionary motive are pretty constant in terms of an individual's decision to hold cash. The decision to hold cash for those motivations is not influenced much by, nor do those motivations influence the interest rate or the marginal efficiency of capital (MEC). It is the **speculative motive** that is influenced by, and influences the **MEC** and the **interest rate.** Keynes pointed out that it is **uncertainty** that mostly determines desire to hold cash rather than tie it up in savings accounts or bonds. He stated how if everyone always knew what would happen, they would set up all their asset purchases, so the right amount of cash would always become available at the right time for the next desired spending opportunity.

Since that is not the case, there needs to be some cash available to spend when the right opportunity comes along. If the interest rate goes high enough, there will come a point when the speculative investor will decide the return on a savings asset is high enough for him to put his cash there; that the interest rate is high enough that he is more likely to get a higher return with the interest bearing account than he would with a venture investment. This is how the speculative motive interacts with the interest rate. Of course, it is going to have the same relationship with marginal efficiency of capital. The investor will use some discretion and will probably hold some cash until the marginal efficiency of capital is a value that he feels waiting for a better opportunity is not worth the risk. Since he will always have the choice between a venture asset and a savings asset, the marginal efficiency of capital and the interest rate will equalize.

Regarding the relationship between holding cash and the interest rate Keynes says "interest has been usually regarded as the reward of not-spending, whereas in fact it is, **the reward of not-hoarding**".[16]

Hoarding here means to hold cash or liquid assets, rather than tying it up in some sort of longer term savings account, or bond. If you increase the available cash for-profit investors have, they will normally put some of that extra cash into purchasing venture or savings assets, in such a way that interest rates and marginal efficiency of capital will equalize. But both will equalize downward, i.e., the value of both the available interest rate and the marginal efficiency of capital will be reduced, since that is what happens to both when more of each of those assets is purchased.

But also, as more spending is done to purchase venture assets, there is a counterbalancing effect. If the economy is at less than full employment, the venture spending will lead to an increase in employment and via the multiplier effect an even larger increase in income and demand. That factor will put pressure to increase marginal efficiency of capital and interest rates. Additionally, as interest rates the banks pay on deposits go down then loans become cheaper and this leads to more venture spending, again putting pressure to increase marginal efficiency of capital and interest.

This secondary effect caused by the increased demand cannot be greater than that primary effect of increasing the available cash because if it were, the primary effect would never happen in the first place. The secondary effect does modulate the primary effect, however. It is typical in economics for there always to be counter-balancing effects. At any rate, increased cash available to for-profit investors would be expected to lead to reductions of marginal efficiency of capital and interest rates, even if the total effect is modulated somewhat by counterbalancing effects. And vice versa: decreased available cash would increase interest rates and marginal efficiency of capital, even if the total effect is modulated.

How does inflation affect all this? Inflation will make it more likely that the cash investors are holding will be put into some asset that gets a return. This is true because inflation means hoarded cash, which is getting no return, will be losing

---

16 [The General Theory of Employment, Interest and Money by John Maynard Keynes, Chapter 13, Section V, Paragraph 1

value compared to inflation. This will lead to more spending to obtain both types of assets, venture and savings. The increased spending could possibly stimulate the economy leading to increased employment and demand unless you ended up with excess inflation which would adversely affect "real" (inflation adjusted) demand.

CHAPTER 26
Does Investment Equal Savings?

In this chapter I are talking about the situation where we have marginal efficiency of capital enticing money into venture assets on the one side, and interest enticing money into savings assets on the other side.

I DO NOT call spending to acquire venture assets the same thing as what I called investment in Chapter 2. In fact, spending to acquire venture assets could be investment or it could be consumption, but since it is spending, each bit of it must be categorizable as either investment or consumption.

I do not call spending to acquire a savings asset the same thing as savings. Spending to acquire a savings asset is spending not savings. It is also categorized as either investment or consumption or some of both. Spending to acquire a savings asset is not the same thing as the savings that is the preservation of investment, but if part of the spending to acquire a savings asset qualified as investment spending then that part will become part of the savings that is preservation of investment. The same goes for the spending to acquire a venture asset. Any part of that spending that meets the criteria for investment as outlined in chapter 2 becomes part of the savings that is preservation of investment.

If we exclude the part of savings that is net production, if we only include savings that is the preservation of investment, that savings will always equal investment for the simple reason that they are the same money. This is not an "equilibrium" that the system moves towards. The same money (as defined in chapter 2) will always equal itself.

On the other hand, spending to purchase a savings asset does not have to equal spending to purchase a venture asset. Spending on venture assets and savings assets will cause the economy to tend towards an equilibrium. But that equilibrium is not reached when total spending to acquire venture assets equals total spending to acquire savings assets. That equilibrium is reached when two other things are equal. That equilibrium is reached when the interest rate equals the marginal efficiency of capital. That is what must be equal at equilibrium.

The absolute amount that one puts into savings accounts and bonds does **not** have to be equal to the absolute amount put into spending to purchase a venture asset. In fact, it is a very low probability that they would be exactly equal. Unlike the savings that equals the preservation of the investment money, they are not the same money, in fact they **compete** for the available money. This confusion is caused by not realizing that the savings that is the preservation of investment is not the same thing as spending to purchase a savings asset or that investment is not the same thing as spending to purchase a venture asset.

We are talking about for-profit investors here. There is other spending besides venture asset spending and savings asset spending. There are other types of spending that count as investment and consumption and add to overall demand. Overall spending defines overall demand, and any spending will also affect both the above-mentioned types of spending done by for-profit investors. Total demand affects marginal efficiency of capital, because you will have customers to sell your product to. And an overall increase in income will also make more people and more businesses qualify for loans and this will increase the amount of interest banks can charge on loans and pay on deposits.

Spending done for the purpose of having an asset that increases in monetary value, does not account for all spending. Instead of an asset that will increase in monetary value there may be other things the spender is hoping to get. The "return" they hope to get might be food or shelter or transportation, it might be leisure activities, or having a good feeling about helping someone through charity. Or having a well maintained and developed infrastructure paid for by taxes that allows the government to fund those things. Or it might be government spending for public safety that results in having police, fire fighters, and other first responders, or paying for doctors to keep us healthy, or giving income to the poor, disabled and elderly so they can pay for food and shelter and be part of their family's lives. So, spending made with the expectation of a monetary return, though essential, is not the only kind of spending, and not the only spending that contributes to overall demand.

CHAPTER 27
Monetary Policy

Monetary policy is controlled by the Central Banks and is utilized to affect demand. Either increase demand or lower it depending on the macroeconomic conditions at the time. This chapter attempts to explain the basic principles as they historically applied. In 2008, there was a dramatic shift in how monetary policy is implemented. This is also discussed here.

The typical historical explanation of monetary policy:

WE CONTINUE WITH the situation of interest on one side trying to attract savings account deposits, i.e., purchase of savings assets, and the marginal efficiency of capital on the other side trying to attract spending on venture assets. Let us consider more of the effect of the size of the liquid money supply on interest and on marginal efficiency of capital in a situation where the economy is at less than full employment.

If the amount of liquid money were added to by some outside source, then this would increase spending on savings assets and venture assets, putting pressure to decrease both interest rates and the marginal efficiency of capital. Regarding interest: with more available cash, obtaining deposits would be easier for banks. The banks would not have to offer as much interest to get their money needs met. This would also mean all the banks could offer loans at reduced interest and still make a profit. Any bank that did not do so would presumably lose loan customers and have reduced overall profits. One also knows that marginal efficiency of capital would go down as well, for reasons explained in previous chapters.

The new equilibrium point, after the injection of that extra cash, would occur after more bank deposits were made but also after more venture spending was done. This extra venture spending is the type of spending that would increase demand for labor, goods, services, and other desired outcomes and would be expected to lead to increased employment and production. Also contributing to overall spending would be more affordable loans due to decreased interest rates and more qualified borrowers due to increased incomes. The increase in loans increases the money the borrowers have available for spending.

Remember, before the injection of cash, money was being put into venture spending, loans were being made, incomes were being earned, money was being put into bank accounts, i.e., money was moving through the economy. The injection of cash does not change the fact that economic activity was occurring. It simply influences the equilibrium points.

This leads us into the discussion of the first type of monetary policy called Open Market Operations. This is another name for the procedure where the Central Bank (known in US as the Federal Reserve Bank) buys bonds with money it has created, to increase demand, along with increasing the money supply, or sells bonds to decrease demand, and in the process reduces the money supply. One way that Open Market Operations work is by influencing the interest rate banks can charge on loans and therefore the interest rates they can pay on deposits. As we know, Commercial Banks (heretofore in this chapter referred as "banks") are required to keep a designated amount of money in "reserve". These reserve requirements (aka required reserve, heretofore RR), are usually around 10% of the amount of their deposits. At the end of the day, or "overnight", the banks, are required to show they have this RR amount, which is usually kept in accounts at the Central Bank ("owned by the Commercial Bank but possessed by the Central Bank"). If the balance in those reserve accounts of a given bank, at the end of the business day, (averaged over a couple weeks period), falls below the RR, the bank will have to borrow to get those balances up to the RR amount. To do so the banks generally borrow from each other. Those banks that not only have the RR, but also have money in excess (excess reserves heretofore ER) will be able to lend to those banks that have a shortfall. The interest rate the lending bank charges the other bank is whatever rate the two banks negotiate.

However, the Central Bank has ways to influence that rate. If you think of it, the money the banks borrow to replenish their reserves, is "replacement money" for money they were able to loan to customers during "daytime operations". So, one assumes that the rate they are charged for replenishing these funds will directly influence the interest rates they can charge their customers, and therefore also the rates they can pay on deposits. Here is where the Central Bank's "money creating" authority, comes into play. And this is one of the main ways the Central Bank uses "Monetary Policy" (MP) to influence the economy. If the Central Bank wants to increase or decrease demand (spending) in the economy, they can target the cost of borrowing (interest rates). They do this by trying to influence the interest rate banks charge each other for replenishing their reserves. The target rate they aim for is something referred to as the Federal Funds Rate (heretofore FFR). To reduce the rate banks charge each other, the Central Bank will increase the money supply by buying treasury bonds (Treasuries) which then will cause the sellers of these Treasuries to have more money which generally will end up deposited in banks. This means more banks will have ER of cash, and will be able to lend money to other banks, and less banks will need to borrow to replenish their reserves. Since more banks can lend and less need to borrow, the interest rates the lenders will be able to demand is lower, so the overnight rate (effective Federal Funds Rate, eFFR) will be lower. This will allow interest rates the banks charge their borrowers to be lowered as well. Lower interest rates allows for more borrowing which leads to more spending and increased aggregate demand.

If the Central Bank wants to lower demand, then it does the opposite. It sells Treasuries it owns. This causes withdrawals from bank deposits to pay the Central Bank for those Treasuries and leads to lower cash holdings of those banks. Thus, more banks will need to borrow to replenish their reserves, and less banks will have ER to lend. This will increase the rate the lending banks can charge the borrowing banks. That in turn will increase the rates banks need to charge their loan customers, and the rates they will need to pay depositors to get funds for lending. The result of increased rates will be less borrowing, less spending and decreased aggregate demand.

Generally speaking, at least historically, to maximize profits, banks would be expected to try to lend out the maximum amount they are allowed. The maximum amount they are allowed is determined by the reserve requirement. They will lend out as much of their reserves as they can since, in the past, any money held as excess reserves is not making money for them, so competition by banks to lend to the max will drive interest rates for borrowers down until the banks have loaned out all they are allowed. The interest banks can charge for loans is highly influenced by the amount they have to pay to get funds to lend. This is why the so called "overnight interbank lending rates" (eFFR) would be so important in determining the cost of the replacement funds banks will need to keep lending, and thus the interest rates charged on loans.

Something called the "discount rate" (DR) is a rate of interest that the Central Bank will charge for creating money and directly lending it to banks. This rate is usually set at about one half of a percent above the targeted FFR (tFFR). The idea behind a DR is that it provides a source of funding, to replenish reserves, that is available to banks who are otherwise having trouble getting those funds at a cheaper rate. This sets a ceiling on how high the "effective federal funds rate" (eFFR) can go. The eFFR is the average of the ACTUAL rate banks end up charging each other. (vs the targeted FFR, the rate the Central Bank is trying to achieve). The reason it sets a ceiling on the eFFR is because with money available to borrow at the DR, whenever a bank needs to replenish its reserves, there will be no need for that bank to ever pay a higher interest rate than the DR to another bank. In terms of expanding the money supply, this is an example where the Central Bank buys debt obligations directly from banks, rather than expanding the money supply by buying Treasuries. Of course most of these loans to the banks at the discount rate are very short term loans, so they do not have much effect on the long term size of the money supply.

Something called "quantitative easing" (QE) is another part of monetary policy. This is when the Central Bank embarks on a regular and large amount of bond buying over a specified time period. This is Open Market Operations on steroids, and one can think of this as an attempt to squeeze every bit of venture spending out of the economy, driving the rates as low as possible. The holder of a treasury sells it to the Central Bank. As with Open Market Operations in general, any money used to buy a bond becomes owned by the seller of the treasury, and instead of holding a bond and getting a return the seller now has cash. The idea is that seller will now want to find a venture or savings asset to purchase with that money, to start getting a return again, any return, and with savings rates being driven to zero, hopefully those "for-profit investors" will maximize venture spending, and stimulate the economy, maximizing incomes, employment and production.

Now if for whatever reason, (say these interventions work), and spending and demand were considered to be getting too high, then the Central Bank can reverse these interventions by selling treasuries instead of buying them. This will lead to the opposite effect. There will be less money in circulation, less money in bank reserves, less banks with excess reserves they can lend on the overnight market, and more banks seeking to borrow on the overnight market. This will drive up the interest rates banks charge each other and that will force banks to charge more interest on loans made to borrowers. This will lead to less lending and less spending and cause an overall decrease in demand.

Another monetary strategy that can be used to increase spending and demand, that the Central bank is authorized to do, is to reduce the fractional reserve requirement, (fRR) the percent of deposits commercial banks are not allowed to lend. For example, suppose they decided to reduce the fRR from 10% to 5%. This could increase the amount of loans banks issued. This also would probably, through competition for customers, lower the interest rate charged for loans by the banks. If you increase the amount of loans people acquire, you can increase their total spending. My understanding is, in the past, this intervention was rarely used. Similar to other types of Monetary Policy, if the Central Bank wanted to reduce demand, by reducing the amount of loans it could do the opposite, i.e., raise the fRR.

All these tools mentioned are controlled by the Central Bank and are part of Monetary Policy.

The Game Changer: The New Monetary Policy

In 2006 the banking laws in America were changed in such a way that the way Monetary Policy is implemented is completely different. The factor in that law that made such a difference is the decision to have the Central Bank pay interest on bank's reserve funds. This giving interest on **Required** Reserves is not the game changer. The game changer is that this law, not implemented until 2008, **also** authorized the Central Bank **to pay interest on "Excess Reserves" (ER)**. That is, instead of having a situation where the banks are always encouraged to lend out as much money as they can, they now have incentive to keep money in ER if they are able to earn more interest money there. This keeps a floor on how low the eFFR can go. No bank with ER would lend to another bank at a rate lower than the interest paid on excess reserves (IOER). Open Market Operations will not be able to cause the eFFR to fall below the IOER rate. It also puts a floor on what rate customers will be able get on a loan. No bank would lend at a rate lower than the IOER rate since they could earn more by just keeping their money in ER.

What I just stated is not completely true because after a loan is dispensed, it generally comes back to the banks to be part of bank reserves, it's just that the lending bank has no way of knowing that particularly money is going to end up back in its own reserves. However, if a particular bank were able to both loan out the money to borrowers AND have the money come bank to its OWN reserves, the bank could end up getting paid both interest on the loan by the borrower, and IOER on that same money because it came bank to be part of its commercial bank reserves.

This situation would be much more likely to occur if the number of commercial banks were small, or if certain large banks had a large percentage of the loan market. And of course it would be much more likely to occur if banks were able to collude with each other, which again is more likely to be able to occur if there were less banks dominating more of the market. It is also possible that if a bank knew that a certain percentage or amount of its loans was going to come back and be part of their commercial bank reserves, it might be able to offer borrowers loans a little below IOER and have its total profits still be greater than if they did not loan it all. This would give a competitive advantage in terms of loan rates such a bank could offer. Since large banks, or banks that are colluding, are more likely to be able to reliably predict a certain percentage of their loans coming bank into their commercial reserves, they would be the ones with the competitive advantage and this would carry the risk of them driving competitor banks out of business. This could lead to increasing monopoly power of banks remaining, especially the larger banks.

Since the new law allowing interest to be paid on excess reserves went into effect, the amount of money held in excess reserves by banks increased from a couple Billion Dollars to over 2 Trillion Dollars. That is an increase on the order of 1000-fold. I suspect that the Quantitative Easing implemented as an attempt to help the economy to recover from the Crash of 2008, after IOER was implemented may have played a role in this. The combination of increasing the money supply by large amounts, with most of that increased money landing in commercial bank reserves, and then having the Central Bank guarantee the banks interest on those increased reserves, would not only reward banks for not lending, but would also have the banks support enlarging the money supply, and consequently their reserves, as much as possible. It would further give strong incentives for the banks to oppose any attempt to reduce the size of excess reserves.

With Interest being paid on excess reserves, Open Market Operations will no longer be effective to **lower** effective rates. Further, in the current situation, they will also be powerless in **raising** the eFFR. This would be the case because, with ER balances being so high, one can imagine that most, if not all banks would have ER and can use that to meet RR requirements, and so those banks with excess reserves will never need to borrow money from other banks. This was an essential ingredient in having Open Market Operations affect the interest rates. IOER, puts a ceiling on rates banks will pay depositors. A bank will never have to pay a depositor an interest rate higher than the IOER rate to get money to lend. If a bank has enough money in ER, it would be cheaper to liquidate some of those reserves to access money to lend, rather than paying a depositor an interest rate higher than IOER rate.

You can see from this discussion that IOER can also put restrictions on the possible rates of return obtained on venture investments, because if the marginal efficiency of capital falls below the IOER rate the investor would be more likely to want to put their money in a savings asset, where the interest rate of that deposit is going to approach the IOER rate. If a bank could increase their excess reserves by paying an interest rate **less** than the IOER rate, even if it is not that much less than the IOER rate. They are likely to do it (with consideration to cost of bank operations) because the bank will make more money from IOER than would have to pay the depositor in interest payments..

In 2013 the Federal Reserve Chairman announced that the eFFR would be mainly determined by the IOER rate.[17] This was not a policy choice but simply a statement of reality. The primary tool the Central Bank currently has to change the interest rates charged to customers of banks is to change the IOER rate. Open Market Operations can still be used to increase or decrease the money supply. But with all the money being held in excess reserves, I do not see much of a current need to increase the money supply. One could reduce the money supply by having the Central Bank decrease its balance sheet by selling assets. If this caused the amount kept as ER to get low enough that some banks were occasionally in need of borrowing to meet RR then perhaps normal Open Market Operations could begin to influence the eFFR again. Until that happens, if that happens, we will continue with the current situation where the IOER rate is effectively serving the role the eFFR previously did. The IOER rate is now the important interest rate, the one the Central Bank changes to raise or lower the "interest rate".

Where does the money to pay the IOER come from? It turns out the IOER is paid for as part of the Central Bank's operating cost. Since any profits from interest left over, after any operating costs are paid for, gets transferred to the Treasury's general fund, the IOER is, in essence, paid for by the Treasury ("taxpayers").

The rationale for paying interest on Required Reserves was that the banks should be compensated for money they CAN'T loan out. With IOER banks are being paid interest on money they CAN loan out. This means they are rewarded for basically doing nothing. This system supports having that money not being spent and not moving. Paying people for "not doing anything" when the economy has low demand, if one knows those people are likely to spend that money, and increase aggregate demand, is one thing. Giving money to institutions, when that supports those institutions NOT SPENDING either that interest received or the money they already have in ER, is a whole different story. Who benefits from this

---

17   https://seekingalpha.com/article/3015696-the-interest-rate-on-excess-reserves-is-the-new-fed-funds-rate

IOER? Well clearly the banks and their stockholders should. If the banks began to compete with each other for depositor's money by raising interest on deposits, they could if need be, increase interest on deposits until those rates got close to, or almost all the way to the IOER rate. Then you could say the depositors of the banks would definitely be sharing some of the benefits of IOER. There is certainly a danger, however, that this interest money being "paid for nothing" will lead to an increase in monopoly power, and have the benefits go disproportionately to the wealthy and cause significant increases in inequality.

As with the old system of Monetary Policy, the effect of the new law on the economy will be determined by who benefits from this economic structure that has increased the value of the ER so much. Ultimately, its effect should be judged by what happens to spending, incomes, employment, net production, and by what happens to the standard of living, and quality of life for everyone.

In most of this book I have been attempting to describe Macroeconomic principles that Keynes discovered (prior to IOER), and that, for the most part is what is described in this book, in both preceding and later chapters. I would just like to mention that in order to understand macroeconomics as it exists today, one must modify some of what is contained in this book, to incorporate IOER.

Just to show how different monetary policy can be with IOER, at the time of the writing of this second edition, the required reserve ratio for commercial banks in the United States has been lowered to 0%, that's zero percent!. And yet the IOER has been able to keep lending from being too excessive and lead to a hyperinflation situation.

Fiscal policy, which is also used to increase demand, is direct spending by the government. Fiscal policy is not controlled by the Central Bank, it is usually controlled by the legislature. Monetary or fiscal policy used to stimulate the economy can only increase employment if the economy is at less than full employment. In Keynes' model if the economy is at true full employment and we try to stimulate the economy it would just cause increased prices. In the NAIRU model, if the unemployment level is equal to or less than NAIRU and we try to increase demand by monetary or fiscal policy, we would get excess inflation.

CHAPTER 28
Capital Goods

Economists sometimes refer to investment as meaning spending to purchase something called Capital Goods, and consumption to mean spending to acquire something named Consumption Goods. I discuss that here.

THERE IS A model where the economy is divided up into those who are involved in making what are called "consumption goods" which are intended to be sold and those who are involved in making what are called capital goods which are goods not intended for sale. The first group is commonly referred to by economists as consumption goods workers. The second group is referred to as capital goods workers.

To make this concept understandable in terms of the model in this book I make the condition that capital goods workers are paid by investment spending, that is they are paid by money being used for spending for the first time in the given time period. The capital goods workers include anyone involved in the venture that creates capital goods who earns income from that venture.

I also make the condition that Consumption goods workers are paid their income from out of money earned from sales of consumption goods. Included in those I am calling consumption goods workers is any person who earns income as a result of the production and sales of those consumption goods.

While the totality of the sales of those consumption goods goes completely into the consumption goods workers income, (and that is all the income they get), the income of the consumption goods workers is not enough to pay for the totality of the sales. That is because the consumption goods workers do not spend all of their income, they save some of it. This means that some other source of money must be used to pay for the purchase of that portion of consumption goods not purchased by the consumption workers.

In this scenario, the capital goods workers have gained an income from investment spending. Unlike the product made by the consumption goods workers, the investment goods do not have to be sold. So, nobody's income need be used to buy investment goods, meaning the investment goods worker's income can be used to pay for the rest of the sales of the consumption goods. That will make the economy described in this scenario viable.

Note that the income of the consumption goods workers from this time period was paid for by sale of consumption goods and then part of their income was re-spent to pay for more consumption. That re-spending of consumption goods workers income, to pay for that part of the sales is consumption spending by definition. It is spending paid for our of current income. The income of the capital goods workers was paid for by investment and then out of that income, the capital goods workers paid for the remaining portion of the sales of the consumption goods, the portion the consumption goods workers did not pay for. That spending by the capital goods workers is also consumption spending, since that spending was paid for out of the capital goods workers current income. This means when the consumption goods workers and the capital goods workers spend to purchase consumption goods it is all paid for out of their current income and is categorized as consumption spending.

Using the definition for consumption from chapter 2, all the spending to purchase consumption goods is consumption spending. And in this restricted model any spending to pay for the production of the capital goods is classified as investment spending. That is why capital goods are sometimes called investment goods. It is the paying of the money acquired in a previous time period, that investment spending, that provides income to the capital goods workers, which allows for the extra spending necessary to pay for all the sales of the consumption goods necessary to provide the income paid to the consumption goods workers. It is this investment spending that allows the described economic scenario to be viable.

That is about as clean as I can make this model, so the reader can get a good grasp of it. Capital goods, by the way, are said to mean things like buildings, machines, computers, vehicles, raw materials, inventory, research and development, staff training etc. Mostly when economists talk about capital goods they mean things that facilitate or are directly used in the manufacture of consumption goods.

CAPITAL GOODS

It is important for me to introduce these concepts, because the reality is, that in current economic textbooks, when reference is made to investment spending, which Keynes knew was essential to have a viable economy, the most common explanation is that they are referring to the money paid to produce or purchase capital goods, and that is the only thing considered to be investment spending.

Actually, often the textbooks go one step further because, since the standard teaching is that income and wealth are the same thing, the textbooks will interchange what they call investment, sometimes calling investment the money paid for the capital goods, sometimes calling the investment the capital goods themselves.

I have applied my definition of investment to the above scenario, where investment is spending paid for with money being used for spending for the first time in the given time period, but allowed the restriction that the only spending considered to be investment is the spending to pay for the capital goods. Even working within the confines of that restriction, it would make no sense to have investment be the investment goods themselves. Investment would still have to be the spending to pay the income of the capital goods workers, to give them money to be able to pay for consumption goods, to have this scenario be viable. This investment spending is part of spending and income, it is measured on the income axis. The value of the capital goods produced, which may or may not match the amount of money used to purchase them, is measured on the wealth axis, not on the income axis.

In the most general application of my model, when I refer to sales, it is a measure of the sale of anything, including paying for goods, services, **labor** or any other desired outcome. In that application, for example, when the labor that produces the capital goods is paid, the payment is considered paying for some sales, the sales of their labor by the laborers. Also, in my model, the sales are paid for by both investment spending and consumption spending, not just consumption spending.

In my model, although I realize that some of the goods produced may be sold and some of the goods may not be sold, I do not have to worry so much about what the investment spending pays for as long as some investment spending occurs. (using my definition of investment from chapter 2 of this book). The investment spending can pay for goods, services, labor or any other desired outcome. The consumption spending could pay for anything as well, as long as the spending is paid for out of current income. And the items that are sold could be produced in any time period; past, present or future.

Suppose that I said all the goods are intended to be sold, that is one does not make any distinction between consumption goods and capital goods. In my model it makes no difference. Even if you considered all the workers to be consumption goods workers, you still will need some investment spending to make the economy viable. The pay of the workers who sold their labor to make any product and the pay of the employers who then sold the product will both count as current (gross) income, and in either case the spending could be investment spending or consumption spending.

Not having to make a distinction between what counts as capital goods and what is consumption goods, is an advantage of my model, because trying to specify what is a capital good and what is a consumption good is often an arbitrary decision anyway.

It seems the belief that changes in wealth equals income leads to the belief that one can think of the investment goods as the investment. In my model the investment good is not investment nor is the value of the investment good calculated on the income axis. Believing that the value of any wealth produced as a result of the spending is income leads one to believe that one can have a net income in the macroeconomy. In the macroeconomy, one can have a net wealth production, but as I have shown, if I define investment and consumption as I do in chapter 2 net income will always be zero. Transactions can result in the creation of assets and wealth, but they do not create money, nor do they destroy money. Spending just transfers ownership of money from one person or entity to another. No money is created in that process. For net income to be greater than zero, the series of transactions would have to have created more money. This is not possible, since money can only be created by the central bank. Commerce may result in wealth creation, but it does not result in (base) money creation.

In the limited model where investment spending is limited to paying for capital goods one can make a viable economic model, but I believe that this is too restrictive and that the much broader model I have described is a better model and able to give a more accurate picture of how spending is affecting the economy.

Capital Goods

If one is restricted to only acknowledging as sales, purchases of items produced in the current time period, such as currently produced "consumption goods", then one ignores all sorts of spending and income that affects total demand, including paying for labor, paying for the selling of product made in a different time period, government transfers, charity, etc. All this is discussed in greater detail starting in the next chapter.

At any rate in my model, investment is **any** spending paid for by money acquired as income in a previous time period and being used for spending for the first time in the current time period. It does not have to be paying for capital goods to count as investment. And also, in my model, what qualifies as consumption is any spending paid for out of current income and could include the purchasing of what may commonly be referred to as capital goods.

CHAPTER 29
GDP – THE PRODUCTION APPROACH

GDP stands for "Gross Domestic Product". It is a commonly used macroeconomic term and therefore deserves analysis here in terms of the concepts introduced in this book. The next three chapters are my attempt to do that.

IN ANY INTRODUCTORY or intermediate macroeconomic text book I have seen introduced as irrefutable fact something called "The Fundamental Identity of National Income Accounting", which states the following:

Total production = total expenditure = total income

Students are told it is "true by definition", it's a "tautology."

"In propositional logic, a **tautology** (from the Greek word ταυτολογία) is a propositional formula that is always true. In other words, a tautology cannot be wrong."[18]

Here is a definition for tautology that I feel is more appropriate for the given situation: "Tautology (Rhetoric) In rhetoric, a tautology is an argument which repeats an assertion using different phrasing. The proposition, as stated, is thus logically irrefutable, while obscuring the lack of evidence or valid reasoning supporting the stated conclusion"[19]

In other words, "The fundamental identity of national income accounting" must be true, because it has been defined as being true, even though no definitive evidence is presented to support the statement. This has the effect of making

---

18   https://simple.wikipedia.org/wiki/Tautology_(logic)
19   https://simple.wikipedia.org/wiki/Tautology_(rhetoric)

it impossible to question its validity. This allows it to then be applied as a basis for structuring more economic models, theories, and policy recommendations. It would be a big mistake to structure economic models and theories on this "identity" if it were not true. I assert that this is the case, it is not true, or at least only partially true.

I agree that total expenditure (spending) equals total income; the definitions in my model are explicit about this. I do not agree that either of those things equals total production. In my model, income and production are calculated on different axes, income is on the income axis and production is accounted for on the wealth axis. I have already discussed this repeatedly and in detail in previous chapters and will not repeat it here.

The standard economics textbook approach of GDP is to give three different definitions of GDP and set them equal to each other. They have a definition which is based on collecting data on what has been produced, in the given time period (production approach) and a definition supposedly based on spending in the current time period (expenditure approach), and a definition based on data they collect about incomes (income approach).

In analyzing each category, I hope to describe these 3 definitions of GDP in the terminology I have been using in the model presented in this book. Specifically, I will be focusing on where these definitions are describing wealth, and where they are describing income. In analyzing these definitions, I will make suggestions as to modifications needed to allow the production approach to represent an accounting of wealth production, to allow the expenditure approach to be an accounting of spending, and to allow the income approach to accurately describe all income. I will later use these modified definitions when analyzing models, assertions, and policy recommendations that are derived in part based on the definitions of GDP as standardly taught.

The Production Approach to GDP

There are usually very intelligent and well thought out descriptions of how to calculate the amount of production in an economy during a given time period. I believe, reading the descriptions of the way the production approach to GDP is calculated in any of the standard college macroeconomics textbooks can provide one with pretty solid and well thought out descriptions of wealth produced by human efforts, wealth that can be reasonably easily valued in terms of the amount of money it would sell for, at the time of production. The production approach as normally presented does account for, i.e., subtract off, any wealth depleted as part of the production process, like intermediate products. It does not appear to account for wealth depleted outside of the production process. I might like to see, added to the list, those things that are not so easily valued in monetary terms, or things created by nature. The production approach to GDP describes current production, that is, it includes only that which is produced in the current time period.

I want to emphasize that the production approach to GDP is a calculation that occurs on the wealth axis, not the income axis. Whether the formula includes all possible contributors to net production or only some, each element in it, is all still something that is added to or subtracted from total wealth. The accounting of each element in the production approach to GDP occurs on the wealth axis.

The next two categories are the income approach to GDP and the expenditure approach to GDP. Unlike the production approach to GDP both are, or at least in my view should be, measures of income and so I will analyze them to see how accurate these descriptions are as measures of total income in the macroeconomy.

CHAPTER 30
GDP – The Income Approach

LET US LOOK at the income approach to GDP. Since it is labeled the "income approach" I will be trying to determine what counts as income in the private domestic economy. This means I will not be adding the change in value of wealth to the total. Change in value of wealth is accounted for on the wealth axis, not the income axis.

The way standard economics textbooks typically structure the income approach to GDP is to add these things to the total: salaries and benefits, interest income, proceeds from the sale of goods and services. Typically, not included as income are transfer payments received from the government, interest the government pays on its debt to our country's individuals and firms, and charitable giving.

All of these things mentioned should be included as part of the total income because they involve the transfer of ownership of money from one individual or entity to another for a purpose. In all these cases the spending is targeted at an entity whose income becomes part of the total income for the private domestic economy, and therefore, should be included in the income approach to GDP. More complicated to explain is how taxes and something called "net foreign factor income" affect income.

Taxes

First I would like to address the issue of whether the income approach to GDP should count as the income earned in the private domestic economy only or if it should include income earned in the private domestic economy plus income earned by the government.

Government income is generally considered revenue from taxes. If one were to see GDP as a measure of spending and income, then taxes would be a transfer of ownership of money from the private sector to the government for a purpose. A toll is a tax, and you have just paid for the service of being able to cross that bridge or use that road. Similarly, property taxes pay for being allowed to live in that town and benefit from the towns services and infrastructure. Social Security taxes pay for the ability to be able get income when we either become retired or disabled. Income taxes and sales taxes pay for all the benefits we and our society gain from what the state, local or federal government provides. In short, taxes do count as spending because they are transfers of ownership of money for a purpose, with the purposes including causing those outcomes just mentioned to occur.

In some descriptions of income approach to GDP some taxes such as Sales taxes are included in GDP, but many other taxes are not. In my model, you can't do that. If the income approach to GDP is going to be a pure measure of income, you must include all spending and not pick and choose. This means if one is going to include government income in GDP then one must include all spending that causes income to government recipients, which certainly means including all taxes but also means including other spending, which I discuss more of in the next chapter.

It is my view that including all taxes and other things that generate income for a government in our expression for the income approach to GDP would cause it to be a radical departure from what is usually included in standard definition. The standard definition is closer to what one would get by just including income occurring in the private domestic economy. Therefore, my modified definition of income approach to GDP will not include government income but will be strictly a measure of private domestic income. By a similar argument, and because in the macroeconomy spending and income are equal, my modified version of the expenditure approach to GDP will also be solely a measure of private domestic spending (=private domestic income).

GDP – The Income Approach

Net Foreign Factor Income

Net foreign factor income is defined as income our domestic firms and individuals earn abroad, minus income foreign entities earn here. While the income approach to GDP, Gross Domestic Product, includes all income earned by anyone in the domestic economy, adding net foreign factor income to GDP converts GDP into something called GNP, Gross National Product. GNP is formed by taking GDP and adding to it any income gained by domestic entities in a foreign country, and subtracting off income earned in the domestic country by people or entities who are from foreign countries. GNP is income domestic people or entities earn, no matter where they earn it, and GDP is income earned in the domestic economy, no matter who earned it. In the United States, GNP just redefines what we call our economy from what happens in America to what happens to Americans.

So, choices have to be made about what we are going to call our economy. Do we just count any income earned in this country no matter who earns it, whether a domestic entity or a foreign entity? Or do we only count income earned by domestic firms and individuals, whether they earn it in this country or a foreign country? Or perhaps you could even define as your private domestic economy any transactions that occur in the world using your domestic currency?

These are difficult questions and the analysis is further complicated by the fact that we have multinational corporations that cannot be easily identified as belonging to any particular country. It is complicated by an international financial structure that allows transactions to occur all over the world involving individuals and firms from many different countries. This makes it difficult to determine, not only what countries the participants in the transaction belong to, but even to say in what country the transaction is occurring. In fact, since these transactions are occurring in many different currencies interacting via exchange rates, we are really utilizing a worldwide money supply.

Regardless of these complications, I believe adapting the concepts covered in this book to an analysis of the worldwide economy, with multiple currencies and exchange rates. can be done. I leave it to the chapters on international trade at the end of this book to present an approach that allows us to resolve some of these issues.

GDP – The Income Approach

In analyzing the concept called GDP, the model presented in this book requires us to include all of the following as income, in the income approach to GDP. Included are salaries and benefits (the money paid for benefits is most often paid directly to the benefit provider, but it is still spending and income) , interest income, proceeds from sale of goods and services, transfer payments received from the government, interest the government pays on its debt to our country's individuals and firms, charitable giving and money foreigners pay to recipients in the domestic country for exports.

◈◈◈

I would add that since loans are a transfer of ownership of money from one entity or another they should be added to total income. This may sound odd but if you understand that the income referred to is gross income, then it becomes more comprehensible.

◈◈◈

Note that transferring ownership of a non-monetary asset in exchange for another non-monetary asset is a barter. Barter always plays a small roll in our economy and has been ignored in my descriptions mostly for that reason. A barter introduces the utilization of product as currency and complicates the picture. If all we want to do is account for how much the barter adds to total spending then one can look at is an equivalent monetary transaction.

For example, person 1 trades item A appraised at 20 dollars to person 2 for item B. This is equivalent to person 2 giving 20 dollars to person 1 for item A and then having person 1 give the 20 dollars back to person 2 for item B and that counts as 40 dollars of income. If a private domestic entity donated an item of wealth to another private domestic entity, that would be equivalent to having the donator give money to the recipient of the donation who then gives it back to the donator in exchange for the item. Both of these entities would be considered to have received "gross" income in the private domestic economy in such a situation. If the government possessed an item of wealth and gave it to some person or entity as a benefit, this would be equivalent to the government giving money to the beneficiary and the beneficiary giving back the money in exchange for the item of wealth. If the item were assessed to be valued as 10 dollars then that would count as 10 dollars private domestic income, and 10 dollars government income. Since only private domestic income counts

GDP – The Income Approach

as part of my modified definition of the income approach to GDP, then GDP would have increased by 10 dollars.

But as discussed at the end of Chapter 16 the real way to add barter transactions would be to assume at least one item was functioning as a currency and to multiply the number of units of that item that exist by the velocity of spending of that item. Then use the exchange rate between that item and the dominant currency (the average cost of that item in terms of dollars for example) to find out the amount of spending use of that item as a currency added to the economy. Actually, one could do that for as many possible barter items as one wanted and add their contribution to the totals for spending in the given economy. But since the velocity of spending of barter items is infinitesimal for the most part, I have chosen to view barters as making an insignificant contribution to total spending and income and, for the most part, to ignore barters in my discussions of GDP.

CHAPTER 31
GDP – The Expenditure Approach

THE EXPENDITURE APPROACH to **GDP** is the approach that is most like Keynes' expression where **Y = I + C**. When presented in textbooks, normally GDP is designated as **Y**, however, because of the national accounting identity, it is generally assumed **Y** equals both income and production. In Keynes' expression **Y** is a measure of income only, not a measure of production.

The way the equation for the expenditure approach to GDP is defined in standard textbooks, it makes it partly a measure of income and partially a measure of production. To show how this **Y** that is described by expenditure approach to GDP is not the same as **Keynes' Y = I + C** one has to look at each element one at a time. I will show how they are not the same and how the definitions of the components of the expenditure approach to GDP needs to be changed so that it is essentially the same thing as **Keynes' Y = I + C**. This is important because the expressions for GDP cannot be both an expression of production and income at the same time. I believe the production approach to GDP should stand alone as a measure of new production, but that the income and expenditure approaches to GDP must be pure measures of income, not a mixed bag.

The expenditure approach to GDP is typically defined by this expression

$Y = I_p + G + X - M + C$

Y = income or gross domestic product

I_p = private investment

G = government investment or purchases

GDP – The Expenditure Approach

C = consumption

X = exports

M = imports

The term I_p is used here instead of **I** to distinguish the I_p in the formula for GDP from the **I** in Keynes' formula **Y = I + C**.

X - M is usually put in parenthesis like **(X-M)** or referred to as "Net Exports" or **NX**. I do not put them in parenthesis for reasons that will become clear later. The expression **(X - M)** is referred to as a trade surplus if **X>M** and **(X - M)** is positive or as a trade deficit if **X<M** and **(X - M)** is negative.

I have seen where Taxes are included in expressions for spending as being subtracted off and reducing the spending. If this were added as a component of the expenditure approach to GDP then the expression would become:

$Y = I_p + G - T + X - M + C$

Where **T** = taxes

In analyzing all these elements I will include **T** in the discussion for completeness. So we will go through all the elements of this expression one by one:

$Y = C + I_p + G - T + X - M$

I will be analyzing these elements to see to where this equation for the expenditure approach to GDP may represent income, and where it may actually represent something that should be calculated on the wealth axis. We will also discuss what modifications are needed to make it purely a calculation of income, not wealth.

Private Investment I_p

What I call investment and what the standard teaching for GDP defines as investment are different things. For the expenditure approach to represent private domestic income, I need to have I_p represent investment spending by private domestic entities directed at other private domestic entities. Consumption spending by private domestic entities aimed at other private domestic entities will be categorized as part of C. My model defines I_p as spending by private domestic entities to purchase labor or goods or services or other outcomes, from other private domestic entities, and have that spending be paid for by money being put into income for the first time in the given time period.

Contrast that definition with the commonly taught definitions. Here is a typical standard definition from Investopedia website:

"What is an 'Investment'?"

"An investment is an <u>asset</u> or item that is purchased with the hope that it will generate income or will appreciate in the future. In an economic sense, an **investment** is the purchase of goods that are not consumed today but are used in the future to create wealth. In finance, an **investment** is a monetary asset purchased with the idea that the asset will provide income in the future or appreciate and be sold at a higher price"[20]

Let us start with the main differences between the definitions of investment in that quote and my own definition. I say investment is spending, including spending to buy an asset. In the first sentence they say investment is the asset itself, not what was paid to acquire the asset, but the actual asset. I say the investment would be the actual spending, the transfer of ownership of money, done to purchase an asset, not the asset itself.

Then in the next sentence they say that investment is the "PURCHASE of goods not consumed today but used in the future to create wealth". In this sentence they have totally changed their definition of investment from the value of a piece of wealth, the asset, to the SPENDING to acquire the asset. My definition would allow that interpretation, provided the money used to pay for the asset was money being put into income for the first time in the given time period.

Remember in a previous chapter how I talked about capital goods, how spending on capital goods could subsidize the income of people who made their income from sales of consumption goods, so there is enough for all the income earners to spend some and save some, and still pay for all the sales? This is why I brought that up, because a lot of economists, and even Keynes at times, look at investment as being spending pay for capital goods. That is the explanation for why capital goods are sometimes referred to as investment goods. Unfortunately, probably in part because they equate income and production, economists began to look at investment as the capital goods themselves, not the spending to acquire the capital goods.

---

20   https://www.investopedia.com/terms/i/investment.asp

GDP – The Expenditure Approach

I would like to note that it does not matter if the private spending is paying the income of a capital goods worker, paying the income of a consumption goods worker, or paying for any other desired outcome. As long as the private spending is paid for by money being used for spending for the first time in the given time period, it is part of I_p, private investment spending.

In the next sentence in the quote they go back to calling the asset itself the investment when they say, "an investment is a monetary asset.", which pretty much proves my point that economists view the paying for the asset as identical to the asset itself.

The way investment is taught in standard textbooks, not all of what I call investment would be allowed to be classified that way. For example, some of what my model would put into I_p, the standardly taught model would classify as consumption (C). An example would be money be used for spending for the first time in the given time period to pay for "consumption goods", so called final products intended for sale. **My model** would have to include as part of I_p, **any** private spending that is paid for out of money being put into income for the first time in the time period. This might include things not usually thought of as being spending that led to a "product" and increased GDP, such as spending to pay for things like charity, which produces outcomes I have discussed elsewhere that can be considered part of our total wealth (I sometimes refer to charity as private transfers to make them analogous to government transfers).

Further, my definition of investment does not require that it only include spending done for the purpose of earning a personal monetary return such as acquiring or increasing the value of an asset that will gain in monetary value. As long as the private spending is paid for out of money that is entering income for the first time it would count as part of I_p. This is important because if GDP is going to represent all spending, all income, that is, all transfers of ownership of money, then all spending has to be accounted for in the available categories.

All the spending that I have specified as qualifying to be counted as private investment is part of **Keynes' I** in the expression **Y = I + C**. But I_p does not account for all the spending that will qualify as being part of **Keynes' I**.

A critique of this description that I might face at this juncture of my presentation of GDP could come from those believing that if something is going be included in the expenditure approach to GDP it must have some production directly attached to the spending. That criticism would be connected to the belief that GDP must be a measure of production. Since the term Gross Domestic "Product" includes the word product, then some would interpret that as meaning it must be a measure of production. I would prefer to eliminate this complication by calling the expenditure approach something other than GDP, But since I believe that the expenditure approach to GDP was derived from or at least strongly influenced by **Keynes' Y = I + C**, then I feel I need to keep calling it the "Expenditure Approach to Gross Domestic Product", so we don't lose that connection. The connection I want to be able to make, which has importance in looking at macroeconomic models that use the concept to GDP, is that, like **Y = I + C**, the expenditure approach to GDP should be a measure of spending, not a measure of wealth. My modifications are intended to accomplish that, that is, to make the expenditure approach to GDP be a pure measure of spending and income, not a measure of production.

Before I leave the category of private investment I would like to talk about another difference in my model and GDP as taught. That is the issue of intermediate products. The short explanation is that spending does not get counted as part of the standard explanation of GDP it you are paying for "intermediate products". Intermediate products are not "final products" but will, after more production phases, become part of a final product. This is an attempt to make the income in GDP be "net income", and at the same time it is an attempt to equate the value of the final product with income. This concept is best explained using an example:

A unit of product in this scenario will be enough to make one loaf of bread as the end product. Suppose a farmer pays 1 dollar per unit to workers to grow wheat. The farmer sells the wheat to a flour mill for 2 dollars per unit. The mill makes flour and sells it to the baker for 3 dollars per unit. And the baker makes a loaf of bread and sells it for 4 dollars per unit. Gross income, i.e., total spending equals 1 + 2 + 3 + 4 = 10 dollars per loaf of bread produced, but the final product is worth only 4 dollars. In the standard way expenditure approach to GDP is taught, they only consider what is paid for the end product to count as part of income. They do not count any income earned for making what they call "intermediate products". This is perfectly appropriate if the expenditure approach to GDP were to describe the value of production in the given time period. As I am modifying the expenditure approach to be a measure of gross spending and income, and since **Keynes' Y = I + C**, is a measure of gross income, spending for intermediate products must be included as part of I_p, if it qualifies as investment spending by the definition given for investment in chapter two, or consumption if it meets the criteria for consumption in the same chapter. In the example given, the gross income that occurs as a result of making a loaf of bread is 10 dollars, not 4 dollars.

GDP – The Expenditure Approach

The reality is that often what qualifies as being called an intermediate product is not easy to determine. Is the food the final product or is the person it feeds the final product. Or is the bus that person was able to help build because they had enough food to eat the final product. Or is it the bus when it is combined with fuel and can run the final product, or is the people being transported on that bus the final product, like the school janitor riding the bus to work, or is the clean, well maintained school the janitor produces the final product, or is it the teacher using that clean classroom to teach the final product, or is the educated student the final product. or is it the educated student designing a new tv the final product, or is the combination of the tv with the cable service the final product, and so on and so on. Intermediate products can be difficult to define. But more importantly, in macroeconomics, when one is talking about income, one is talking about gross income, so all income earned in the production process, gets counted as part of Keynes' **Y**.

Let us go to the next element of $Y = I_p + G - T + C + X - M$

G GOVERNMENT SPENDING

In standard teaching, **G** means government spending. In the standard description they include government spending on goods and services needed to run the government, and also government spending paid to support producing and maintaining public capital goods. **G** includes all government spending, including, paying for infrastructure production and maintenance, but also **G** includes paying for schools, law enforcement, medical care etc.

What is excluded from **G** in the standard model is what are referred to as government transfers like unemployment, food stamps, social security etc. Since this is the transfer of ownership of money for a purpose, in my model it is part of spending and income, and therefore must be included in the expenditure approach to GDP if it is going to be a true measure of all income. Therefore, I include the government transfers as part of **G**.

As a technical point, I categorize all government spending as part of Keynes' investment, not Keynes' consumption in our calculation of private domestic income. Since any **government income** would be categorized as spending directed at the government, then that income does not count as income occurring in the private domestic economy. Since I have defined the expenditure approach to GDP as a calculation of private domestic income, government spending cannot be considered consumption spending in the private domestic economy, because to qualify to be called consumption spending, the spending must be paid for by money owned by private domestic entities that was earned as income in the current time period. This is not the case with money used for government spending, since money being used for spending by the government is money the government owns, not a private entity. Since all spending must be categorizable as either Keynes' consumption spending or Keynes' investment spending, and since this spending cannot be categorized as Keynes' consumption spending then it must be categorized as Keynes' investment spending. The fact is, it might be money that is hopping back and forth between being owned by the government and private entities but we really don't know when it was acquired or from whom, so I find it provides for a consistent model if we just count all government spending aimed at entities in the private economy to be considered as part of Keynes' Investment. Allowing for the classification of government spending as being part of Keynes' investment spending also ensures that this spending will be included in the elements for GDP, as all spending aimed at private domestic entities must be.

Another way to look at this is using the savings equals investment identity. Any money the government does **not** pay to some entity in the private domestic economy will not exist at the end of the given time period as savings owned by some private entity and will NOT be added to the savings that is the preservation of investment. But any money the government **does** pay to private entities **will** exist and be owned by someone in the private domestic economy at the end of the given time period and become part of the (private) savings that is the preservation of investment. (That is, unless it was later removed from the private domestic economy by taxes or some other means before the end of the given time period). Since that is part of the savings that equals investment, then it must logically follow that government spending should be considered investment, i.e., part of Keynes' I. That is another reason why government spending is best characterized as investment spending, part of **Keynes' I**. In my model, when modifying expenditure approach to GDP to be a true measure of income, G will always be considered part of **Keynes' I**.

In a later chapter I discuss a way one could combine private and government domestic economies into one, but here we are looking at the expenditure approach to GDP which is solely a measure of private domestic income.

$Y = I_p + G - T + C + X - M$

Next we look at T, i.e., taxes

GDP is a measure of private income, it does not include government **income**. Taxes are spending by private sector entities targeted at becoming income for the government. Taxes are a transfer of ownership of that money from the private sector to the government. In the expenditure approach equation for GDP, taxes are sometimes considered as changing the value of certain elements, being something that is subtracted off the total for private income. As it turns out, it is not valid to include taxes in that way, as part of the calculation of total private domestic spending. If the expenditure approach to GDP equation is going to be considered a measure of gross income, it is incorrect to have the expression **-T** be part of it. Here is why:

After the tax money has become owned by the government it is no longer available to be used for spending by entities in the private economy. One might assume that because that money is no longer available to be used for private spending that it has reduced private spending by the same amount and should be subtracted off the income, meaning that taxes should remain an element in GDP. That is incorrect. This is because the effect of taxes cannot be to undo spending that has already occurred. In the macroeconomy, spending is a measure of gross spending. Once a given amount of gross spending has been deemed to occur, there is no negative gross spending that can occur to reverse previous spending. (Gross) spending either occurs or it doesn't occur. There is no negative gross spending. One cannot subtract taxes off the totals for spending that has already occurred. The values the elements of GDP have taken, such as **I_p, and C, or even G** are measures of spending that has already occurred. The real effect of taxes is to influence the amount of spending that will occur, not to reverse spending that has already occurred. The **effect** of taxes is not shown as an extra element in the formula for GDP. The effect of taxes is to influence what the values of **I_p, G, C and even X** will end up being, not to subtract off what they already are.

We do not know what effect taxes will have on total spending, however. If taxes were taken from money that was not intended to be spent, then it may have no effect on the value of the components of GDP. If taxes did prevent private investment spending from occurring, spending that would otherwise have happened but for the taxes, then they have stopped that money from being put into income at all, and this may affect the value other elements of GDP end up being. Taxes may remove money that has already been put into spending, that has already become acquired as someone's income, and cut short any further spending of that money. In either case, we do not know how, or if it will affect total spending and total income. This is not only because we do not know how much taxes will affect the total initial investment spending, (part of Keynes' I), be we also don't know how taxes would have affected further re-spending of that money (Keynes' Consumption). For example, it could have been that had that money not been removed from the private economy it still would have been spent multiple times over, in which case the reduction in total income would be greater than the amount of the taxes. Or it could be that none of that tax money would have been used for any spending in the given time period, in which case that portion of the taxes may have no effect on reducing total income. Also, since taxes are revenue for the government, taxes collected could affect the level of government spending **G** in that if more taxes are collected it might make more government spending possible. So, the reality is, one does not know if taxes will result in a lot less spending, a little less spending, no change in spending, or even contribute to causing more spending. Taxes certainly can influence the amount of spending, but they should not be included as an element in the formula for the expenditure approach to GDP as subtracted off total spending. There should not be a **-T** in the formula for GDP.

The effect of taxes on that part of savings that is the preservation of investment is different, however. Taxes taking money out of the private sector means that any sum of money that had become used for spending in the private sector will not remain in the private sector. That will reduce the amount of money, that have been put into spending as part of Keynes' I, that ends up preserved as savings in the private sector. That money will still exist, just be "saved" in the government's pocket instead of being owned by someone in the private sector. Overall the Savings equals Investment identity holds, it is just that some of that saved money is not existing in private hands any more, it is saved in government hands.

The contribution of taxes to the savings equals investment identity changes the equation of the relationship between savings and investment (not including net production) so the saving equals investment identity becomes: "Private Savings equals Keynes' Investment minus any taxes paid for by current income". Taxes that prevented investment from occurring in the first place (i.e., taxes that remove money from the private sector before it gets used for any spending), do not affect the savings equals investment formula because that money was never part of investment and never contributed to any income and would not be part of what one considers the savings that is the preservation of investment. If, however, taxes take money that has already been used for spending in the private domestic economy, (in the given time period) and cause that money to leave the private economy and be owned by the government, then the savings equals investment identity is affected. At the end of that time period, that money would no longer exist in the private economy and will not be owned by some private entity. Therefore, that part of the money used for spending would not be around to count as part of the savings. That is why the equation for savings (not including the part of savings

GDP – The Expenditure Approach

that is net production) becomes "private domestic savings equals investment minus taxes paid for out of current income".

There is something related to taxes that should be discussed here. Taxes are income to the government. They are spending by the private sector directed at the government as the recipient of that spending. There is another thing that I include as "spending by the private sector directed at and creating income for the government". In my model, the government borrowing from the private sector counts as income for the government. That is, it counts as spending by the private sector to buy an asset from the government (Treasury note, savings bond whatever). In that case the government is selling a loan obligation to the private sector. The spending by the private sector to buy that asset becomes income for the government. However, since it is spending directed at the government it is income for the government and not the private sector. Therefore, it is not counted as part of the expenditure approach to GDP. Its effect on GDP is similar to taxes, that is, it influences the values the other components of GDP take, but the amount of borrowing by the government is not an element in my modified expenditure approach equation for GDP. The contribution government borrowing makes to the total value of GDP is the effect is has on what value I_p, **G, C and X** end up being.

The difference between taxes and government borrowing is how Government spending **G** is affected and the effect that has on the multiplier. With taxes the government is free to spend the money how it wishes. With borrowing, in the future, not only will the money have to be paid back to the private lenders (bondholders etc.), but interest will be paid to them as well. The investors in government bonds will, on the average, tend to be wealthier. This means that when the government is paying off bonds with interest one would expect the multiplier effect of money being paid to those wealthier bond holders will be lower than the multiplier effect of other government spending in general. This would be expected to be true because one would expect that a larger fraction of the other government spending would be targeted at programs that benefit less wealthy people.

Of course this government borrowing could also affect the savings that is preservation of investment and so that formula would become:

"private domestic savings equals investment minus taxes paid for out of current income and minus purchase of debt obligations from the government paid for out of current income"

In fact if loans are part of government revenue and can affect the savings equals investment identity then we should also consider of things that can affect the savings equals investment identity. Sometimes the government sells things of value to private entities even though these payments are really purchases not taxes. That too, like taxes, will be spending by entities in the private domestic economy causing creating income for the government. That money too, will be money leaving the private domestic economy and will no longer be owned by entities in the private domestic economy. Therefore that money also will no longer be available to be considered as "saved" in the private domestic economy.

Therefore the savings equals investment formula would become "private domestic savings equals investment minus taxes paid for out of current income and minus purchase of debt obligations from the government paid for out of current income and minus any sales of items made by the government to private domestic entities paid for out of current income"

As we can see this expression is getting very complicated and unwieldy. For simplicity I propose that, (even though it may not be the most accurate nomenclature), in this discussion of GDP, any spending from the private domestic entities directed at recipients in the government, be classified under the heading of, and included in the total value of, **Taxes.** That is when I use the word Taxes in determining the savings that is the preservation of investment, I will mean that to include actual taxes, loans to the government by the private sector, and any other items the private sector may pay the government to acquire.

This will allow us to use the more simplified version of savings equals investment:

"private domestic savings equals investment minus taxes paid for out of current income"

I am spending so much time on this savings that equals the preservation of investment because I want to emphasize that the money supply can be identified, defined, and followed through its chain of spending. And to emphasize that money is not created or destroyed by commerce, and the money supply can only be changed by the central bank, at least legally.

One of the benefits of producing this modified version of the expenditure approach to GDP is to be able to identify what can be consider Keynes' I and what

GDP – THE EXPENDITURE APPROACH

can be considered Keynes' C. This will allow us to get an idea of which elements are playing what role in determining the multiplier effect, for example.

As I understand it, Keynes viewed the multiplier effect as manifesting through a private sector response to investment spending, and then only when at less than full employment.

Once at full employment Keynes believed that one could focus on maximizing the efficiency of utilization of resources so as to maximize production. To some, maximizing production means letting the private sector function unencumbered. I believe that there are certain things that only government can properly provide. It is my opinion that maximizing efficiency, production, quality of life and standard of living, requires a combination of private and government spending along with properly designed and implemented laws and regulations.

At any rate, by analyzing GDP and understanding the place and function of each element of GDP, in terms of what counts as investment, and what counts as consumption, and how to properly calculate the (total) gross spending and income, may help one get a better grip on the effect spending decisions of private and government entities have on the overall economy

As an interesting sidelight, if expenditure approach to GDP were a measure of wealth and not income, it would still not be valid to include taxes in the expression for GDP, as being subtracted off. If the accounting of I_p, **G**, **C** and **X** are all measures of production which has already occurred then for the amount of taxes to be subtracted off, taxes must reverse some of that production. While it is true that in this imaginary scenario, that taxes could influence the economy so that some of that production does not occur in the first place, taxes do not eliminate any production that has already occurred. So even if the expenditure approach to GDP were a measure of production, you still would not subtract taxes off the total.

I have discussed in detail the role of taxes in GDP and have concluded that the expenditure approach equation for GDP cannot validly include the term **-T**, i.e., minus taxes, as an element.

Because of how we must handle taxes this $Y = I_p + G - T + C + X - M$, the expenditure approach to GDP becomes:

GDP – The Expenditure Approach

$$Y = I_p + G + C + X - M$$

In addition, as regards savings, if we exclude net production, the expression for savings in the private sector becomes:

Private Savings equals Keynes' Investment minus any taxes paid for from current income.

Moving to other elements of

$$Y = I_p + G + C + X - M$$

We next look at exports minus imports, (X – M), also referred to as NX which stands for net exports.

This category may seem straightforward and obvious especially to people who have been seeing it mentioned in economic textbooks and papers and economics statistics for years. **X** stands for exports and is spending by a foreign entity aimed at becoming income in the domestic economy. The spending to pay for the exports, must be considered investment spending (part of Keynes's I). It cannot be consumption because to be consumption it must be paid for by money acquired as part of private domestic income. Since the money used for buying the domestic economy's exports is paid by some entity belonging to a foreign country, then the spending to pay for the exports is NOT spending paid for using money a private domestic entity received as income in the current time period, which is what would be required for that spending to count as consumption. Therefore, spending to pay for exports will be classified as investment spending, like government spending is.

When the export is purchased the money **X** is received as income, and since our expenditure approach to GDP is only counting income in the private domestic economy then **X** is an accounting of spending by a foreign entity to purchase an export from a private domestic entity. For our modified version of GDP **X** will only include payments to private domestic entities and not government entities. And it is also included as part of **Keynes'** Investment spending.

M stands for the amount of spending paid for imports. Imports are paid for by transferring ownership of money from domestic private entities to foreign entities. It is spending targeted at creating income for a foreign entity. It is not calculated as directly affecting income in the private domestic economy.

Government interacting with the foreign economy, that is, government getting paid for exporting items to a foreign country or government paying of imported items, would not change the calculation for income in the private domestic economy either.

Private domestic spending to pay for imports does not get subtracted off of GDP. Like taxes, the effect of spending to purchase imports is not to undo domestic spending that has already occurred, but to affect the amount of spending that will occur. Again, we do not know exactly how this spending of imports will affect domestic spending. It may reduce it a lot, a little, or not at all. And it is even possible that the imports will spark more domestic spending. The items imported may be raw materials that lead to more jobs and production and more spending. Or just the presence of the imports may spark desire for other products and lead to more production and jobs and spending, or just the re-selling of the imports may draw out extra investment spending or consumption spending. We do not know the effect of imports on total income, but we do know that, like taxes, the effect of spending on imports gets baked into the value of the other elements of GDP. There should not be a separate term **-M,** (i.e., minus imports) in the expenditure approach equation for GDP.

Also, even if one considered the expenditure approach to GDP to be a measure of production, (which I do not), then imports still cannot validly be an element of the equation, for the same reasons taxes cannot.

If we ignore the portion of savings that is net production, the effect of imports on savings is similar to taxes. Any money acquired from current income used to pay for imports will be subtracted from private domestic savings. Any spending using money that had not already been used for spending in the current time period will not have been part of domestic spending at all and therefore, would not gave been part of the savings that is the preservation of investment spending.

The savings equal investment identity, as applied to the private domestic economy, when imports are considered, becomes **Savings equals Keynes' investment minus any spending to acquire imports paid for out of current income.**

The savings equals investment identity, as applied to the private domestic economy when **both taxes and imports** are considered becomes:

Savings equals Keynes' investment minus any taxes or imports paid for by money acquired as current private domestic income.

There is one thing I should mention about the relationship of savings and imports. When calculating what is not left of that money being used for spending in the domestic economy, we are not just concerned with the money paid for items that will physically be transported to the domestic country, and not just services utilized by entities in the domestic country. Any money spent to pay for something acquired from a foreign country will be money no longer available for domestic spending. That means we have included spending to acquire items that stay in a foreign country as something that reduces the savings that is the preservation of investment. Even though that money still exists, since it has gone to a foreign entity, it is no longer owned by anyone in the private domestic economy, at the end of the given time period.

The equation for expenditure approach for GDP should therefore not include the element minus taxes (**-T**) or the element minus imports (**-M**). We now understand that the equation for GDP should be $Y = I_p + G + X + C$ with the idea that taxes and imports affect the values of the other variables, but the effect is contained in the values I_p, **G, X,** and **C** take, they are not subtracted off the value they have become.

$Y = I_p + G + C + X$

Next we look at C

In the standardly taught definition of GDP, **C** stands for consumption. The standard definition of consumption describes consumption as purchasing of goods or services that are **produced in the current time period.** Further, students are taught that the money used for paying for that consumption spending can come from money acquired in a previous time period and newly put into spending and causing income, OR it can come from money that has been acquired as income in the current time period. In other words, what they call consumption, by my definitions, would be sometimes classified as consumption and other times classified as investment.

So, the standard teaching of this expenditure approach to GDP says consumption means two things, it **only** includes purchases of goods or services **created in the current time period,** but it can be paid for by money acquired in any time period.

GDP – The Expenditure Approach

(At least here, what they call consumption is referring to the spending itself, and not the item purchased, whereas in their description of private investment there was some confusion as to whether the investment is the item itself or the amount of the spending needed to purchase it).

I have an **opposite interpretation** for what C needs to be to correlate with **Keynes' C**:

First of all, in the model described in this book, C needs to be restricted to that spending which is paid for out of **current** (private domestic) **income**, and second, consumption includes purchases of things (goods, services, labor, any other desired outcome) **produced in any time period**, and produced **by anyone**, (including, by the way, things produced by nature), as long as the recipient of the payment is some person or entity in the private domestic economy. Consumption paid for by money not earned as part of current income, counts as part of **Keynes' I**, i.e., I_p, it is not part of **Keynes' C**. My definitions make totally clear what spending is investment and what is consumption.

In comparing Keynes' equation **Y = I + C** as it applies to the private domestic economy in the expenditure approach to GDP, as modified in this chapter, then the C in the GDP equation has the same meaning as **Keynes' C** whereas **Keynes' I = I_p + G + X**.

Y = Keynes' I + Keynes' C becomes Y = (I_p + G + X) + C

The Modified Expenditure Approach to GDP is GDP = I_p + G + X + C

This makes this modified expenditure approach to GDP completely correlate to Keynes' **Y = I + C**, and be solely a measure of private domestic income.

This concludes my analysis of the expenditure approach to GDP and my comments on what modifications need to be made in collecting our data so that it will be a true measure of total spending = demand = gross income.

Now that I have defined what **Keynes' I** would be in our modified definition for the expenditure approach to GDP the expressions for the **savings that is preservation of investment becomes:**

When taxes but not trade is considered:

Savings equals Keynes' I minus any taxes paid for out of current income, that is **Savings equals (I_p+G) minus any taxes paid for out of current income.**

Similarly, the savings equal investment identity when trade is considered becomes:

Savings equals (I_p+G+X) minus any spending to acquire imports paid for out of current income.

The savings equals investment identity when both taxes and imports are considered becomes:

Savings equals (I_p+G+X) minus any taxes or imports paid for by money acquired as part of current income.

So here, both taxes paid for out of current income and imports paid for out of current income get subtracted off of savings, but no part of **T** or **M** gets subtracted off the expression for GDP.

Note that if taxes or imports are paid for out of money that has not been put into spending at all yet (targeted at private domestic entities) and has not been received as part of current private domestic income, that money will not be subtracted off the savings that is preservation of investment. The reason is that the spending was targeted at recipients that were outside of the private domestic economy, such as foreign entities or the government, but since the money used was never received as part of anyone's private domestic income, it would never have become part of Keynes' investment and would not be eligible to be part of the savings that is preservation of investment.

The money that was put into spending as investment, is preserved, even in an economy that interacts with government and interacts with foreign economies. It is just that some of that money may be owned by the government or foreign entities, and not by entities in the private domestic economy.

The total amount of money does not change unless the central bank changes it. In a closed economy that only includes interactions between the private domestic economy and the government, the total amount of money cannot change. This means that the total net income, if adding the net income of the government to the net income of the private economy, will always be zero. If it is not zero, that is because the central bank has changed the amount of money in the money supply.

That may confuse things and make it harder to do an accounting because the central bank is always increasing and decreasing the money supply. Perhaps to someone doing an accounting of the macroeconomy somewhere this might make it look like commerce alone can cause net income to be different than zero. It cannot. In fact, if we account for all the transactions that occur and combine the net incomes of the private domestic economy, the government, and all the foreign economies, the only way net income can be different than zero is due to creation or destruction of money being used for spending, and the only ones who have the legal right to do that are the Central Banks.

CHAPTER 32
Calculating Different Multipliers Using Various Inputs Looking at the Effect of a Change from a Baseline

*You could use the idea of a multiplier to determine the effect of changes in any sort of input that might affect the total **income**. In fact, you could use the idea of a multiplier to determine the effect of changes in any input that might affect the type or value of output **production**.*

LET US CALL k a multiplier and use subscripts to identify what a specific multiplier applies to. We would end up with something like this:

Suppose factor **A** changes and we want to determine how much of a change this would cause in income **Y**. This gives us $\Delta Y = k_A * \Delta A$, the change in **Y** equals k_A times the change in **A**

Since we know any of the factors mentioned in the expenditure approach definition of GDP, I_p, **G, T, X, M, C**, can affect the total for **Y**, we could end up with equations that look like:

$\Delta Y = k_{Ip} * \Delta Ip$
$\Delta Y = k_G * \Delta G$
$\Delta Y = k_T * \Delta T$
$\Delta Y = k_X * \Delta X$
$\Delta Y = k_M * \Delta M$
$\Delta Y = k_C * \Delta C$

Calculating Different Multipliers Using Various Inputs

Or if we wanted to see how these variables affect the total value of production at a certain point in time one could create different multipliers, say call the multiplier **K** and production **P**, we have

$\Delta P = K_{Ip} * \Delta Ip$
$\Delta P = K_G * \Delta G$
$\Delta P = K_T * \Delta T$
$\Delta P = K_X * \Delta X$
$\Delta P = K_M * \Delta M$
$\Delta P = K_C * \Delta C$

You could do all that and you could figure out what K or k is by plugging in values from gathered statistics, or you could try to come up with a formula that allowed one to calculate the expected value of each multiplier, utilizing whatever factors one decided were pertinent.

People do these sorts of things. They do not necessarily use the type of symbols I am using but my point is people use the term multiplier as applying to many different types of analysis. Keynes' investment multiplier is only one analysis.

If you wanted to use the modified expenditure approach to GDP equation, to figure out Keynes' Investment multiplier, this is how one would do it:

Y = I$_P$ + G + X + C, where **Keynes' I = I$_P$ + G + X**. Then if we considered a change from an established baseline we get:

$\Delta Y = \Delta I_P + \Delta G + \Delta X + \Delta C$

MPC would equal $\Delta C / \Delta Y = \Delta C / (\Delta I_P + \Delta G + \Delta X + \Delta C)$

The change in Keynes' investment would be $\Delta I_P + \Delta G + \Delta X$. If we let **k = 1/(1-MPC)**, then $\Delta Y = k * (\Delta I_P + \Delta G + \Delta X)$ and that would be equivalent to **Keynes' $\Delta Y = k * \Delta I$**

Calculating Different Multipliers Using Various Inputs

Most of the time when one is calculating propensity to consume and multiplier effects the values of the factors are based on changes from a previously established baseline, as we have just done.

Most of the time one is looking at what would happen to **Y** if one changed one of the other values.

That is why Keynes uses the term marginal, because by marginal he means what is going on if any changes are happening relative to our established position, not the total effect.

So **MPC** stands for MARGINAL propensity to consume.

$$\Delta C/\Delta Y = \Delta C/(\Delta I_p + \Delta G + \Delta X + \Delta C)$$

That is why we use the Δ symbol meaning "change of"

What if we wanted to try to derive the propensity to consume multiplier effect for the entire time period under study? How would be do that?

One difference would be that if we calculate the effect of small changes we can use linear approximations, that is the changes of the result is proportional to the changes of each factor. But when calculating a multiplier for the whole time period a linear relationship is unlikely. I propose a better way to look at it.

The propensity to consume for an entire time period is really a velocity of money thing. If one knows the total spending, and one can determine how much of the spending was investment spending, then the rest of the spending must be consumption spending. And then it is easy to calculate the propensity to consume. One knows the total spending, I + C, and one knows C. Propensity to Consume for the whole time period is $C/(I + C)$.

This is true in this model, even though what one calls investment and what one calls consumption are often judgement calls. What is not a judgement call is that total income, the total spending will be the same value. If one decides some spending of money should be classified investment instead of consumption or it should be consumption instead of investment that does not change the total of I + C; total spending remains the same.

We can also say that if we look solely at the money that gets into spending as investment, the greater the amount of consumption, i.e., the greater the amount of re-spending of that money, the higher the velocity of that particular money.

Calculating Different Multipliers Using Various Inputs

Another way to look at things is this: For the existing total money supply, the higher the velocity of the money for the given time period, the more spending has occurred. The more times the money put into investment spending gets re-spent, the higher the velocity of that money. For a given total money supply, total spending in general, investment + consumption, is completely determined by velocity of money.

CHAPTER 33
The Multiplier Effect is Really About the Velocity of Money

AS WE HAVE already seen, all the money put into spending during a given time period gets designated as saved by the end of that time period. All the money put into spending for the first time in the given time period (investment spending) may, in that time period, be used again for spending (consumption), or may not be used again for spending, but in either case, that amount of money continues to exist somewhere. This is the savings that is the preservation of investment money. If one knows the amount of investment spending, then the determining factor on how much total income is going to result from that amount of investment, is **how many times** each chunk of money gets spent. The multiplier effect is really about the velocity of money. In this case I am talking about the velocity of **some**, but not all of the money supply. I am talking about that amount of money that was put into spending as investment, in the given time period. For a given amount of investment, the more times the money is spent, the greater the total income.

Remember, the investment multiplier (**k**) determines how much total income changes (ΔY) for a given change in the amount of investment (ΔI). That means the investment multiplier is really a measure of re-spending of the money put in as investment. And how many times a given amount of money is spent in a given time period is a measure of the velocity of that money. Therefore, as mentioned, the multiplier effect is really a measure of the velocity of money.

Why is that significant? Because now we know that if we have a certain amount of money and we target the spending of it so as to give income to a certain group of people or entities, that money will have a certain velocity. Having a certain

The Multiplier Effect is Really About the Velocity of Money

velocity is equivalent to saying it will have a certain multiplier effect. If we can show that having spending targeted at a different group of persons or entities creates a different velocity of money, then, by necessity, it would also have a different multiplier. If we show that targeting spending in one direction leads to a greater velocity of money than if the money is targeted in a different direction, then we have shown that the multiplier is also greater for the first direction.

As regards the part of savings that is the preservation of investment (excluding net production), it does not matter at what point, in the given time period, it is used for spending for the last time. What does matter is that all the money that went into spending, for the first time in the given time period, will still exist and be owned by someone at the end of that time period (and be called savings). The money could be owned by a bank, or a firm or an individual. It could be virtual money, paper money or coins. It could exist only on a ledger or in a vault or in someone's wallet, in a mattress, behind the couch; it does not matter, the point is it still exists. It is the same money that was put into spending as investment spending; still existing and being owned by someone somewhere. It exists because it is part of savings that is the preservation of investment. As far as the multiplier effect that occurs with a given amount of spending, the amount saved is not the important thing. The important thing is how many times in the given time period each chunk of that money was spent, the velocity of that money, not the fact that it is eventually saved. This means that for the multiplier effect what one needs to pay attention to is not where the money ended up, but how many times it was used for spending.

To review, if more spending is targeted in a direction where velocity of money is higher, then the multiplier is greater, if more spending is targeted where velocity of money is lower, so is the multiplier.

CHAPTER 34
This Changes Everything

KEYNES' FORMULA FOR the multiplier is based on the propensity to consume, which is the fraction of income used for further spending, or it is based on its complement which they often call the propensity to save, which is the fraction of income NOT used for further spending. What I am now going to say is going to confuse the whole picture and will cause us to question everything that, heretofore, has been stated about Keynes' Investment multiplier.

I bring to our discussion the idea from previous chapters that putting money into the bank does not count as savings, it counts as spending, and the money put into the bank account can be further reused for spending, in the given time period. This means that the simplified model Keynes used to describe the multiplier is no longer the proper model. Why do I say this? **Because in reality people and firms save very little of their income, they spend almost all of it, rich or poor they spend almost all of it.** This renders useless the idea of using the propensity to consume in the calculation of the multiplier effect.

Most of what we normally consider as saved is put into some kind of interest bearing account. And putting money into a bank account is not the same thing as savings that is preservation of investment money. Putting money into a bank account is spending. It is spending to purchase an asset. Starting, or adding money to, a bank account is purchasing an asset. The value of the asset purchased is the amount of money the depositor just put into the account, which has become a debt obligation of the bank to the depositor, plus all the other benefits that come with having a bank account, including collecting interest, keeping wealth safe, and facilitating transactions. Bottom line, putting money into a bank account is money spent, not money saved.

People purchase a bank deposit as a way to preserve their wealth. It is an asset although normally people think of it as money because it is an easy asset to turn into cash, by withdrawing the money. Withdrawing the money is more accurately described as selling all or part the asset back to the bank.

The savings Keynes talked about in the first 10 chapters of "The General Theory" is a different thing. That savings is simply the preservation of the money used for investment. If the time period ends before the person gets that money into the bank it is "saved" with the person still having ownership of the money. If the period ends after the money is put into the bank account and before the bank can lend it, the money counts as "saved" with the bank having ownership. And if the period ends after money was issued as a loan but before the borrower could spend it, that counts as saved with the borrower having ownership of the money. If the borrower has spent the money before the end of the given period, and the recipient of the borrower's spending has not yet further spent the money, then money is saved "in the pocket of" the recipient of the borrower's spending, and so on.

For all these situations I am talking about Keynes' concept where the money that is "saved" is the same money as what was first put into spending as investment.

If we accept that the amount put into a bank account becomes income for the bank, that is, the ownership of the money is transferred from the depositor to the bank, then we must accept that it is not the same thing as this savings that is the preservation of investment. This is an important distinction because in the Keynes' model, once the money is designated as saved, it will no longer be used for spending in the rest of the given time period. When money has been put into a bank deposit it becomes owned by the bank, and it can, and often will, be used for further spending.

CHAPTER 35
Direct Spending

I WANT TO propose a definition. The term I will be defining is "direct spending." By direct spending, I mean all spending other than the purchasing or selling of a debt obligation, an asset called a loan. By direct spending I mean spending to purchase labor, goods, services, or some other outcome except if the outcome is a loan. Putting money in a deposit account is a loan, it is purchasing a savings asset, which is lending the money to the bank. It does not count as direct spending. Withdrawing your money from that bank is the bank purchasing back some of that asset they sold you when you deposited your money. The bank is spending to buy back some of that asset to reduce their loan obligation to you. That does not count as direct spending. The bank giving a loan to a borrower is purchasing a loan, a receivable debt, and does not count as direct spending. All of what I call purely financial assets are based on loans. Any purchasing of a purely financial asset or paying off a debt obligation on a purely financial asset does NOT count as direct spending. When money is used to purchase a mixed asset, where part of the asset is based on loans and part of the asset is based on other wealth, the amount of the purchase price paying for the part of the asset based on loans **is not** direct spending. The amount of the purchase price paying for the part of the asset based on other wealth **is** direct spending.

Paying off all or part of any principle owed on a loan is buying back part or all of that asset called a loan. Paying back a loan does not count as direct spending either. Paying interest on a loan is direct spending. It is presumed to pay for the legitimate services the bank provides, see Chapter 5.

Purchasing loans in general, no matter who owes the debt, is never considered direct spending. You could be buying back your own loan, so you no longer have

Direct Spending

a debt obligation, or you could be buying the asset from a lender who lent the money to a different borrower so now that borrower owes you. That can be what happens when one purchases a bond. Purchasing debt that other people have the debt obligation for is still purchasing a loan and still does NOT count as direct spending.

Lending creates an asset, a store of wealth, but it also creates a debt of the same value. It provides no increase in total wealth. That is the reason I separate it out from direct spending. The function of loans is to get the cash to the person or entities who have a desire or need to directly spend the money for the purpose of acquiring labor, goods, service or some desired outcome other than creating or liquidating a purely financial asset. Though the system of lending is not direct spending itself, it does help position the money so someone else is able to directly spend.

All spending is ultimately driven by the desire to get something that adds to wealth, that adds to quality of life, that meets some need or desire. Spending on loans is usually driven by someone's desire or need to do direct spending, or least position one's self to be able to pay for direct spending should the occasion arise, but it does not count as direct spending itself. Economic activity that leads to production of labor, goods, services, or other desired outcomes depends on direct spending. Spending on loans is only useful in that it may facilitate direct spending that otherwise would not have occurred.

All spending is classifiable as either direct spending or spending to purchase, or pay back, a debt obligation. Therefore, those two categories account for **all** the spending and all income.

※※※

Now I will look at something I have not addressed before. This discussion will allow us to integrate major concepts introduced in the first half and the second half of Keynes' General Theory.

When money changes ownership, the recipient of that money, can now use it again for more spending. If that recipient uses the money to purchase goods, services, labor or some other outcome, other than purchasing a loan, it is direct spending. It is only because we have direct spending that the idea of an economy has any meaning at all. It is only direct spending that pays for the production of those things that support and enhance life. To paraphrase Keynes "that which is acquired by direct spending is the ultimate goal of all economic activity".

Direct Spending

His exact quote is: "Consumption— to repeat the obvious— is the sole end and object of all economic activity."[21]

⚖︎

Spending, whether direct spending or spending to purchase assets called loans, can lead to more spending. But spending known as direct spending is different than spending to purchase a loan. Whereas money put right into direct spending only need be spent once to accomplish direct spending, money put into a bank account has to be spent three times to cause any direct spending to occur.

Here is a description of how spending occurs if a person deposits money into a bank. This involves 3 spending steps:

Depositor purchases a bank deposit; the bank incurs an equal debt obligation and ownership of the money.

Depositor withdraws his money, meaning the bank spends to purchase back that asset and eliminate the banks debt obligation, transferring ownership of the money back to the depositor.

Depositor now uses that cash for direct spending.

Only the third time that money is spent does direct spending occur, but each step counts as spending and each time the amount of spending gets added to total (gross) income. Putting money into a bank account still counts as spending, but it will be spent three times before it is used for direct spending. If that money is then used again, straight off, for direct spending then it will have been used only once for direct spending. This means the velocity of that money would be greater if it were put into a bank account, than if it were put right into direct spending, even though in both cases, the direct spending, the important spending, is the same.

Suppose that person A gets paid cash at work on payday and uses that money to buy a widget. Person B gets paid by direct deposit and withdraws the same amount of money and buys a widget.

For that period of time the velocity of person B's money is greater than the velocity of person A's money, yet their real impact on the economy is the same. There are 2 direct spending steps here. Their paycheck paying for their labor is

---

21   Keynes, John Maynard. The General Theory of Employment, Interest and Money (Illustrated) (p. 84). Green World Publication. Kindle Edition.

direct spending, and buying the widget is direct spending. Once the employee gets their pay there are more re-spending steps for person B than for person A.

Person A gets paid and spends their money once, buying the widget. That is two direct spending steps.

Person B gets paid but instructs the employer to purchase an increase in his deposit account, a savings asset, for him. That is two spending steps, step 1) Person B is paid for this labor, that is direct spending, step 2) the putting of the money into his deposit account is another step of spending but it is not direct spending. Then step 3) Person B then withdraws the money which is the bank spending to reduce his debt obligation to Person B, that also is not direct spending. And step 4) Person B buys the widget. That counts as direct spending.

For both Person A and Person B the same amount of direct spending occurred but the total amount of spending was twice as much for Person B. That means the transactions with Person B will cause total gross income and purportedly total demand to be twice the amount as it is for Person A. Now of course half of the spending of Person B is NOT direct spending, but still, by the strict definition of spending as the transfer of ownership of money, the gross spending (equals income) , is twice as much just because person B used a bank. That is twice the total gross income being created, and, one could argue, twice the demand was created.

The bottom line is that if you do not make a distinction between direct spending and buying a loan, then velocity of money will not be a good measure of demand for labor, goods, services, or other outcomes. For example, if we go back to the chapter on effective demand the only spending that is going to increase the demand for employment and increased output is the direct spending. Demand for loans does not directly increase employment or production. We really have to modify our understanding of that chapter somewhat.

Spending really only has a multiplier effect if at least some of the spending is direct spending. When I discuss aggregate demand, I am talking about demand for labor, goods, services and other desired outcomes other than creating a purely financial asset. Therefore, the only type of spending that will directly increase aggregate demand is direct spending. When I am calculating the total demand for an economy I must revise what I said previously, that demand is equal to spending because when it comes to increasing production of wealth, it is only direct spending that actually provides that demand. It is the purchase of goods, services, labor or any other desired outcomes, other than purchasing a purely financial asset, that has any effect on increasing employment, production and income.

Direct Spending

Buying purely financial assets is just switching money around. If no direct spending ever occurred, and the only things ever purchased were purely financial assets, then no goods, services, labor or other desired outcomes would be produced (other than the creation of purely financial assets and their matching debt obligations). That would create no opportunities to get paid for labor, no one would put money into ventures to meet demand for goods and services. There would be no customers. There would be no employment opportunities, there would be nothing produced. If a quantity of money never gets used for direct spending, but is only used to purchase purely financial assets, that spending contributes nothing to aggregate demand.

So, if we are looking at total direct spending demand we calculate it as the direct spending velocity of money times the money supply. That is the average number of times each unit of the money supply has been used for direct spending in the given time period.

Let total direct spending = Y_{DS}

And direct spending velocity of money = V_{DS}

And **M** equals total money supply. Then $Y_{DS} = M * V_{DS}$

We can also calculate total direct spending by looking at the average price of direct spending transactions times the number of direct spending transactions

Let P_{DS} = average price of direct spending transactions and

T_{DS} = the number of such transactions then $Y_{DS} = P_{DS} * T_{DS}$

We can always assign the direct investment spending to mean the first time an amount of money was put into the economy as direct spending and direct consumption spending to mean every time an amount of money first used for direct investment spending in the given time period is used again for spending.

$Y_{DS} = I_{DS} + C_{DS}$.

But it turns out that is not so useful because **any** type of spending that causes the transfer of ownership of money including something like dispensing a loan, can get money into a chain of spending that leads to direct spending occurring.

If the initial spending that starts the chain of spending is direct spending then it counts as part of the total direct spending, but if the initial spending that starts the chain of spending is not direct spending, then it is not included as part of direct spending.

DIRECT SPENDING

In such a case, where the first spending step or steps are to purchase purely financial assets, then the first direct spending step must count as direct consumption spending not investment.

In either case I assume the equation $Y_{DS} = I_{DS} + C_{DS}$ would apply but it is possible that in some chains of spending the first direct spending step would be direct investment spending and in other cases the first direct spending step would be direct consumption spending.

This creates problems in calculating the multiplier effect, we cannot just take:

$$\Delta Y_{DS} = \Delta I_{DS} + \Delta C_{DS}$$

And then say the total direct spending is determined by a multiplier times ΔI_{DS}, i.e., $k * \Delta I_{DS}$ where $k = (1/[1 - MPC])$ and set MPC equal to $\Delta C_{DS}/\Delta Y_{DS}$.

Because for one thing, the change in spending, the amount of new money being introduced into spending as investment may not be direct investment spending, it may not equal ΔI_{DS}. It may be that the first spending, the investment, the spending that started that chain of spending was a loan, spending to acquire a purely financial asset. In that case ΔI_{DS} would equal zero. If such were the case then $\Delta C_{DS}/\Delta Y_{DS}$ would equal one implying that k is infinity.

$$(1/(1-[\Delta C_{DS}/\Delta Y_{DS}])) = 1/(1-1) = \infty$$

The reality is that if money got into the chain of spending first as a loan and $\Delta I_{DS} = 0$, that money could be used for spending zero times or any number of times, even though, if $\Delta I_{DS} = 0$, then ΔY_{DS} will always equal ΔC_{DS} and $\Delta C_{DS}/\Delta Y_{DS}$ will always equal one. $\Delta C_{DS}/\Delta Y_{DS}$ would equal one, if someone investment spends to purchase a debt obligation. But clearly, this initial spending will not result in total direct spending being infinity. The reality is that this initial spending could result in any amount of further spending, including any amount of direct spending. What determines the total direct spending for a given amount of investment is the total number of times the money, which was put into spending as investment, gets used for direct spending, in the given time period. It does not matter whether that spending would count as direct investment spending or direct consumption spending. The number of times that particular money is used for direct spending is the direct spending velocity of that money.

Let the total spending to purchase purely financial assets equal Y_{PFA}, then total spending Y = total direct spending plus total spending to purchase purely financial assets. $Y = Y_{DS} + Y_{PFA}$ but it is only the total direct spending that will determine

263

our aggregate demand. And it is only the change in total direct spending, Y_{DS}, that occurs as a result of some new spending that is important in terms of creating new employment and increased production.

⚜

Here are some other ways spending requires multiple steps if it involves creating purely financial assets:

The depositor purchases an asset called a bank deposit. the bank loans that money, i.e., purchases an asset called a loan from the borrower, then the borrower uses the loan money for direct spending. That is three times the money is spent and only one time is the spending direct spending.

Whenever loans are involved, generally only one of the three steps is direct spending. The same can happen with a private loan. A person loans money to someone else, that is not direct spending. The recipient of the loan buys something with it, that is direct spending. The borrower pays the money back, that is not direct spending. Even though it is a personal loan it's still an asset, even if there is less chance it will retain its value, meaning if there is less chance it will be paid off.

In all this spending, the steps that are not direct spending just involve the repositioning of money, not the creation of any wealth.

Charity is direct spending to purchase outcomes I have previously described, and then if that money is put into a bank deposit that step is not direct spending. There are lots of ways to develop examples of what is direct spending and what is not.

⚜

Focusing on how much is saved, in the sense Keynes meant it in the first 10 chapters of The General Theory, leads one off in the wrong direction. We know how much that savings is. The savings that is "the preservation of investment" is equal to the investment. Propensity to save is misleading because then one thinks in terms of, for a given amount of total income, how much are we saving. That is a microeconomic concept. In the macroeconomy, savings is determined by the investment amount, and consumption does not change or decrease savings. Savings is fixed by the amount of investment, consumption just gets added to the total income. Increased consumption just means the money is being used for spending more times in the current time period.

Direct Spending

It is the spending, not the savings, that should be focused on, and here I am saying that when it comes to accounting for the effects of spending that directly causes production of wealth, the spending that we must be concerned about is direct spending. Spending that buys or liquidates purely financial assets may affect how much direct spending is done, by positioning money to be used for direct spending, but it is that actual direct spending that counts, no matter what influences caused the direct spending to occur, it is the amount of times the money that was first put into spending as investment that gets used for direct spending that causes the multiplier effect and determines the level of employment and influences the amount of production.

In a system with loans the income that paid for the direct spending in not always caused by direct spending, not always received as income caused by direct spending. A person who direct spends his income could have gotten that money from a loan, for example, which is a transaction where the bank pays to acquire a purely financial asset. It is possible that the money can move through spending steps which are both direct spending and spending to purchase a purely financial asset, in the same chain of spending. The system of lending makes it possible that, if a possessor of some money is not ready to re-spend that money right away, and instead puts the money into a bank deposit, or otherwise lends it, someone else may acquire that money and use it for direct spending, increasing the direct spending velocity of that money.

Only the direct spending steps count when we are determining the aggregate demand. It is direct spending demand that influences employment level in the chapter titled "effective demand". When I use the term aggregate demand in that model, the only valid way to describe it is to say it is referring to total direct spending demand. In Keynes' model for the investment multiplier, the multiplier effect only occurs because the initial income is used to pay for some production that causes someone else to get income that they use to purchase something that causes income to the next person etc. Production draws out more spending and increases sales and income leading to demand for more production and more sales etc. (with production and sales of production meant in the most general way possible, as previously described). If the only wealth created is assets backed by the creation of an identical debt obligation, there is no net wealth production, and there will, ultimately, be no reward for any spending. If there is no reward for spending, there is no reason for spending and all spending will cease. It is direct spending that drives everything in the economy.

Keynes' original model for the multiplier makes no sense unless all the spending is considered to affect employment and net wealth production. Therefore, the only spending he can be considering is direct spending. In Keynes' calculation of the multiplier all the investment must be direct spending and all the consumption spending must be direct spending, and the total spending that equals total income must be total direct spending, i.e., total direct spending income. In Keynes' model, all the direct consumption spending is done by people or entities who got that money as income as a result of someone else's direct spending. Any further spending with that money counts as direct spending consumption, which affects employment and production. This means, that Keynes' multiplier model does not consider income caused by spending to acquire a purely financial asset. Keynes' model is really a model that does not consider the effect of the system of lending on the economy.

CHAPTER 36
Keynes' Multiplier Modified to Include the Effect of Loans and the Concept of Direct Spending

Since we have an economy where money "saved" in bank accounts can be used for lending, the simple formula for the investment multiplier given by Keynes is not valid. This chapter shows a different approach to understanding the investment multiplier effect.

THE MODEL DEVELOPED in this chapter modifies Keynes' original model for the multiplier effect to one that applies in an economy that has a system of lending. In Keynes' original model all the spending would count as direct spending. In this model I consider purchasing purely financial assets as spending and income, but I do not consider it as direct spending and direct spending income. We must exclude spending to purchase a purely financial asset from total spending to determine our direct spending totals. The actual borrowing of money does not affect the demand that affects production and income and jobs. It is only when the borrower uses that money for direct spending that the spending of that money can increase such demand.

As I analyze how to modify the calculation of the multiplier effect I need to address one of Keynes' main points, that income going to poorer people will result in a larger proportion of the income being spent, and a larger multiplier effect, than if the same amount of income goes to richer people. In Keynes' model, the multiplier was larger if more of the income is spent and smaller if less of the income is spent.

Keynes' Multiplier Modified to Include the Effect of Loans

This is an issue because of what I pointed out earlier, that all people spend almost all of their income, rich or poor. When adding to our model the effect of having loans, we cannot include all spending to determine the multiplier. We can only include direct spending. In an economic model where we consider the effect of loans, instead of the multiplier being determined by the fraction of total spending that is consumption spending, the only multiplier effect we are really concerned with is the amount of total direct spending that results due to some new money introduced into spending, i.e., as investment, whether that investment is direct spending or not.

I have discussed how the multiplier effect is really a measure of the velocity of money. If more direct spending is done, in a given time period, that means the direct spending velocity of money is greater for that time period. If I can show that spending targeted to cause income in group A leads to more total direct spending than spending targeted to cause income in group B, then I have shown that the direct spending velocity of money, and therefore the multiplier, is greater when spending is targeted at group A. Two important groups to compare in this regard are richer people versus poorer people. What happens to total direct spending if the income of poorer people was increased compared to what happens to total direct spending if income to richer people is increased.

This chapter will be integrating the main concepts in the first 10 chapters of Keynes' General Theory, where he introduced the concept of the multiplier, with the concepts starting in chapter 11 of the General Theory where he introduced the relationship between the marginal efficiency of capital and interest rates.

There are two main important concepts that come out of Keynes' original multiplier:

That if an additional amount of spending is introduced into the economy, total spending will be increased by an amount greater than that additional amount due to a multiplier effect.

That poorer people will spend a larger fraction of their income than wealthier people, and that will make the multiplier effect greater if more income is given to poorer people as compared to wealthier people, and vice versa.

In Keynes' formulas, the change in total income from an established point is calculated by these equations:

$\Delta Y = \Delta I + \Delta C, \Delta Y = k\Delta I$

ΔI is the original additional spending, **k** is the multiplier, and ΔY is the change in total spending that occurs as a result of the original additional spending. ΔC is the amount of re-spending of that money used for the additional spending ΔI. ΔC is what determines the size of the multiplier effect.

In Keynes' model **k = 1/(1-MPC)** where **MPC = $\Delta C/\Delta Y$**.

MPC stands for marginal propensity to consume. For Keynes, the model was simple, increase propensity to consume and you increase the multiplier and total income for a given amount of initial extra spending. Poorer people have a higher propensity to consume, give them more money and you have a greater increase in total income than if you give that same money to richer people.

I try to show, that, with an economy that has loans, both those things remain true, except that the focus is not on all the spending, it is the direct spending that we are concerned with. Keynes' two important points get restated (assuming the economy is not at full employment):

1. An initial amount of extra income will generally lead to an increase in direct spending. The total increase in direct spending will have a multiplier effect, because it will cause increased employment, production and sales; the income from which will cause further increases in employment production and sales, etc.

2. A specific amount of income going to poorer people will cause a greater increase in the overall amount of direct spending than the same amount of income going to richer people. That is, the direct spending multiplier effect is greater if spending is targeted at poorer, rather than wealthier, people.

In this analysis I propose to divide spending in an economy into two types:

1. Spending to acquire items when the spending is not done for the purpose of seeking a monetary return. This is spending to purchase items the spenders want for personal use, for example.

2. Spending to acquire assets or shares in assets that will give a monetary return or at least are purchased in the hopes that they will maintain their

value and can be considered to have value as a store of wealth. This is the type of spending done by "for profit investors" where they will spend to acquire a venture asset or spend to acquire a savings asset.

I think it is reasonable to assume that the fraction of poorer people's spending that is type 1 spending is larger than the same fraction for richer people. This is because, in general, there are limitations to one's appetites. There are limits to how much one person can use, and therefore, to how much a person will spend for items that are purchased simply for personal use, with no consideration of its value as a store of wealth, or as something that may increase in value. One may argue this point. One might claim there are no such limits on type 1 spending. They may argue, for example, that a richer person may buy multiple houses which they intend to use. However, such purchases also are made with the idea of selling them in the future. They are bought with the hopes of generating a return or at least maintaining their original value. In other words, a large part of purchasing of those houses is better categorized as type 2 spending.

I believe it is also reasonable to assume that the fraction of richer people's spending that qualifies as type 2 spending is greater than the fraction of poorer peoples spending that would be categorized as type 2 spending. Type 2 spending is the type of spending done by "for-profit investors". Richer people will certainly have a larger fraction of their income available for such spending opportunities than poorer people.

No one could make the case that there is always a monetary return sought from spending. It is reasonable to assume that a lot of products for sale will not be something people buy thinking it will increase in value. These are things people will buy for personal use, which they intend to use up, or which are purchased because they want to have it and use it, even if it is more durable. In other words, a large amount of spending is done for the purpose of acquiring something without any consideration for whether that item will hold its value or increase in value over time. A large part of spending is type 1 spending, which is always direct spending.

The second type of spending is part direct spending, i.e., the purchasing of venture assets. But the other part, the purchasing of savings assets is not direct spending, it is spending to purchase a purely financial asset. The money spent to acquire a bank deposit could lead to direct spending, because it could lead to a loan being dispensed and the amount of the loan could be used for direct spending.

Keynes' Multiplier Modified to Include the Effect of Loans

I want to make a distinction between two categories of bank deposits. One type is bank deposits that are short term, low or no interest, or even charging fees. These assets are easily converted back to cash; people are always depositing money or quickly withdrawing it. This type of account has deposit totals that are constantly changing because those accounts are always involved in those three step transactions mentioned previously.

The second type is bank deposits which are intended to stay in the bank longer and usually get a higher interest rate. The difference is, that money, which stays in the bank longer can be loaned out.

It is possible that those shorter term accounts always reliably run a certain balance, and it would be safe for the banks to loan that money out as well. That is, even though the banks will have to dedicate a certain amount of money to never be loaned out, to be kept available for these short term transactions, they can keep another portion that is able to be loaned out, that will not be continually be withdrawn and deposited and used in those three step transactions which the banks perform all the time at the behest of their depositors. For our purposes one could consider the amount of deposits that reside in the shorter term accounts and can be loaned as being part of the "longer term accounts". Only the amount of money in shorter term accounts that never gets loaned out, that is kept around to service the constant request for deposits and withdrawals and three step transactions is what I will consider as short term account deposits.

The money deposited in those shorter term bank deposits, since it is never loaned out, is just like cash as far as direct spending goes. It is either in the bank or in the would be depositor's pocket. If the depositor wants more cash for spending, the asset is converted to cash, i.e., money is withdrawn from the bank account, and spent. Since the money is never loaned out, i.e., it only goes back and forth between the bank and the depositor, those transactions add nothing to direct spending totals. All that constant spending to purchase the bank deposits and then the spending by the bank to purchase back the debt obligation to the depositor when the money is withdrawn from or deposited in these short term deposits is considered spending (to purchase purely financial assets), but it is NOT direct spending and adds nothing to the direct spending totals and can be completely disregarded in the analysis. That money is just considered the same as if it were held as cash in the wallets of the depositors. Money held as cash in someone's wallet can be used for direct spending, but the point is, the transferring of that money back and forth from cash to those short term bank accounts is not that direct spending and, as I said, adds nothing to direct spending totals.

One might argue that the banking system increases the convenience and speed of electronic transactions and this would mean having these short term accounts, even if the money deposited in them never gets loaned out, will still increase the velocity of money. However, that fact is not something that plays a role in this analysis because I am mainly looking at the difference in the multiplier effect of money going to richer people versus money going to poorer people and I assume that the convenience and speed of transactions done by both groups of people is similar and that those factors do not play a significant role in the difference between the amount or type of direct spending each group does.

Only transfers of ownership of the money that pay for goods and services, labor or other desired outcomes other than purely financial assets are included in the accounting of direct spending totals. Unlike the purely financial asset transactions with short term accounts, those transactions involving longer term accounts cannot be ignored. This is because longer term deposits can be part of the chain of spending that results in a loan, the amount of which can be used for direct spending. The transactions that only buy these purely financial assets that are longer term accounts, still do not count as direct spending, but one cannot totally disregard them because spending to produce them, even though it is not direct spending, can become income for a borrower who may direct spend that money. The transaction that caused that money to be gained as income by the borrower was the borrower agreeing to owe a debt obligation to the bank in return for the money, a purely financial transaction, and the borrower uses that money for direct spending. Because of that, in situations like that, I will have to say the loans caused "income" to the borrower which was used for direct spending, rather than "direct spending created income was used for direct spending". The income to a person that they then use for direct spending could be income caused by a direct spending payment to that individual or it could be money the individual obtained as a loan (still counts as gross income in my model) which is not direct spending.

Paying interest is a type of direct spending that occurs with the banking transactions. The interest the borrowers give the banks is direct spending by the borrower and creates direct spending income for the banks. The banks then give a portion of that interest payment to the depositor. This is direct spending by the bank to create direct spending income for the depositor. This is the interest paid on savings assets that gets balanced with the marginal efficiency of capital, which is the return on venture assets.

Interest payments are direct spending. Why are they direct spending? Interest payments to the banks pay for all services mentioned in Chapter 5 on the function of banks. Interest payments by the bank to the depositor is payment for the service of being allowed to use the depositor's money. It is this interest payment that causes the deposit to occur in the first place. The depositor would not agree to trading cash for an asset that is only a recording of a debt obligation if they got nothing in return. The interest is paid to the long term account depositor for the depositor's inconvenience of not having the money available immediately for other desired uses, and for having to worry about getting it paid back.

Longer term deposits that can be loaned out to borrowers who will use the money for direct spending are different, (because of the interest rates they earn and because they result in direct spending by the borrower), than shorter term deposits that this model regards as being the same as cash. Those shorter term deposits never end up being part of loans to borrowers outside of the bank, and are just in the bank for safe guarding, and convenience of transactions. The portion of short term deposits that banks feels safe loaning out I count as being, in effect, a part of the longer term deposits, and it is that part that probably allows the banks to pay that very small amount of interest these short term accounts sometimes earn, though often the fees charged are more than any interest paid anyway.

Fees charged by banks, paid by short term depositors to maintain an account and any conveniences are direct spending payments for those services. But that is treated no differently than any other direct spending the short term depositors will do with their cash. The same would be true of any fees charged when borrowers apply for a loan. That is considered direct spending to pay for services the bank is providing by processing the loan application and is direct spending.

So, even though the purchasing of longer term savings assets is not in and of itself direct spending, it does involve direct spending; the direct spending involved is the interest payments and the fees. Direct spending is also involved when the borrowers use the money obtained as loans to pay for their direct spending purchases.

Most people would agree that wealthier people do more of the second type of spending compared to poorer people. So, if an extra amount of spending were given as income to richer people one might assume that would lead to increased type 2 direct spending and that would create a multiplier effect, and this is true. However, this multiplier effect will not occur because of type 2 spending alone. Ultimately, these ventures will have to lead to the production and sales of items often referred to as end products. End products will include some items that are acquired by spending that can be considered type 2 spending, i.e., the items are purchased because they hold or increase in value. But I think it is reasonable to assume that most end products sold are not intended as items to be purchased as a store of wealth, or as items to be purchased for the purpose of getting a monetary return. Most of the end products sold are intended for personal use, to be used up or to have for personal use or enjoyment.*

It is the type 1 spending done to purchase these end products for personal use that drives all spending. In order for ventures to be viable at all, their efforts will ultimately need to contribute to the production of, and sales of, large amounts of end products. It is mainly this type 1 spending to purchase end products that makes the multiplier larger when more income goes to poorer people.

(*Although many end products preserve and enhance "human capital", and preserving, enhancing and increasing "human capital" can lead to all sorts of "returns" in the future, that is not what I mean by the type of return type 2 spenders are seeking. In my definition, the type of return type 2 spenders are seeking is an increase in the monetary value of the assets they buy. They may have awareness of, or hope that, if people buy their end products, and this has beneficial effects for those people, that over time this will also preserve or enhance their own wealth as well. But it is the sale of those end products that gives the type 2 venture asset purchasers the return they seek.)

If the economy is at less than full employment, then increased (direct) spending on these end products can lead to increased employment and increased production overall. Increased spending on intermediate products, products that are not themselves end products but will be used in the process of creating end products, will cause increased income that will help pay for sales of end products. But if spending on end products is not increased sufficiently as a result, this will just cause increased inventories that will slow or cease that extra spending to pay for intermediate products. So ultimately, at less than full employment, even in the case where the initial extra spending is type 2 spending (which includes spending to produce intermediate products), it is increased type 1 direct spending to purchase end products that leads to

Keynes' Multiplier Modified to Include the Effect of Loans

the multiplier effect of increased total direct spending income, and to increased employment and production.

Due to limitations into how much one person can actually use, and due to the fact that once one has saturated such appetites, the extra type 1 spending richer people will be doing will be limited, even if their total income is significantly increased. There is only so much spending an individual can do to pay for things like servants, private jets, bottles of wine, yachts, collector's items, expensive vacations, and expensive meals purchased for the purpose of satisfying one's personal needs or desires for end products. And actually at least part of the spending to buy yachts, planes and collector's items must count as type 2 spending, that is purchasing something that will maintain its value or increase in value, which they can later sell. My point is, if you want to increase total direct spending income, employment and production this will mean increasing type one direct spending. That will ultimately mean having to increase the income of the poor and the middle class. This is because, compared to richer people, the appetites for end products of the poor and middle class are far from satiated.

This is where Keynes' quite reasonable assumption that poorer people spend a larger proportion of their current income fits into this analysis. It is this greater unsatisfied appetites for end products poorer people have compared to richer people which is the main cause of the multiplier being greater when more income goes to poorer people than richer people. It is ultimately this type 1 direct spending to purchase end products, that poorer people will do more of, that leads to increased overall direct spending income and drives the whole economy.

Additionally, increased direct spending income will make more people eligible for loans and this will further increase total direct spending and direct spending income and demand. I would allege that loans obtained for the purpose of direct spending to purchase end products is more common for poorer people than richer people. Richer people tend to be net lenders not net borrowers, and richer people or entities tend to obtain more loans for the purpose of type 2 spending than poorer people. That is another way more income to poorer than richer can increase type 1 direct spending and total direct spending income, direct spending velocity of money, and the multiplier effect.

After we get to full employment the same effect will not apply and increased spending, whether targeted to create more income for the poor or middle class, or targeted to create more income in richer people is only likely to cause inflation, with no increase in employment, production, or buying power. But up to full employment increased direct spending will increase employment and production, and if increased direct spending leads to increased income to poor and middle class people, this will cause the total direct spending to increase faster or to a larger degree than if the increased direct spending causes increased income to richer people.

In summary, any additional increased amount of spending will normally also increase direct spending, however, it is the amount of type 1 direct spending that can have the strongest effect on total direct spending income. Type one direct spending is more likely to increase as more income goes to the poor and middle class, as opposed to the rich. Type one direct spending directly leads to other type 1 direct spending, but it will also draw out more venture spending (Type 2 direct spending) by increasing marginal efficiency of capital, because of the increased demand for product. Type one direct spending will also increase lending because of more qualified borrowers, and this will attract savings asset purchases, since banks will have to increase interest rates they pay depositors to get the added cash they need to meet the demand for loans. As a result of all those factors, increased income to poor and middle class increases total direct spending more than increased income given to richer people, which means the direct spending velocity of money is greater, which is the same as saying the multiplier is larger.

There will also be compensatory effects that modulate the direct spending increase, such as, if direct spending increases caused the income of poor and middle class to increase, and the demand for loans increased, that can allow banks to increase interest rates charged on the loans, making them more expensive and decreasing somewhat the amount of loans dispersed. The increased interest rates on the loans will, in turn, lead to increased interest rates on deposits since banks will be competing for deposit money and because they will have the ability to pay more interest. These increased interest rates on longer term deposits will draw money away from venture spending, which will reduce overall direct spending.

But these compensatory effects only serve to modulate the primary effect, they do not change the direction of the primary effect, only reduce the magnitude of it some. But this does mean that having a system of lending has some stabilizing effect on the economy. If (gross) direct spending incomes of poor and middle class are reduced, the economy with a system of loans compensates to prevent the direct spending income from being reduced as much. If direct spending incomes of poor and middle class are increased, the economy with a system of loans compensates to prevent the (gross) direct spending income of poor and middle class from being increased as much.

The main danger with too much borrowing and lending, is when the repaying of the loan principle begins to shift too much spending away from direct spending to spending to pay off the debt obligation on that purely financial asset, and when the direct spending called interest payments begins to shift spending away from creating income for poorer people, who are more likely to be borrowers, creating income for longer term depositors who are more likely to be wealthy.

Keynes had no need for the concept of direct spending. In his model for the multiplier, all spending is direct spending. As far as I can tell his concept of savings did not recognize that putting money into a savings account is not the same as what he meant by savings in the first 10 chapters of "The General Theory". He did not recognize that putting money into a savings account is not the same thing as the investment money continuing to exist at the end of the given time period. Keynes did not consider that putting money into a savings account is spending and that the same money can be used for further spending in the given time period. In his model there was no need to distinguish between spending to purchase an asset based on a debt obligation, (that is, a purely financial asset), and direct spending.

It was in those first 10 chapters that he showed the concept of the investment multiplier and aggregate demand. His theories of aggregate demand were based on direct spending income and his formula for calculating the multiplier is based on direct spending as well, whether he knew it or not. In the model presented in this chapter, the calculation of the multiplier is also based on direct spending, but because this model recognizes that income can occur, i.e., money can change ownership, in a way that is not considered direct spending income, by the purchase of purely financial assets, the analysis is not as simple.

Spending is anytime money changes ownership for a purpose. It is only direct spending we are concerned with when we calculate the level of aggregate demand. It is only the effect of a given amount of spending on total direct spending that is important for the economy so the only multiplier effect that is important is how much a given amount of new spending increases the amount of total direct spending. If we know the change in the direct spending velocity of money that occurs as a result of some new spending, we know the multiplier effect of that new spending. Showing that direct spending will be greater when spending is targeted in one direction compared to another, for a given time period, is the same as showing the direct spending velocity of money has increased more in the one direction as compared to the other. In this chapter I have made the case that, as long as the economy is at less than full employment, increased income going to poor and middle class has a greater effect on increasing the direct spending velocity of money and leads to a greater multiplier effect than increased income going to richer people.

We still have a multiplier that occurs as a result of increasing spending. We cannot use this formula, **k = 1/(1-MPC)** to calculate the multiplier because the initial spending that ends up starting a chain of spending that includes increased direct spending may be the bank or the government dispersing a loan, or it may be someone putting money in a deposit account that ultimately results in a loan being given to a borrower. The investment spending does not have to be direct investment spending, but it must lead to direct spending or it will be of no consequence in terms of causing any change in production or employment.

I have used the term "less than full employment" in this chapter when what I really meant was "when the unemployment rate is greater than the Non Accelerating Inflation Rate of Unemployment (NAIRU)." I did this on purpose because I thought it would make the document more readable, and allow me to get my points across without distracting the reader as much. But strictly speaking I should have said "unemployment rate greater than NAIRU" rather than less than full employment, because in reality the economy never reaches what Keynes' called full employment because we will normally get excess inflation prior to reaching that point.

Inequality

Inequality in wealth develops because the richer on average get a proportionately greater amount of new net production. Or because they get more of the money supply and everyone else gets less. Or because they get more of the purely financial assets and less of the associated debt obligations.

Meaning the poorer get a proportionately smaller amount of net production, or they end up with less of the money supply, or they end up with more of the debt obligations and less of the purely financial assets.

And that's how inequality of wealth develops and increases.

Inequality of income is a different thing. If one person has greater income than another there is no guarantee that they will end up increasing their wealth more. Their wealth may increase or possibly decrease. It all depends on how the income is spent and the results obtained from current and prior spending.

There will definitely be a correlation between inequality of income and inequality of wealth for the simple reason that those with higher incomes are able to purchase more wealth.

Sometimes economics writings appear to consider inequality of wealth and inequality of income to be the same thing. I wanted to point out they are not the same thing.

In this chapter I have revealed that the Keynesian multiplier as normally presented is flawed. The flaw is the assumption that the money designated as saved can be money put into a savings account. But in Keynes' model the money that is considered saved will no longer be spent in the current time period. It is not considered eligible for use in further spending. Any further spending of that money would mean that more consumption spending is occurring and the marginal propensity to consume is increasing. I have shown that putting money into a bank account actually counts as spending not saving. Putting money into a bank account is consumption spending, (or investment spending). Therefore, putting money into a bank account in and of itself would affect the marginal propensity to consume. Putting money into a bank account is not necessarily the end of the use of that money in that time period. That money can still be used for further spending in that time period. Only when the "bell whistles" indicating the end of the given time period will that money, wherever it ends up, be considered saved in the way Keynes meant it in the first 10 Chapters of the General Theory.

Keynes' Multiplier Modified to Include the Effect of Loans

This brought up a bigger concern. If so much of what we call spending is actually spending that involves purchasing an asset called a loan or purchasing to reduce a debt obligation (i.e., purchasing back part of that asset called a loan), then what really does all that spending do? And what group is more likely to spend more if spending includes buying of and paying back loans?

It is true that the banking system and the system of lending facilitates direct spending that could increase the direct spending velocity of money, if the money gets loaned out, but the spending being done to purchase or pay back a debt obligation will not cause any increase in direct spending demand. When that spending is included in our calculation for total spending, we lose the correlation between spending that increases demand for goods, services, labor or other outcomes, (except demand for purely financial assets) and total spending.

One of the main ideas of the Keynesian multiplier is that poorer people spend more of their income than richer people. I developed the concern that since calculations of spending includes transactions that involve buying and selling purely financial assets this would no longer be true. All those transactions by richer people buying and selling purely financial assets would count as spending and probably to a large degree count as consumption spending. This would greatly increase the propensity to consume of the rich, perhaps making the propensity to consume of the rich, calculated this way, to be similar to or possibly be even greater than the propensity to consume of the poor. This is what has to happen if we follow the definition of spending I described in chapter 2. Further confusing the issue, one could have the picture previously described where we have two ways of purchasing an item and one way the transaction would show three times as much spending, income and demand as another way. A good example of that is the transaction described in chapter 4 where Bob buys something from George but they decide to do it as a direct bank to bank transaction. This would be similar to paying for something with a debit card. According to my model this requires at least 3 steps that count as spending.

1. Bob's bank purchases back some of the asset called Bob's deposit account and lowers his debt to Bob, the money is then briefly owned by Bob. That is one step of spending and income, but the only spending was buying back a debt obligation, the bank buying back the asset sold to Bob when he put money into the account in the past. This step is not direct spending.

2. Bob indicates ownership of that money should go to George and George gives Bob the purchased item. That money is then briefly owned by George. That spending pays for the good being purchased. That is direct spending.

3. George then directs the money be put into his deposit account. This is spending by George to acquire a larger balance in the asset known as his deposit account. That counts as spending to purchase a savings asset, a purely financial asset.

Compare that to spending paid for by paper currency. Bob gives George money, George gives Bob the item purchased. One round of spending paying for the good. For the 3 step electronic transactions, in terms of economic activity, other than some shuffling of the value of accounts at the bank, the same thing happened as when Bob paid George with paper money. But in terms of total spending the electronic transaction creates three times as much spending and three times as much (gross) income. The connection between spending and economic activity was beginning to lose its meaning in my mind. That is when I realized I needed to distinguish between spending to purchase a purely financial asset and the type of spending I call direct spending.

This dilemma was solved by the realization that it is only the spending on labor, goods, services, and other outcomes (except buying a purely financial asset) that creates demand for those things that lead to increased employment and production and affects our standard of living and quality of life. I decided on the term "direct spending" for that type of spending. I defined direct spending as including all spending except spending that pays to acquire all or a part of a purely financial asset.

So now my model can not only account for the fact that putting money in a deposit account does not stop that money from being used for more spending, but the concept of direct spending resuscitates the most basic tenets of the Keynesian multiplier, i.e., that increased spending causing income to be used for direct spending will lead to even more direct spending due to a multiplier effect, and that the multiplier effect is larger for income that is given to poorer people, who will not only use more of their money for direct spending than wealthier people, but who, more importantly, will use larger fractions of it for type 1 direct spending.

I realized that it is the direct spending that drives everything. It is total direct spending that determines aggregate demand and it is total direct spending that occurs as a result of a given amount of investment spending (direct or not) that determines the "direct spending velocity" of that investment money and thus the multiplier. Total direct spending divided by the investment amount will be your direct spending multiplier, whether the initial investment spending was direct spending or not.

Let the direct spending multiplier k_{DS} be defined so that for a change in investment spending ΔI, the change in total direct spending income ΔY_{DS} is equal to $k_{DS} * \Delta I$. $\Delta Y_{DS} = k_{DS} * \Delta I$. Therefore $k_{DS} = \Delta Y_{DS}/\Delta I$.

For an amount of investment spending ΔI..............the change in total direct spending is $\Delta Y_{DS} = \Delta I_{DS} + \Delta C_{DS}$ where ΔI_{DS} is the change in the amount of direct investment spending, if any, and ΔC_{DS} is the change in the amount of direct consumption spending. This means the direct spending multiplier is calculated as $\Delta Y_{DS}/\Delta I = (\Delta I_{DS} + \Delta C_{DS})/\Delta I$.

If the extra investment spending ΔI is direct spending then it equals ΔI_{DS} and if it is not direct spending it cannot equal ΔI_{DS} because then ΔI_{DS} **must = 0**. If $\Delta I_{DS} = 0$ then all the direct spending would be direct consumption spending, ΔC_{DS}. That means, in the case where the increase in the investment spending is a loan, then $\Delta I_{DS} = 0$ and $\Delta Y_{DS} = \Delta C_{DS}$ and the multiplier would be $\Delta Y_{DS}/\Delta I = \Delta C_{DS}/\Delta I$.

The change in total direct spending income divided by the investment amount is the investment direct spending multiplier. If the investment is direct spending investment then the change in total direct spending includes the investment amount added to the direct consumption spending amount. If the investment is not direct spending, the change in total direct spending income is equal to the change in direct consumption spending.

A couple examples:

If the investment is all direct spending, and equals 1 dollar and that dollar gets re-used for direct spending 10 times, we have the change in investment $\Delta I = \Delta I_{DS} = 1$ and $\Delta C_{DS} = 10$ then investment direct spending multiplier k_{DS} is **(10+1)/1=11**

And if the change in investment spending is a loan of one dollar, then the change investment $\Delta I = 1$ but $\Delta I_{DS} = 0$ and if again $\Delta C_{DS} = 10$, the investment direct spending multiplier k_{DS} would be **(10+0)/1=10**

My approach in this book is to develop the ideas in a step by step fashion, to maintain our connection to macroeconomics as usually taught, and progress gradually as new concepts are covered. Although I did not include this concept of direct spending earlier, we should make a mental note that all previous discussion of aggregate demand and the multiplier must now be modified so that when doing an accounting of aggregate demand, the only spending that one uses is direct

Keynes' Multiplier Modified to Include the Effect of Loans

spending. Now that I have defined the concept called direct spending, when looking at other chapters in this book, whenever demand that affects the employment level is discussed we should substitute the term direct spending for spending, and direct spending demand for demand. Any time in this book where the multiplier effect is discussed understand that we really need to be concerned with how much of an increase in total direct spending occurs as a result of an initial increase in spending. As long as we are at less than full employment (unemployment greater than NAIRU, actually) any increase in direct spending can increase employment and production and potentially standard of living.

Once the economy gets to full employment the only way improvements in standard of living occur is by improving productivity and efficiency. The improvement in standard of living, of course, is also guided by the wisdom behind spending choices. It is not just how much we produce, but what we produce.

Let us say that α is the fraction of new spending that creates income for type 1 spenders.

And **(1-α)** is the fraction of new spending that creates income for type 2 spenders.

Let ρ_1 and ρ_2 be the direct spending multipliers for when a certain amount of extra income is given to type one spenders and to type two spenders, respectively. We know from the previous discussion that ρ_1 can be expected to be greater than ρ_2.

Let ΔI be the amount of that extra income with the fraction α of that amount going to type one spenders and the fraction **(1-α)** of that amount going to type two spenders. The total increase in direct spending income can be expected to equal the change in direct income cause by the fraction of the increased income going to type one spenders which equals $\rho_1 * \alpha * \Delta I$ plus the change in direct spending income caused by direct investment income going to type two spenders which is $\rho_2 * (1-\alpha) * \Delta I$

Let ΔY_{DS} be total increase in direct spending including the multiplier effect and this gives:

$$\Delta Y_{DS} = \rho_1 * \alpha * \Delta I + \rho_2 * (1-\alpha) * \Delta I$$

$$\Delta Y_{DS} = \rho_2 * \Delta I + (\rho_1 - \rho_2) * \alpha * \Delta I$$

This shows that, since $\rho_1 > \rho_2$ that as α increases, as the fraction of that extra income that goes to people more likely to "type one direct spend it" increases, the total amount of direct spending income increases.

Let $\rho_1 = 4$ and $\rho_2 = 2$ as an example. Then the formula becomes:

$$\Delta Y_{DS} = 2*\Delta I + 2*\alpha*\Delta I$$

If $\alpha = 0$ then $\Delta Y_{DS} = 2*\Delta I$

If $\alpha = 1/2$ then $\Delta Y_{DS} = 2*\Delta I + 1*\Delta I = 3*\Delta I$

If $\alpha = 1$ then $\Delta Y_{DS} = 2*\Delta I + 2*\Delta I = 4*\Delta I$

In this example the more the extra income goes to type 1 spenders the greater the total direct spending income and demand. This is more likely to be the case if more of the initial extra spending and income goes to poorer people as compared to richer people. I just wanted to devise a simple way to show how type 1 direct spending might have a greater effect on total income than type 2 direct spending. That being said, one cannot have an economy function without the occurrence of both type 1 and type 2 direct spending. If there was only type 1 direct spending and no type 2 direct spending the economy would not be viable.

CHAPTER 37
Grow Like Crazy or Have a Depression?

The previous chapter on capital goods (Chapter 28) explains how economists viewed investment as paying for capital goods, also known as investment goods. That, of course, counts as direct spending. Keynes, at one point in the General Theory, wrestled with that definition of investment and some of the problems it would create. A student of Keynes, Alvin Hansen, was also influenced by this idea. This is my understanding of the issues of concern that arise if we restrict investment to mean purchasing capital goods, when analyzing that idea using the definitions and concepts discussed in this book.

IF THE ONLY thing that counts as investment is the paying for capital goods, and if the value of the direct spending multiplier, **k**, is fairly stable, one would need to keep the amount of investment in capital goods from decreasing, or total direct spending income, demand and employment would also decrease.

Let ΔY_{DS} equal total direct spending. Since $\Delta Y_{DS} = k * \Delta I$ if the amount of investment drops, total direct spending income which equals total direct spending demand drops. We now also make the reasonable assumption that when below full employment if we increase direct spending demand, by increasing direct spending investment (or the direct spending multiplier acting on that investment) we increase employment and production.

Working on a model where what is counted as investment is mainly spending on capital goods, the concern was how to keep the spending on capital goods just enough to give us a value of aggregate direct spending demand adequate enough to make effective demand occur at full employment. What if spending on capital goods was optimal to maintain full employment but the investment spending at that certain level caused production of excess capital goods? Then we assume that inventories would build up and eventually those paying for the creation of the capital goods would cut back on their spending. When that investment, i.e., the spending on capital goods, falls, then total direct spending income and demand would fall below the level necessary to maintain full employment and involuntary unemployment would ensue. If nothing further was done, then the only thing that would lead to recovery is when the inventories of those capital goods began to get depleted and investment spending on capital goods resumed.

In this scenario, the depletion of the capital goods, which are used to make consumption goods, would occur only as fast as the consumption goods can be sold. The sales of the consumption goods, and the time to recovery, would be delayed even further, as a result of the decreased spending and income, caused by increased involuntary unemployment. The quandary to those working with this model became how to find ways to maintain investment spending at just the right level to maintain full employment, in order to prevent involuntary unemployment.

Too much investment could lead to inventory buildup, causing the scene we just described. Too little investment would cause aggregate demand to be insufficient to reach full employment.

One thing that would keep the need for investment from falling and to prevent the inventory of capital goods from building up would be if population kept growing. If population kept growing you would need to increase or maintain the rate of production of capital goods because there would be more need and demand for consumption goods preventing the capital stock from building up. That actually would be an increase in the propensity to consume and the multiplier effect, because the proportion of total spending to purchase consumption goods would be greater compared to the proportion of investment spending. This leads to the idea that we need to keep increasing population or we will go into a depression.

Another way to keep investment into capital goods from falling is to keep developing new products and new technologies. Capital spending would be necessary to develop the new products and set up the production process, the advertising, supply and sales chains, etc. This led the conclusion that if the new technologies were not always being developed, investment in capital goods would be inadequate to keep spending sufficient to maintain full employment and we would go into a depression.

Another way to keep investment into capital goods from falling is to keep exploiting new territories or resources. Capital spending would be necessary to develop the new uses of land or natural resources. This led the conclusion that if new resources are not available, investment in capital goods would be inadequate to keep overall demand sufficient to maintain full employment and we would go into a depression.

In this scenario we are limited to considering production of investment goods as the only investment and paying for the purchase of consumption goods as the only consumption. Just for completeness, in that setting, I would add another way to match up investment spending with consumption spending so that inventory or capital does not build up. This would be to make the production of investment goods less efficient, and in that way not as much will be produced. That can mean the employers will continue to need to pay for production of capital goods, reducing the chance that investment spending will fall off. That is unlikely to be the strategy used.

Or we could keep efficiency of investment goods production the same and increase consumption goods production, i.e., produce and sell more consumption goods. This way the consumption goods production would be using up the inventory of capital goods, so they would not build up. This could occur with the increased efficiency of the consumption goods workers, as long as their pay goes up as much so there is enough spending power in the economy to buy those extra consumption goods. Or rather than increased efficiency of the consumption goods workers, increase their work hours, and in that way their total wages and ability to direct spend to purchase consumption goods could increase along with the increased production more working hours allowed. Or as mentioned, from increased population with new workers going into consumption goods production. The last three scenarios all have the fraction of spending that is (direct) consumption spending increase and the fraction that is (direct) investment spending decrease, which means the direct spending multiplier will be increased.

Eventually, the concern is, that we would fall short on all these measures and investment spending to purchase capital goods would not remain adequate, due to not enough consumption demand and inventory buildup. This would cause a demand deficit and involuntary unemployment would develop and increase, that is, the economy would fall below full employment.

Hansen believed that, if the private sector were left to itself, inevitably, we would find ourselves in a situation where investment in capital goods is inadequate to maintain full employment. His reasoning is based on his belief that, in the late 1930s, the economy was reaching a limit on how far and how fast technology would develop, and we were running out of new resources to exploit and this would lead to a situation of inadequate investment and involuntary unemployment. He also further believed that population growth was slowing, and that population could possibly even decrease, eliminating another way to keep investment adequate. For all of these reasons, he became concerned that our economies would always tend towards a state where the economy has inadequate demand and a certain level of involuntary unemployment and will be in a chronic recession or depression. He called this state of the economy "secular stagnation".

The legacy of this model, where investment only includes spending on capital goods, is the belief that in order to have a viable economy you must have a constant and relentless increase in technology, and/or a constant discovery of new frontiers or resources, and/or a constantly increasing population, and/or a constant increase in productivity, and/or a constant increase in the amount of spending on goods and services by consumers. In other words, grow like crazy or have a depression.

After World War 2, Hansen was proven wrong in his concern that the develop of technologies would slow significantly, and as a result he lost some of his influence. As a result of our ability to keep investment in capital goods increasing, and the economy viable, there was no real need to challenge the idea that the only thing that counts as investment is spending to obtain capital goods. However, Hansen's concerns about the possibility of this "secular stagnation" eventually occurring is on solid theoretical ground **IF** we restrict our understanding of what counts as investment spending to be spending on capital goods. If, however, one understands investment spending as it is defined in Chapter 2 of this book we do not have to be trapped in this mind set.

My much more general definition of investment shows how spending on capital goods is not the only way we can keep demand adequate to maintain full employment, or at least keep unemployment levels from becoming higher than NAIRU.

Increased (direct) investment spending can include government transfers, such as unemployment insurance, welfare, and food stamps. It can include government spending on infrastructure, government spending on research, paying for maintenance and staffing of national parks. It can include spending on the arts, and spending on sports and recreation. It can include spending on cleaning up the environment. It can include spending on all sorts of government services.

But it is not just direct government spending that can keep the economy going. Private investment spending on research and development, training, education, even charity can help reduce that demand deficit. And as we have seen in Chapter 36 loans can start the chain of spending that increases total direct spending and aggregate demand. That is, the investment does not even have be restricted to direct spending, much less restricted to purchasing capital goods. Oh and just to mention, it is spending, period, that is needed to increase direct spending demand, so even though government spending is always classified as investment spending, increases in private spending could be either increases in investment spending or increases in consumption spending (as per the definitions of investment and consumption in chapter 2)

It is undesirable to have inadequate aggregate demand, because not only does it cause the suffering of the unemployed and increase poverty, it also reduces wealth production and wealth building and keeps our standard of living from attaining the level it might otherwise.

The point is this is a completely unnecessary situation. We do not need continued population increases, or continued growth in the per capita amount of personal spending on consumption goods, or, *even though it is desirable*, we do not need to be constantly, (and some would say frantically), increasing our productivity and technology and variety of products to maintain adequate aggregate demand. We can maintain adequate (direct spending) demand with or without those factors. In fact, even if all we are doing is maintaining the same standard of living, we can still maintain adequate demand. It is easily done, if we understand that investment spending can be many things other than just paying for the production of capital goods. And if we understand that any spending that results in an overall increase in the direct spending velocity of money will increase aggregate demand.

Critics will express the concern that if we used government spending to increase total investment (Keynes' I) this will make people lazy and unwilling to work and they would not contribute to production. They are worried that government transfers intended as a safety net will actually end up decreasing production in the long run, not increase it. Or they might worry that the government might pay for ventures that are inefficient and produce limited or no benefit to society and are unworthy of being supported. They will express concern that those programs decrease wealth production overall and make us poorer not richer. These are valid concerns and it is better if government spending programs are intelligently and responsibly designed and administered. But these concerns should not be used as a total refutation of the validity of the concept of inadequate aggregate (direct spending) demand. The fact is, we can use government spending, at times, to boost investment and keep the economy from going into a depression.

Critics will argue that government spending will just decrease private spending by the same amount because ultimately the government spending must be paid for by the private sector. The answer to this criticism comes from the statement that, in the macroeconomy, spending is not the depletion of wealth. If spending slows, it is because those with the money to spend decide not to spend it. If the economy has inadequate aggregate demand it is in a state where, due simply to lack of (direct) spending, output is reduced compared to its potential. In such a situation the solution is to increase (direct) spending, so as to increase the direct spending velocity of money. If the private sector, whether through charity or investment in new ventures, or investment in research and development, decides to increase their spending and make up for the demand gap, then increased government spending may not be necessary. But if the private sector does not make up for the demand deficit by increasing spending, then in order to prevent demand shortages, government spending will be needed to increase the direct spending velocity of money. Assuming that government spending will benefit some of the poorer factions of society more than the wealthy, that factor would be expected to give a further boost to the direct spending velocity of money and decrease the demand shortage.

As for where the money for the spending comes from, we have to consider that, as long as we don't have an inadequate money supply, this is situation where demand can be increased by increasing the direct spending velocity of money. If that is not occurring, then we need to get the money away from those who are not direct spending it as much, and into the hands of those who will be direct spending at a faster rate.

One of the functions of loans is to take money from where it is not being spent and put it in the hands of those who will spend it. Borrowing and then direct spending by individuals or the government can help make up for direct spending deficits. Yes, loans have to be paid back, and if the only thing that increased direct spending was loans by the private sector, then the burden of debt would begin to reduce direct spending as more of the income of indebted individuals would be diverted to paying the loans.

As for government borrowing, who has to provide the government with the tax revenues to allow the government to pay those loans back is important. Making the poor and middle class pay more of the increased taxes will slow direct spending and direct spending velocity of money more than if wealthier people were made to pay more of the taxes. Of course, government loans would not be necessary if taxation, instead of borrowing, was able to directly generate the money for government spending. Again, who bears the burden of that taxation, or who bears the burden of paying back loans, is essential to whether it leads to increased aggregate demand or decreased aggregate demand. Tax the poor and design government programs that help the rich decreases overall spending and demand. Tax the rich and design government programs that help the poor increases aggregate demand. If the way to get increased spending power to the poor and middle class is increasing their debt obligations due to borrowing, instead of increasing their income by paying them more, this can, over time, slow the direct spending velocity of money, as more and more of the poor and middle classes income gets diverted to paying off debt obligations.

The advantage to wealthier people of an economy that does not have a direct spending demand shortage is that they usually are ones who take possession of and sell the increased production that results. Therefore, one would expect the wealth of the wealthier factions to go up, not down, even with taxes factored in. Assuming that the government spending is responsibly managed and production increases, taxing the rich more to pay for government programs that keep spending at an optimal level, does not harm the wealthy, in fact, on the average, it probably helps them, perhaps helps them the most.

Repeating the main message of this chapter. The bottom line is that investment spending includes a lot more than just spending to produce capital goods. There are many other types of spending that can keep aggregate direct spending demand adequate to prevent a recession or a depression. Policymakers should keep the valid concerns of the critics mentioned above in mind, but at the same time, understand that there are remedies for times of inadequate aggregate demand.

Keynes wrestled with the same ideas, and he advocated other possible ways to increase investment spending than just spending on capital goods. Keynes, I believe, in analyzing this particular scenario, was mainly looking at what happens to the economy if investment spending is completely controlled by for-profit private concerns. It was in this context that he presented the above mentioned explanation as a theory about how business cycles might work, that is, where the inventories could build up and lead to less investment, leading to decreased direct spending demand and involuntary unemployment until capital goods are depleted and investment spending starts again.

I do not believe Keynes thought that secular stagnation was inevitable because he advocated all sorts of remedies for situations when the economy has inadequate aggregate demand including government spending.

Another concern that people have, a concern also expressed by some economists, is the idea that as the population ages we are going to have problems because there will be a lower percentage of the population working and supporting us. This is a purely supply-side concern. The only way we could end up with a decrease in standard of living due to less people working is if production is inadequate. The concern that this will be so is used as a reason to cut retirement benefits and increase retirement age. The belief that we should be concerned about this has no credibility. Our constantly increasing productivity makes this a moot point. With less workers the economy will easily be able to produce enough to take care of an aging population. (Of course, if we destroy our economy through destruction of the environment, including the influence of climate change, or from war, that can cause supply side shortages and economic depression).

Adequate production due to productivity increases does not automatically mean that individual people will have enough income to pay for their spending once they stop working. It just means that if they have the money, the product will be available for purchase. But that situation is easily solved. If the economy is producing enough, despite a lower number of workers, so that nobody's standard of living has to go down, and if the only reason retired people's standard of living has gone down is because they don't have enough income to purchase the products they need to maintain their standard of living, then just give people more income in their retirement. That is, have society spend to purchase the outcome that, when retired, people can maintain a better standard of living.

That so many economists do not tout this obvious solution, I believe, is in part due to the disproportionate influence of a self-interested investor class. Some seem to believe that nobody should get paid unless they are making something the investor class can get a profit from. It also comes from the idea that investors should do anything and everything to maximize profits. Even if the means avoiding any taxes, or not paying into pensions or 401ks, or any other spending that would support increased retirement pay. In other words, avarice of the investor class could be playing a strong role in creating an artificial crisis. One way this is playing out is propagating the idea that we must cut retirement benefits, or we will have a supply crisis in the future, and then using that concern to justify decreasing retirement incomes and raising retirement age. This influence is felt both in not giving enough income to people during their working years to allow a good retirement nest egg, and in always fighting against taxation that would allow government funding that could be used to increase retirement income and benefits in general.

If the economy is below full employment and not producing at maximum, any type of (direct) spending increase will increase demand and should help increase production and employment. That is true whether the population is going up, staying the same or going down. It can be either an increase in investment spending which increases the ΔI which increases total direct spending according to the formula $\Delta Y_{DS} = k * \Delta I$, or it can be an increase in direct consumption spending which increases the velocity of money and increases the direct spending multiplier, k, in $\Delta Y_{DS} = k * B$.

Increasing the velocity of money by increasing spending can be accomplished easily without the need for population increases. This extra spending could be supported by the population increasing but it is not required. Increasing the amount of spending on consumption goods per person, including the increase in quantity and variety of these goods, can keep investment spending on capital goods adequate to prevent a depression. But those things are not necessary to prevent a depression. Although generally we are consuming more per person, and the variety and quality of items available keeps changing, that does not mean we cannot have a situation where we keep the same production and productivity and still have a viable economy. Recognizing all the things that count as investment spending, and recognizing that we can increase aggregate demand by increasing direct investment or direct consumption spending will give us the knowledge as to how to maintain adequate demand and full employment (as Keynes would say), unemployment rate = NAIRU as modern economists would say.

Although, generally speaking, growth is a desirable thing, during periods when aggregate demand is not sufficient, as mentioned, there are remedies available to policy makers, so that economies do not have to suffer through a depression or recession, and can maintain or increase level of wealth. **Understanding what counts as investment spending is key to understanding how to design such a remedy.**

A key point in designing a solution includes the need to monitor its effect on production. If after a reasonable amount of time production does not start recovering, or even worse if it is decreasing, then the government should take a closer look at their strategy and consider making adjustments.

CHAPTER 38
Choice of Units

This chapter shows an interesting way Keynes developed to count employment levels and calculate income. He thought it helpful to define two particular units.

KEYNES DEFINED IN his chapter about choice of **units** the **labor unit** which can be used to measure the employment level and the **wage unit**, i.e., W, which is the amount of pay per unit of time per labor unit.

The total number of labor units N employed is not exactly <u>EQUAL</u> to the number of people employed.

Let us start with the basic labor unit, the lowest skilled job… That person would count as one labor unit.

Then let us say there is a skilled laborer who is paid twice as much, that person counts as two labor units etc.

You could even have a person count as 2.75 labor units or 1.5 labor units, or 5 labor units.

But generally speaking, the more labor units, the more people employed and certainly the more wage units paid out to workers.

If you had one basic laborer (1) plus one skilled laborer paid twice as much (2) and a highly educated manager paid 3 times as much (3), then in that case N equals 1 + 2 + 3 = 6 even though there are only 3 workers… N = 6 labor units, not 3.

The number of labor units employed, as defined above, **corresponds** to the number of people employed but is not equal to it.

Choice of Units

The wage unit is how much you pay each labor unit.

Now the distribution of wages in **real life** tends towards a relatively stable distribution, so that in reality as N increases, the number of people employed increases in a similar proportion. That means, this concept can be **useful** as a measure of employment.

Plus, it makes it a lot easier to calculate total income. Just multiply the number of labor units N by W, i.e., the wage unit.

CHAPTER 39
Flexible Wage vs Flexible Money Policy

Keynes discussed both these policies in "The General Theory". The flexible wage policy is still taught in macroeconomics courses, although it is not specifically called that anymore. I will show why I consider the reasoning behind the flexible wage policy to be incorrect, and therefore, the policy recommendations stemming from it to be invalid.

IN THIS CHAPTER I describe concepts that are commonly taught in standard economics textbooks. They are presented as I understand them. Generally speaking, the concept of direct spending is not included in these concepts as taught. For that reason, I exclude using the term direct spending in my presentation in this chapter. That being said, all of the spending referred in this chapter is direct spending.

Flexible wage vs flexible money policy are policies designed to deal with demand shocks. Keynes talks about this in "The General Theory of Employment Interest and Money". A form of the flexible wage policy is discussed in every modern macroeconomics text book as a basic concept.

I think the best way to look at this concept is to break these two policies into two simple, or rather, simplistic models.

Both models start with a demand shock. Another term for a demand shock is a "spending decrease". A sudden spending decrease, or a relatively fast spending decrease, or an atypical spending decrease, but a spending decrease nevertheless.

In both models the assumption is made that that the pattern of spending remains the same, that the proportion of total spending targeted in any direction remains the same. In other words, the types and distribution of transactions remain in the same proportions no matter what the total demand is.

A Simplistic Flexible Wage Policy Model

We know demand = income which is equal to average price times number of transactions.

Demand= **P∗T**, where **P** is the average price of transactions and **T** is the total number of transactions.

In this simple model, as already stated, the assumption is made that the types and distribution of transactions remain in the same proportion, no matter what the value of **T** is. If **T** is the same, then the amount of production and sales of everything in the economy remains unchanged.

In the simple flexible wage policy, wages are assumed to always be a constant fraction of prices. If wages are increased or decreased by a certain percent, prices are increased or decreased by the same percent.

The idea in the flexible wage model is that we can keep the number of transactions constant by lowering the **prices**. If $T = T_0$ a constant, then if demand (**Y**) is lowered by a certain percent, lowering price by the same percent will allow the equation $Y = P*T_0$ to hold.

If **Y**, which represents total spending and total income, is suddenly cut in half but price, **P,** is cut in half the equality will still hold and the number of transactions will remain at T_0. The total production and sales is preserved.

The flexible wage policy says that if demand **Y** is cut in half that if **wages** are then cut in half that **prices** will also be cut in half and the total employment and output will remain the same. This means that **even if wages are cut in half**, since prices are also cut in half, the worker can buy just as much stuff and **nothing changes**. Though the wages are reduced, their **buying power** is the same, meaning real, inflation adjusted wages are the same. There is no depression, and the economy does not miss a beat. Nobody's financial position suffers.

In terms of Keynes' units, the wage unit would be reduced in the same proportion as demand and this would mean that demand in terms of wage units remains the same. If prices went down in the same proportion as wage units did then the buying power of a wage unit would remain the same.

A Simplistic Flexible Money Policy

For the simplest model of the FLEXIBLE MONEY POLICY when demand goes down somehow or other, presumably by some sort of government intervention, the decrease in demand is reversed. More money for spending is made available, and somehow the spending pattern is the same and nothing changes in the economy. Everyone has the same income and the same amount of spending happens, the same amount of product is produced and sold, and the same level of employment is maintained.

In the flexible money policy if demand, (that is the **Y** in **Y = P∗T$_0$**) is reduced, instead of changing prices, you find a way to increase demand **Y** back to the previous level, so **T** can remain at **T$_0$**, at the same average price **P**.

FIGURE 39.1
A GRAPH OF THE FLEXIBLE WAGE POLICY

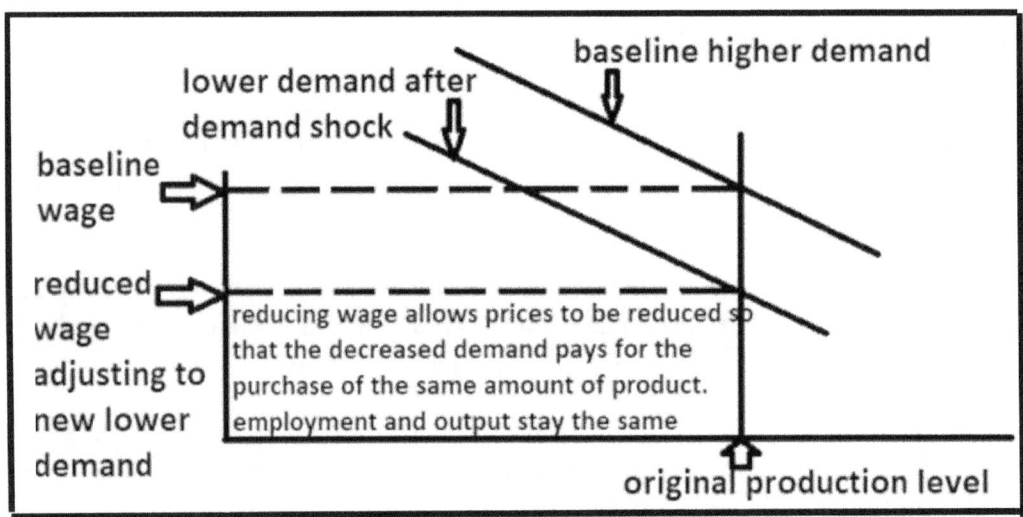

This is what proponents allege will occur if the simple flexible wage policy could be fully and consistently implemented. They recognize however that the flexible wage policy is never in reality able to be consistently and fully implemented. Those proponents teach that the only thing that gets in the way of the simple flexible wage policy working just as outlined, is factors that keep wages from adjusting downward.

Wages that do not adjust downward immediately are called sticky wages, where workers resist a cut in wages, and sticky prices are prices that do not immediately adjust downward, because sellers resist lowering their prices. If not for sticky wages and sticky prices, proponents say, we would never have a depression or a recession, and the economy would keep functioning at maximum level. My observation is that sticky wages generally appear to get more blame than sticky prices.

Here is how economists might say "sticky wages" interfere.

Let us say the economy has a demand shock and wages and prices do not adjust downward, that they stay the same. Based on Demand, which equals $Y = P*T$, if prices remained the same then transactions must be reduced proportional to Demand, which in the sticky wage model means employment level and the output will be reduced proportional to demand as well.

FIGURE 39.2

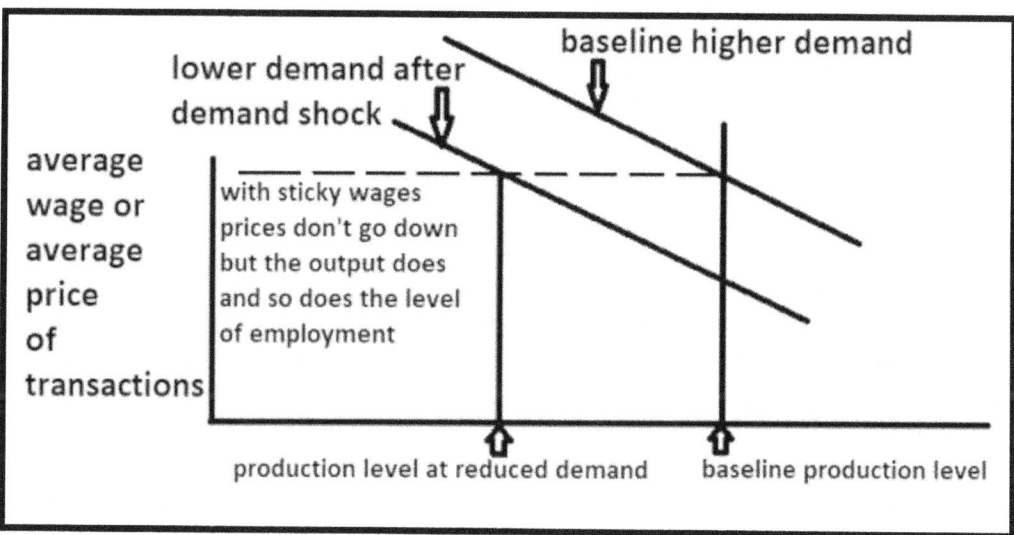

The proponents of the flexible wage policy would say that even though wages initially do not adjust downward, that since unemployment has increased due to the decreased demand, that competition for jobs will slowly push down the wages. And slowly over time, even though we have the reduced demand that occurred after the demand shock, production and employment will increase and return to baseline levels, albeit with workers getting reduced nominal wages. This means the wages would gradually go down and production will go up as the system moves along the reduced demand line from point 1 to point 2 as shown here in figure 39.3.

FIGURE 39.3

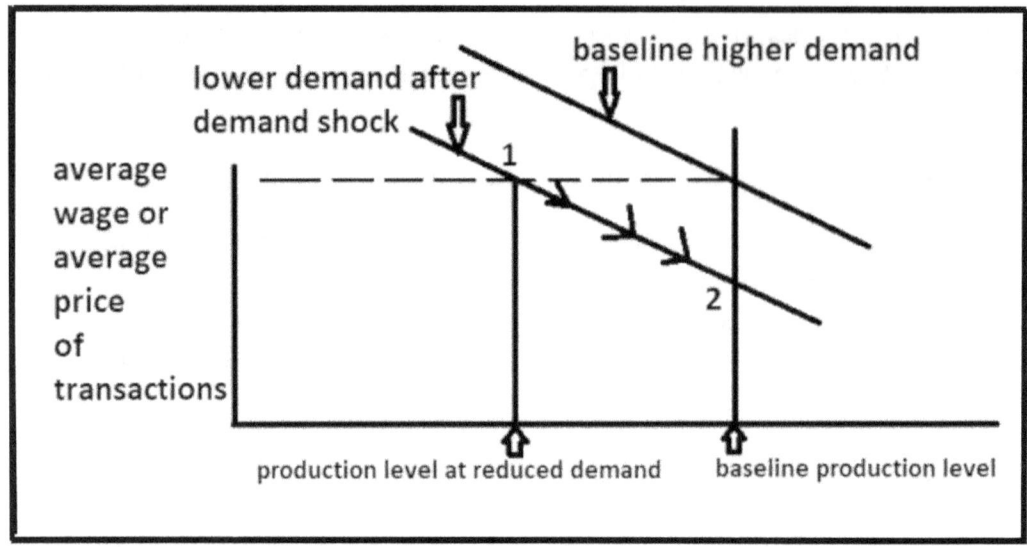

They like to say that this means the economy is "self-correcting". That even with "sticky wages" and "sticky prices" the economy will come back to NAIRU and maximum sustainable employment levels and production, without any "artificial" government intervention.

But figure 39.3 is erroneous, it cannot happen that way.

This model is presented as showing the economy as recovering to the same REAL demand, the same inflation adjusted income with the same amount and distribution of transactions, and wage earners having the same buying power.

But if, when you had the demand shock, employment decreased. That means the amount of production and the amount of transactions decreased. And when you reduce wages and average prices to compensate, you do not go down the same reduced demand line to point 2. In other words, if you reduce wages, you decrease total demand even further, you jump to a line representing even lower demand. You move to point 3 on the next graph. By reducing wages and prices at the current reduced number of transactions you cause demand to go down further. Graphically it looks like this:

FIGURE 39.4

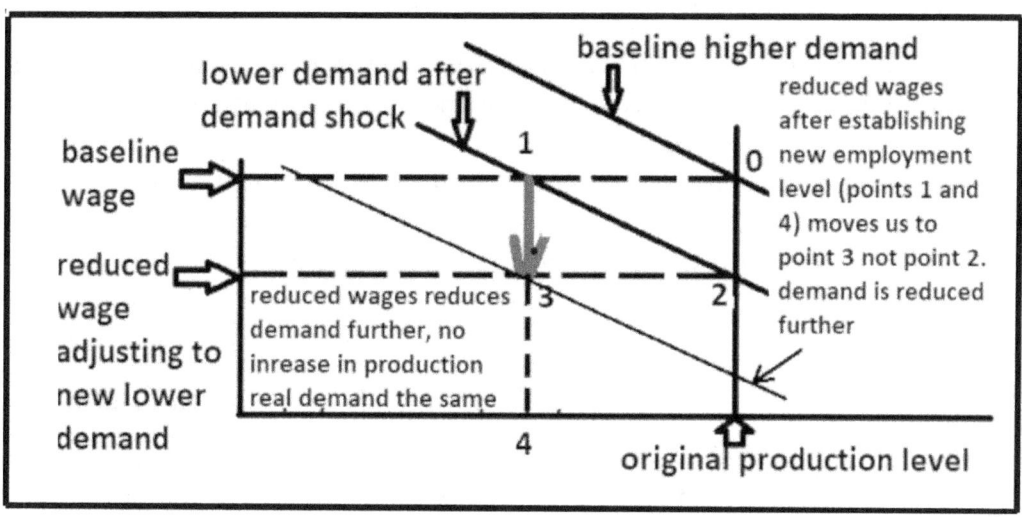

In terms of demand $Y = P*T$, at point 0 we have demand, price and transactions Y_0, P_0, and T_0. $Y_0 = P_0 * T_0$.

After the demand shock we move to point 1. At point 1 we have demand now changed to the lower value Y_1, the price remains the same (sticky prices) at P_0, but due to the demand decrease the number of transactions is reduced to the lower level T_1. $Y_1 = P_0 * T_1$.

The next step is to reduce prices by reducing wages and the way this model is usually taught is that this gets us from point 1 to point 2, and we are back at full employment.

But since we now have the lower number of transactions, if we reduce wages and prices go to a lower value P_1 then demand reduces further to $Y_2 = P_1 * T_1$

Following the flexible wage policy model where wages are a constant proportion of prices, reducing wages does not increase transactions in the macroeconomy, all it does is keep the transactions the same.

Reducing wages causes demand to go down further, so as wages decrease, if the prices decrease by the same proportion, then the new lower demand will, due to the price decrease, be able to keep output and total transactions the same, but output and total transactions will not recover at all and will not increase back to the starting point as implied in figure 39.3.

What it means is that real buying power of the wages does not increase, real buying power stays the same.

The only way to increase the demand is to increase spending. Decreasing wages is not a magical way to increase real demand. It is not a way to get back to the previous level of employment output and number of transactions. If real demand is decreased, the only way to return to the previous level of real demand is to increase the amount of real, inflation adjusted, spending. But that could be done at any level of wages. Reducing wages does nothing to cause recovery.

FIGURE 39.5

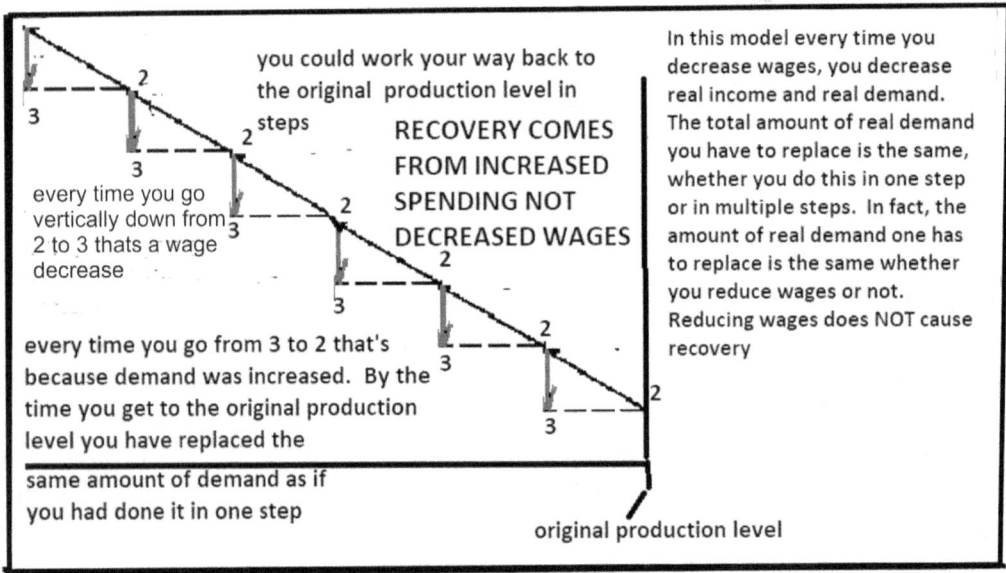

Why do so many economists think that the economy recovers from a demand shock by having sticky wages eventually get lower?

I do not know, perhaps it comes from the simplistic flexible wage policy scenario where they imply a simultaneous decrease in wages, that occurs along with the demand shock would mean that real demand never changes. For that to actually occur, that would mean all incomes and all prices across the entire economy would have be reduced simultaneously whenever there is a change in the amount of spending. Good luck with organizing that.

Perhaps they figure that it is because in real life depressions put downward pressure on wages and wages do go down in depressions and yet, usually, the economy does recover. But when that recovery occurs, it is because of spending increases, not wage decreases.

Most likely though, economist's views are influenced, at least in part, from looking at this scenario from a **microeconomic perspective**. If, for an individual firm demand for their product suddenly went down, if workers took an immediate pay cut they could ship as much product for the lower total amount of money offered to buy their product, and the company may be able to continue to produce at the same level and perhaps not lose market share.

In the macroeconomy, you cannot increase real demand by decreasing wages, all else being equal. If you decrease nominal wages all you do is decrease nominal demand further, and at best, real demand does not increase, it stays the same.

To go from point 3 to point 2 you must increase real demand. To increase real demand, you must increase either real consumption spending or real investment spending or both.

So, in this simple flexible wage policy, after the economy has a demand shock, which due to sticky wages and sticky prices gets the economy to a reduced level of employment, reducing wages only causes a further reduction in nominal demand, and an identical level of real demand. Reducing wages does not help recovery of employment level or production. The only thing that helps increase employment and production back to the previous level is increased spending. When you have a spending decrease that causes a depression you must have a (real) spending increase to have recovery from that depression. The bottom line is, in the macroeconomy, there is no magic way to increase demand by making people take pay cuts.

Discussion of The Flexible Money Policy

And this leads us right into the flexible money policy, because from the description of the flexible money policy given above we see that the goal is, if we have a demand shock, a spending decrease, then the solution of the flexible money policy is to find a way to replace the missing demand, replace the missing spending.

Government policy such as fiscal and monetary interventions are intended to replace missing demand. And of course, they cannot replace everyone's missing income in such a way that everything remains the same, but the idea is that they increase spending, direct spending and this gets us back up to higher levels of employment and production.

Keynes would have liked us to get up to true full employment but nowadays people aim to get to the NAIRU.

⁂

Keynes described another significant problem with the flexible wage policy. It is not just the lower paid workers who are the income earners. There are higher paid workers, executives, entrepreneurs and rentiers. These people are generally not the ones targeted to have their income decreased. In fact, in many cases when the employers try to reduce low paid workers' wages, it is with the goal of having the higher paid people's pay increased. There are also fixed nominal expenses based on contract that will not decrease.

What this means, is that to support a price decrease, lower paid workers pay must be reduced even further in such a way that not only does the real pay of workers who kept their jobs not increase, but real inflation adjusted pay of those workers will go down. Their real pay will go down while the real pay of the others involved in the economy will go up. This is a redistribution of income from lower paid workers to higher paid workers. As was discussed earlier, this will reduce the direct spending and slow the velocity of money and reduce overall demand even further, making even more of a spending increase necessary to achieve a recovery.

This simple model as presented also did not include the existence of a baseline inflation, but all the concepts are identical if we just add a preexisting baseline inflation, then one would simply label the y axis inflation instead of prices which has been shown elsewhere. (Compare the graphs in the chapter "Keynes, Phillips, and NAIRU" and the chapter on stagflation for an example of how to do this)

Also, if there was baseline inflation, one expects interest rates on loans to be adjusted to that baseline inflation, to inflation adjusted prices. But if inflation adjusted wages are reduced more than inflation adjusted prices this makes the loan burden greater (percentage of income needed to make loan payments). Richer people tend to be net lenders. (we make interest on our bank deposits because banks are able to loan out the money gained from our deposits, a bank deposit is a loan by the depositor to the bank). Poorer people tend to be net borrowers. So, that is another factor in reducing the total buying power of poorer people, that is, their real wages go down further than prices and their debt burden increases. This will further reduce aggregate demand of the economy as a whole.

Keynes believed flexible wage policy hurts lower paid workers.

As he puts it:

"It can only be an unjust person who would prefer a flexible wage policy to a flexible money policy"[22]

When Can Reducing Wages Help Recovery

Suppose because of inefficiencies workers productivity started to go down. It could be an inflexible work force or inflexible work rules. It could be employment structures that reward laziness, it could be all sorts of obstacles that are solvable *if* everyone acted reasonably, but the people were not acting reasonably. It could be that production and productivity was reduced because of situations that most people could not do anything about, such as depletion of vital natural resources requiring replacement options that need more labor efforts to produce, or total net production could be reduced by destruction from wars and natural disasters.

Whatever the cause, let us assume productivity went down. So, for the same wage level, and the same employment level, prices would go up meaning buying power of the wages would go down.

This is a true supply side cause of reduction in real wages. This could cause people's standard of living to go down, or down relative to what it could be. In some of the situations it may be more difficult to maintain standard of living.

In other cases, however, at times, particularly when workers are being lazy and unreasonable and overly rigid, it is possible that wage decreases for some may be necessary as part of the management strategy to motivate those workers. These are situations where employers may need to structure compensation in such a way that it rewards efficiency and hard work. It is rational that in some situations this might involve targeted real, inflation adjusted wage reductions or even workforce reductions, using competition for jobs to encourage hard work and efficiency that can increase productivity and standard of living for all.

---

22 Keynes, John Maynard. The General Theory of Employment, Interest and Money (Illustrated) (pp. 216-217). Green World Publication. Kindle Edition.

There is the danger, though, that such interventions could be implemented simply to support the short-term greed and profit of certain individuals and not for the ultimate welfare of everyone. Nevertheless, it would be naive and foolish to ignore the fact that such realities exist. However, if one is going to justify such interventions, it should be supported by a rational and objective understanding of the situation. It should not be justified as rational based on incorrect models like the ones that support implementing a "flexible wage policy".

The fact of the matter is that like it or not, our current economic policies have developed the way they have for a reason, and not always for bad reason. As a result of what Gurdjieff would call the crystalized consequences of the organ Kundabuffer, and self-calming, mankind can be extremely lazy and as such needs structure, designed to motivate people to contribute to the general wealth and to discourage harmful behaviors.

Whenever I think of this issue I always recall one of my favorite stories in Beelzebub's tales to his grandson, in "CHAPTER 15 Beelzebub's first descent to the planet Earth"[23]

---

[23] Gurdjieff, G. I.. Beelzebub's Tales to His Grandson (p. 104). BookMasters. Kindle Edition.

CHAPTER 40
NATIONAL SAVINGS

This topic is also commonly taught in macroeconomics textbooks. I address this topic because I believe the arguments used in presenting this concept are erroneous, leading to the wrong conclusions and damaging policy recommendations.

HERE WE DISCUSS the concept known as "National Savings" is discussed. National Savings is considered the amount of savings one gets when adding up private and government savings. The conclusion presented by standard economics teaching is that we will increase national savings by reducing direct consumption spending and government spending. I show how the opposite is true. If the economy is at less than full employment direct spending will increase wealth and total savings, not decrease it.

In this chapter the spending referred to is assumed to be direct spending, and income is assumed to be direct spending income. Therefore, I will not be using the terms direct spending investment, direct spending consumption, or total direct spending income because I am presenting the model as typically taught, where the concept of direct spending is either taken as a given or not considered. Even if they were counting purchasing purely financial assets as part of the spending, it would not invalidate anything in this chapter because we are not calculating aggregate demand to determine employment level or calculating a multiplier effect.

The expenditure approach to GDP is comparable to **Keynes' Y = I + C** in that it is a bunch of terms that count as investment spending plus consumption spending.

NATIONAL SAVINGS

The standard expenditure approach is **GDP = I_p + G + X - M + C** where **X** stands for exports and **M** stands for imports.

If that is a valid equation for income, then **Keynes' Investment I** would equal I_p + G + X - M

However, as I have proven in Chapter 31 on the expenditure approach to GDP -M does not belong in this equation because the effects of that factor are already contained in the values the other variables take. In that Chapter I also showed how the effects of taxes T^{24} is also already contained in the values I_p, G, C, and **X take**. So, the proper expression for expenditure approach to GDP will be Y = I_p + G + X + C. This means, in **Keynes' Y = I + C, Keynes' I** or Keynes' investment would equal I_p + G + X

I have never seen a formula for expenditure approach to GDP that does not include imports subtracted off. All equations I have seen for expenditure approach to GDP includes the term **[X - M]**, exports minus imports, or its equivalent **NX**, short for net exports. Since I have shown previously that it is improper to include imports subtracted off, whenever it is usual to put the expression **NX or [X - M]** I will simply use **X** for exports. If one wants to make comparisons between the typical proofs they present, and my analysis, simply substitute in **NX** where I have **X** and the main points I make in the analysis will still be valid.

The model as taught in standard economics courses attempts to show how we can increase savings by **decreasing spending.** It attempts to show how decreasing spending increases total wealth in the macroeconomy. When this concept is taught net production is not included as part of the savings. The savings they are talking about is only the savings that is preservation of investment. As I have pointed out it is impossible to increase or decrease wealth without including net production in your definition of savings. The savings that is the preservation of investment, is just the preservation of the money used in spending. That portion of savings does not represent a change in the level of wealth. As such, their model must make some assumptions that are in conflict with the concept of savings as it has been defined in this book.

---

24 In Chapter 31 on the Expenditure Approach to GDP, I defined Taxes **T** to include taxes, loans by private domestic entities to the government and any spending by private domestic entities to purchase anything else from the government. I continue that convention is this chapter.

I think these types of conclusions are often not challenged because they are true in **microeconomics** therefore it seems to a lot of people to make sense that it would be true in macroeconomics as well. In microeconomics, it is simple. An individual or firm spends less of their income and they have more left over for savings. In the macroeconomic sphere, when one person cuts down on their spending their personal savings increases, but we also have the compensating fact that the person, who would have been the recipient of that spending, does not receive that money and has less money, in the exact same amount that the would-be spender has saved by not spending. That increases the holdings of money for the one person but decreases the holdings of money for the second. There is no increase or decrease in the amount of money people in the whole economy are holding.

If the lack of spending had somehow caused an increase in the total wealth, it would have occurred not in the money supply but in net production. This would be unusual because, when you decrease demand, production is typically decreased. It would be unusual for decreased spending to lead to increases in net production of wealth.

As regards the money supply, which is a form of wealth, there is actually a way to increase that amount of wealth. The only way to have the amount of currency increase (or decrease) is if the central bank increased (or decreased) the money supply. The explanation for National Savings as normally taught does not include wealth and savings being increased by the Central Bank creating more money. Therefore, to be consistent with that, in this analysis, the money supply is assumed constant.

"National Savings"

Now I would like to examine the standard teaching of the concept called national savings. The proponents of this concept purport to prove that if everyone in the aggregate, "spends less" total savings will increase. Again, the only savings involved is that which equals the preservation of investment. Net production is ignored. I will show how the concept as presented leads to the wrong conclusion and that, in the macroeconomy, decreased spending does not increase the savings that is preservation of investment.

The typical textbook explanation of the concept of National Savings starts with the concept of "Private disposable income" Y_D defined as:

$Y_D = Y - T$

By so defining it, it is implied that the taxes referred to are paid for out of the current income Y, leaving the remainder to be the money left over to spend, i.e., the disposable income. If $Y = I_P + C + G + X$, then $Y_D = I_P + C + G + X - T$.

Government income, which I will designate as Y_G is said to be equal to taxes, that is $Y_G = T$. Although taxes are considered income, i.e., government income, they are not part of Y, as the expression $Y = I_P + C + G + X$ shows, and so therefore we must assume that in this model Y only includes **private** income. If Y did include government income taxes T would be added to the total and the expression for total income would be $I_P + C + G + X + T$. Since $Y = I_P + C + G + X$ without the T added on then $Y = I_P + C + G + X$, the expression for expenditure approach to GDP (which I analyzed in detail in chapter 31) defines Y as an expression for private income only.

The amount of **private SAVINGS** (S_P) is defined as what is left of disposable income after "consumption". I am certain that what is meant here by savings does not include net production. The only savings being talked about is the savings that is the preservation of investment money. I assume by consumption what is meant is any spending of money judged to have been acquired as part of the "disposable income". Since it is spending paid for by current income then it would meet my definition of consumption too. Consumption, as defined in that equation appears to account for all of the consumption spending in the economy during this time period, so we can reasonably assume that definition of consumption C, would meet the definition of consumption I gave in Chapter 2. Private savings (S_P) becomes defined as $S_P = Y_D - C = Y - T - C$ where C stands for consumption.

From Chapter 31 I showed that private savings in a closed economy, one that has no international trade, is properly defined as being equal to Keynes' Investment minus that part of taxes which is paid for out of current income. I have stated above that in this standard explanation for "National Savings" T is completely paid for by current income. We also know that Keynes' investment equals Y–C. That would give us the same formula for private savings, $S_P = Y_D - C = Y - T - C$ and so that equation would be in agreement with my model for the definition of the savings that is the preservation the investment money. This is saying that private domestic savings is Keynes' investment (Y–C) minus taxes paid for out of current income, which equals T, because it is stipulated by the definition of disposable income that all taxes are paid for out of current income.

Government savings (S_G) is defined to be government income which is taxes T minus government spending G. $S_G = Y_G - G = T - G$. If we add them both together we get "total savings" (S_T).

$S_T = S_P + S_G$

$S_T = (Y-T-C) + (T-G)$

$S_T = Y-C-G$

In the standard explanation, this equation ($S_T = Y-C-G$) for total savings is used as "proof" that any consumption (**C**) and government spending (**G**) decrease national savings, and therefore, we can increase national savings by reducing consumption (**C**) and government spending (**G**).

The taxes are said to decrease private savings but then increase government savings by the same amount and so taxes drop out of the equation.

Here is how the standard explanation purports to "clinch" their proof. They assume **Y** is constant. I show now that **Y** is not constant.

Now from above we have the expenditure approach to GDP, **Y**

$= I_P + C + G + X$

Then the stipulation is made that this is a closed system, meaning there is no trade with outside countries, net exports are not in the equation, **X** is not occurring, and so **X** is dropped from the equation and we get

$Y = I_P + C + G$

This equation shows that government spending increases private income, that is, it does increase **Y**. As **G** increases that would increase **Y** dollar for dollar and increase disposable income dollar for dollar, so in the equation for private savings, $S_P = Y-T-C$, increasing **G** would **increase** private savings dollar for dollar due to its effect on **Y**. On the other hand, based on the definition of government savings, $S_G = Y_G - G = T - G$, government savings is reduced by government spending, dollar for dollar. This means that, overall, government spending would be both added to total savings and subtracted off total savings. Government spending has **no effect** on the value we get by adding private savings and government savings together. Government spending has no effect on total savings.

That <u>contradicts</u> the usual assertion that increased government spending will decrease total National Savings.

I have shown that the flaw in the standard model is that it does not account for the fact that, since **G** increases **Y** dollar for dollar, increasing or decreasing **G** will not change the total savings. Knowing that, it is actually easer to see this using the formula above for total national savings, $S_T = Y-C-G$. In that equation increasing **G** would increase **Y** by the same amount and S_T would remain unchanged.

Doing a similar thing with consumption **C** since $Y = I_p + G + C$ we see that increasing **C** increases private income **Y** dollar for dollar too. Then using the derived formula for total savings = $S_T = Y-C-G$ the value of C will be added to S_T since the value of C is contained in the value of **Y** and then C is subtracted off S_T, meaning changing the value of **C** has no effect on S_T.

To summarize, since total National Savings in a closed economy, as defined in this model, equals $S_T = Y-C-G$, and since increasing either **G** or **C** causes an identical increase in the value of **Y**, increasing or decreasing either **C** or **G** has NO EFFECT on the value of "National Savings". Changing the amount of consumption spending has no effect, nor does changing the amount of government spending. The recommendation that we must decrease spending to increase national savings is based on an incorrect model.

How and why do the textbooks get it wrong? Because of the stipulation that **Y** is a constant. The justification for this may be in part based on the idea that production and income are the same thing. The descriptions of this model give as a rationale, for saying **Y** is constant, that the current economic infrastructure and organization is a pretty stable thing and that it is unlikely to change much, meaning we can expect production (and therefore total income) to stay constant.

If **Y** did remain constant, then total savings $S_T = Y-C-G$ would indeed be decreased by government spending or consumption. But in this model **Y** is a measure of income, not production, and production is not equal to income. Subtracting income off production is mixing up things that do not belong together in the same equation. As shown, **Y** does not stay constant when **C** or **G** change.

What is really being alleged here, is this:

We know that total investment is all the money being put into spending, and that amount is still around at the end of the given time period. That money is what gets preserved as total savings, S_T, which equals $S_T = Y-C-G$. If when **C** or **G** is increased **Y** stays the same, then S_T will be reduced. Since S_T is the preservation of any money being used for spending during the given time period it cannot be reduced, unless some of that money magically disappeared, or perhaps was purposefully destroyed. If, when **C** or **G** are decreased, **Y** stays the same, then S_T will be increased. Since S_T is the preservation of any money being used for spending in the given time period it cannot be increased, unless some new money magically appeared or was created by counterfeiters or something. It could have been created by the central bank, but I already pointed out that is not allowed in this scenario, the money supply is assumed constant.

So, what this explanation of the concept of National Savings is actually alleging is something like the following:

If you reduce consumption and/or government spending, counterfeiters will create more money or more money will magically appear, and we will have increased National Savings. If you increase consumption and/or government spending that will cause someone to destroy money or money will magically disappear, and National Savings will be decreased.

<hr>

The point is, since **net production** is not included as part of savings, the only thing that is being considered is the money supply. Any money used for spending in the given time period will be preserved. Economic activity does not increase or decrease the money supply, only the central bank can do that.

The reason proponents give for **Y** to be constant, that we have an established economic infrastructure and our output is unlikely to change much, is a description of wealth production, not income. If we did not have employment and production maximized, increased spending would increase employment and, very likely, production. Saying increased government spending or private consumption spending would not increase production also implies the economy is at full employment and producing maximally. If the economy is at full employment and producing maximally then it also means there is a good match between spending and production so why would anyone want to mess with that situation? If we decrease spending, "to increase savings" (which I have just shown is a false premise), that could hurt employment and reduce production. That would make the recommendation to decrease government spending and consumption spending irrational. That is of course what I am saying; decreasing government spending and consumption spending to increase national savings makes no sense in the macroeconomy. It is not rational, it does not work, it doesn't accomplish the alleged aim of increasing national savings.

If the economy were producing maximally, all you would accomplish by decreased spending is decreased demand which would probably decrease net production and have an adverse effect on total savings. The savings that is preservation of investment would still equal investment and that part of savings would not be describing any change in the level of wealth and would not represent any change in the total money supply.

The savings that is preservation of investment will decrease if investment is reduced, but again, that does not change the total amount of money in the money supply and is not an accounting of what has happened to wealth. Since government spending normally is best categorized as investment spending then decreasing government spending would decrease the savings that is preservation of investment, while not representing any change in total money supply or the value of total wealth.

Consumption spending has no effect on savings that is the preservation of investment, and the consumption spending itself does not represent a change in the level of wealth, nor does it represent a change in the size of the money supply. The only thing that changes the level of wealth is net production. The only way the size of the money supply changes is if the central bank changes it. Normally, reduced spending will reduce, not increase, net production. Whatever other conclusion may be drawn from this chapter, the message is, if you decrease consumption spending and government spending, you do not increase savings or increase the production of wealth, you probably decrease both.

CHAPTER 41
Uses of Savings

I include this topic for a couple of reasons. First, I want to disprove the strange allegation that you can "increase net exports or domestic investment by increasing savings." To increase savings, as typically presented, the recommendation is that people increase savings by decreasing spending, which in the macroeconomy is incorrect.

Second, I want to show how it is the part of savings that is net production which must increase to draw out more investment spending and that it is net production that will allow us to have more products to sell as exports.

THIS IS THE way this concept is typically presented in macroeconomic textbooks:

..........*"which tells us that saving either goes into investment— acquiring capital goods and boosting the capital stock—or, alternatively, into net exports—selling goods to foreigners in exchange for foreign currency assets. In other words, a nation that saves can invest in its capital stock or acquire assets from foreigners."*[25]

This quote is saying that savings "goes into" exports, or private investment. I assert that this is a misinterpretation of what is going on, the part about savings going **into** exports particularly. It might make more sense if they allowed consideration for the part of savings that is net production, but when this model is presented in textbooks they are restricting themselves to that part of savings which is the preservation of the money used for investment spending.

To be fair, since the standard teaching of macroeconomics is that production and income are the same thing, there is no awareness that net production needs to

---
[25] Mishkin, Frederic S. Macroeconomics: Policy and Practice (Page 77). Pearson Education. Kindle Edition.

USES OF SAVINGS

be considered as a component of savings. The exponents of the standard model, believe that the savings that equals investment spending includes net production. This quote is really not wrong, if it is describing the part of savings that is net production. (I describe what counting net production can do for domestic investment and exports later in this chapter). However, since the savings this model is using is only the savings that is the preservation of investment spending, it does not include any component describing production of wealth. I will show how this leads to incorrect policy recommendations.

Here is the derivation as typically presented:

Using the expenditure approach equation to GDP we have $Y=C+I_p+G+NX$. Notice I am using net exports instead of just exports, that is because this is how it is taught. I will try to account for exports and imports properly after I run through the standard exposition.

The next step is to sub in for **Y** in the equation:

$$S_T = Y - C - G$$

This means the savings that is being looked at here is total savings in both the private domestic economy and the government. However, this is an open economy and exports and imports are part of the picture. Foreign savings is not being look at in the calculation of total savings. What this turns out to mean is that this equation:

$$S_T = Y - C - G$$

is not correct for an economy that has international trade, it is only correct for what is called a closed economy, a closed economy being an economy that does not have foreign trade. I will correct this expression but first I want to present the concept as it is normally taught.

Substitute for **Y** by putting the expression

$Y=C+I_p+G+NX$ into

$S_T=Y-C-G$

This gives

Uses of Savings

$S_T = C + I_p + G + NX - C - G$

This makes C and G drop out giving us $S_T = I_p + NX$

This

$S_T = I_p + NX$

is what they call the "Uses of Savings Identity". From that equation they conclude that increasing savings gets put into increasing exports or increasing private investment. In other words, the standard explanation is that savings **causes** private investment and or net exports.

I interpret the statement in the opposite way. I say private investment money will get preserved as savings, and money paid for exports is money coming from foreign countries and being used for spending in our economy. That money too, will be preserved as savings.

On the other hand, imports (**M**) will cause money to leave our economy, and if that money came from current income, the amount spent on imports will reduce the amount of money that gets preserved as savings (in our domestic economy) by the same amount. (That money will still continue to exist in the foreign economy as part of their savings). In other words, savings is the preservation of these elements of investment spending. Savings is NOT causing the investment but is a **result of** the investment spending.

There are several things that need correcting to make these equations strictly correct. The equation for savings $S_T = I_p + NX$ is not correct. The error comes in because $S_T = Y - C - G$ is not correct for an open economy. It needs a couple adjustments.

We formerly approved the formula $S_T = Y - C - G$ as being an acceptable definition for a closed economy, with the stipulation this can only be considered true if taxes were assumed paid out of current income. I allow that assumption to stand, even though it may not be a completely accurate description of reality. At any rate, corrections are needed to this equation because of net exports. But we must do this correctly. I showed in Chapter 31 how imports should not be a part of the expenditure approach equation for GDP. I will then correct that in this chapter and will make **Y= I_p+G+C+X**, removing the **NX** (**X-M**) and just leaving the **X**, that is removing the imports and leaving the exports.

This would make $S_T = Y - C - G = I_p + G + C + X - C - G = I_p + X$.

$S_T = I_p + X$

USES OF SAVINGS

But that is still not correct. This is because money paid for imports is money leaving the domestic economy. And if those imports are paid for out of current income, i.e., using money that is already part of current spending, the that will cause a reduction of the amount of investment money that remains in the current economy and will cause a reduction in the savings that is preservation of investment.

What this means is that the formula for investment money still saved in private sector and government pockets changes from $S_T=Y-C-G$ to:

S_T=Y-C-G-imports paid for out of current income.

Substituting in for **Y** one gets S_T=**I$_p$+G+C+X-C-G-imports paid for out of current income.**

Which reduces to S_T= **I$_p$+X-imports paid for out of current income.**

So that would be your uses of savings equation, properly formulated. Remember, in the uses of savings they are counting private domestic savings and government savings. They are not counting savings occurring in foreign economies as a result of these transactions.

Calling this equation a "uses of savings" equation, starts us off as implying a wrong interpretation. The real interpretation of S_T = **I$_p$ + X − imports paid for out of current income,** is that S_T represents the preservation of the money being put into income as investment spending that has not been given to entities in another country. **I$_p$** is private investment spending in my modified version of GDP, and **X** is defined as money coming in to the economy from a foreign country and **both** meet the definition of investment from Chapter 2. **Imports paid for out of current income** describes money, that has been introduced into spending as investment spending, being taken out of our economy and that will no longer be around to count as savings for the private domestic economy to the domestic government, This reduces the total government and private domestic savings that exists at the end of the given time period, (not including net production).

Savings that is the preservation of the investment is equal to investment money minus any of that investment money that may have been taken out of the country. The savings equals investment identity holds because all the money used for investment still exists, even though some of it is owned by an entity in a foreign country and it is not part of the domestic savings. Bottom line, the savings that is the preservation of investment money takes what value it does BECAUSE of the domestic investment and money obtained from selling exports. Savings that is preservation of investment is just that, it does not CAUSE the exporting of items or

USES OF SAVINGS

the domestic investment spending. The proponents of the uses of savings concept are implying that not spending increases the money supply. It does not. Only the Central Banks can increase the money supply.

<hr />

All that being said, there is a way that savings can facilitate increased exports. **You <u>can</u> increase savings by increasing that part of savings called net production**. By producing more things to export, you can increase exports. By having more product to sell domestically, you can draw out domestic spending, investment or consumption, to purchase those products. **In that way, by increasing net production, we can effect an increase in both domestic private investment and in exports being sold**. That is the proper way to explain how increased savings can lead to an increase in exports and private investment.

This is a very important point to make, because what proponents of this concept are attempting to promote is, once again, the idea that people in an economy must "not spend" so that they can "save" so that people have money to "invest" or get foreigners to pay us money for exports. Since "not spending" is much more likely to decrease net production, "not spending" is much more likely to reduce exports and reduce domestic spending. The recommendation that reducing spending is the way to increase exports and domestic spending is completely opposite to what the recommendation should be.

<hr />

Savings is a measure of wealth, monetary and non-monetary, coming out of the current economic situation. Money is wealth, but income is not the money itself, income is the change of ownership of money. It is the change of ownership of money, the spending, that motivates the labor that causes the production, in this time period or any time period. It is net production which can lead to changes in the total level of wealth.

If you want to calculate the total savings you need to add net production to the savings

The savings would be $S_T = I_P + X$ **–imports paid for out of current income + net production.**

You could design a model where you tried to figure out the contribution to net production of the various contributors to total income if you wanted. Something like

Uses of Savings

net production attributed to **X,M,I$_p$,C,G,T**, being designated as $S_X, S_M, S_{IP}, S_C, S_G, S_{Taxes}$ where S_{Taxes} and S_M might be negative.

If one makes total savings from net production equal S_{NP} and set $S_{NP}=S_X+S_M+S_{IP}+S_C+S_G+S_{Taxes}$ then one could have a fancy final formula for total savings in the combined government and private domestic economy to be:

$S_T=I_p+X-$ imports paid for by money obtained as current income$+S_{NP}$

That would be a more accurate way to calculate a value for "national savings", at least if we want to include the contributions to net production of wealth from all those items we categorize as spending.

CHAPTER 42
Combining Private and Government into 'One Economy'

I have shown a model I call a modified version of the expenditure approach to GDP. This model makes the expression for GDP into an expression that calculates total spending and income in the private domestic economy only. It does, however, like the standardly taught expression for GDP, include discussions of interactions between the private domestic economy and the government as well as interactions with foreign countries. This chapter shows a way to extend the formula for GDP to include both private domestic income and government income. I also comment on how one would do the same with the private domestic and foreign economies.

TO COMBINE THE private and the government economies into one economy we need to change the way we look at interactions between the private domestic entities and the government. This will change some of what we call investment spending and some of what we call consumption spending. Also be aware that that the spending and income measured are gross spending and gross income, same as it was for my modified version of the expenditure approach to GDP.

The trick to using the equation for GDP and combine private domestic with government spending into one economy is to **treat the government like it was a large firm in the private economy.**

Integrating the government and private economies would mean that taxes would be viewed as spending by the private sector to purchase things from the large firm called the government. That spending would be able to be classified as either investment or consumption depending on what is more appropriate, using the definitions of consumption and investment spending described in Chapter 2. Taxes are spending and would be added to total income. These taxes would become income for the large firm called the government. These taxes are purchasing things like shared government goods and services.

Taxes would count as part of gross income and not only that, in a closed economy, all the money used to pay the taxes would still exist at the end of the given time period, owned by some entity in the private domestic economy or the government, and might be counted as part of the savings that is preservation of investment. If the taxes were paid out of money being put into spending for the first time in the given time period, it would count as investment and that money used would become part of the savings that is preservation of investment. If the taxes were paid for out of current income it would be consumption and that spending would not increase or decrease the savings that is the preservation of investment.

Government spending would be considered spending by that large firm called the Government, aimed at and creating income for entities in the private sector. Here too, that spending could be considered consumption or investment depending on whether it is paid for by current income of the government or not. If the government was treated like a large firm in the private economy, then government spending would become gross income for the combined government/private economy. The money used for any of the spending would still exist at the end of the given time period as savings.

Something similar would occur when integrating a foreign country with the domestic economy (including government). That would be as simple as just assuming the two economies are one. It might cause some difficulty because of two currencies, but the two could be treated as one currency using the exchange rate to determine what a given amount of money is worth. If we integrated our economy with a foreign country's economy, and treated its economy as integrated into ours, private investment, government spending, taxes, consumption and exports would all be included as part of total spending, but purchasing imports would also count as spending and be added to the combined total income of both countries. In a combined economy, purchasing of either imports and exports count as just spending, no distinction made between them. Combining foreign and domestic economies would mean all spending is part of total gross income **Y**.

CHAPTER 43
Ricardian Equivalence and Debt Financed Government Spending

Many economists and policy makers have the belief that any attempt by the government to stimulate the economy will serve no purpose and may even cause harm. Ricardian Equivalence is an example of a theory intended to support that notion. This is discussed here.

"WHAT IS THE 'Ricardian Equivalence'? Ricardian Equivalence is an economic theory that suggests that when a government tries to stimulate an economy by increasing debt-financed government spending, demand remains unchanged. This is due to the fact that the public saves its excess money to pay for expected future tax increases that will be used to pay off the debt. This theory was developed by **David Ricardo** in the 19th century but was revised by Harvard professor Robert Barro into a more elaborate version of the same concept."[26]

Ricardian equivalence says that government spending financed by debt, or tax cuts, (which worsen the government's position due to loss of revenue), will not cause increased demand. This is because people will account for it and not spend the extra income; because they know they will need the money to pay the inevitable increased taxes the government will have to levy in the future, for the purpose of paying its debt, or to recover the lost revenue caused by tax cuts.

When the model says people will not spend any of that extra income and will save it, it must allow for people to put that money into bank deposits. This is how most people "save". More generally, using the terminology in this book, this means

---

26   https://www.investopedia.com/terms/r/ricardianequivalence.asp#ixzz5TOHgCnZI

that, in addition to just holding cash, what the model allows for is an increase in **spending to purchase purely financial assets.** This implies that the Ricardian Equivalence model is not excluding a change in the level of all spending, only a change in the level of **direct spending.** This means the Ricardian Equivalence model must be saying that debt financed government spending or tax cuts will cause no economic stimulus because it will result in no increased overall **direct spending,** in the private sector. That is to say, the implication is, that debt financed government spending or tax cuts, will cause no overall increase in spending, by people or entities in the private economy, to purchase labor, goods, services, or other outcomes, other than the outcome of creating purely financial assets.

Some of the logic behind the concept of the Ricardian equivalence is explained in this quote:

"The forward-looking consumer understands that government borrowing today means higher taxes in the future. A tax cut financed by government debt does not reduce the tax burden; it merely reschedules it. It therefore should not encourage the consumer to spend more."[27]

It is common for economists to express disagreement with the Ricardian Equivalence model, but still **agree** with the premise that that consumers who gain income from debt financed government spending **should not** increase their direct spending. Those economists would agree that to do so will increase future debt and decrease future "investment", causing reduced future demand and economic depression. For such economists, they agree with saying that people **should not** increase direct spending. They only disagree with the Ricardian equivalence theory because they believe that most people **will** increase their direct spending if they get more income. The reasons commonly stated for believing this to be the case is that those income earners either need the money and have no choice, or because they are "short sighted", or "selfish", or do not understand "the consequences" of their spending.

The basic belief underlying the Ricardian equivalence model is that debt financed government spending, or tax cuts, will cause no increase in direct spending and therefore no positive effect, because people will save to pay the future taxes, or that if it does increase direct spending, any positive effect on demand now will be reversed in the future when the debt has to be repaid, because that money they used for direct spending is gone, and when people get the tax bill in the future they will have to use other money, that otherwise could have been used

---

27 Mankiw, N. Gregory. Macroeconomics (Page 567). Worth Publishers. Kindle Edition.

Ricardian Equivalence and Debt Financed Government Spending

for direct spending, to pay the taxes. That is how it is alleged that spending now, decreases spending and demand later.

I will show here an explanation of why these assumptions are false. That is, if private income is increased by debt financed government spending or tax cuts, and this results in an increase in direct spending, that will not necessarily result in increased future debt and decreased future demand. In fact, the opposite is more likely to be true, the debt may be easier to pay off and future demand may be greater, if income from debt financed government spending is used for direct spending.

Let me reformulate these concepts using the language of this book, including the idea that putting money in the bank is not "saving" but instead is spending to purchase a "savings asset". Let us say the government agrees to a debt obligation to a lender from the private sector, in exchange for cash. That is, the government borrows some money. The government then spends that money with the spending directed at, and causing income to, recipients in the private sector.

For this government spending I are not talking about the government taking that money and lending it out. To do so would just transfer the debt burden from the government to those that borrow from the government. That would not lead to any net government debt, therefore it would not cause a need to increase taxes. That means transactions that involve government borrowing so the government can then spend to purchase purely financial assets is not the type of government spending being referred to here.

The relevant **government spending** the Ricardian equivalence model must be talking about is direct spending, by the government, aimed at creating income for recipients in the private sector. This spending is paying to acquire goods, services, labor to produce goods or services, or other outcomes that are not purely financial assets. This newly created wealth may increase the governments wealth or could be sold to help pay for other government spending that may create or preserve wealth. Or the wealth could be a shared asset that the private sector benefits from as well. Or that increased wealth the government obtained could be distributed to people in the private sector. For example, if it purchased food, the food could be used to feed hungry people. Or that which the direct spending could be paying for is the outcome that people have income to pay for housing, or food, or medical care. So, that first round of direct spending done by the government, is only relevant to the discussion to the extent that it is direct spending, and it does have some benefits and further, that money has not disappeared, it still exists as it is owned by those who were income recipients as a result of the government's direct spending of the money it borrowed. And this shows that some of the spending will clearly lead to re-spending for at least one more round of spending.

But let us say those people that got money as income, from the government spending of the borrowed money, have "seen the light" and are "not selfish" and they decide to strictly follow the Ricardian equivalence model, i.e., no direct spending. In those referenced passages above it is implied that the recipients of that money as income "save" that money to have it be available to pay taxes in the future. I have shown that although this "saving" partly, and probably in a minor way, takes the form of holding the cash privately, mostly this savings refers to people putting the money into a bank deposit. That is, this saving refers to spending to purchase a bank deposit or some other purely financial asset. When one "saves" by purchasing a purely financial asset they are spending to cause the creation of an asset, but they are also causing the creation of a debt obligation. Unlike the direct spending the government did with the money they borrowed, the spending of those recipients of income from the government spending will not cause the creation of any net wealth (if they do not use it for direct spending). The value of the asset they purchased when they "saved" is based on, and offset by, the value of the debt obligation.

If those, who get private income directly from the government spending of the government loans, do not use it for direct spending, in the future, when the tax bill comes, those people will be able to just give the government the cash they are holding, or they will sell the asset called a bank deposit back to the bank for cash which they can give to the government. The government will then be able to pay off its debt.

One would also assume that the government pays interest on the loan so that might require the taxes to be higher than the initial money spent by the government. Of course, the people might have earned some interest on those bank deposits and that could partially offset the extra needed to pay the tax bill. But still, if the money given by the government spending is never used for private direct spending, some of the private sectors pre-existing wealth, may have to be liquidated to pay some of the taxes because of interest the government owes on their loans.

In order to obtain the cash for taxes, purely financial assets could also be sold to others besides the bank or other entity who owes the debt obligation. This means the person who owned the asset sells it to someone else for cash, and then the someone else is owed the cash by the person or entity with a debt obligation. This could occur if someone used their new income to purchase a bond, which they later sold when they needed the cash, for example.

If, after that initial debt financed direct spending by the government, no further direct spending occurred, the money still could be used to purchase more and more purely financial assets. But those assets are always matched by debt obligations of the same amount. The creating of more and more savings assets with matching debt obligations does nothing to increase wealth. At any rate, the holders of those purely financial assets would have them, to cash in if needed, to pay taxes when the time came. In terms of total wealth, if no money is used for direct spending, the private sector will be no better or worse off after they pay their extra taxes caused by the government's borrowing, than they were before the government borrowed and spent the money in the first place. So, the message proponents of Ricardian equivalence is that debt financed government spending causes no beneficial effects, it just requires a lot of extra accounting work, for no real purpose. It may actually make things worse for the private sector because of interest charged on the loans.

The model alleges it would be even worse if those who received that government spending as income **did** use it for direct spending. The implication is that if the money is used for direct spending it would be gone, disappeared, and not available to pay for those government taxes. The result would be that in the future, when the taxes are due, those people would have to dig into other money they had, money they could have used for direct spending, to pay the taxes, and that will decrease overall direct spending demand in the future. Any increase in demand from direct spending now, will decrease direct spending and demand in the future. That is the stated rationale behind the Ricardian Equivalence Theory. The authors of that theory then say that since people know this, they will not, as a result, use that extra income for direct spending now. They will purchase a savings asset, to have the funds to pay the taxes later, and the result will be that all that government borrowing and spending is a complete waste of time.

Now, how is this false? First and foremost, in the macroeconomy, spending to purchase anything does not cause the money to be "gone". That money still exists somewhere. The recipients of that money used in direct spending can be holding the money as cash, which can later be used to pay taxes, or the money can be used to buy assets called bank deposits, which can later be cashed in to pay the taxes. The only difference is, it might be someone else beside the original income earner from the government's spending, who owns the cash or the asset they can sell to pay the taxes.

There is nothing in this model that says people who were not direct recipients of the debt financed government spending, cannot be the ones paying the future increased taxes. The model just assumes that someone, unspecified, will have to pay the taxes. And that after the individuals who pay the taxes do so, they will no longer have that amount of money available for direct spending. But up until the point where the extra taxes are paid, someone in the private economy will possess the money obtained from the increased government spending. So, the idea that, overall, direct spending has caused the private sector to no longer have the money to pay those taxes when the bill comes due, is incorrect. What I am saying is that if money acquired as income from debt financed government spending is used for direct spending, it will not disappear, it will still exist, owned by someone else in the private sector, and the private sector as a whole will be just as capable of paying the taxes as it would be if no direct spending had occurred at all. This leads to the conclusion that, overall, direct spending now will not decrease the ability of the private sector to direct spend in the future, and the ability to direct spend in the future will not be any less than the ability to direct spend was before the government spending occurred. In fact, since the government spending increases private domestic income, then it is more likely that the ability of the private sector to direct spend is increased, not decreased.

Again, the logic behind the Ricardian Equivalence model seems to be that direct spending, unlike spending to purchase a purely financial asset causes money to disappear, that somehow direct spending reduces the money supply.

Like so many theories promulgated as macroeconomic concepts, this is really a microeconomic concept. If an individual or firm spends their money, that money is gone from their wallet. But in the macroeconomy the money still exists, just who owns the money has changed.

The money used for direct spending is not destroyed. In fact, it is not only purely financial assets that can be sold to get the cash to pay taxes. Any type of asset that has value can be sold to get money to pay the taxes. This includes forms of wealth referred to as "other assets" in Chapter 14 titled "The Forms of Wealth". The assets that could be sold to get the cash include goods, services, labor, or any other outcome that would draw out someone's spending to cause that outcome to occur (not including the outcome of creating a purely financial asset and a matching debt obligation). If the direct spending causes the creation of assets that can be sold then that direct spending has caused to be created more assets that can be sold to pay taxes, not less.

When one sells a purely financial asset to get the cash, either the value of the assets is eliminated, to eliminate the debt obligation or the asset still exists but so the does the debt obligation. Purchasing and causing to be created those purely financial assets does not increase overall wealth. But those "other assets" created and sold as a result of money being used for direct spending, do increase overall wealth. And some of those "other assets", those items of wealth will be able to be sold to get the money to pay the taxes if need be.

Those "other assets" could exist only for a short time, such as the labor paid for that only exists at the time it is being provided, or it could be an asset that is more durable, such as whatever the labor produced. Whatever the case, producing all those other assets contributes to increasing the standard of living. Both the short term perishable items and the longer term more durable items will have contributed to increasing the overall wealth, and standard of living, of those people living where that economy is operating. Using income obtained from debt financed government spending for direct spending will not cause us to be poorer in the future, and it is not likely to decrease "investment" in the future. It is far more likely to cause us to be richer in the future.

Now, it is true that, if the tax burden of paying for the government debt fell on poorer people, and at the same time, any increased direct spending, caused by the debt financed government spending, resulted mostly in increasing the income of richer people (who direct spend far less of it), that could result in decreased overall demand of an economy. This situation would likely cause a decrease in the total amount of type one direct spending (see chapter 36) leading to a decrease in overall direct spending. That would decrease overall demand and adversely affect total employment and production of wealth. This reduction of total direct spending income and the slowing of direct spending velocity of money could be expected to decrease standard of living. But that is a distribution of wealth and income thing. That is a regressive tax policy thing. That is not something that can be blamed on "too much direct spending".

The conclusion here is:

If one obtains income as a result of debt financed government spending or tax cuts, direct spending of that money is likely to cause increased production and therefore to **make it easier to pay government debt,** because of the increased production of assets, and therefore the increased number of assets available to sell for money to pay the taxes. Direct spending could potentially lead to the production of assets, whose value would allow that society to pay its taxes multiple times over. Not that we would want to. But the point is direct spending is **less** likely, not more likely, to "saddle future generations with debt". In fact, it is much more likely to make future generations richer and have a higher standard of living.

This does not mean that debt financed government spending or tax cuts are always a good idea. An example of a situation where it is a bad idea would be if we had an economy at full employment and more labor is not available. In that case, more direct spending would only cause prices to increase. Or perhaps more accurately stated, accounting for the phenomenon of excess inflation, debt financed government spending or tax cuts would be a bad idea if the unemployment rate equaled NAIRU and increasing direct spending would lead to excess inflation and end up harming real demand. In that situation having the government acquire debt to increase spending would not be recommended. At that point, the only government spending should be for the purpose of paying for things considered essential, entitlements and safety net included. But also needed to be funded by the government are all the essential services government provides for, including infrastructure, law enforcement, military, government, education, medical care, etc.

This belief or concern that spending is the same thing as the depletion of wealth, this microeconomic concept, is what makes it so easy for people to buy into concepts like Ricardian Equivalence.

Spending is not the depletion of wealth, it is the transfer of ownership of money. And that transfer of ownership of money activates the economic activity that creates and maintains wealth. If we look at the overall economy from a macroeconomic perspective, if the economy is at less than full employment, if there is inadequate overall aggregate demand, then we need increased direct spending to correct that situation. Overall, too much "not spending" will prevent recovery of employment levels and production. Slowing the velocity of money by reducing direct spending does not improve the macroeconomic situation. Loans and lending, even when the borrower is the government, can be useful to the economy if it results in taking stagnant money and getting it into the hands of people who will use it for direct spending. When the economy is depressed, loans and lending can stimulate the economy by increasing the direct spending velocity of money.

Can spending facilitate the depletion of wealth? Absolutely, if it causes the recipients of that income to quit their jobs where they are more productive and go into positions where they are less productive without the old job going to some unemployed person. In other words, if the increased spending causes a decrease in wealth production, that could reduce net production or even make it negative. Or, if the spending facilitated the irresponsible depletion of natural resources, that could cause net production of wealth to be negative. Or if the spending facilitates the degradation of the environment or if it facilitates the production of weapons that are used to destroy other forms of wealth including "human capital", both of these things can lead to loss of total wealth. There is, however, one way spending does not facilitate the reduction of wealth. Spending does not facilitate the reduction of wealth by decreasing the money supply.

CHAPTER 44
Where You Spend Affects Total Income

IN CHAPTER 36, I calculated the multiplier effect from an analysis of the velocity of money used in direct spending. We know that the multiplier effect applies when the economy is at less than full employment. I have shown that the change in total income from direct spending, and therefore, usually, change in total production of wealth, will be greater if more income is given to poorer people than to richer people. That means it matters where we spend. New spending can be targeted to create income for people or entities that will cause a higher multiplier effect or to people or entities that lead to a lower multiplier effect.

Suppose we analyze the effect of targeting spending in different directions. We would look at what would happen if one chose to put the spending in certain direction and compare that to what would happen if we chose to put the spending in a different direction. Now let K_{LM} be the direct spending multiplier for a lower multiplier spending choice. And let K_{HM} be the direct spending multiplier for a higher multiplier spending choice.

The difference in total income would depend on whether we changed the direction of spending from going to a higher multiplier place to a lower multiplier place in which case total income would be decreased versus if the direction changed from a lower multiplier to a higher multiplier place, in which case total income would increase.

※※※

Formally, if one were changing the spending from a lower direct spending multiplier direction to a higher direct spending multiplier direction: If ΔM is the

WHERE YOU SPEND AFFECTS TOTAL INCOME

amount of money changing places, then the change in **Y** (direct spending total income) would be calculated adding the amount of income that the new spending path would cause, plus $K_{HM}\Delta M$, minus the amount of spending that would be lost since the money is no longer going along the other path, minus $K_{LM}\Delta M$

$\Delta Y = K_{HM}\Delta M$ minus $K_{LM}\Delta M$

Or

$\Delta Y = (K_{HM} - K_{LM})\Delta M$

Let us call the overall multiplier K_{OA}

$K_{OA} = K_{HM} - K_{LM}$

Since the way I have defined things $K_{HM} > K_{LM}$ then K_{OA} is positive. That would cause an increase in total income. ΔY is positive.

If the money went into the other direction, for example, if you took income from poorer people and gave to richer people then K_{OA} would equal $K_{LM} - K_{HM}$ which is less than zero. That would cause a decrease in total income. ΔY is negative.

In reality, money is not just spent once, it is spent multiple times and we do not just account for where it is spent in the "first round" of spending. Every time that money is re-spent it goes to a new person or entity and the likelihood that they will re-spend it, and whether that re-spending is direct spending, affects what the total multiplier effect will be. On top of that, where the money is spent in one time period will affect the total amount of direct spending in future time periods as well.

We could randomly pick a starting time and calculate the multiplier effect from that point. We could specify the time period to be of any duration. We could calculate the total income and total velocity of money for any starting time and for time periods of any duration one wished.

The point is, if one wanted, and had access to a proper accounting of all the spending and its results, one could calculate the influence and effect of any spending on total direct spending demand.

Perhaps more to the point, every decision to spend, every bit of spending affects the total direct spending velocity of money, every bit of spending has its own multiplier effect. What I am getting at is every decision about how much and where to spend, at any time in the given time period, affects the magnitude of the multiplier effect. The multiplier effect of a given chain of spending does not depend solely on the first spending of a given amount of money, i.e., the investment, it depends on the direction and amount of all the resulting spending.

For example, supporting businesses that compensate their lower paid employees well is likely to cause a greater overall multiplier effect, than supporting businesses that do not. This is so because the lower paid employees are more likely to use a greater fraction of their income for direct spending than higher paid employees, or investors are.

If a greater portion of the money keeps going to places where it will be used for direct spending more often, in the given time period, the total direct spending income, the direct spending demand, will be greater than if it goes to a place where it will cause less overall direct spending. All of us, and our decisions where to spend, affect the multiplier and overall demand in the economy. It is not just a matter of government policy or government spending to increase aggregate demand, but all the spending that occurs after that.

There will be those who argue that the spending of those who are wealthier is "smarter" even if that causes total direct spending income to be less. They might argue that the lower direct spending of wiser and richer people, who are getting more of the income, leads to spending that has a greater effect on wealth because it is done in such a way as to lead to much more net production. And that it will lead to production of things that in the long run are far more beneficial to society. They may argue that the spending of these richer people would in the long run cause a greater increase in the standard of living for people of all income levels.

Perhaps there is some validity to that, but this is something they would need to prove, and I doubt it is something that could legitimately be proved to be universally and consistently true.

Besides, as previously discussed it is not rational to assume that richer people will be able to do enough of the type one direct spending that really drives the economy, and that is the type of spending that promotes the maximization of wealth production and standard of living for all. At any rate, even if it were just a matter of how much more valuable rich people's spending choices are than poor people's spending choices, in terms of what that does for maximizing net production, and standard of living, does anyone really believe that richer people's spending choices are 400 times smarter and more valuable than poorer people's?

Where You Spend Affects Total Income

Because that is the difference in pay some CEO's get compared to the average workers.

Anyway, every spending choice, made by every person, is constantly affecting what the total direct spending velocity of money will be. Every spending choice affects total overall income and the value of the direct spending multiplier.

CHAPTER 45
The Capital/Labor Split

The next three chapters are about something called the capital/labor split or theories that integrate the capital labor split into their models. These models discuss what these theories call income, investment and consumption. At first look, one would assume all these things belong on the income axis, however, I will show that none of those things are actually measures of income. They are in fact all measures of change in the level of wealth. It is for that reason that I thought it was important these chapters be included in this book. Believing that something which is in fact a measure of change in wealth is a measure of income, can lead to incorrect conclusions.

THE CAPITAL/LABOR SPLIT concept applies to output functions, and attempts to explain what happens to output when the inputs are changes.

Suppose you are a company and you want to maximize your output and the two adjustments you can make are you can spend more money to hire more workers to produce the product or you can spend more money to acquire or improve the things the workers use to produce the output. These "inputs" are referred to as labor and capital, respectively. Typically, when the concept is presented labor is designated with an upper-case **L** and capital is designated with an upper-case **K**.

Then a typical model would say that output is a function of **K** and **L**

Output = f(K,L)

The question is, does the company want to hire more people or do they want to purchase a machine or something else that helps them produce more product without hiring more workers? The decision is made by the firm based on what maximizes their output. Do they increase their output more by putting money into more hires, or do they increase their output more by putting that money into buying more "capital"?

This is obviously a simplistic scenario because workers are not a homogenous bunch who can just be plugged in to any situation and give the same results. People have all different levels and types of intelligence, skills, education, ethical code, endurance, ability to concentrate, to avoid mistakes, to stay on task, different life situations and influences, different health status, all of which would affect output. We could probably use Keynes' idea of creating labor units and having more skilled workers count as more than one labor unit.

The idea of what counts as capital could be open to very broad interpretations or narrow ones, and even with narrow ones, the question is still which capital one should spend to acquire or increase the amount of output the most. Capital includes the stock and quality of raw material, types of machinery, level of technology, buildings, and vehicles. Some would count spending on training as spending on capital. Some would count spending on research and development as capital spending. Just about anything one can imagine could be included such as power sources, internet availability and speed, and software. If one expands the idea of capital enough, they could think of our education system as spending on human capital.

One thing important to notice is that these output functions that include capital and labor as inputs, do not describe **how** the sales of the output are paid for. These models are not macroeconomic models in that sense.

In the Capital/Labor split models, it is common to look at the amount of capital, **K**, as the total amount of capital in the economy. On the other hand, sometimes the capital is described as including only part of the total capital in the economy, such as only counting capital that is used by the labor in the production process. When having **K** signify all the capital in the economy, typically included is any capital existing no matter when it was made or when it was acquired. The only labor that is counted is people employed during the current time period.

These models do not mention the income of labor or the income of the sellers or providers of capital directly. They assume that the output production is the income and that it will end up being given to pay the wages of the providers of labor. The rest will go to those who provided the capital.

The Capital/Labor Split

The models talk about something called the marginal productivity of labor and the marginal productivity of capital. This means how much output increases for a unit increase in labor, or capital, respectively.

The MPL (marginal productivity of labor) is presumably designated in units of currency for the value of the output, and labor units. For example, it is the change in the value of output in dollars per change in the number of labor units.

The MPK (marginal productivity of capital) is presumably designated in units of currency for the value of the output, and units of currency for the change in the value of capital. For example, it is the change in the value of output in dollars per change in the value of capital, in dollars.

It is frequently stated that the wage paid per labor unit is equal to the marginal product of labor. In other words, the amount paid to hire one more labor unit, is the amount of increased value of output product that occurs as a result of hiring one more labor unit. If that is true then every labor unit previously hired is paid a different amount, because their wage would be what the marginal product of labor was at the level of employment when they were hired. Let me show this graphically using a typical Cobb Douglass production function curve, which incorporates diminishing returns:

FIGURE 45.1

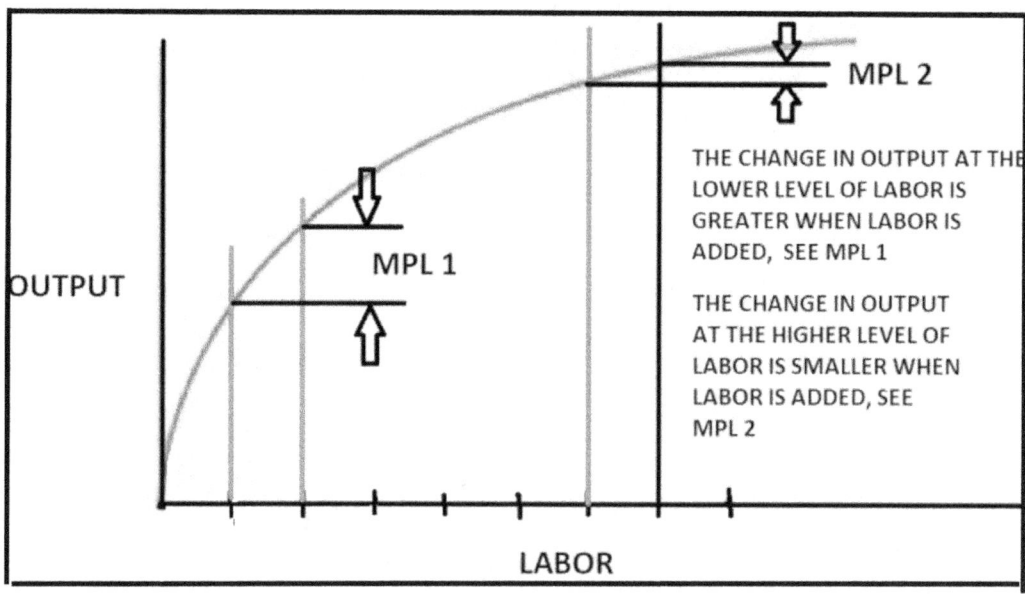

This graph for this output function shows that if the marginal product of labor is the wage, then the wage will be lower as each new person is hired.

This raises questions:

1. Is the wage paid to each labor unit the MPL paid when they were hired, meaning each labor unit is paid a different amount? Or

2. Does the wage for all the labor units change to match the current MPL as each new labor unit gets hired? In this scenario that would mean each time a new labor unit is hired every labor unit's wage would be reduced to the level of the current MPL. In this graph that would also mean that labors overall percent share of the total output would continue to be reduced as each new labor unit is hired. Or

3. Does this mean that the current MPL gets added to the total wages paid and then the total wages are divided by total labor units to get the pay of each labor unit? That would give everyone the average wage and still in this graph the average wage would go down as MPL gets lower, but the average wage would not go down as much or as fast as in 2. But at least, if this were the way wages were adjusted, labor would continue to get the same percent share of overall output

The Capital/Labor Split

These issues as I have outlined describe the problem with economic models that just state wage equals the marginal product of labor, without specifying how those wages are going to be distributed. Most people would say that of the three options outlined above that number 3 is the fairest and the most workable. One could say that even if nominal wages stayed the same, that due to diminishing returns that average REAL wages are going to decrease, mimicking, in real wage terms, the situation described in 3. That is, due to diminishing returns in production, buying power of the labor units goes down even for the same nominal wages. But buying power does not just have to do with product made in the current time period, it has to do with all the product available, made in any time period, and one cannot assume that prices of things made in different time periods is going to adjust so quickly or predictably.

One can assume, reasonably, that in these Capital/Labor models, any share of the value of output that does not go to pay wages of labor, goes to capital. What do that mean, that it goes to capital? It means that the value of the output that does not go to labor, goes to one or more of the people who own a share of the capital, or alternatively who have provided funds to buy capital that is used in the production process.

Let us look at a model where capital is the amount of money spent to add to the stuff used by labor to produce the output. An entrepreneur pays for whatever mix of labor or capital he needs to maximize his profits. The entrepreneur pays for labor, pays for new or replacement capital and keeps what is left of the value of the output. They keep the money for the output that **was** sold, and any output left that was not sold, and they subtract off any money paid for labor and capital to get their net change in wealth. This model does not include information on who actually paid for the output that was sold. This model all works perfectly if it is assumed to exist in the microeconomic sphere. But if one tries to analyze it with the macroeconomic definitions used in this book there are problems, such as: Where does the money paying for the sales come from? If someone pays for capital, like machinery, and it is produced in the current time period shouldn't it count as output instead of input, because it is production from that period? And isn't part of what is paid for the capital really going to the laborers who produced the capital? Shouldn't that be categorized as labor not capital?

As for a model where capital is considered to be all capital, i.e., all wealth, the Solow Growth Model is an example and I look at this in more detail in chapter 46. Another model that is built on the idea of a Capital/Labor split is Piketty's model in trying to analyze inequality which I discuss in more detail in Chapter 47.

CHAPTER 46
THE CAPITAL/LABOR SPLIT AND THE SOLOW GROWTH MODEL

In this chapter I analyze the Solow Growth Model[28] as typically taught in standard macroeconomic textbooks. I do this analysis with a goal of explaining what is consistent with my model and what is not, and where the explanation is not consistent I give what I believe is the proper interpretation. The typical way that economics textbooks teach the Solow Growth Model is utilizing graphs. It would not be possible to provide a useful analysis without providing similar standard graphs, with my analysis. The Cobb Douglass function is typically used on these graphs as the output function. I follow this convention and attempt to use labeling that will allow the reader to be able to compare my charts with the charts as typically taught.

TYPICALLY, THE VARIABLES used in the Solow Growth Model function are defined as follows:

Y is a measure of the output. In this Solow model, **Y** is the value of the total output generated for the time period, or the rate of the amount of output produced per unit of time. The output is measured as the value of how much money it would sell for if it all sold in the period of production. Or it could be seen as a measure of the value of product produced per unit of time. Either way of looking at it will fit into the Solow Growth Model.

---

28 Robert M. Solow, "A Contribution to the Theory of Economic Growth," Quarterly Journal of Economics (February 1956): 65–94.

The Capital/Labor Split and The Solow Growth Model

K is an input and is considered to be the total capital "stock". That is, it is my understanding that in this model **K**, represents total capital, total wealth and total accumulated savings.

L is an input and it stands for labor units

K/L = k is the total capital stock per labor unit

Y/L = y is the value of output produced per labor unit for the current time period or the rate of production per unit of time for each labor unit, at the current level of **k**.

The Solow Growth Model assumes that some of the current production gets used up in the current period or is being used up at the current rate . This new production used up is, by the common usage of the word, considered consumed, and as such, is called consumption. There is a certain amount of output being used up for the given time period, or alternatively, as output is being produced at a certain rate, a fraction of that output is being used up at that current moment, for the given value of the input **k**. In the Solow Model consumption means the amount of wealth that gets used up in the given time period or the rate at which current output is being used up. This means that consumption is describing something measured on the wealth axis. That is a different definition than what I call consumption in Chapter 2, which is a measure of income, not wealth.

New production that gets used up counts first as new wealth when produced and then when used up it counts as wealth depleted. The Solow Model's consumption is part of wealth depleted. As such it is part of the calculation of net production, or it could be alternatively understood as part of the calculation of the current value of the rate of net wealth production.

What the Solow model refers to as **savings** is new production not used up for the given time period, or alternatively as the rate at which new production is being preserved and "not used up". That is also part of the calculation of net production for the given time period, and therefore part of savings, since production is part of what I define as savings (Savings equals investment plus net production). Wealth "not used up" contributes to net production and therefore I am in agreement that what the Solow Model calls savings is part of what I call savings. Alternatively, it could be considered the current rate of wealth being added to by new wealth production; the rate of preservation of current output. Either way, when measuring that which the Solow model refers to as savings, that is a measurement of something occurring on the wealth axis.

The Capital/Labor Split and The Solow Growth Model

The standard teaching of the Solow Model, however, assumes that what the model calls savings **is**, in fact, something measured on the income axis. The model assumes that what they call savings is the part of savings that is the preservation of investment. That is incorrect. It is not the same thing as the savings that is preservation of investment money, it is part of net production.

Because the model assumes that what is being called savings is the part of savings that is preservation of investment, they also assume that what they call savings equals investment, i.e., that new production not used up, is the same thing as investment.

Investment does not equal new production not used up. Investment spending is a measurement of the amount of money being put into spending in the current time period which still exists at the end of the given time period when it is called savings. That part of savings, the preservation of investment, does not represent new wealth, and cannot change the level of wealth. What they call savings in the Solow growth model, does represent new wealth production, and can change the level of wealth. The amount of total new output production "not used up" is a measure of a change in the value of total wealth and is something that must be accounted for on the wealth axis, not the income axis. New production not used up is part of the calculation for net production. The total calculation of net production in the Solow growth model is total output, minus new production used up, (what the Solow model calls consumption), minus depreciation, which represents the total for the loss of value of preexisting wealth. Net production in the Solow model is new output, minus the total of "newly produced wealth depleted plus old wealth depleted".

The rate of new output being preserved does not equal the "rate of investment". Even though all common textbook descriptions of the Solow growth model repeatedly use the word investment, investment is not even included in the Solow Growth Model (with investment as described as a part of spending and income in chapter 2 of this book). In fact, all the quantities described in the Solow model, other than time and the amount of labor, are measures of wealth. There is not a single quantity that describes spending and income in the Solow model, (using my definitions for spending and income). Descriptions of, or measurements of, demand are not measured anywhere in this model, as it is described in standard economics textbooks. This is why I say the Solow Growth Model is not a fully macroeconomic model.

The Solow Growth model includes a quantity "s" (for savings apparently) which is the **fraction** of output not used up in the given time period. This means the value of output not used up would be **s∗Y**, (we will just designate this sY, … s times Y). That means **s∗y,** or **sy,** is the amount of output not used up per labor unit.

Or, alternatively, **sy** is the rate of preservation of current output per labor unit; that rate at which new wealth is collecting, with **s** being the rate of preservation of new output divided by the rate of total new output production.

⁂

Textbooks typically use the Cobb Douglass equation as the output function when presenting the Solow growth model:

$$Y = A*K^{\alpha}L^{(1-\alpha)}$$

α is a fraction from 0 to 1

K is total capital stock existing at the current time period and **L** is the amount of labor units employed at the current time period.

Dividing the whole equation by L we end up with:
$$Y/L = [A*K^{\alpha}L^{(1-\alpha)}]/L = [A*K^{\alpha}L*L^{-\alpha}]/L = A*K^{\alpha}*L^{-\alpha}\ Y/L = A*(K/L)^{\alpha}$$

Labeling **K/L = k** gives us **k**, the total capital stock divided by the number of labor units.

And we also designates **Y/L = y**. **y** is the value of the total output, produced in the given time period, per labor unit employed during that period. Alternatively, **y** is the value of the amount of output being produced per unit of time per labor unit.

so, **Y/L=y=A∗(K/L)$^{\alpha}$=A∗(k)$^{\alpha}$ ……….y=A∗(k)$^{\alpha}$**.

This Cobb Douglass has some properties that make it attractive to economists. Those properties include the function being monotonic, meaning the value of the output keeps going up as the value of the inputs increase. But it also "curves downward", meaning the rate of increase in output slows compared to rate of increase in the value of the inputs as the total value of the inputs become greater.

This fits with the concept of diminishing returns, a phenomenon described by Keynes to occur when one gets close to full employment. Diminishing returns is accepted as commonly occurring in economic models.

The output function as described by the Cobb Douglass graphically looks like this.

FIGURE 46.1

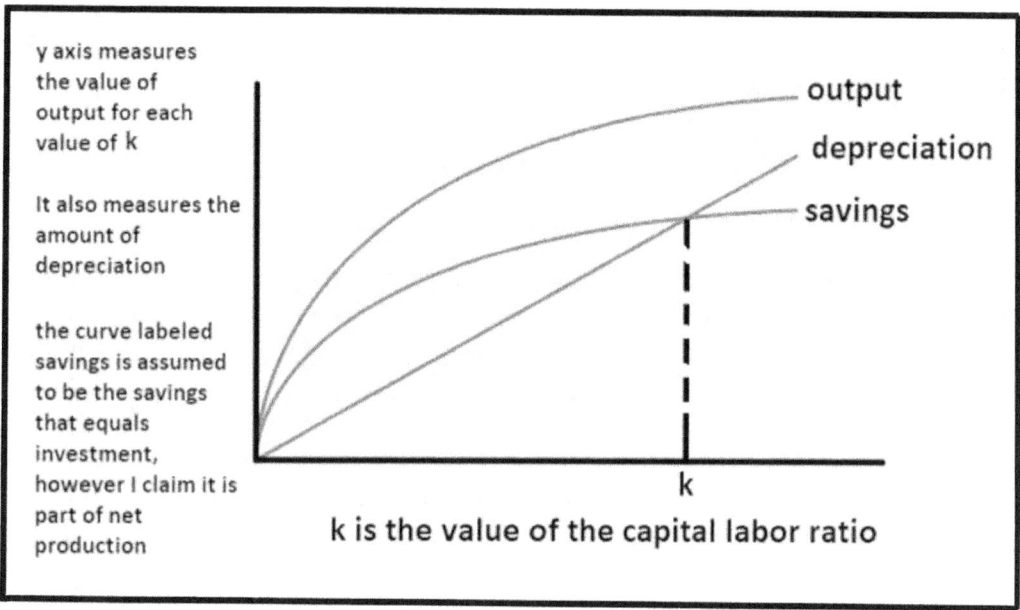

I need to explain this graph. The top curved line is the output production function.

$(Y/L) = y = A*(k)^a$

It describes all the current output production per labor unit for each value of k. It describes the value of all the new output in a given time period per labor unit or the current rate of output per unit of time per labor unit at the current moment.

The bottom curved line is defined by this equation

$s*(Y/L) = sy = sA*(k)^a$

which is the fraction of current output not used up, the fraction of current output saved (as part of net production)

The way the Solow growth model is presented is to say that this curve represents savings, but as mentioned this savings is represented to be the preservation of investment, when it is not. It is really part of net production. This curve represents the amount of new production not used up for each value of **k**.

The Capital/Labor Split and The Solow Growth Model

Both the first equation, total output, and the second equation, the amount of output not used up, describe things happening to wealth, not income.

Subtracting the Solow "savings curve" from the output curve, is subtracting that part of the new production not used up from the total new production. This then must be the amount of new production that has been used up, which as I have already said, the model labels consumption. That is also describing something happening to wealth. None of what is being referred to here are measures of income. None of these quantities are measures of the change of ownership of money. They are all measures of something added to or subtracted from our calculation of total wealth.

The other line, the straight line is the depreciation line. This line represents how much of the **existing capital** is depleted for a given amount of time for each value of **k** or alternatively it is the rate at which capital is being depreciated for each value of **k**. This depreciation is also a measure of something happening to wealth.

When the rate of increased wealth from the amount of new production not used up equals the rate of depletion of previously existing capital, the economy has reached an equilibrium. The value of total wealth (total capital) per labor unit (**k**) will stabilize. That is what is represented on the graph as the intersection of the line called savings and the depreciation line.

Since the proponents of the Solow model believe that the savings curve is the part of savings that is the preservation of investment, they believe that what they call savings is what equals investment and so the terms savings and investment are interchangeable on the chart. The Solow Model proponents view the chart below to be equivalent to the chart above. The only difference is the word investment replaces the word savings.

FIGURE 46.2

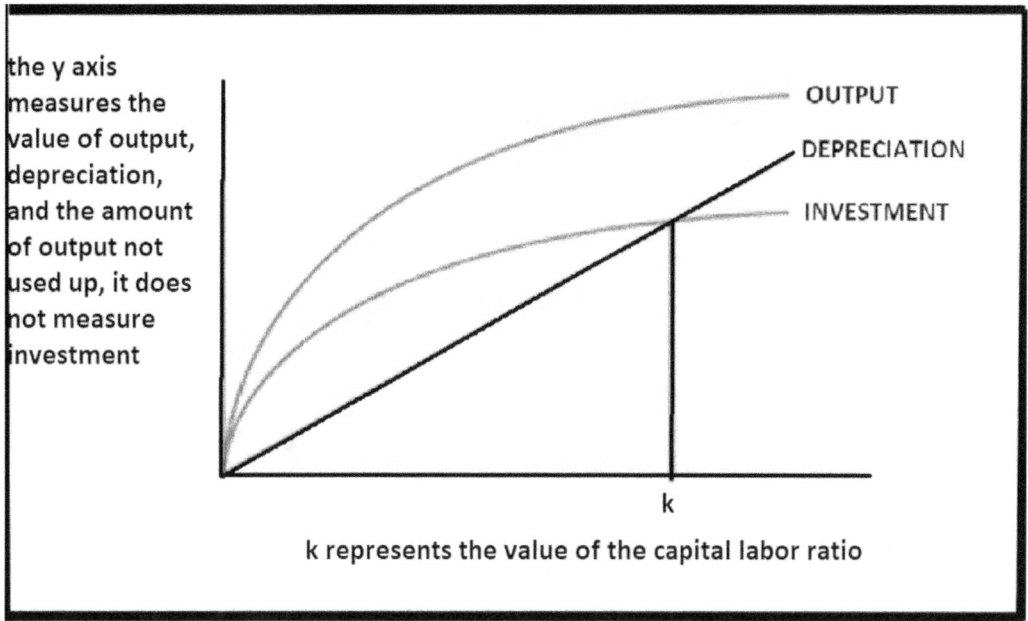

To me, it makes no sense that the value of the amount of new production "saved" at the end of the time period would always equal the amount of **money** put into spending for the first time in in the given time period (definition of investment from chapter 2). If the value in dollars of the investment spending equals the value in dollars of the output not used up, then it is pure coincidence. But the fact is, the usual way the Solow Model is presented, is in fact implying that this occurring would not be a coincidence. The Solow Growth model is representing that it is always true that the amount of money put into investment spending, equals the amount of new production not used up. This comes from the belief that income and net production of wealth are the same thing.

FIGURE 46.3

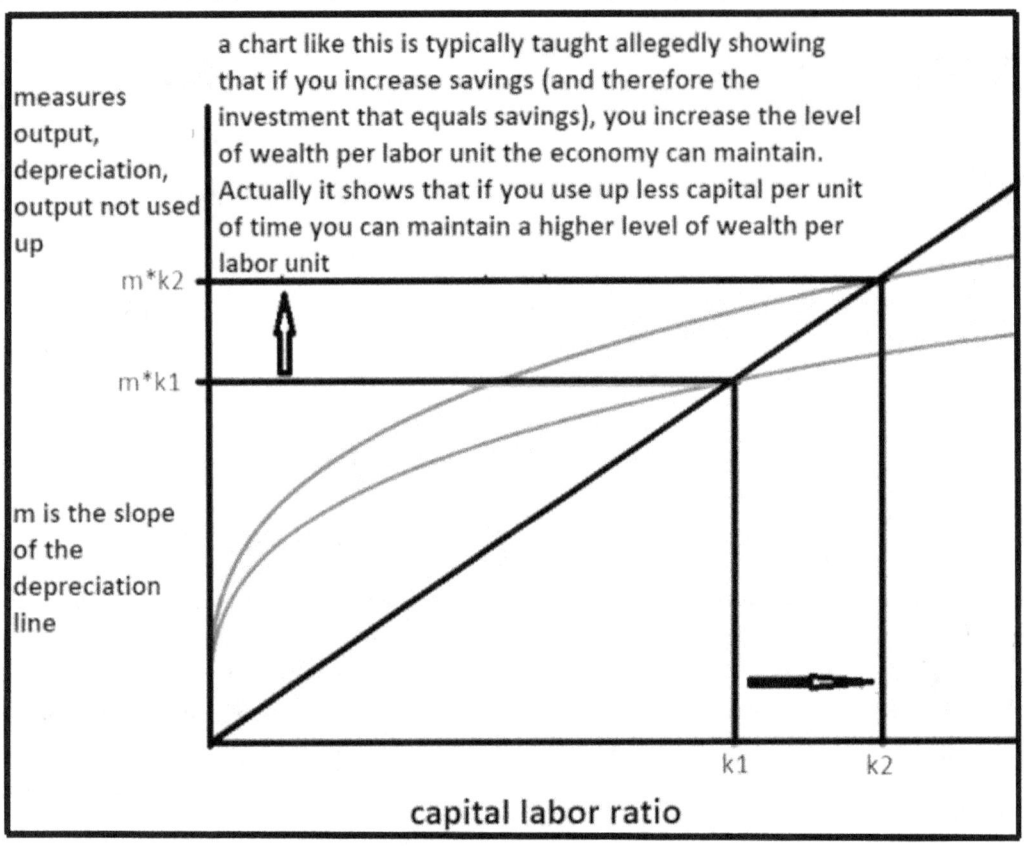

This shows what the graph looks like if the amount of output not used up is increased to a larger fraction of total output, that is, if s is increased. If the amount of output not used up is increased, i.e., if the amount of new wealth being preserved and added to the total wealth keeps growing, this will mean the depreciation rate has to increase to match in order to establish a new steady state. But on this graph, the depreciation rate will only increase if the total wealth per labor unit increases. This means equilibrium will be achieved at a higher level of total wealth per labor unit, a higher value of **k**.

The opposite would happen if the amount of output not used up decreased. Meaning if **s** decreased. In that case the rate of collection of new production being saved would decrease, and depreciation would be in excess of the amount of new production causing **k** to decrease until the depreciation rate was low enough to match the new, lower rate of new production being saved. This is saying that if we decreased the amount of new production we do not use up, then the total amount of capital per labor unit maintained would be reduced.

That all makes sense to me as long as one recognizes that the savings this model is referring to is part of net production, and not part of the savings that is preservation of investment.

Calling the part of new production that **is** used up consumption allows one to allege that it is consumption that determines how much wealth an economy is able to maintain. In other words, increased consumption leads to less wealth, and decreased consumption leads to more wealth. What is being called consumption is the using up of new production, which is part of the depletion of wealth. This definition of consumption is not the same as my description of consumption from chapter 2. It is a measure of the change in level of wealth, **it is not a measure of spending or income**. The error comes in when one equates the amount of "new production used up" to spending (paid for out of current income). This then leads to the extremely damaging recommendation that to increase wealth, the people and entities in this economy have to decrease spending, so we do not deplete as much wealth. In reality, consumption spending is spending, the transfer of ownership of money, it is not the depletion of wealth.

Let me repeat that spending is not the depletion of wealth. Quite the opposite spending often promotes the production of more wealth. Consumption, as described in chapter 2, is spending. What the Solow Growth Model calls consumption is not spending. What that model is calling consumption is the using up and depleting of part of the new production.

Further what is being called investment is not investment. If the definition of investment was the amount of new production not used up, then what is called investment in this model would be investment. But I have never seen a definition of investment stating that investment is the amount of new production that is not used up. It is, apparently, just assumed that because the savings/investment identity says that "savings = investment" then all one need do is substitute the word investment for savings and this gives identical charts. But the definition this model gives to investment is not a measure of spending, it is a measure of wealth, and therefore the only reason it is even part of the measure of savings in this model is because it is part of the net production of wealth. They are not measuring the money put into spending that is preserved as savings at the end of the given time period. Yet that is what this model is alleging by making their definition of savings (new production not used up) equal to investment, (which I define as the amount of money previously obtained, used for spending for the first time in the given time period). What the Solow model calls investment is something that is

The Capital/Labor Split and The Solow Growth Model

measured on the wealth axis, not the income axis. What I call investment in chapter 2 is a measure of spending and is measured on the income axis

Here the implication is that for a given amount of output at a certain level of **k**, if you increase consumption spending, it comes at the expense of savings, and therefore investment, causing wealth to drop. From Keynes' **Y = I + C**, if at less than full employment for a given amount of investment spending, increased consumption spending increases total income. Increased consumption spending increases total income, total demand, and will probably promote increased production output. Increased consumption spending does not decrease investment spending, unless the demand got so high that it led to excess inflation, and this led to a decrease in inflation adjusted demand (spending), see chapter on NAIRU and stagflation.

The bottom line is this, the advice to decrease consumption spending to increase wealth is a wrong interpretation of the Solow Growth Model. The graph below shows that if the output curve were total income, and investment spending was represented by the lower line what would actually happen if you were at less than full employment and you decreased consumption spending.

FIGURE 46.4

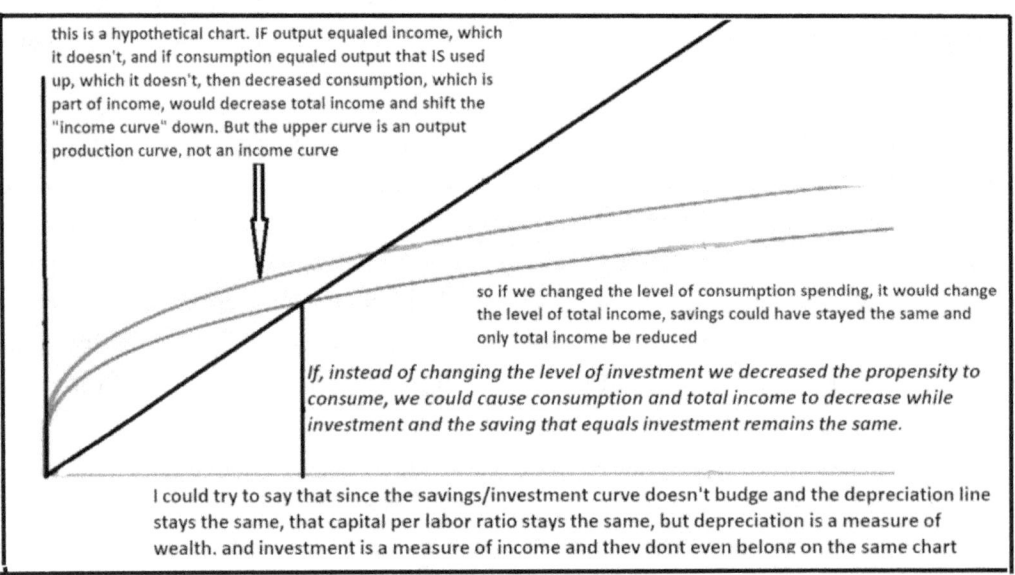

Decreasing consumption spending does not increase investment. It does not increase savings. It does however decrease income. Decreasing income decreases demand, which would probably decrease, not increase, production. If one reduced

production one would probably also cause the amount of new production not used up to decrease. That could cause the total wealth per labor unit to be decreased.

⌘

Often shown in textbooks when the Solow Growth Model is discussed is the so-called bathtub model.

It shows total wealth being the water in the bathtub. And water coming out of the spigot is labeled "investment" and it is shown as "increasing the wealth". And then at the bottom the drain is the "depreciation" of the already existing wealth, draining water out of the tub.

The big mistake here is claiming that it is investment flowing out of the spigot. What should be shown coming out of the spigot is the amount of production not used up. That is how wealth is increased no matter what the amount of investment spending was in that time period. The assertion is that investment is increasing the wealth directly. In reality investment spending does not increase wealth directly, it is just the transfer of ownership of money. It can spur production, but it is not in and of itself production.

To correctly label the bathtub model one would realize the combination of new production of wealth minus new wealth used up equals total new production not used up. Total new production not used up comes out of the spigot. The value of preexisting wealth being depleted is what is called **depreciation** in the Solow Growth Model, and it is that amount flowing out of the bathtub drain. Total new production not used up minus depreciation equals net production. It is net production of wealth that determines whether the amount of water in the bath increases, decreases or stays the same. All of the quantities shown in the bathtub models, when properly labeled, are measures of wealth, that need to be accounted for on the wealth axis not the income axis.

The belief that water coming out of the spigot is investment spending results from believing that what is called savings in this model, new production not used up, is that part of savings that is preservation of investment. That then allows one to use the Savings equals Investment Identity, which is the expression for savings that ignores net production, to assert that new production not used up equals investment.

The Solow Growth Model, as normally presented, depends on the incorrect belief, derived from the incorrect Fundamental Identity of National Income

Accounting, asserting that **Y** equals both the value of total new production and the total income; that they are identical quantities.

The proper definitions of these variables if **Y** equals income are:

Y = total spending = total income

I = investment spending = spending with money being used for spending (and causing income) for the first time in the given time period

C = consumption spending, i.e., spending paid for out of current income.

Instead, the Solow model, as taught, has **Y** = total output, and **I** = new production not used up, and **C** = new production that is used up.

The Solow model has **Y**, the total output, as a function of **k**, (the amount of total wealth per labor unit), and the amount of **Y** that gets saved can vary if you alter the values of what the Solow model calls investment and consumption. All of those things are measures of wealth. If what is called **I** and **C** in the Solow growth model, were actually investment and consumption, then increasing either would cause **Y** to increase. But in the Solow Growth Model one can leave the output curve the same and increase the value of what Solow model calls **I** (output not used up) for each value of **k**, by reducing the value of what the Solow Model calls **C** (output used up) for each value of **k**. For a given output curve **Y**, increasing what Solow Model calls I must decrease what it calls C, and vice versa.

When those values **Y, I,** and **C** are representative of spending and income, not wealth, (using the definitions of total income, investment and consumption from chapter 2), changing the values of **I** and **C** will also **change** the value of total gross income **Y**, provided the economy is at **less than full employment**. (At true full employment, however, increasing investment spending, could replace some consumption spending and reduce the total for consumption. That is, at true full employment total spending would not increase if investment increased, or at least inflation adjusted spending would not increase if investment spending increased since at full employment increased spending would not increase employment and production).

Since the model, as typically presented, has incorrectly asserted that the rate of increase in wealth, the amount coming out of the spigot, is **I**, in Keynes' **Y = I + C**, then the model uses that incorrect application and concludes that one will increase **I** by decreasing **C**. This allows one to make the damaging and wholly incorrect conclusion that, even when an economy is at less than full employment, consumption spending decreases investment and savings and makes our society poorer. This is a very damaging conclusion and leads to the 180-degree wrong recommendations on how to grow our economy, when at less than full employment. It leads to the recommendation that **not spending** will increase wealth in the macroeconomy. If an economy is at less than full employment, or rather if unemployment is greater than NAIRU, we need increased, not decreased direct spending, to increase aggregate direct spending demand.

The concepts in this chapter are a perfect example of how recommendations that may make perfect sense when applied to an individual or firm, are unsound when applied to the whole macroeconomy.

One thing that, in my opinion, prevents the Solow Growth Model from being a complete macroeconomic model is that it does not account for where the funds come from that pay for the sales of the output. The model does not describe whether the output is sold and how much is stored. It does not tell how much of the spending to pay for the output sold is investment spending and how much is consumption spending. As I said, there is no quantity referred to in the Solow Growth model that is a description of spending.

Another thing not mentioned in the standard explanation of the Solow Growth Model, is **L** is a measure of how many workers. **L** is not a measure how much they are paid. There is no reason to assume that a specific fraction of the value of the output will be paid, as income, to the workers. In fact, there is no reason to assume that a specific fraction of the value of the output will go to pay for the true total cost of having that many workers. In a perfectly competitive market one could make that assumption, but this model does not deal directly with that issue. If this model assumes a perfectly competitive market, I have not seen it explicitly stated.

Many people, whether they know it or not, when talking about the Capital/Labor split are automatically making the assumption that we have a perfectly competitive market at full employment. They talk about a labor share of the output. The amount of increased output that is caused by an increase in spending to hire more labor would be given to pay the true extra cost of labor, wages and benefits included. This only happens in a perfectly competitive market.

The Capital/Labor Split and The Solow Growth Model

A Comment on Convergence

The Solow Growth Model is used to explain a concept called convergence. The idea behind convergence is having poor countries wealth per capita grow, allowing them to get closer to richer countries in that metric. Will this result simply from people or firms spending on ventures in those countries? Is it the flow of money into their incomes which leads to their increased average net worth in terms of wealth?

If I put money into ventures in the foreign country that results in income for some of their citizens, part of that income will be preserved as savings, so in that sense, yes, it will increase the wealth of that country because the currency I gave, that ended up being saved, is wealth. But that is not new wealth overall for the world as a whole, that is just me giving some of my money from my country to the people in that country.

As that money can reasonably be assumed to be money being used for spending for the first time in their country, then we can classify it as investment spending. The people in that country will be able to use that investment income to purchase things, and to the extent that the purchases lead to income for people in the same country then their overall income will grow. But so far, the only thing mentioned that increases their wealth is the amount of currency sent over to their country.

If the new spending leads to production of new wealth, then whether that new production increases the wealth of that particular country depends upon who ends up owning that particular wealth. Let us say all the product is owned by investors from other countries. If that product is taken out of the country and sold it adds nothing to the wealth of the poor country. If the product, owned by investors from other countries is sold in the poor country then the product stays there as wealth, but money of presumably equal worth leaves the country, so that transaction adds nothing to the new wealth of that country.

So far in this scenario the only new wealth that becomes owned by the people of the poor country is that money they are paid by investors from other countries for their labor, plus any wealth acquired, minus any money paid to foreign interests to acquire that items of wealth. Paying each other for labor does not increase their wealth unless that labor produced something of value that people in the poor country could keep. In terms of increased overall wealth, items of wealth that last beyond the current time period will show as contributing to increasing in total wealth. during that time period. But we also must remember that even the effect of perishable forms of wealth that do not last beyond the given time period, can have an overall positive effect on wealth production, if that wealth being used up helps preserve wealth. This, for example can occur when the perishable wealth, such as food, helps keep humans alive and healthy, i.e., preserving that wealth known as human capital.

The point here is that it is only to the extent that the people of the poor country get to own part of the output production or get to keep their wealth from being reduced, by using products that preserve wealth, that the wealth of the poor country will be able to increase.

In explanations of convergence it is then stated that since it is cheaper and easier to maintain a smaller amount of wealth than a larger amount of wealth, that it does not take much increase in ownership of wealth by the poorer country to offset the depreciation. It is much easier to have a growing amount of wealth in a poorer country, because since poor countries have so little wealth, they have so little wealth depreciation. That is certainly true.

As for a wealthy country, it is likely they have achieved an equilibrium state where new production not used up is equal to depreciation, and that the level of wealth stays the same. Due to productivity increases, in the long run, there will be growth in the rich countries, but not as fast as growth of wealth as in the poorer countries, which makes sense.

That is where the convergence concept comes from. That is where the idea comes from that it doesn't take much investment in poorer countries to lift their wealth and standard of living. That may be so, but I am trying to point out that it is only from the amount of their net production that the poor countries are able to **keep,** that their wealth increases, it is not the amount of investment spending that directly increases the wealth.

If all the new production becomes owned by investors from other countries, that production does not add to their wealth, except in that the workers there are paid for their labor efforts. And if the investors from other countries end up taking other wealth, like natural resources, out of the country without fair compensation then the total wealth of the country could decrease instead of increasing.

The presentation of the Solow Growth Model as taught in textbooks sometimes seems to imply that when rich countries spend in poor countries it is almost by definition going to be the case that the wealth of the poor country will increase and that the investment will help lift them out of poverty, but as we can see from this discussion that is not automatically the case.

Wealth that is contained in the humans that inhabit the poor country, i.e., human capital, could also be impacted by the influence of these investors, for better or for worse. Destruction of that wealth by crime or violence, if that occurs as a result of the influence of investors from other counties can lead to the depletion of all sorts of things one may consider wealth. It is not such a simple thing as it is often presented.

One must raise such concerns lest the convergence concept be used by certain individuals as a rationalization for exploitation which, in reality, may be causing more harm than good for the poor country.

Here are some charts that are frequently shown in text books and lectures related to the Solow Growth Model with my labeling and my comments.

FIGURE 46.5

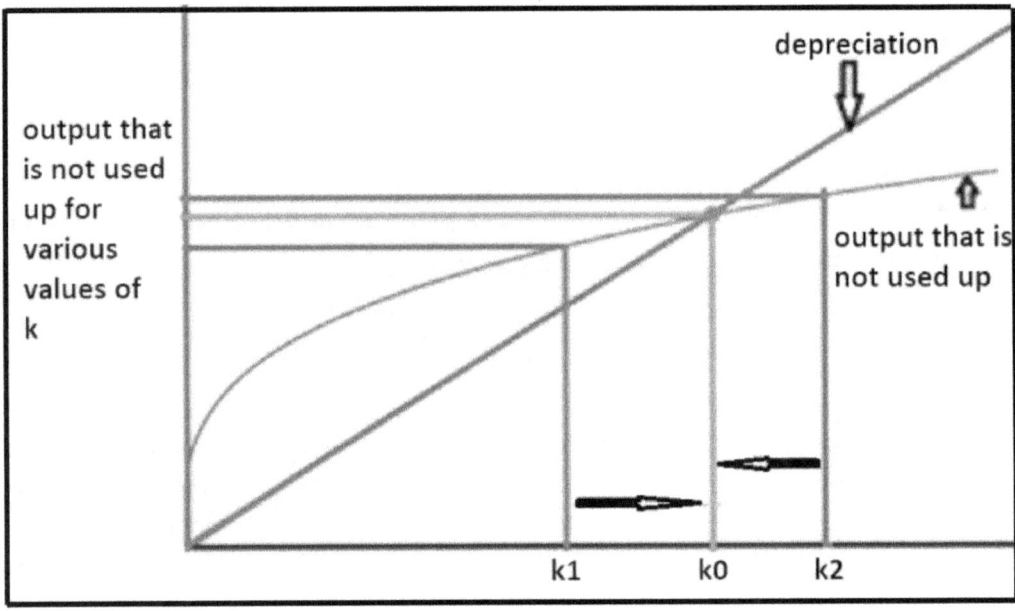

k is total wealth per labor unit.

and at **k1** "current output that is not used up" will be greater than current depreciation, causing an increase in total wealth per labor unit that will increase until you reach equilibrium at **k0**.

And at **k2** "current output not used up" will be less than current depreciation so that total wealth will decrease down until one reaches equilibrium point **k0**. All the variables in that chart are measures of wealth except labor and time.

FIGURE 46.6

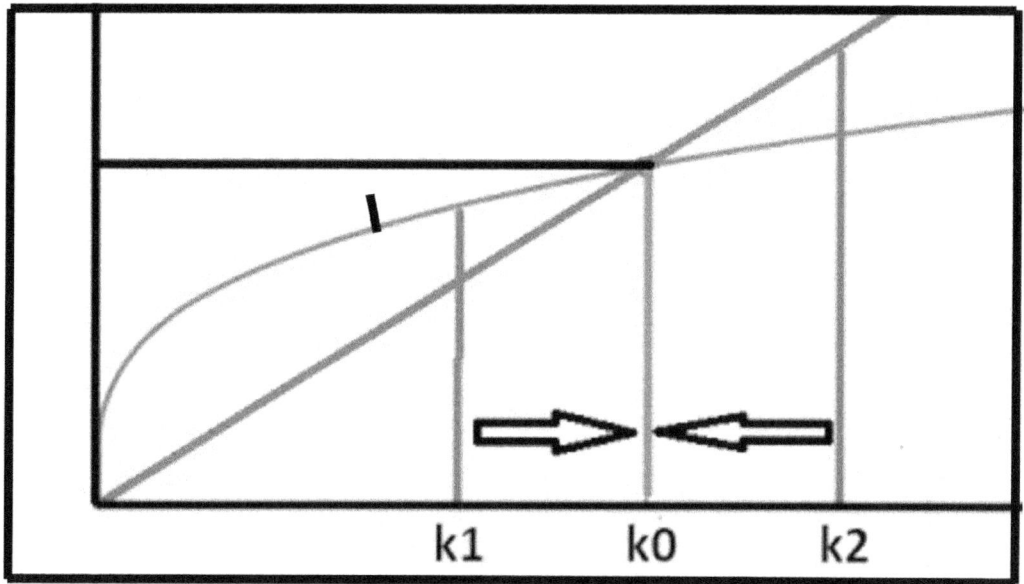

This chart represents when **k** changes due to changes in population.

k1 represents if population increases then presumably the total amount of labor **L** also increases and **K/L**, i.e., **k** is smaller

k2 represents if population decreases then presumably labor also decreases and **K/L**, i.e., **k** is greater.

This is saying that total production will not change right away, so production per labor unit, **k**, initially is smaller like at **k1** or larger like at **k2** but then eventually the total production will decrease or increase to match the new number of workers, that is productivity will tend to return to the baseline productivity levels for either scenario and **k** will return to **k0**.

In other words, if population increases then wealth per worker will decrease but eventually go back to the same value, and similarly, if the number of workers were decreased then wealth per worker would increase, but the remaining workers would be unable to maintain the level of production needed to maintain that

The Capital/Labor Split and The Solow Growth Model

total level of wealth and in both cases the wealth per worker ratio would come back to the same level.

Again, other than measures of labor and time, this chart only shows measures of wealth, not income.

FIGURE 46.7

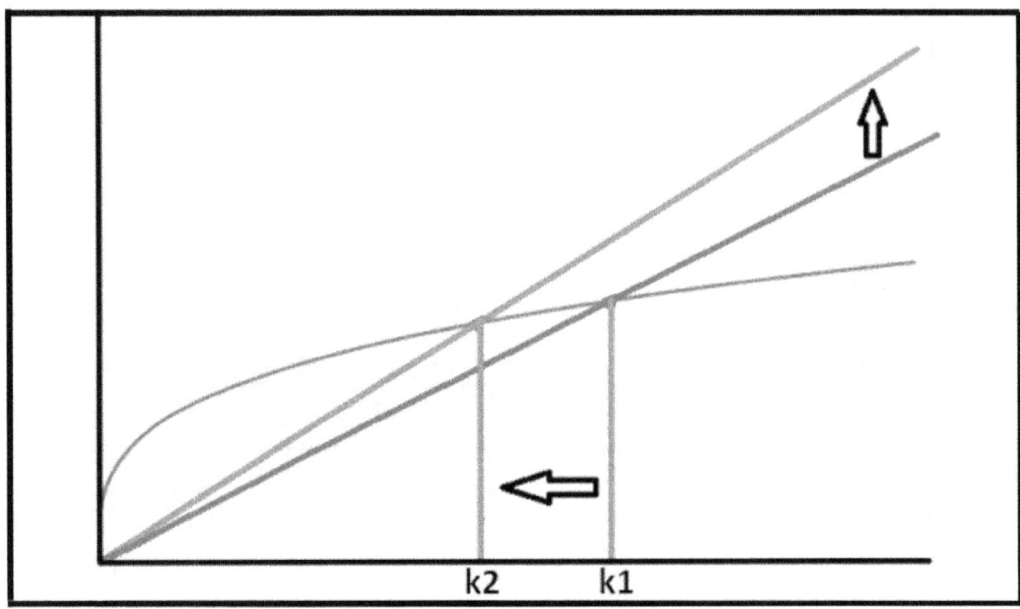

This shows that by increasing the rate of depreciation one could decrease the total wealth of a society. Have wealth be depleted more rapidly and the slope of the depreciation line increases, and it will intersect the line representing "new output not used up" farther to the left, meaning you will have a steady state at a lower level of wealth per worker. So, increasing the rate of depreciation, depletion, decay, and destruction of preexisting wealth could lead to reduced wealth of a society. And of course, preserving wealth at a greater rate could lead to increased wealth of a society. Again, the chart only shows measures of wealth, labor and time.

FIGURE 46.8

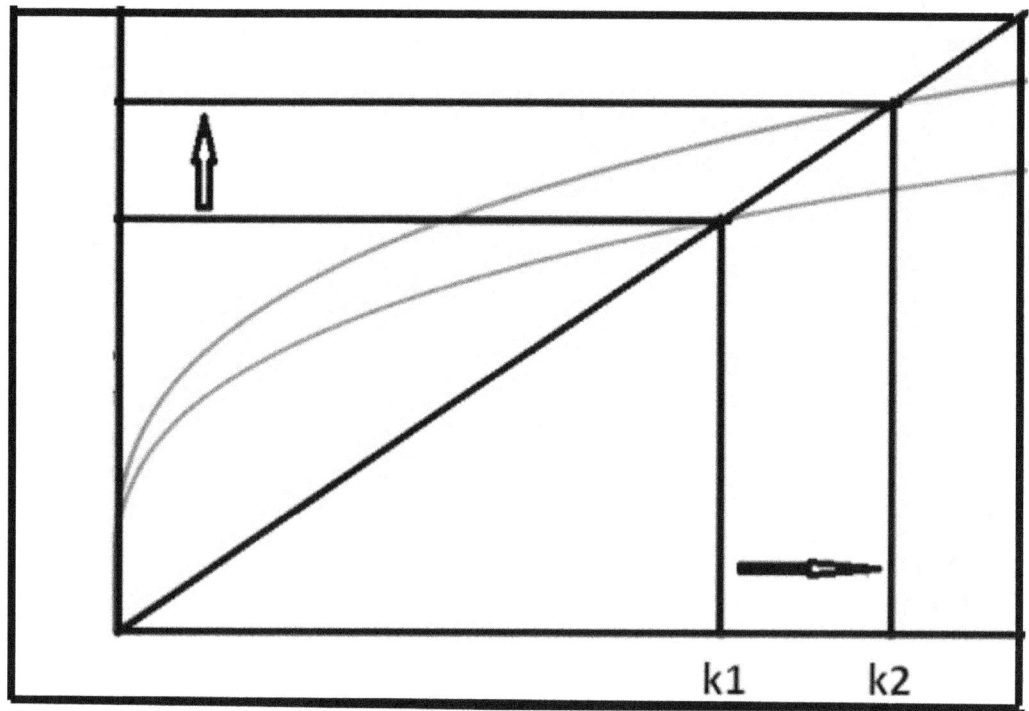

This is what happens if productivity increases, causing an increase in total amount of output produced, which presumably would correlate to an increase in the amount of production not used up. This chart compares the two curves showing the amount of production not used up for each value of k. The lower curved line is the fraction not used up for a lower level of production and the upper curved line represents the fraction of production not used up with a higher level of output production after productivity has increased.

Increased productivity increases the total amount of production and, in this chart, also the total amount of production not used up for the given time period. If the depreciation rate per level of **k** (wealth per worker) remains the same, then **k** will increase until depreciation rate is the same as the rate of wealth accumulating, that is, at the same rate the amount of output not used up is accumulating.

The Solow Growth Model does not show any measures of income, only measures of wealth and changes in the level of wealth. **Y** in this model equals output and it does not equal investment plus consumption, it does not equal money times the velocity of money, and it does not equal average price times the number of transactions. There is nothing showing the income axis. Nothing identifying who is paying for the output, and who is paying the workers, and how much they are paying.

CHAPTER 47
THE CAPITAL/LABOR SPLIT - PIKETTY MODIFIED

I BELIEVE THAT Piketty and his colleague's work on wealth inequality was an enormous contribution to our understanding of this issue. It is hard to fathom how much labor must have been involved in all the research necessary to collect and organize the data their work has provided us. In my opinion, their work, which culminated in the book "Capital in the 21st Century" is one of the most important contributions economists have made to the world in recent times.

My issue with his work has to do with some of the equations he uses, not his data. His equations are based on believing in the truth of the generally accepted "Fundamental Identity of National Income Accounting". Specifically, the part where Production and Income are considered as identical. That meant to me, that my understanding of his work would never be satisfactory unless I could find a way to reconcile the differences in a theoretical construct based on accepting that income and production are descriptions of the same thing, and my model, which does not accept that premise.

This Chapter presents Piketty's theoretical framework as I understand it. It simplifies his model into certain basic definitions and concepts, which are then analyzed in terms of the model of macroeconomics I have presented in previous chapters of this book. It is not intended to be an authoritative or officially sanctioned representation of his work. His model as presented is my own interpretation.

Before I start to talk about Piketty's model, I am going to make one statement that I think is indisputable. If you consider production to be any process that produces or increases the value of wealth, then the change in the level of wealth that comes out of a period of economic activity equals net production, i.e., production of new wealth minus any depletion of wealth. No matter where or how the change in wealth occurs, it, all added together, equals our net production. Any theory about the change in wealth and distribution of wealth has to be about who ends up with how much of the net production from a given period, and the effect of the sum of the changes over multiple time periods.

There is a big difference in the terminology that Piketty uses and the terminology that I use in this book. The most important difference is that I keep the accounting of spending and income on one axis and the accounting of wealth on another. Piketty says, in essence, income is production, that is, he is talking about something that is accounted for on the wealth axis only. For this reason, when his model calls something income, I will keep reminding that he really is talking about a change in the level of wealth. That he is really talking about something that is part of net production. I will be calling this "Piketty's income", to distinguish it from what I call income, as defined in Chapter 2, where I define income as the transfer of ownership of money from one person or entity to another, for a purpose. My income is calculated on the income axis, "Piketty's Income" is calculated on the wealth axis.

Since his book is about capital which he says is equivalent to wealth (same as my definition) and the main thrust of his book is about inequality of wealth, then I will try to find a way to link his terminology to mine in such a way that we can understand his work using my terminology.

Piketty's definition of income is similar to my net production, that is new production minus any wealth depleted. He uses the term depreciation instead of depletion, so I will follow suit.

In my model, figuring out what depreciation should equal is easy, just subtract off the value of any wealth lost or depleted in some way. That would include adding to depreciation any new production that was used up before the end of the time period.

The Capital/Labor Split - Piketty Modified

With Piketty, there is an attempt to link depreciation to capital that is necessary to the process of production, that is, capital that must exist pre-production to be available for use in the production process. In fact, I believe he makes the jump to assuming all existing capital is necessary to the process of production, so depreciation would include the loss of value of all wealth that existed prior to production, which I will call "old wealth", and which I assume is all the wealth existing at the start of the given time period. And so, it is expected that some new production is used up or loses value prior to the end of the time period, but that is not what he intends as part of depreciation. Therefore, the distinction between my net production and what I will be calling Piketty's income is that my net production would include as depreciation all of the wealth used up no matter when or how it was produced, and his only includes the loss of value of old wealth.

Piketty has this thing called β which he describes as the ratio of capital (total wealth) to income (Piketty's income). From what I gather, Piketty assigns the value of capital to be that wealth which is possessed or mainly possessed by those who are wealthy, that is people who get their increased wealth by owning a lot of wealth in the first place. He refers to those people who possess the capital (wealth) as Capital. They are said to be contributing capital (wealth) to the production process rather than labor.

His model shows that Labor (those who contribute labor to the production process) gets a portion of the new production as pay. His model, however, does not seem to allow for those who gain their Piketty's income from labor to save any of that income. He seems to imply that the only wealth people who get their money from labor ever have is what they earned in the current period, because any wealth earned in a previous time period they use up in that time period, there is no carry over or building up of capital by Labor.

Now it is possible that he considers people to have a Labor side and a Capital side. In other words, everyone can contribute some capital and some labor, and their Capital part is the part they can save and build wealth. And in that case there would perhaps be some whose contribution is all, or mostly all, labor, but who still can own, provide and receive some capital. And there could be some that have a lot of wealth and are assumed to have mostly contributed capital but little or no labor, who end up with large portions of the increase in total capital. And one could imagine all sorts of combinations. People being simultaneously part of both

The Capital/Labor Split - Piketty Modified

groups is possibly what Piketty meant, it is just nothing that I saw explicitly stated in his book. So, I will divide them completely in my analysis.

Piketty estimates that total depreciation during a given time period is about 10% of GDP. What I am calling new production is what he refers to as GDP, the production approach to GDP at any rate. Therefore, to a reasonable approximation, depreciation of **total wealth** in any given time period, is 10% of the value of **new production** from that time period.

Next I describe how Piketty's model addresses the "Capital/ Labor split"; where he looks at where the new production he calls income goes. How much of the total income (Piketty's income, really wealth) goes to Labor, people who acquire wealth by selling their labor; and how much of Piketty's income goes to Capital, those who contribute capital.

The capital that Capital gives for the production process is all old wealth. We know a certain amount of old wealth gets depreciated (10% of GDP). And we also know that, as defined, before Piketty's income can be positive it must at least equal the total value of depreciation. This means that in essence the value of any of the depreciated old capital must be replaced before Piketty's income takes on any positive value. I bring this up at this point only to point out that the value of any depreciated capital gets replaced and when replaced it gets owned again by Capital, i.e., by those who own all the capital. This is different from my model, because in my model you can have positive income even when total wealth is being reduced, such as during times of war or natural disasters, but this is not the case if income is defined by net production of wealth. This is because if income is defined as the change in level of wealth, then income cannot be positive when the change in level of wealth is negative.

Piketty's income, i.e., what is left of new production after subtracting the depreciation, then gets divided up between what goes to Capital ("the ones who make their income by contributing capital") and what goes to Labor ("those who make their income money by contributing labor). Let us say Labor is to get 70% of Piketty's income and Capital 30%. These are typical numbers given when Capital/Labor split is discussed in standard economics texts.

If labor is to get 70% then they will only get 70% of the value of new production **after** the depreciation, which is in essence saying that 70% of the value of depreciation is deducted from labor's take of "Piketty's income". In other words, Labor would have gotten 70% of that depreciated wealth, if it had not depreciated. And if Capital is to get 30% percent of the Piketty's income then their take is reduced

The Capital/Labor Split - Piketty Modified

by 30% of the value of that depreciation. So, Capital loses wealth in the form of depreciation but then, with the value of the depreciation being fully replaced by part of the new production, Capital regains the entire value of the depreciated wealth. This is because, apparently, in the Piketty model, only Capital gets to keep any wealth that survives and still exists at the end of the given time period. That is, with a depreciation of 10% of GDP (GDP = new production), Capital loses 30% of that 10%, i.e., 3%, but gains back the entire 10% so Capitals total take of new production becomes 37%, i.e., 30% of value of new production, minus 3% lost to help compensate for depreciation but add back 10% (100% of the value of the replenished depreciation). Labor, on the other hand, had to contribute 70% of value of depreciation, 7% of the total value of new production, to make up for depreciation. But Labor does not get keep any of that depreciation that was replenished. That means Labors total take of new production is 70% minus 7% equals 63%.

In our example, using the typical Capital 30% Labor 70% split of net output production. Labor will end up paying for 70% of the of the total depreciation. Capital is paying to make up for 30% of the total depreciation. After looking at those figures, it leads to the question: Who is really contributing the capital used in the production process?

The next thing to point out about his model is that it appears to be that the amount of (Piketty's) income that goes to Capital is assumed to be totally saved and added to total wealth of "Capital". The total amount of Capital's share of (Piketty's) income is added to and increases the total wealth of the capital owners.

Capital gets to "save" their portion of Piketty's income in its entirety and add that to their total wealth. The same cannot be said for Labor. The amount Labor gets might typically be around 70% of Piketty's income. But it is not explicitly stated, in his model, how much of that 70% of Piketty's income gets saved. In fact, there is no mention at all about labor having any savings at all. It seems to be that the amount of wealth Labor has is all represented in their (Piketty's) income from the current time period. Labor gets a significant fraction of Piketty's income every year (say 70%) but none of it carries over. All the value of Labors share of Piketty's income gets used up or otherwise depleted so that none of that wealth carries over until the next time period. The only wealth that Labor seems to possess that continues to exist, and can perhaps even grow, from one time period to the next is human capital, the capacity to provide labor, in terms of both quality and quantity is the only wealth Labor is allowed to "save" from one period to the next.

The Capital/Labor Split - Piketty Modified

Piketty presents his β, which is the ratio of total capital (total wealth) to Piketty's income, as a good way to evaluate inequality. The comparison is between the total wealth of people with capital (who get to watch their wealth grow because they have capital) and the amount of new production. Since labor gets a definite proportion of the new production, it does represent, to some extent, a comparison of total wealth to Labor's current share of new production. His model shows that generally, absent some significant disruption in the economy, Capital's total wealth increases every year and also shows that the amount by which the capital is increasing every year also tends to increase. Labors part of income (Piketty's) increases every year, but none of that increased production that went to labor gets saved. Labor acquires more new production every year but uses up all of it up and none of it gets saved and carries over. Labor keeps getting richer in that they acquire more new wealth each year, but they still do not save any of it and their wealth does not build up. That is what I think the model in effect describes.

The fraction of Piketty's income that becomes possessed by Capital is symbolized by a small letter **s** in Piketty's model. This means that the amount of new capital saved, the amount by which total capital increases that year is **s** times Piketty's income. Piketty also defines something he calls by the small letter **g**, which is the fraction by which Piketty's income increases every year. The amount by which Piketty's income increases each year is **g** times Piketty's income.

The significance of these two values is they describe a comparison of the amount by which total wealth of Capital grows from the previous year (s times Piketty's Income) as compared to how much the Piketty's income is growing from the previous year (g times Piketty's Income). It is implied in the model that this is a comparison of the change in level of wealth of Capital from the previous year to the change in the level of wealth of Labor from the previous year.

Piketty explains how if **s** and **g** are constant, how after enough years the value of β gets closer and closer to **s/g**. β is the ratio of total wealth to (Piketty's) income. Since his model is looking at inequality, this is the measure that determines, in his model, the level of inequality. This is the explanation for why β will eventually equal s/g if s and g stay constant:

The Capital/Labor Split - Piketty Modified

Let K_0 be the total capital at time zero

And G_0 is income (Piketty's income) at time zero Assuming that **s** and **g** are constant

And that the Piketty's income in the year n is G_n

The total capital gets added to each year by the amount **s** times the G from the previous year

Capital after n+1 years becomes:

$K_0 + sG_0 + sG_1 + sG_2 + sG_3 \ldots + sG_n$

That capital starts with the original amount and the savings from each year are added year by year to the total

Income (Piketty's income) after n +1 years is $G_0 + gG_0 + gG_1 + gG_2 + gG_3 + \ldots + gG_n$

Because each year G increases by **g** times the previous year's Piketty's income

So β, the Capital to income (Piketty's income) ratio for the nth year is

$(K_0 + sG_1 + sG_2 + \ldots + sG_n)/(G_0 + gG_1 + gG_2 + gG_3 + \ldots + gG_n)$

$(K_0 + s[G_1 + G_2 + G_3 + \ldots + G_n])/(G_0 + g[G_1 + G_2 + G_3 \ldots + G_n])$

as n increases the term K_0 will become insignificant compared to $s[G_1 + G_2 + G_3 + \ldots + G_n]$ and the term G_0 will become insignificant compared to $g[G_1 + G_2 + G_3 + \ldots + G_n]$

so, the value as n increases of the capital to income (Piketty's income) ratio will become

$s[G_1 + G_2 + G_3 + \ldots + G_n]/g[G_1 + G_2 + G_3 + \ldots + G_n]$ which equals s/g

that means as the number of years increases the savings rate over the growth rate of income (Piketty's income) **s/g** becomes the capital to income (Piketty's income) ratio β, provided **s** and **g** remain relatively constant.

Piketty used this explanation to show how if **s** and **g** are changed, it can take a long time to establish a new equilibrium, many years in fact.

The Capital/Labor Split - Piketty Modified

That's the best I can do in terms of understanding the basics behind Piketty's main theoretical model that he presents in his book "Capital in the 21st Century". In order to understand his work in terms of my model there are things I would do to modify his theoretical model. For example, if I were interested in comparing level of wealth I would not compare wealth to income, I would compare wealth to wealth. I believe that modification would give a more accurate description of the difference in total wealth between those who increase their wealth by being rich and those who survive by labor.

Although that modification may make a more accurate description of the difference in wealth than comparing wealth to income, doing it Piketty's way may be a more useful comparison because the actual comparisons in the level of wealth may be so extreme that it does not do the best job of reflecting resources available to each group, Capital and Labor. Perhaps what one has to look at is how much is the total capital worth compared to how much the "stock of the labor" is worth. In other words, how much money can labor earn in the given time period, and therefore have to spend, even if the model does not credit them with being able to save any of that income. If that was how one looked at it, as the value of total wealth possessed by Capital, compared to the amount of income (as I define it) Labor earns in each time period, it might be a useful comparison. I suspect that is probably the comparison Piketty is implying anyway.

The fractional or percent rate of growth of total wealth is **r** Piketty's most famous expression is **r>g**. This equation would describe a situation where total wealth of those considered Capital grows faster than the "Piketty's income" including Labor's portion of Piketty's income. If one defined income as I do in chapter 2, then this might be viewed as comparing the total increase in wealth of Capital as compared to how fast the amount of income labor can generate increases. In Piketty's model since the amount of capital growth is a fraction of Piketty's income, (like 30%, for example) if the rate of growth of Piketty's income is limited, that will put a ceiling on how high r can go. The percent of Piketty's income that goes to Capital could be increased but eventually the total value that Piketty's income can attain is limited by **g**, so there remains limits on how high **r** can go. For example, we see that the if s and g are constant then over time β becomes a constant. Since β is the ratio of wealth to income that would mean wealth is growing at the same rate as income, meaning r is not greater than g, r is equal to g. In this model g determines the rate of growth of Piketty's income and it is Piketty's income from which the increase in total wealth comes. So I am not quite sure what use **r>g** is in terms of a model to analyze what is occurring. EXCEPT that it shows what Piketty's research showed is occurring. In real life, based on the enormous labor intensive amount of research he and his colleagues did, he was able to show that as time went on, if there was not a disruption occurring in the economy, such as one might get with war, that **r** indeed is greater than **g**. But is **g** addressing the total increase in wealth labor is allowed to keep (in the model above it appeared not to be) or the increase in the amount they can earn through their labor each year. Once again, I believe the confusion here is caused by accepting the truth of Fundamental Identity of National Income Accounting, and believing that income and production are always equal and can always be substituted for each other, at any time, and in any equation. As stated repeatedly throughout this book, I disagree with equating income and production.

I'll end this chapter with some comments about a couple things that affect the distribution of wealth, and a comment on human capital.

Stock buy backs

I want to look at something called Stock Buy Backs. Let us say companies ended up with more cash because of a tax cut. Let us say that instead of investing in the company, the leaders decided to use the extra money from the tax break to buy back company stock, which makes that stock no longer exist. Stock buy backs increase the value of the still existing stock, by decreasing the total number of stocks in the company. The value of the company is temporarily increased with the tax cuts, but then that extra value of the company gets reduced again when the money is given to pay for the stock that will be retired. So, the end result is that the value of the company is the same but there are less stocks, so the value of individual stocks is greater.

For those, whose benefit derives from the value of the company in terms of what it produces in terms of employment and output, stock buy backs are not helpful. In other words, it is not likely to increase most of the employees pay, except perhaps highly paid executives and board of directors, whose "performance" the stockholders appreciate. These stock buy backs are not likely to increase the benefit this company gives society in terms of increased production. It is unlikely to increase aggregate demand if at all, because increasing the worth of rich people's stocks is not likely to lead to much spending.

The theory behind tax cuts helping the economy is supposed to be that it increases aggregate demand, by spurring investment spending by the company that got the tax break. If the stock buy backs are paid for by tax cuts and the tax cuts in turn lead to a decrease in government spending on programs that benefit the poor and middle class then the tax cuts that support the stock buy backs can be harmful, while the stock buy backs themselves may do nothing for the economy at all, and only help increase the income of the wealthy stock holders.

Stock buy backs help both the stockholders who don't sell because the value of their stock goes up. And Stock buybacks help the ones who sell the stocks that are "bought back" because they can command a higher sales price, based on the increased demand for (spending to acquire) that stock the stock buy backs cause.

Since a lot of stock buybacks are announced, that is automatically going to increase the price of that stock, since if people know the value of the stock is going to go up, why would they sell it at a lower price??

One could make a case that the money those who sold their stocks earned will be used for spending that stimulates employment and production. Since people who are selling stocks usually are wealthier, and this money is mostly ear marked for buying assets that give a profit, that money will not be used so much for buying end products. It may be put into investments of some sort that can have a positive effect on demand.

Proponents of stock buy backs sometimes allege that stock buy backs just move the money to supporting ventures that will give a bigger rate of return and are going to provide more benefit for society. They would allege that those who sold that stock will find better places to invest their money and this will stimulate the economy.

Those buy back proponents might allege that if the company that got the tax cut was such a good opportunity then the company would keep the money and spend to exploit those opportunities; that stock buybacks are proof the money is better spent elsewhere.

They might allege that this would more than make up for any cuts in government spending because private for-profit spenders are more intelligent in where they put their money, and that is what maximizes production and wealth, and that will ultimately increase employment, production, and increase the velocity of money and income, causing an increase in tax revenues.

But, the fact of the matter is, if there were spending opportunities with a better return, then you would think the stockholders of the original company would sell their stocks in that company and buy into the opportunity with the better return anyway. You don't need a tax cut to have that happen. Further it is known that corporations and wealthy individuals are already hoarding trillions of dollars of cash[29] or easily liquidated assets with low yield because those better investment opportunities are not there.

Are all the consumer appetites satisfied? Are there no longer any desires for more products or outcomes? Or is the economy at full employment and unable to produce anymore? If so, on either score, then why would policy makers be attempting to increase demand with tax cuts. If either was the case, then increased production is either unnecessary or impossible. The point is, if the economy is not at full employment, or if all our appetites are not satisfied, then perhaps it is an aggregate demand problem that is not being improved by giving tax cuts to corporations who then just divert the money into already very deep pockets.

Dividends

Let us say tax cuts increased the value of a company. Let us say the leaders of the company decided to pay out that increased value as dividends to stockholders. Dividends are analogous to stock buy backs, in that it takes value away from the company and gives money to the stockholders. Except in this case, instead of having that money going to a few people who sold their stocks, the money gets distributed to all the stock holders. The value of the company goes down, but the stockholders are compensated by that exact amount.

Again, if the value of the company was increased by a tax cut the money could have been put into the company, but if, instead, it is distributed to the stockholder, then the tax cuts will not benefit society through that company increasing employment, wages or production. If the tax cuts lead to a decrease in government spending it could even create an overall adverse effect.

Proponents of dividends would allege that if it were worthwhile to invest in the company that got the tax cuts they would have done so, and they would allege instead, that giving that money out as dividends will be giving the money to

---

29   https://www.cnbc.com/2019/11/07/microsoft-apple-and-alphabet-are-sitting-on-more-than-100-billion-in-cash.html

The Capital/Labor Split - Piketty Modified

people who will find better places to invest their money, and this will stimulate the economy. They would allege that this would more than make up for any cuts in government spending because private for-profit spenders are more intelligent in where they put their money, and that maximizes production and wealth. They might say it will even increase tax revenue by increasing employment and income, or at least the real spending power of the tax revenue that does exist. Again, I say, if there were better opportunities out there, why wouldn't the stockholders just sell their stock and buy into the better opportunity. You don't need a tax cut for that to happen.

Stock buy backs and dividends are a way of liquidating some of the worth of the company and giving that value to the stockholders. In the past tax policies have been designed to encourage reinvesting in the company, to keep the worth of the company growing and strengthening it. This is what happened when marginal tax rates for individual tax payers were much higher. If they took profit from selling stock or getting dividends, their tax liability might be considerable. In such a situation, stockholders would likely be happier if the decision makers kept putting extra revenue, such as from tax cuts, back into the company rather than dispersing that value into stock buy backs and dividends.

Piketty says:

"There are many reasons for excluding human capital from our definition of capital. The most obvious is that human capital cannot be owned by another person or traded on a market (not permanently, at any rate)."[30]

Some ideas on how human capital is included in our valuations of wealth:

A large percentage of what investors are buying, all of the time, is human capital. Every time someone purchases a stock in a company they are buying human capital, not the people themselves, but their placement in terms of location, where they go every day, what they do, what they know, how they interact with each other, the whole operation that is referred to as a firm or a company is run by people. People who have the knowledge and ability to implement the process. The value of that asset depends almost completely on human capital. Mistreating those humans that have that knowledge and ability could cause the worth of that asset to collapse very quickly.

---

30 Piketty, Thomas. Capital in the Twenty-First Century (Kindle Locations 871-872). Harvard University Press. Kindle Edition

Even when we purchase purely financial assets like bank accounts we are really ultimately purchasing an asset whose value depends on the ability of the people who borrow from the bank to pay that loan off. We are investing in the "human capital" the borrowers possess that will allow then to be able to acquire the funds to make their payments. It they don't make their payments, then the bank can't pay interest on our deposit. If the borrowers don't make their payments then when we need to withdraw the money, the money won't be there since most of it is loaned out.

Almost every possession that any person or entity has involves utilization of human capital in producing, maintaining and/or safe guarding it. In general, whenever any entity, person, firm, government, whatever, spends to purchase something, whether it is expected to last and give some return or benefit, or whether it is intended to be used up quickly, human capital is probably involved in some way in giving that which we are purchasing its value.

CHAPTER 48
Zero Lower Bound

At zero lower bound, which I will define here, I show that monetary policy loses its ability to stimulate the economy, at which point fiscal policy is necessary. This is problematic because while monetary policy is controlled by the Central Bank, fiscal policy, i.e., direct government spending, is controlled by other parts of the Government.

MONETARY POLICY USES real interest rates. That is the nominal interest rate adjusted for inflation. If the nominal interest rate **increases** relative to the inflation rate, the real interest rate increases. This makes loans more expensive, reduces the amount of lending, and reduces direct spending and aggregate demand. If the nominal interest rate **decreases** relative to the inflation rate, it decreases real interest rates, makes loans cheaper, increases the amount of lending, and leads to an increase in direct spending and aggregate demand.

If the inflation rate remains the same over a long period then the economy has adapted, so that everything has adapted, wages, pensions, prices, and interest rates have all stabilized. Let us say we have an established inflation rate and we develop a period of inadequate aggregate demand where we judge that the unemployment rate is greater than NAIRU. This decreased demand could end up causing wages to fall due to decreased bargaining power, and prices to fall due to decreased demand, meaning the inflation rate would slow as well. That is one of the main ways Central Banks judge that unemployment level is "too high", i.e., one of the ways that they determine that the unemployment rate is higher than NAIRU, by seeing the inflation rate fall.

The Central Bank would respond by lowering nominal interest rates more than the inflation declined, so as to lower the real interest rates. Hopefully, this would increase aggregate demand and stabilize the economy and return the unemployment rate back to NAIRU, at which point inflation would stop falling. Let us say it wasn't enough and the rate of inflation kept falling. This would cause the Central Banks to continue to lower nominal interest rates faster than the amount inflation falls, so as to continue to lower real interest rates. If the inflation rate continues to fall, eventually this would lead to the Central Bank bringing the nominal interest rates all the way down to zero. When the Central Bank has lowered the nominal interest rate to zero, and cannot lower it any further, this is called the Zero Lower Bound.

Notice what happens here if the inflation rates dropped further. If inflation kept going down, real interest rates would then start to increase. That means that lowering interest rates cannot help stimulate the economy after we reach zero for the nominal interest rate. This shows what happens if we reach zero lower bound:

Real interest rate(r) = nominal interest rate(i) minus inflation(π)

$r = i - \pi$

but at zero lower bound nominal interest rate(i) is zero, nominal

interest rate (i) can't get any lower

substitute in 0 for the nominal interest rate i and you are left with

$r = -\pi$

in terms of changes in real interest rates vs changes in inflation rates we have

$\Delta r = - \Delta \pi$

At zero lower bound as inflation gets lower, real interest rates increase. This is the opposite of what normal monetary policy tries to accomplish.

The table below shows how normal monetary policy would affect real interest rates before nominal interest rates reach zero and after they reach zero.

TABLE 48.1

Nominal Interest Rate	Inflation Rate	Real Interest Rate
12	8	4
10	7	3
8	6	2
6	5	1
4	4	0
2	3	-1
0	2	-2
0	1	-1
0	0	0
0	-1	1
0	-2	2
0	-3	3
0	-4	4

This table shows the normal policy whereby nominal interest rates, controlled by the Central Bank, are reduced when inflation rate decreases, but by MORE than the decrease in the inflation rate. This causes real, inflation adjusted rates (nominal rate minus inflation rate) to be reduced as well. Deflation is a sign that the economy is slowing, reducing real interest rates increases demand by making loans cheaper, to help stimulate the economy.

This works well until nominal interest rates reach 0%. Nominal rates cannot be reduced below 0%, or at least not very much below 0%, so as the inflation rate continues to fall, real interest rates start to rise. This has the opposite effect on demand as it begins to make the inflation adjusted cost of loans more expensive and loans are less affordable.

This is the equation for real interest rates at zero lower bound: $\Delta r = - \Delta \pi$. As inflation falls, the change in inflation rate is negative so the change in real interest rates is positive.

Sometimes economists will say the economy loses its "self-correcting mechanism" at zero lower bound, implying that somehow prior to reaching that point the economy corrects itself. But there is no "self-correcting mechanism", just specific monetary policy designed based on an understanding of the effects of real interest rates on real aggregate demand and employment levels. I am talking about the specific **policy** where if inflation increases, the interest rates controlled by the Central bank are increased even more, or if inflation decreases the interest rates are purposefully reduced more the inflation decrease. If inflation increases, nominal interest rates are increased more than the inflation rate increase so as to keep inflation and demand from getting too high. This is not by some natural occurrence but by policy.

Let us look at the balance of purchasing savings assets versus purchasing venture assets in this scenario. If one decreases Federal Funds Rate or IOER rate, this can make loans cheaper and increase aggregate demand, but also make purchasing shares of ventures (venture assets) more attractive. This will lead to increased spending on venture assets and lower the marginal efficiency of capital until it can go no lower for that particular interest rate, which means this intervention can provide no more stimulus at that particular FFR or IOER rate. If the interest rates (Federal Funds Rate or IOER rate) were to be lowered further, this would loosen money for purchasing savings assets and venture assets, causing returns on both of them to go lower until they reach an equilibrium for that interest rate (Federal Funds Rate or IOER rate) and by the time the economy reaches zero lower bound, when FFR or IOER rate is zero, the return on savings and venture assets would have been driven lower until each reached zero. And so at that point one would expect the Central Bank buying bonds, to have little, if any effect.

At zero lower bound, Monetary Policy, which is directed by the Central Bank will not work, so the only government option then becomes fiscal policy, which is not controlled by the Central Bank. Fiscal Policy is controlled by the Government. In America that would be the legislative branch and the executive branch. Fiscal policy is direct spending by the government to attempt to increase aggregate demand. Below is a chart attempting to illustrate how fiscal policy might affect aggregate demand and inflation rates to bring us out of a zero lower bound situation. It shows how much more of an effect fiscal spending has while at zero lower bound, and how the effect is reduced after the economy has escaped zero lower bound. This is assuming the standard monetary policy of increasing interest rates to control inflation is used after zero lower bound, counteracting somewhat the effect of continued or increasing fiscal policy.

FIGURE 48.1

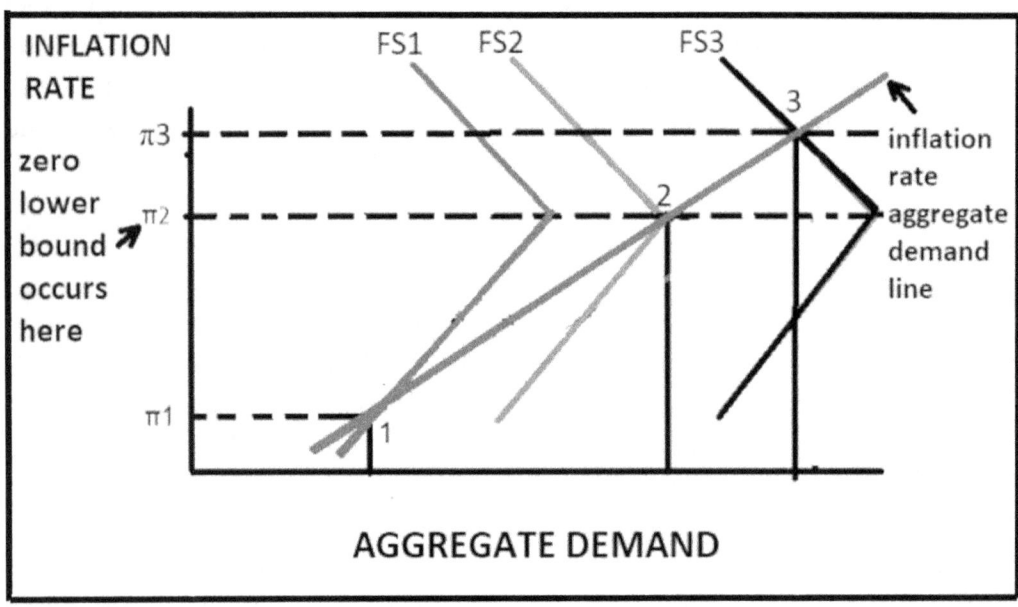

FS stands for the level of fiscal spending, new spending by the government (FS1, FS2, FS3 on the graph). How far the FS curve shifts to the right is the measure of the increase in fiscal spending. The total increase spending (AGGREGATE DEMAND) for each level of fiscal spending is measured on the horizontal axis as AD1, AD2 and AD3. On the vertical axis, π is a measure of the inflation rate. Zero

Zero Lower Bound

lower bond is designated as occurring at π2 in this scenario. The upward sloping line represents the value inflation will take for a given level of aggregate demand. The higher the aggregate demand the more prices generally can go up. Obviously, using straight lines, this is a simplification to make the point.

The important point to note on this chart is the large increase in aggregate demand (horizontal axis) for a smaller increase in fiscal spending when the economy is below the zero lower bound (FS1 to FS2). Then notice the relatively smaller increase in aggregate demand associated with a larger increase in fiscal spending when the inflation rate is above zero lower bound (FS2 to FS3).

The total level of spending, i.e., aggregate demand, is influenced by both monetary policy and fiscal policy. Below zero lower bound only fiscal policy has any effect. In that case increasing fiscal spending can have a large effect on aggregate demand because it operates unabated by monetary policy. This explains why we move so far up inflation/aggregate demand line from point 1 point 2.

Once the fiscal stimulus causes the inflation rate to reach the level that corresponds to zero lower bound, it is still a situation where further fiscal stimulus will continue to work to increase aggregate demand, and increase inflation rates. But this graph shows how monetary policy can work in the opposite direction. By increasing real interest rates in response to rising inflation, it reduces demand, and opposes the effect of fiscal policy on inflation and aggregate demand. This is shown on the chart by moving from point 2 to point 3. That explains why the movement up the aggregate demand/inflation line is so much less, even though the increase in the amount of fiscal spending was so much greater.

An advantage of having the inflation rate be above zero lower bound, and perhaps by a reasonable margin, is that will allow the monetary policy of lowering the interest rate to be effective, if needed, in the future. Specifically, it will give room for the interest rate to be lowered, to increase demand, without as much of a risk of getting into a zero lower bound situation.

Just to mention an interesting phenomenon. We see that not only does Fiscal policy directly increase demand, but one of its important effects is to increase inflation. Another way to increase inflation is convince people that inflation will be increasing. Expectation of inflation alone leads to inflation and this can be a way out of the zero-lower bound. This means if the Central Bank can make people believe that they are going to consistently follow policies that will increase inflation, that in itself, will help accomplish it.

Obviously, it is not only government spending or fiscal policy that increases aggregate demand, it is private spending too. The idea behind fiscal and monetary policy both, is not to take over for private spending but to stimulate it. Increased demand can lead to an increase in the amount of product available for purchase, and this will draw out spending including from private sector sources. The income earned by people involved in causing that increased production will have a multiplier effect causing an overall increase in velocity of money. In fact, one thing the Central Bank can do is just defer the monetary policy of increasing interest rates if we saw inflation rising. At that point, it is likely that private spending and employment level and production are recovering and, if we deferred the interest rate increase, it would allow the economic recovery to get on much firmer footing before the Central Bank returned to "normal monetary policy".

The idea behind monetary and fiscal policy in general is to increase demand so that private economic activity takes on its own inertia. The term "priming the pump" is an expression used to describe that dynamic.

This chapter is a typical explanation of the idea of Zero Lower Bound, based on how Monetary Policy was prior to the implementation of paying interest on excess reserves. Since the IOER has become the de facto effective Federal Funds Rate, the amount of excess reserves has become enormous, over a trillion dollars in America. Due to that, I suspect even minor adjustments to the interest rate paid to excess reserves will have much more major effects, so even when rates appear to be very close to ZLB, where monetary policy will no longer have an effect, they may not, in reality be so close. Additionally, with so much money in excess reserves, we should not be so quick to raise rates either, as that could also have major effects on the economy. Nevertheless, if nominal interest rates cannot be lowered any more, the concepts in this Chapter are valid.

CHAPTER 49
Trade - Balance of Payments

The purpose of the project that culminated in this book was to develop a complete and thorough understanding of the material presented by John Maynard Keynes in "The General Theory of Employment, Interest, and Money". I then hoped to be able to share that understanding with others. In the process I found it is not possible to understand Keynes work isolated from current macroeconomic thought. Throughout this book I have attempted to express my personal understanding of both Keynes' work and relevant standard macroeconomic teachings. It will be no different in these next few chapters on trade. In the next chapters I will, for the most part, not be introducing any original material. I will just be explaining how I understand these concepts. I will also try to integrate some of the material presented earlier in the book where I find it instructive.

IN DISCUSSIONS REGARDING trade I would like to remind the reader that, as noted in chapter 31, the expression used for my modified version of the expenditure approach to GDP, $Y = I_p + G + C + X$, referred only to spending and income that occurred in the private domestic economy. I also, after modifying the definition of each element, showed how this expression was equivalent to Keynes' expression $Y = I + C$. (also written as Y = Keynes' I {(Keynes' Investment} plus Keynes' C {Keynes' Consumption}). I then went on to explain which elements of GDP could be considered part of what I call Keynes' I ($I_p + G + X$) and which we should consider part of what I call Keynes' C (C). In that Chapter, I mentioned **trade** in describing **X** (for exports) as being considered as part of Keynes' **I** and also I showed how, for the purposes of the expenditure approach to GDP, **M** (for imports) should not be overtly considered part of the GDP equation, its true effect being to influence the values of other parts of the expression for GDP.

I later showed in Chapter 42 how there is a way to devise an equation for GDP that combines government and private spending, which requires some modification of what spending would count as part of Keynes' Consumption and what spending is included as part of Keynes' Investment.

What I want to mention here is that though the equation $Y = I + C$ (Income Y = Keynes' I plus Keynes' C) can be used, and be valid if properly applied to models that describe private domestic spending and income, it can also be applied and be valid in models describing and combining private domestic spending and domestic government spending. It could even be accurately applied to describe models that combine, as one economy, all the spending in private, domestic and any foreign economies that interact with the domestic economy, as long as one accounted for the fact that, while one would need to be using exchange rates, the total money supply used for spending includes more than one currency. And if $Y = I + C$ is valid for any of those models, then so is $Y = M*V$ (where M stands for the value of the money supply, not imports) and $Y = P*T$, as long as the income measured is known to be earned in the defined economy.

(For the model where all the countries are combined as one economy, to calculate M [here M stands for money supply, not imports] and therefore be able to calculate M*V, we would define one unit of measure for the money supply and use exchange rates to see how many units there are in the totality of all the money supplies involved. For example, if the unit of the money supply is one dollar that means 100 yen is also a unit of the total money supply, approximately. V will still be how many times each unit of the money supply is used for spending on the average).

In these chapters on trade (49 through 51) we will be looking at models that combine domestic private and government economies as they interact with foreign economies. The task is to figure out which definition of an economy would best help us to analyze international trade. It turns out that, in my view, none of the three definitions of an economy, already mentioned in this chapter, qualify for being the best to use in this application. I will use a new definition altogether.

When I analyze the interactions occurring in trade I will draw boundaries in a couple different ways. One way defines who is doing the spending and receiving the income from the spending. To this end I will recognize trade as being defined as occurring between different sovereign countries. How one wants to define what counts as being part of a specific sovereign country is up to the person developing the model. At any rate, all entities (people, organizations, businesses, governments etc.) involved in any spending, including any spending that can be stated as affecting trade, will need to be identified as belonging to and being a part of a particular sovereign country. Things that are happening to those entities, like acquiring income, or changes in level of wealth, etc., are considered, in the aggregate, to be happening to that country to which they belong.

No entity can be considered to be part of more than one sovereign country, except that there may be certain entities, such as multinational corporations that can be considered to have specified parts belonging to one country, and other specified parts belonging to another country, or multiple other countries. However, if one of those parts belonging to a specific country has any financial transactions with a part of that company belonging to another country, that transaction must be accounted for on the Balance of Payments calculation for either of those countries.

The same would be true if one had a dual citizenship and used that status to be able to conduct foreign trade. In this case, when that person is participating in any transaction, we must be able to identify which country that person should be considered part of for that transaction. This brings to us the interesting situation where all the wealth and all the financial assets that this dual citizen person owns must be assigned as being owned by an entity belonging to either one or the other of the countries. For the purposes of their economic identity, this person is divided into two different entities, each belonging to a separate country. Any transactions or shift of assets that person attempts, that would cause it to be considered as shifting from occurring in one of those country's economy to the other, must show up in calculations for the Balance of Payments. Just taking from one bank account to another would be considered part of international trade if the assets ownership was considered to be moving from being owned by the part of that person belonging to one country to being owned by the part of the person belonging to the other country.

In general, across the whole world, all specific entities, or specified parts of an entity, that is involved or can be involved in spending, especially spending involved in trade will have to be identified as being part of one and only one specific country. However, each entity will still have the ability to transact using the other country's currencies and be able to "own" foreign money and foreign assets denominated in foreign currency.

In the concept called the "Balance of Payments", another way I will describe a boundary is to separate transactions by **which currency** is being used in the spending to conduct a specific transaction. Is it a domestic or foreign currency? To simplify: In order to understand the "balance of payments" most easily, we can look at each entity involved in trade as belonging to a specific country, and look at the "economy" of that country as including the money supply denominated in that currency, and all the transactions that are conducted using that country's currency. A country's currency is defined as being that currency which is issued by, and whose supply is controlled by, that country's Central Bank. What this means is that for the purposes of analyzing international trade, a country will be defined by all the entities who belong to it, and the wealth of that country will be all the assets, financial and non-financial that are owned by entities belonging to that country. But when we refer to the economy we will be referring to an accounting of everything that happens to the money supply of that country, including where the money supply exists and who owns it, who controls the spending of it and all the spending done with that money supply.

This definition of an economy is distinct from the three mentioned above (private domestic being one, domestic including private and government combined being another, and domestic combined with foreign as one economy being a third). However what remains true with this definition of an economy, that is, an economy defined as including all the existing currency of a given denomination and all the transactions occurring in using that specific currency, is that the expressions, $Y = I + C$, and $Y = M*V$ and $Y = P*T$ will all still be valid. That is, these expressions will be calculated and hold true for the money supply of each and any of the currency denominations. That is, those equations apply **separately** for the currency created by the central bank of any sovereign country in the world that has its own currency. What allows this to be true is that all of those listed equalities define measures of spending not wealth.

Having the economy of a given country so defined, we need to recognize that the spending occurring using a given currency is influenced by which entities and countries own any wealth, what wealth they own, in what quantity and how that wealth may be involved with any spending or in any international trade. But also influencing the spending of a given country's currency is the spending of currency belonging to other countries.

Using this definition of the economy, what is also true is that the "Savings equals Investment Identity", (i.e., the part of savings that is the preservation of investment) will hold true, and hold true separately for the economies of each country that produces its own currency. In other words, if, for each sovereign country, we consider an economy to be defined as including **any transactions** being paid for with the currency created by that country's Central Bank, commerce involving that currency will not cause the supply of that currency to increase or decrease, and that currency will still exist in that country's economy.

This definition of a country's economy is different from my modified equation for the expenditure approach to the private domestic GDP of a given country, where there is no accounting for a given amount of currency used to pay for an import, since once it is acquired by a foreign entity that money left the private domestic economy (see chapter 31). Instead, in this model, where the economy is defined as the money supply of a given country's currency and any transactions conducted using a given country's currency, for example, the money paid by a domestic entity for imports, would all be considered as occurring in the economy of the country to whom that currency belongs. All of that spending is contained in the expression $Y = I + C$ for that **currency,** no matter who has gained that money as income. This is true because just the fact of someone being the recipient of some spending done with that currency, means they have gained income in that currency. Since that transaction occurred with that currency all of that transaction, both the spending and the income, is considered to have occurred in the economy of the country whose Central Bank produces that currency.

If the transaction involved a foreigner buying something with domestic currency that transaction occurred in the domestic economy. It could be something like that foreigner using domestic cash to buy a debt obligation, such as putting domestic money in a domestic commercial bank. All that spending occurs in the domestic economy. The money becomes owned by the commercial bank, and remains in the domestic economy. The debt obligation the foreigner acquires from the commercial bank, that asset, is not strictly money, and is not in the money supply. However since the depositor controls the spending of that money, that depositor is still involved with and has an interest in, the economy. So, because of having control over the spending of that money, from a practical perspective that asset owner and that asset are integrally involved in the economy and will be counted in the balance of payments. In other words, even though, with virtual money, the bank officially owns the money, for the balance of payments it is the one who controls the spending of the money that this money is really considered to "belong to". If money in a commercial bank is owned by a foreign entity, it is not the money the bank owns, but the asset the foreign depositor owns that gets counted. It is the amount of money that asset owner controls the spending of that gets counted in the balance of payments.

So with this new definition of the economy, income can be acquired by anyone who is the recipient of the spending of that currency, including government entities and including foreigners. It is not just entities who belong to the country whose Central Bank issues that currency that can be a recipient of that spending, and therefore considered to have earned income in that country's economy, but any recipient of that spending can be considered to have earned income in that country's economy.

In my modified equation for expenditure approach to GDP, described in Chapter 31, income could only be earned and contribute to GDP if a private domestic entity was the recipient of spending. In the chapter describing a combined government/private domestic economy, income could only be earned by private domestic entities or government entities. In neither of those definitions of what constitutes the economy can a foreign entity be considered as earning income in that economy. This is because if a foreigner is the recipient of any spending, that money would be considered as having left the domestic economy.

With the definition of the economy being the money supply of a given currency and all the spending that occurs using a given currency, then obviously even when there are foreign recipients of spending with a domestic currency, that would still count as gaining income in the economy of the country that issues that currency. This definition of the economy also has the advantage of still allowing us to separate the economies of different countries from each other. This is a more accurate description of how the world wide economy functions than we would have if we tried to make a model where the entire world was one big country with one currency. That is, my proposed definition of the economy as being the money supply and all the transactions occurring using that money supply is a more accurate description and a more useful model than one where we tried to combine all the worlds currencies (after applying exchange rates) and treat them as if they were one money supply and all the world's economic activity was all occurring in one giant country. The model I am presenting, in my opinion, is really the model that is already being used for the balance of payments concept, even if that is not explicitly stated or recognized to be the case.

Another issue that we might need to consider in analyzing trade is what happens on the wealth axis. How do we determine who owns any wealth. Any items of wealth that have been traded will simply be owned by whoever acquires them and ownership of that wealth will be assigned to the whichever country that entity belongs to. Similarly, any money, no matter which country's central bank produces it, will be owned by some entity, no matter what country that entity belongs to. And the country to whom that entity belongs can consider that money as part of their wealth. Any asset owned that gives the asset owner control over a given amount of money, is also going to be, like money, considered as owned by some entity that belongs to some specified country. But for the purposes of balance of payments, even though, for example, it is the commercial bank that owns that money (and a debt obligation to the asset holder, such as the bank depositor) it is really who controls the spending of that amount of money that will credited with being the "rightful owner" of that amount of money. In other words, it is the claim that a foreign entity has on some amount of domestic currency by owning a debt obligation from the bank, (for example), that will allow one to designate that foreign entity as having a stake in the domestic country's economy.

For the concept known as The Balance of Payments, we look at what happens to the money in the money supply as it relates to international trade. We look at the spending of that money, what situations the spending of that money create, where the money ends up, and who controls the spending of that money.

Introducing the Concept Known as the Balance of Payments

One contribution the Balance of Payments makes to understanding international trade is it helps us to follow where the money goes when trade occurs. One can imagine that if the domestic country ran a trade deficit and did so for an extended period of time, the money used to buy the imports would keep going to the foreign country and never come back to the domestic country, leading to a money shortage in the domestic country. The Balance of Payments, specifically the part called the Capital Account, allows for a very good understanding of this issue, and where the money spent goes. Perhaps an even more important contribution Balance of Payments makes is what another component called the Current Account, measures. This component measures trade balance, that is, whether the domestic country is running a trade deficit or a trade surplus. And as an advantage over the GDP model mentioned in Chapter 31, it measures all of a countries trade including trade conducted by both the private sector and the government.

Before going further with the idea of Balance of Payments, I think it might be useful to try to give the simplest possible explanation of the basic concepts:

Balance of Payments has two components, Current Account and Capital Account (we can think of the word "account" as meaning "accounting").

Suppose an American buys an import from a Chinese for which the American pays $500. The Chinese then owns 500 American dollars, which is either owned as physical cash or as a $500 bank deposit, or some combination equaling $500. (For any bank deposit the Chinese owns the asset called the "bank deposit," but it is the bank that owns the cash, usually virtual cash, denominated in American currency, i.e., dollars, but the Chinese will control the spending of that amount of money).

Here we have traced the money traveling from the American purchaser of the import, to the Chinese seller of the import, and then control of the money 'settles', and continues to exist in financial assets owned by the seller of the import, the Chinese. (Both physical money and bank deposits are financial assets.) Since the denomination of the money used is dollars, these activities have all occurred using dollars and the financial assets remain denominated in dollars. What this means, **is that all this economic activity occurred in the American economy, officially**. The transactions did involve a foreign entity, but the transaction occurred using the American currency for payment and therefore the transactions occurred in the American economy, and the financial assets that end up being owned by the Chinese are denominated in dollars.

In the situation described, the 500 dollars paid by the American for the import is the Current Account. The financial assets whose worth totals 500 dollars (combination physical currency or bank deposits), that become owned by the Chinese is the Capital Account. The Current Account is the money paid for the import, and the Capital Account identifies where the money ends up.

That is the essence of the Balance of Payments. For an import, when the transaction is complete, the foreign entity has gained control of the spending of the domestic money. The physical or virtual money remains domestic money, and remains part of the domestic economy, but control of the spending of that amount of money, virtual or physical, has transferred from the domestic entity who purchased the import, to the foreigner who sold it. Thus by gaining control over the spending of some domestic money, the foreign entity has gained an interest in the domestic economy, that is, the foreign entity has gain an asset in the domestic economy.

For whatever reason, it was determined that the Capital Account and the Current Account always differ in sign. If one looks at having a domestic entity pay for an import, the transfer of ownership of the money, (or at least control of the money), occurs with money going from the domestic entity to the foreign entity. So money paid for the import is a positive for the foreigner and a negative for the domestic entity. This amount, negative the amount of payment, represents the Current Account calculation for this transaction for the domestic country and has a negative sign, and therefore is subtracted from the total for Current Account for that time period. But the description of the money ending up as a domestic currency denominated foreign owned asset makes it seem like the money, paid for the import, has "come back" to the domestic economy (even though, in reality, it never left). Looking at it that way could make those foreign owned domestic assets seem like an addition to the domestic economy. In reality they are not adding any money, monetary assets or net wealth to the domestic economy, they are just replacing equally valued financial assets that a domestic entity "used to" own before the domestic entity paid for the import. After paying for the import ownership of the domestic financial asset, and control of the spending of the money, or at least the amount of money upon which the value of the asset is based, was transferred to the foreign entity, with the financial asset still belonging to, and being part of the domestic "economy" since all the transactions occurred as result of domestic money changing ownership (or least a change in who owned control over the spending of an equivalent amount of money).

At any rate, since that foreign owned domestic asset is viewed somehow as an addition to the domestic economy, for this transaction, the Capital Account of the domestic economy is given a positive sign. The Current and Capital Accounts are opposite in sign while the magnitudes are equal. With that way of looking at it, if you add Current Account and Capital Account together, they will always equal zero.

In reality, this simply means, that if some spending to pay for an import occurs using a given currency, when you trace where that money went, you will find out it still exists, in the same amount, with control of the spending of that money having been changed from the spender to the recipient of the spending.

I know this brings all sorts of questions, like what about exports? What if the importer pays in foreign currency instead of domestic currency? What if the money ends up owned by a foreign commercial bank instead of a domestic commercial bank, etc.? All these variations will be shown to have similar explanations. My goal is to help the reader to acquire a clearer, more generalizable, understanding of how to structure and explain all these different situations.

As stated, when I am talking about trade I am making the assumption that there are separate sovereign countries whose boundaries, as far as trade goes, are definable basically by which entities are assigned as belonging to that country. That means, based on these definitions I am giving here, any entity that can or does participate in trade, must be assigned as belonging to one of these sovereign countries. Now this being true, I also note that for the purposes of Balance of Payments calculations, the only important designation is that an entity either belongs to the specified *domestic* country, for whom we are calculating the Balance of Payments, *or* that they belong to *any* of the *foreign* countries with whom entities belonging to the domestic country trade. Calculations of Balance of Payments only applies to one country at a time, but it could be any country. The designated country for which we are calculating the balance of payment is referred to as the "domestic" country. All of the trade partners combined belong to the "foreign" country category. In other words, you would combine Balance of Payments for each foreign country versus the domestic country and then add the results together to get the official Balance of Payments result. Each country's currency would have its own exchange rate with the domestic economy which gets accounted for in the balance of payments calculations for each country individually.

Assigning an entity to a specific country may not always be easy or straightforward, but what is true is that each entity can belong to one and only one sovereign country. An exception, as mentioned, may be for large entities such as multinational corporations. In such cases it may be more appropriate to assign certain segments of each of these corporations to one country or another, but the person doing that analysis must make sure that every part of the company is assigned to one and only one sovereign country. Any movements of ownership of money or other assets from a part of that corporation that belongs to one country, to a part of that corporation that belongs to another country, would have to be included in and calculated as part of the trade between those two countries.

When talking about a trade we are talking about transactions being paid for by money transfers, using one of the official currencies of the trading countries. This does not necessarily include barter. However, if one did account for barter, one would have to do something like I showed earlier in this book where I transformed such barters into the equivalent of a transaction conducted using money for payment. So if Party A traded item 2 to Party B in exchange for item 1, that would be like Party A giving Party B money in payment for item 1 and then party B giving an equivalent amount of money back to Party A in exchange for item 2. It is a little more complicated to show how this would be done when the barter is occurring between entities associated with different countries.

Barter involves an item of wealth being paid for with another item of wealth. If one assumes that both items are of equal value, (which, basically, a barter would be considered as affirming), this will not change the Current Account or Capital Account. This is because each of the participant entity's countries can be considered to be both importing and exporting, paying the same amount, at the same time, and they will cancel out their respective contributions to Current and Capital Accounts. Barters do not change the total value of either component and therefore, for the purposes of Balance of Payments, barters can be ignored.

Cryptocurrency transactions, other than people selling cryptocurrency for money, is a form of barter. Cryptocurrency is often portrayed as an international currency with no boundaries, but for the purposes of this discussion, it will be considered a commodity, not a currency, and it will be owned by an entity who is identified as belonging to a given country.

In this book I showed how the difference between a barter economy and a monetary economy is that in a barter economy change of ownership of each commodity traded counts as spending and income, but in a monetary economy *only* change of ownership of the *money* counts as spending and only receiving money counts as income. This is very pertinent to Balance of Payments because I will be focusing on the movements of money and where the money goes in making any calculations. Although we may know where any item purchased goes, we do not include the non-monetary items in the calculations, just the money, the spending of the money, who ends up owning the money or which entity owns the purely financial assets that allows that entity to control the spending of a specified quantity of that money.

How we decide what counts as a country, which entities belong to each country etc., is up for interpretation and may be adjusted according to the model with which one is working. The important thing to consider is that once the boundaries are determined, they are understood to remain consistent and clearly defined during the period under analysis. In other words, a model cannot allow for an entity switching sides, or switching of ownership of financial assets from one country to another without accounting for it in the Balance of Payments.

Formal Definition of the Balance of Payments

Balance of Payments has two components:

1. Current Account

The Current Account is basically a measure of what I have called "Direct Spending". Direct Spending occurs in international trade when an entity belonging to one country trades the ownership of money from themselves to an entity belonging to another country, in exchange for some non-monetary form of wealth. This wealth being paid for must be defined in the most general way possible so that all payment of money from an entity belonging to one country to an entity belonging to another country are able to be calculated as part of this direct spending. This includes paying for any goods, services, or any other desired outcome. It does not include paying for a purely financial asset (loans).

2. Capital Account

The Capital Account involves measuring cash or purely financial assets that tell us where the money used for the direct spending described in the Current Account ends up. As discussed previously in this book, purely financial assets are basically loans. Loans compose the lion's share of what is measured when measuring the Capital Account. This is in no small measure due to the fact that a bank deposit is a loan, from the depositor to the Commercial Bank with whom the depositor has an account.

Current Account

Current Account is basically determined by the calculation for Exports minus Imports. In other words, when looking at Current Account, economists look at it as a calculation of our Trade balance, i.e., is a country running a Trade surplus or Trade deficit. I will now take a closer look at what is usually included in the calculations of Current Account. I divide my descriptions into how Current Account is affected by exports and situations that are equivalent to exports, then I make the same analysis with imports.

Current Account – exports

For exports the trade balance will be positive and consists of:

1. The amount of money paid to the domestic (exporting) entity by the foreign entity importing that non-monetary product. That amount is added to the Current Account of the domestic country, i.e., it is a positive value for the Current Account.

    In the model as I am defining it, it doesn't matter where the exported item is physically located when it is sold, it could even be physically located in the country of the foreign entity buying the export. Since the domestic, exporting country is defined by the entities who belong to it, as long as the exported item is owned by an entity belonging to the domestic country when it is purchased by the entity from the foreign country, it will count as an export from that domestic country to the foreign country.

    Further, it doesn't matter where the foreign entity keeps that product after it is purchased, including what country it is kept in. Since that foreign country is defined by the entities that belong to it, then as long as the product becomes owned by some entity that belongs to that country, that country owns the item, and it has been "exported" to that foreign country.

    The fact is, for some exports it might even be difficult to determine what country they physically exist in, like computer support services, for example. Although normally we expect most items referred to as having been exported to be something that will be physically transported from within the physical boundaries of the exporting country to within the physical boundaries of the importing country.

2. If some entity in a foreign country donates money to the domestic country, like a charitable contribution, that amount of money is added to the Current Account as a positive value. Just like the money given to pay for an export, this is still money given by the foreign entity to the domestic entity. One could say the "export" being paid for by the foreign country is the product known as "some desired outcome".

3. If a domestic entity owns a purely financial asset in a foreign economy which gives a profit or a return, the money paid as the return is essentially a payment from the foreign country to the domestic entity, like an export, and so counts as part of the Current Account on the positive side. This is, essentially, the same thing as foreign entities causing money to be added to the value of that domestic entity owned foreign financial asset. This means entities in the foreign country are acknowledging they are receiving some sort of value (some desired outcome) for which they are willing to pay. The "some desired outcome" is the export. Whether those earnings are kept as cash or put into increasing the value of the asset, (the debt obligation owed to the asset holder) the effect on the Current Account is the same. The increase in value of the asset is looked at as equivalent to an export for the purposes of calculating the Current Account. The assets I am talking about are not non-monetary assets. They are all strictly purely financial assets, and when their worth increases, it is solely as a result of transfer of ownership of some money and/or the transfer of the control of the spending of some money to cause the increase in the value of the domestic countries foreign assets.

4. If a **foreign** entity owned an asset in the domestic economy and it **decreased** in value, that situation is looked at as if the foreign entity is transferring the lost value of the asset to entities in the domestic economy. This can either be the handing over of money or it could be a decrease in the debt obligation the domestic country has to the foreign entity. In either case, this is equivalent to the transferring owner ship of money, and/or control of the spending of a given amount of money, from the foreign entity to some domestic entity or entities and is equivalent to an export. This is, in essence, the foreign entity acknowledging that they are getting something of value, something worth paying for, some desired outcome, by continuing to hold a financial asset in the domestic economy.

If one is not satisfied that 2, 3, and 4 from above should count as exports then they can be referred to as "export-like". But those things are included in calculations of the Current Account.

Note that contributions to the value of the current account occur due to spending of different currencies. But it is clear in any case which economy's money is being spent in each transaction. When combining the contribution to the totals for the current account and balance of payments in general, exchange rates will need to be used. Typically the value of each currency is converted into what it would be if it were domestic currency, the currency of the country for which one is figuring out the balance of payments.

Current Account - Imports

For imports the trade balance will be negative and consists of:

1. The amount of money paid to the foreign (exporting) entity by the domestic (importing) entity. That amount is subtracted from the Current Account of the domestic country, i.e., it is a negative value for the Current Account.

    In the model as I am defining it, it doesn't matter where the item being imported is physically located when it is sold, it could even be physically located within the borders of the domestic country when the domestic entity buys it and still be considered an import, as long as the ownership switched from a foreign seller to the domestic buyer. Since each country is defined by the entities that belong to it, as long as the imported item was owned by an entity belonging to the foreign country when it is purchased by the entity from the domestic country, it will count as an import to the domestic country.

    It doesn't matter where the domestic entity keeps that product after it is purchased, including what country it is kept in. Since the country is defined by the entities that belong to it, then as long as the product is owned by some entity that belongs to the domestic country, the domestic country owns the item, and it has been "imported".

    The fact is, for some imports it might even be difficult to determine what country they physically exist in, like computer support services, for example. Although normally we expect most items referred to as having been imported to be something that will be physically transported to the exist within the physical borders of the domestic country.

2. If some entity in the domestic country donates money to a foreign entity, for example, as a charitable donation, or foreign aid of some type, that amount is added to the Current Account as a negative value, just as is the money given to pay for an import. This is money given by the domestic entity to the foreign entity. One could say the "import" being paid for by the domestic country is the product known as "some desired outcome".

3. If some foreign entity owns a purely financial asset in the domestic economy that gives a profit or a return, the money paid as the return is essentially a payment from the domestic country to some foreign entity, like an import, and so counts as part of the Current Account on the negative side. This is, essentially, the same thing as domestic entities causing money, or at least control of the spending of a certain amount of money, to be added to the value of that foreign country's "foreign entity owned" domestic financial assets (remember money itself is a financial asset). This means entities in the domestic country are acknowledging they are receiving some sort of value (some desired outcome) for which they are willing to pay. The "some desired outcome" is the import. The increase in value of these assets are looked at as equivalent to an import for the purposes of calculating the Current Account.

4. If a **domestic** entity owned an asset in the foreign economy and it **decreased** in value, that situation is looked at as if the domestic entity is transferring the lost value of the asset to entities in the foreign economy. This is equivalent to the transfer of ownership of money and/or the control of the spending of a certain amount of money going from the domestic entity to the foreign entity or entities and is equivalent to an import. This is, in essence, the domestic entity acknowledging that they are getting something of value, something worth paying for, some desired outcome, by continuing to hold that financial asset in the foreign economy. This counts as an import for the purposes of calculating the Current Account.

If one is not satisfied that 2, 3, and 4 from above should count as imports then they can be referred to as "import-like". But those things are included in calculations of the Current Account.

Capital Account

I have talked about **Current Account,** now let us look more closely at **Capital Account**, maybe better described as "where the money ends up."

In order to make the concept of **Capital Account** as understandable as possible, I will first boil down **Current Account** to its essential ingredient. The essential ingredient of an export is money being paid by the foreign entity to a domestic entity. The essential ingredient of an import is money being paid from the domestic entity to the foreign entity. It is the movement of money (or at least control of the spending of money) to new ownership that is the essential ingredient. For both imports and exports the spending that actually pays for the export or import is direct spending, money that has transferred ownership to acquire some good, service or any other desired outcome,….. (excluding the purchasing of a purely financial asset….which also does not count as direct spending, even though as the transaction unwinds, some money will move in and out of purely financial assets, it is not that spending that pays for the trade, it is the direct spending). So the essential ingredient of Current Account is an accounting of how much direct spending occurs, who does the direct spending, and who is the recipient of the direct spending. Whereas the essential ingredient of the Capital Account is where the money ends up and who owns it. Overall then, the **Balance of Payments** is essentially an analysis of what happens to the money.

Here I will first be looking at what happens to the **Capital Account** with an **Import**.

Three ways payment for the import can happen are:

1. **The domestic entity can pay with domestic money.**
2. **The domestic entity can pay with foreign money.**
3. **The domestic entity can exchange domestic currency for foreign currency and then use the foreign currency to pay.**

Let us look at what happens to the money in these three circumstances.

The first option:

The domestic country pays the foreign entity for the import with domestic money.

First, to simplify, let us say that the transaction was paid for completely with physical money, paper currency and coins. If the domestic entity pays the foreign entity with domestic money, then the domestic entity comes to own the item purchased, while the foreign entity has come to own the domestic money. *<u>This means that (and this is the most important concept with regard to the concept of Capital Account), by owning this domestic money, the foreign entity has obtained a stake in the domestic economy.</u>* Remember, I define the domestic economy as being all of the domestic money (also referred to as currency) existing and any transactions that occur in which the spending is paid for with domestic currency. By receiving that domestic money, the foreign entity has gained money in the denomination of the domestic currency and as such has earned income in the domestic economy. In that way, the foreign entity, by owning that money, has become part of the domestic economy. The money whose ownership transferred from the domestic entity to the foreign entity still exists, only who owns it has changed. The amount of money that has become owned by the foreign entity is added to the Capital account of the domestic country in that time period. The same amount of money would be subtracted from the Capital Account of that foreign country, for that time period.

The rationale behind this is apparently, this money, whose ownership has gone to a foreign entity, has supposedly become a "foreign investment" in the domestic country. The reality is that while the foreign country did transfer the imported items to the domestic economy, it did not transfer any money into the domestic economy, the money was already in the domestic economy and the only thing that changed was who owns it. While the Current Account measures the direct spending done by the domestic entity where money is given to the foreign entity, the Capital Account measures the simultaneous formation of a financial asset for the foreign entity in the domestic economy, that is, the foreign entity now owns domestic currency. When normally taught it seems as if they say money was given to foreign entities to pay for the import and then that money was immediately (and obligatorily) used by the foreign entity to buy a domestic purely financial asset. But that is not the case. In this scenario, by receiving the money as payment for the import, the foreign entity was receiving and therefore owning a foreign financial asset, in this case the cash.

What I just described is what would happen if the money paid was all physical money, coins or paper currency. It is slightly different with virtual money. With virtual money the individual entity never really "owns" the money, its financial institution does, usually a Commercial Bank. The bank owns the money and the individual entity owns an asset called a bank deposit, or deposit account. While the deposit account owner does not own the money, it does gain the ability to participate in controlling the spending of an amount of money equal to the value of the deposit account.

Now, with virtual money, since the Commercial Bank owns the money, that money is able to be, and likely will be, loaned out, that is, that money will still be cycling through the economy being spent and re-spent. So even though the owner of that asset, the bank depositor, controls spending of a certain amount of money owned by the commercial bank, it doesn't necessarily control the spending of any specific money, just an amount of money equal to the value of the bank deposit.

When the domestic entity pays for an import with virtual money, what happens in essence is the domestic entity loses an asset that gave it control of the spending of that amount of money, and the foreign country gains an asset that gives it control of that amount of money. This because it is actually the Commercial Bank or Banks, that will own the money. So after the trade the foreign entity now controls spending of some domestic money. But this money was **not new** to the domestic economy. Just who controls the spending of it has changed. It was not taken from the domestic economy, given to a foreign entity, to pay for the import, who then used it to purchase a domestic asset. That money was part of the domestic economy before the trade and remains part of the domestic economy after the trade. Only control of the spending of it change, that is, only who owned the asset that gave control over the spending of that money changed ownership. There was no obligatory payment by the foreign entity or entities after the trade to acquire a domestic asset. It is simply how payments are made with virtual money. The reason the foreign entity has a domestic asset is because they came to own that asset as a result of being paid with virtual money for the import. The domestic country bought an import and lost ownership of the assets, the physical or virtual money, used for payments. For transactions paid for with virtual money, after the trade is completed, the bank deposits in the amount of the trade owned by the domestic entity no longer exists, but instead an equivalently valued domestic asset called a bank deposit was created and became owned by the foreign entity who was the recipient of the spending. Then, even though the foreign entity's domestic commercial bank would own the money, the foreign entity, instead of the domestic entity who paid for the import, would be able to participate in controlling the spending of that amount of money.

Some may wonder what is gained by the concept of a Capital Account? In my opinion its main utility is that it gives a good way to track where the money goes and where it ends up, which as I already mentioned, is one of the major contributions to the understanding of macroeconomics that this Balance of Payments concept affords us.

To review:

The Capital Account changes as soon as the spending measured in the Current Account occurs. The Capital Account is really just a description of where the money that was acquired as payment for the import goes. The change in the value of the Capital Account is always equal in magnitude but opposite in the sign of the Current Account.

In the case of an import, the Current Account is negative and the Capital Account is positive. This is because the Current Account represents money being paid from the domestic entities to the foreign entities so that the value of that money has changed ownership from the domestic entity to the foreign entity (or in the case of virtual money, from the domestic entity's Commercial Bank to the foreign entity's Commercial Bank). That is a negative for the domestic country.

On the other hand, as soon as the sale is made, the foreign entity has gained an asset in the domestic economy in the form of physical money or a bank deposit. That is considered a gain for the domestic economy (even though it is not, because that money was already in the domestic economy) and counts as a positive addition to the Capital Account of the domestic country. The asset gained by the foreign entity in the domestic economy is exactly equal to the amount paid for the import. Capital Account plus Current Account equals zero.

The second option:

The domestic entity pays for the import with foreign money.

If the domestic country has foreign money to use, this means that the domestic country has a stake in the foreign economy. When this foreign money was originally obtained it was obtained as a result of a payment by a foreign entity to the domestic entity. This would have caused a positive contribution to the Current Account of the domestic economy. When the domestic entity was paid with the foreign currency that would cause the domestic entity to own a foreign financial asset, that is, foreign money or a bank deposit denominated in foreign currency. That would have been looked at as a financial assets somehow moving towards the foreign economy and away from the domestic economy and considered as a negative contribution to the Capital Account of the domestic country at that time.

That means, that come the day when the domestic entity uses its supply of foreign currency, previously acquired (or liquidates a previously acquired financial asset to get foreign currency), to pay for an import, it will not only cause a negative contribution to the domestic Current Account (money paid from the domestic entity to a foreign entity in payment for the foreign country's export), but it will reverse the previous negative contribution to the Capital Account of the domestic economy that occurred when those foreign financial assets, foreign money or bank deposits, originally became owned by the domestic entity. That means the reduction in the value of domestic entity owned foreign financial assets are looked at a positive contribution to the domestic Capital Account. It is treated as if the financial assets are moving back to the domestic country from the foreign country, but the reality is, that none of the financial assets are moving back. The assets are still existing in the foreign country's economy, denominated in their currency but are no longer owned by domestic entities.

I guess we can note that as a result of the amount of domestic owned foreign assets shrinking, that the **fraction** of total assets owned by the domestic country that is identified as domestic assets is increasing, because the amount of foreign assets it owns is shrinking. Perhaps that is the "movement towards" the domestic economy that made economists think of the shrinking of foreign assets as resulting in an increase in domestic holdings, of some sort. Whatever the thinking may be, reducing the value of domestic owned foreign financial assets is considered a positive contribution to the domestic Capital Account.

The reduction in domestic owned foreign assets (including assets based on debt obligations, any money paid) will exactly equal the amount paid to the foreign country for the imports.

The third option:

The domestic country exchanges domestic money for foreign money (currency exchange) then uses the foreign money to pay for the imports.

In the exchange of currency, the domestic entity spends to "import" the foreign currency, that is, it purchases foreign currency from some entity in the foreign country (whether directly or through one of several intermediaries, it doesn't matter, the overall effect is essentially the same, at least over the long run). The foreign entity gets the domestic money which causes it to own a domestic financial asset. The domestic country gets to own the equally valued (after applying the exchange rate) foreign financial asset, i.e., the foreign money. Thus the domestic and foreign entities have each gained financial assets in the other's economy. BUT, when the domestic entity then uses its foreign money to pay for the import, its domestic ownership of that foreign financial asset (foreign currency) goes away, while the foreign owned domestic financial asset that was established by the currency exchange remains.

The domestic entity started with domestic money, exchanged it for foreign money which it immediately gave to the foreign entity as payment for the imported item. The domestic economy received the non-monetary import from the foreign entity, but the foreign entity got the foreign money back it had given in the currency exchange, and also ended up with the foreign owned, domestic financial asset. This means that the Current Account of the domestic economy is negative and the Capital Account of the domestic economy is positive in the exact same amount. This is the same result one would have if the domestic money were used for payment without the currency exchange. The Balance of Payments equals zero.

When an import is purchased, with domestic currency, or equivalently, after doing a currency exchange, the domestic entity gains the item imported, but has given the money and financial assets to the foreign entity. This means the domestic **country** has lost money and financial assets to the foreign **country**. However, the domestic **economy** has **not** lost any money or financial assets. This simply means that the domestic money supply has not been reduced by the international trade. The domestic money supply was not increased or decreased. The only thing that changed was who owns that money, or in the case of virtual money, who owns the bank deposits attached to the money the depositors commercial bank comes to own. So one sees the distinction between the domestic **economy**, which is defined as all the domestic currency existing and all the transactions occurring where domestic currency is the money being used for the spending, and the domestic **country**, which is all the entities that belong to that domestic country.

Tracking the Money Supply

A country's currency has two parts, the virtual money and the physical money (coins and currency). As international trade is conducted, the virtual money is easy to track and this is done in the normal course of any transactions using virtual money. The Central Bank of a given country constantly keeps tabs on and adjusts its records to reflect how much virtual money each domestic Commercial Bank owns at any given time. For an institution to be considered a domestic Commercial Bank they must have a relationship with that countries Central Bank. By relationship I mean Commercial Banks for whom the Central bank tracks and constantly tabulates the amount of virtual money that bank owns, (and in fact all the money, virtual and physical the Commercial Bank owns). For the virtual money I generally describe it as that money "owned by the Commercial Bank but held at the Central Bank", as entries on the Central Bank's ledgers.

It is because this money must be tracked constantly by the Central Bank that virtual money is easy to keep track of. On the other hand, physical money, especially since it can be possessed and owned by entities other than Commercial Banks or the Treasury, will not always be so easily trackable. For physical money, keeping track of the location and quantity of a given amount of money is much harder and this causes some uncertainty in keeping track of the size of the **total** money supply for a given country's currency. If enough paper currency or coins are stored or hidden or destroyed, domestically or in foreign locations it not only makes it difficult to track, but it could also create a currency shortage in that country's economy. This could lead to the need for the Central Bank to create more money. Nevertheless, knowing the size of the money supply or where the money is located, for example, how much of it has become possessed by foreign entities, is less of a concern these days since most international transactions occur using virtual money.

Please note that, without affecting the balance of payments, money can be moved around in a given domestic economy. For example, foreign own domestic financial assets can be traded for domestic owned domestic financial assets. If the assets traded are of equal value, in terms of domestic currency, this does not change the total value of the foreign country's holdings of domestic financial assets. Therefore it does not change the value of the Capital Account for either country. Now, if any of these assets, that have become foreign owned as a result of the swap, later change in value then that will affect the Current Account, and thus, also the Capital Account.

What may become a concern in unbalanced trade, especially if this becomes a chronic situation, is how much of the money supply gets controlled by foreigners. With virtual money this means concerns about the amount of debt obligations Commercial Banks have to foreign entities, that is, how much of the spending, of money owned by Commercial Banks, is controlled by foreigners. And with physical money, if a significant amount were being used in trade, this means concerns about what quantity of that paper currency or those coins is owned and possessed by foreign entities.

Some economists like to believe that all trade is caused by and funded by lending, that no trade is possible without lending occurring. This is not true, but is an artifact of the nature of virtual money, and the limitations of virtual money. Virtual money always exists as a Commercial Bank owning the money and the depositor having an asset called a bank deposit. The bank deposit is an asset whose value is based on a debt obligation of the Commercial Bank to the depositor, so most virtual money exists as owned by Commercial Banks who have assumed a debt obligation in order to own it, meaning that debt is involved in it existing. Commercial Banks can own virtual money without it being attached to a debt, but one expects the vast majority of what they own to be acquired by agreeing to a debt obligation to a depositor. Looking at that one might want to say that almost **all spending with virtual money is based on debt, not just trade**. But this does NOT mean that trade can only be funded by debt. If all trade were conducted with physical money, there would be no doubt that trade can occur **without** someone borrowing to acquire the money to pay for it. Plenty of people and other entities have cash on hand, for which they are not indebted.

If one were able to create virtual money where the Central Bank could track ownership right down to individuals and entities, not just Commercial Banks, or if a country had virtual currency that existed autonomously from Central Banks after issue, similar to the way it is with paper currency or coins, we could also then have trade occur without incurring debt. (This could be something like a Cryptocurrency, only one issued by the Central Bank, not private entities). Even if a country had a virtual currency with these properties, where the money didn't have to be constantly tracked by the Central Bank, this would not change the fact that Commercial Banks would still own most of the base money supply since people would still put their money in banks, i.e., purchase assets called bank deposits in exchange for letting the Commercial Banks own the money. The would do this because of the desire to get a return on that money but also possibly because the Commercial Banks would still be superior in conducting electronic transactions, and at record keeping.

I should mention that it was different when our money was not fiat money.

Formerly we used "representative money" (like gold standard money). Gold Standard money is considered a debt in gold by the Central Bank to the owner of that representative money. Given that, it is easy to see how, when ownership of the representative money switches to foreigners it was considered a switching of the debt, to the foreigner who comes to possess that money by receiving it as payment for an import. Or if the gold standard money is virtual money (which it can be) you would have, like fiat money, a situation where the Commercial Bank owes the bank depositor a debt but the Commercial bank owns the money and the Central Bank owes the Commercial Bank the gold. In any of these cases, the Central Bank continues to keep holding and owning the gold. And in that sense, i.e., in the sense that bank deposits are loans by the depositor to the Commercial Bank , then one can say that with representative money all trade is based on debt. But again, that is no different than saying that **all spending** is based on debt, not just spending occurring as part of international trade.

So when we had gold standard money, the Balance of Payments model probably made a little more sense, in terms of looking at the Capital Account as being totally based on debt. And, as just pointed out, even domestic physical cash, such as gold standard paper notes, being held by a foreign entity, would be able to be looked at like a bank deposit, as an **asset** whose value is based on debt. In that case the debt is the debt in gold of the Central Bank to whomever might own that gold standard note.

Capital Account with exports

This is easy to figure out, it is just like Capital Account with imports but everything is reversed. The three options become:

1. **The foreign entity pays for the exports with its own currency.**

2. **The foreign entity pays for the exports with domestic money.**

3. **Entities belonging to the foreign country exchange foreign for domestic money (currency exchange) then uses the domestic money to pay for the exports.**

The first option:

The foreign country pays for the exports with its own currency.

If the foreign country pays for the exports with its own currency, then the domestic country is receiving payment in that amount which counts as a positive value for the domestic Current Account. But this immediately establishes a stake of the domestic country in the foreign economy by the domestic country owning foreign cash or foreign denominated bank deposits in the case of payment with virtual money. The domestic country increasing its ownership of foreign financial assets counts as a negative for the domestic country's Capital Account. So the Current Account is positive and Capital Account is negative in the exact same amount.

The second option:

The foreign entity has domestic money already and pays with that.

The foreign entity has domestic money already and pays with that. The foreign entity gives domestic cash to the domestic entity to pay for export. That is a positive on the Current Account of the domestic economy. But the size of the foreign ownership of domestic financial assets has been reduced by the same amount. That counts as a negative for the Capital Account of the domestic economy. Current plus Capital Account equals zero.

The third option:

Entities belonging to the foreign country exchange foreign for domestic money (currency exchange) then uses the domestic money to pay for the exports.

Entities belonging to the foreign country exchange foreign for domestic money (currency exchange) then uses the domestic money to pay for the exports. A domestic entity then owns some foreign currency, either as physical or (more likely as) virtual money. Thus the domestic entity has gained a stake in the foreign economy either owning physical foreign money or owning a foreign financial asset whose value is based on the debt obligation of a foreign commercial bank to the asset holder. The foreign entity had temporarily gotten control of the domestic money but gave it back to the entities in the domestic economy when it paid for export.

This means the Current Account of the domestic economy is positive having gotten paid the money for the export, but the domestic economy has obtained, simultaneously, a foreign financial asset which in the Balance of Payments counts as a negative for the Capital Account (accounting) of the domestic country. This is exactly the same situation one would have if the foreign money were used for payment without the currency exchange. The Balance of Payments equals zero

If you look at typical Balance of Payments descriptions of the contributors to a Capital Account they divide a Capital Account up into different categories. I do not wish to go into all these categories just to say that these categories are all subsumed as being purely financial assets whose value is based on a debt obligation of some person or entity, or they are physical money. These assets are tradable between people or entities belonging to the same country, or tradable for assets denominated in the same currency. As long as the total value of the foreign owned domestic assets doesn't change or the total value of the domestic owned foreign assets doesn't change then the values of the Capital Account will remain the same. If the totals had changed then that would mean something happened that would also change the Current Account.

Balance of Payments is applicable with fiat money, and as noted, it can also be applicable with representative money like the gold standard. If the whole world used gold coins as a currency the idea of the Balance of Payments would just mean that whoever gets paid in gold has gold as a result. In today's world if gold is involved in a trade it is treated as a commodity.

The model I have used here to explain balance of payments is not as easily applied in a situation where you have a common currency for multiple countries like the euro. If one treated all the Eurozone countries as one country, this model would fit. But if one were trying to calculate the Balance of payments for each individual country separately it would be different, especially for trade with each other. So one would have to add all the contributions for balance of payments for trade with countries outside the Eurozone, but contributions for trade inside the eurozone, would be different. If some country pays euros for an import from another eurozone country, they would transfer ownership of euros or assets denominated in euros to the country from who they are purchasing the import. This will count as negative for the current account of the importing country, but as the country they purchased the import from would have more euros or assets denominated in euros they would have a bigger stake in the euro economy and this would have to count as a positive in the importing countries capital account. That is how one would have to do it.

So, in my opinion, the important contribution the concept of a Capital Account is to help explain and track "where the money goes". Current Account, which is an accounting of the trade balance, is, in my view, a much more important element of the "Balance of Payments".

CHAPTER 50
Trade - Currency Exchange

EXCHANGING CURRENCY USUALLY requires the help of a broker, specifically licensed and equipped to provide that service. This exchange could involve the exchange of any type of money, physical money for physical money, physical money for virtual money, or virtual money for virtual money. Exchanges always occur in "pairs", that is, the exchange transaction always involves only the trading of currency from two different countries with each other.

In order to trade **virtual money**, the agencies or institutions must have a relationship with that country's Central Bank or at least they need a partner that has a relationship with that country's Central Bank. This is because virtual money can only be owned by a financial institution but is always "stored" on the records of the given country's Central Bank. For most, but not all, of the virtual money those financial institutions own, they have to agree to a debt obligation to a depositor to be able to own it. It is possible for a **bank** to acquire virtual money without having to agree to a debt obligation to own it.

When I say these financial institutions must have a relationship with a given country's Central Bank, I am saying that Central Bank must be able to track what virtual money the financial institution (or their partner) **owns**... ("stored at that Central Bank but owned by" whatever institution or agency one is talking about).

When entities from two different countries exchange currency, one assumes that, by definition, what they are purchasing from each other is equal in value. This is because that is what the exchange rate defines, the value of one currency in terms of another currency and vice versa.

When country A purchases some of country B's currency, that purchase is categorized as an import of currency B for country A and an export of its own currency for country B. That is, country B gets paid by country A for selling its currency to country A. At the same time country A is exporting its own currency to country B. In an exchange, the value of the amount of currency A paid to import currency B, and the amount of currency B paid to export currency A are considered equal, because the amounts traded are determined by the exchange rate.

This means that for country A the current account is negative for the import of country B's currency, and, in an equal amount, positive for the export of its own currency. Because the amount of country B's currency paid for country A's currency (country A's export) is considered equal to the amount of country A's currency paid for country B's currency (country A's import), then current account for country A for its import cancels out the current account for country A for its export. To country A the current account of the import has a minus sign, and is of equal magnitude to the current account of the export which has a plus sign. This means that for country A the Current Account total is zero, and so also must be the Capital Account. By identical logic, the Current and Capital Accounts for country B will also be zero.

Conclusion:

A money exchange does not affect the Balance of Payments of a country.

Strictly speaking, any fees charged for the exchange does affect the Balance of Payments, and depending on who is charged the fee, this will affect the current and capital accounts to a very minor extent.

Now if at some point in time after the currency exchange the exchange rate changes, the change in the exchange rate **will** affect the balance of payments.

Suppose country A's currency appreciates in value compared to country B's currency. That means, a given amount of country A's currency will buy more of country B's currency. I also means that a given amount of country B's currency will buy less of country A's currency. Further it means that any assets denominated in country B's currency will show a decrease in its value in terms of country A's currency…… And that means **foreign assets that entities from country A own** in country B, which are denominated in country B's currency, will show a **decrease in its value in terms of country A's currency**. A decrease in value of a foreign asset counts as an "import like" transaction and is a negative for the Current Account of Country A and a positive for the Capital Account of country A.

An import implies that Country A has given money to country B. Think of this money going from country A to country B as follows: All of country B's assets, will have lost value in terms of country A's currency, but part of the country B currency denominated assets are owned by country A. And for that part of country B currency denominated assets, country A entities will be taking the loss instead of entities from country B. That means that country B, in terms of country A's currency, is a little richer than it otherwise would have been if country A did not own any foreign assets. That's how one can think of this loss of value of country A's foreign assets, in terms of country A currency, as being equivalent to a shift of ownership of money from country A entities to country B entities. Meaning that is how it qualifies as a payment from country A to country B and why this counts as an "import like" transaction when calculating country A's Current account.

On the other hand, since country B's currency has depreciated in terms of country A's currency, this means that country B's foreign assets, valued in terms of country A's currency will increase in value in terms of country B's currency. For country B's balance of payments this counts as an export like situation for country B and as positive for its Current Account and a negative for its Capital Account. In this case, since the value of country B's foreign assets is increased, in terms of its own currency, this is an export like situation.

If there was no foreign ownership of country A denominated assets, then the increase in value of those assets, in terms of country B currency, would all accrue to domestic entities. But since there is foreign ownership of domestic A currency denominated assets by country B, the increase of value of the country B owned, "country A currency denominated assets", in terms of country B's currency, accrues to country B entities instead of country A entities. So the increase in country A assets in terms of country B currency is reduced by the amount of that increase that accrues to entities from country B, those entities who own foreign assets denominated in country A's currency. This is equivalent to money going from country A to country B and that is why this counts as an "export like" scenario for country B, but it also makes it an "import like" scenario for country A.

Now one might conclude that this all means that a change in the exchange rate, solely by itself, with no other factors considered, favors the country whose currency has depreciated, and harms the country whose currency has appreciated. And as far as the value of foreign assets goes, that is true.

But even though country A's foreign assets may have decreased in value, (in terms of its own currency), ALL of country B's domestically owned assets (country B assets owned by country B entities) have decreased in value in terms of country A's currency. Similarly, even though country B's foreign assets denominated in Country A's currency, have increased in value, in terms of its country B's currency, ALL of country A's assets owned by country A entities have increased in value (in terms of country B's currency).

So the change in currency exchange rate between two countries actually favors the country whose currency as appreciated, if one considers what happens to all the financial assets in both countries.

All that said, there **are** ways that having a currency depreciate in value can be favorable to the country whose currency has depreciated in terms of trade balance. However this has more to do with price of exports and employment levels.

What causes an exchange rate to change?

Basically, what changes exchange rates is demand for a currency. Demand in this case equals both actual and anticipated spending for a currency

Increased demand for a currency will tend to cause an increase in the relative value of the currency, decreased demand will tend to cause a decrease in the relative value of the currency. When one asks the question "What things affect the exchange rate?" one is really asking "What increases the demand for a currency?"

If you buy one currency with another currency, that will increase the demand for the currency being bought. So if you buy foreign currency with your domestic currency the increased demand for the foreign currency will be expected to increase price of the foreign currency, which is the same as saying that in such a case one can expect the exchange rate of the foreign country to increase. That means it will take more domestic currency to acquire the same amount of foreign currency. This also can be phrased as saying the domestic currency's exchange rate will be reduced. Another way to say this is to say the domestic currency has depreciated in value compared to that foreign currency. And that the foreign currency's exchange rate has increased, and it has appreciated in value compared to the domestic currency.

So now we are left with trying to figure out what causes each country to want to buy more of the other country's currency.

First note that theoretically it is not the case that you absolutely need a currency exchange to conduct an international trade. For example, the foreign country could already have some domestic currency and could use that up first. Eventually however, over time they can be expected to use up their supply and have a need to do a currency exchange to increase their holdings of domestic currency in order to meet their needs. Or they could pay for the domestic country's export (their import) with foreign money, if the domestic entities will accept it. Eventually however the domestic entities will probably want or need to convert that currency into domestic money, or certainly this will shift the equilibrium such that the domestic entities want to convert less of their currency into foreign and more into domestic currencies. All of this means increased demand for domestic currency, causing an appreciation of the value of the domestic currency. The point is all these situations are pretty much equivalent. It is my understanding that with the sophistication of the current foreign exchange market currency exchange is pretty much routine and occurs automatically and seamlessly for most trades, without people even thinking about it.

At any rate, the foreign exchange market is huge in terms of the volume of exchanges that occur every day.

"The foreign exchange or forex market is the largest financial market int the world – larger even than the stock market, with daily volumes of $5.1 trillion vs. 84 billion for equities worldwide, according to the 2016 Triennial Central Bank Survey of FX and OTC Derivatives markets."[31]

Examples of Factors that Affect the Demand for a Currency

Some examples of factors that affect the demand for a currency.

1. Price

---

31   https://www.investopedia.com/articles/forex/11/who-trades-forex-and-why.asp

Price of goods and services being produced by a country. Lower prices for items will increase the demand for those items and the demand for the currency of that country. This means the inflation rate of a country can affect demand for a currency. If the domestic country's prices have decreased or at least have increased slower than the rate of increase of prices in the foreign country, entities in foreign countries may find it cheaper to purchase imports from the domestic country. This will increase the demand for the domestic countries currency, causing its value to appreciate. One would expect that this is the main way exchange rates get affected, that is, international trade, importing and exporting of items traded is what affects exchange rates the most.

2. Speculation.

Apart from the issue of paying for imports and exports, there is the issue of individuals or entities, purchasing or selling currencies, simply on the basis of expecting the exchange rate for that currency to increase or decrease in the future. If they believe that a currency will appreciate in the future they will try to obtain more of that currency now. If they believe its value will depreciate in the future, they will be less likely to try to acquire that currency and more likely to try to sell it. The futures market plays a role here. Although this may sound like an activity that offers little benefit to society, it actually does play an important role.

Speculators serve to keep currency values and exchange rates from straying too far from what the fundamentals say they should be. Currency rates, ideally would be determined by real costs and prices, by things like wages, productivity, shipping costs, political factors etc. If for some reason, currency values do not accurately reflect what these fundamentals say they should be, then speculators in the currency market are likely to detect it and compensate for it, in the prices they are willing to pay or charge for various currencies. This can modulate the factors that may cause exchange rates to stray from what the rates realistically should be and has the effect of helping stabilize currency exchange rates.

3. Government policy and interest rates.

Central Banks can affect exchange rates when they use monetary policy to affect interest rates. If interest rates of a given domestic country are raised, then people or entities from foreign countries may find they may get a better return on their money if they did a currency exchange and bought domestic assets. Even domestic entities might sell their foreign assets and do a currency exchange to buy some of those higher interest rate domestic assets.

4. Currency Manipulation.

It is possible for countries and institutions to use currency purchases as a way to try to keep the value of their own currency lower. Such a strategy would be implemented for the purpose of gaining or keeping a price advantage in trade so as to maintain or increase its exports and gain or keep a trade advantage.

SUPPOSE THE ONLY MONEY IS GOLD.

Suppose the only money was gold. There would be no exchange rate, just gold as money. Now in trade one would gain more money, i.e., gold by exporting items and would lose gold by paying for imports. The country with the most gold can pay labor and induce production domestically and presumably, with a larger and more active work force, increase productivity at a faster rate than countries with less gold. This increased productivity makes their products cheaper. This will increase the amount of items they are able to export, and bring in more gold. This extra gold will fuel more employment, opportunities to earn wages will increase and this will put upward pressure on wages as employers compete for labor. As wages increase items of production become more expensive and this will begin to affect prices of exports.

Meanwhile, in other countries who have less gold, and have been at a disadvantage in international trade, employment opportunities will be scarcer, and this will put downward pressure on wages, and workers will compete with each other for available jobs. The decrease in wages will reduce cost of production and reduce prices of items. This will make that country more competitive in trade and increase their exports. As exports increase so will the amount of gold that country possesses. As the amount of gold they possess increases the more labor they will be able to hire and the higher their production and productivity will become, further decreasing prices and increasing exports. Eventually when employment levels get high enough workers will be more in demand and employers will be competing with each other to hire workers and wages will increase. This will increase prices of exports.

Meanwhile in the country that was originally doing the best, as demand for its exports decrease, the amount of gold coming into the country decreases, demand for production decreases, employment decreases, wages decrease until eventually exports prices decrease and they become competitive again, etc.

This is a natural cycle, and it is probable, that if this process was allowed to continue unencumbered, without interference from certain domestic or foreign factors, that, overall, we would have productivity levels increase such that, over time, total wealth and standards of living in the world would be increasing.

But there always seems to be factors interfering with this process, such as those who would use violent means to accomplish their ends. Not the type of violence or threatened violence that every stable country will have to resort to occasionally to prevent anarchy, but violence implemented for the purpose of satisfying greed and lust for power. In the past, when gold was used as a currency, people and groups with such goals would attempt to acquire gold by whatever means and hinder its free use in fair trade. In the past countries have used their navy to plunder other countries merchants to acquire their gold and riches so as to maintain their advantage in trade. And of course, individuals have used violence to possess more of the land and to exploit labor and keep wages low. Countries have conquered other countries and basically treated the citizens of those countries as slaves, or they have committed genocide, plundered their resources, taken all the profit generated from their labor, and from their exports, etc.

There is also a natural cycle that occurs with the type of fiat money we currently have. There too, it is possible for people or groups to interfere with the natural functioning of an economy, usually due to the same motivators of greed and lust for power. I talk more about how international trade functions and things that can disrupt it in the next chapter.

CHAPTER 51
TRADE – AN OVERVIEW

I wanted to look at analyzing trade using some of the concepts discussed in this book. I do this because I think this model will allow us to understand some of the dynamics of trade better. I am going to analyze trade from the perspective that except when there are sanctions that prevent any trade at all, the main factor that determines whether one purchases an import or a domestic product, is the price.

EARLIER IN THIS book when I began to look at the various definitions of GDP it was explained how the definitions for GDP were broken up into one for Income and one for Expenditure. I explained how since in the macroeconomy spending and income are always equal that the equations for income and expenditure approach to GDP, done properly should also be equivalent. This assertion is in agreement with the concept known as the "Fundamental Identity of National Income Accounting", which states they must be identical, and that this is true by definition . However the "Fundamental Identity of National Income Accounting" also states that these two quantities must be equivalent to the amount of or value of any production of goods and services made or delivered during the time period in question. I have shown repeatedly in this book, that I disagree with that assertion.

I have stated that such spending and income are measures of the change of ownership of money, and that this is calculated on one axis, whereas the measurement of production is part of the calculation of wealth, which is accounted for as an independent variable, on a different axis. I explained how even though spending and wealth production are variables that affect each other, they still remain independent variables, that is, these two variables together, mathematically describe a system that has two degrees of freedom.

Trade – an overview

I found that the standard definition for expenditure approach to GDP needed to be modified to make sure that it was purely an expression of spending, specifically gross spending. I modified that equation to make if fit that criteria. I showed how and why it is best to consider this modified version of the expenditure approach to GDP to apply only to the private domestic economy. I explained how that definition most closely represents what is standardly taught as the expenditure approach to GDP. I showed how one of the complications of representing GDP, as a measure of spending and income in the private domestic economy only, is that when we combine interactions with the government, the savings equals investment identity becomes not strictly true, because money could become owned by the government at which point it leaves the private domestic economy.

The reason that knowing the savings equals investment identity[32] remains true is important because the savings equals investment identity represents that portion of savings that is the preservation of money. Since, in a monetary economy, spending represents the transfer of ownership of money, it is important that we are able to understand and calculate exactly what the money supply is and the quantity of money that exists. If we are going to track spending we cannot just have money disappearing or showing up out of nowhere, without any accounting of where it was, and where it is going to. When money is created one must understand that it is the central bank only that creates it and how and when and in what quantity. This is why I have always been so careful to identify bank deposits as assets not money, and insist that bank loans do not create money, that the only thing that should count as money is base money. This is why I have been so insistent that we consider money owned by the treasury as being IN the base money supply.

So it has always been somewhat problematic that with GDP in a closed economy (no trade), the savings equals investment identity seems not to apply. I solve this mystery by noting that it does indeed remain true if we follow the money wherever it goes, that is, if when looking at savings we included both money owned in the private domestic economy and money owned by the government, then we will be able to show that any money first put into spending in that time period still exists either in the hands of the government or in the hands of some entity in the private domestic economy.

The same difficulty occurs with trade because money can leave the private domestic economy and become owned by foreign entities. If you include the money that is owned by foreign entities, at the end of the given time period, as part of

---

32 The measurement of the part of savings that does not include "net production"

what is saved, again, any money put into spending in that time will still be shown to exist, even it if exists in the hands of some foreign entity. Still, it complicates following and accounting for the money supply and appears to break up the money supply in terms of how and where the spending is done.

The modified version of the standard definition of GDP and how trade and taxes and government spending interact with the private domestic economy may have its place, but to get a better understanding of trade, and specifically how the money supply for any given country functions in trade, (that is the money supply created by the given country's central bank), I find the concept introduced in Chapter 49 to be more useful. Specifically I am talking about the model where I consider all entities involved in international trade to belong to a specific country, but I define the economy of a given country as the total money supply of that country's currency plus any transactions paid for by that currency, that is any spending occurring using that country's currency. This means any entity using a given country's currency for spending, no matter where and by what method, and no matter to what country that entity belongs, is causing that transaction to occur in economy of the country whose central bank issued the currency being used.

Such a concept means that no money ever leaves the economy of any country, since it is the spending of the money of that country that defines that country's economy. Therefore all money first put into spending as investment will remain in the that economy and continue to exist as savings in that country's economy, at the end of the given time period. The savings equals investment equation holds, and all money saved is in that country's economy, because the spending and ownership of that money is what defines that country's economy. Therefore, whenever that money is spent the recipient receives ownership of that amount of money as income just by the very nature of receiving money in the denomination of a given countries currency that income has occurred in that country's economy. I should also mention that when we are defining a country's economy it is important to recognize who controls the spending of a given amount of money. For example, with virtual money, the commercial bank will own the money, but the bank depositor controls the spending of that money. So how financial asset holders, such as holders of bank deposits, decide to use the money they control is integral to what is happening in that country's economy. So the economy of a country, so defined, focuses on the spending and what happens to the money. As for who owns the wealth, any wealth will always be owned by some entity belonging to some country, (including the money which is part of the wealth) and therefore that particular wealth will be said to be part of the total wealth of that country the entity belongs to.

It is the combination of these two definitions that I think is best suited to understanding trade, defining the country as the sum total of all the entities that are considered to be a part of or belong to that country, and the economy of a given country as being the money supply of that country's currency and all the spending transactions occurring using that currency for payment. For the purposes of this chapter one need not be too concerned about how one would obtain the data to calculate the actual values of these transactions. More important is to just try to understand the basic concepts. However, using these definitions one will have measures of spending and income that are clearly defined and for which, when talking about international trade, the savings equals investment identity, as presented in chapter 2, will always be true, and so will all the expressions for income: $Y = I + C = M*V = P*T$. For each economy thus defined one will be able to understand what is spending and what are the results of that spending on the multiplier. This will also be useful in defining any spending, and in which country's economy it occurred allowing us to get a better picture of what effect any spending has on prices, the trade balance, and on net production of wealth in individual economies and for the world economy as different countries' economies interact through the conduction of trade.

I have discussed spending and income as being the amount of transfers of ownership of money from one person or entity to another, this being true no matter what amount of net production results from that spending. And I have discussed the amount of net production as having to be calculated separately from spending, on a different axis, the wealth axis. I have discussed how the amount of net production can not only determine the change in level of wealth achieved in a country, but is also involved in determining the buying power of a given amount of money.

One confounding factor in understanding buying power of a given amount of money or currency, is the fact that, in general, in most countries in the world today, we have a baseline inflation. Having a baseline inflation means the buying power of a given currency is always decreasing. This tends to obscure the effect of increased productivity on prices. In this setting increased productivity will not be causing the buying power of a currency to increase. Instead it will be 'causing to be decreased', **how fast** the buying power is decreasing. That is, the effect of increased production will show up as a decrease in what the inflation rate would otherwise be, not as a deflation.

Trade – an overview

Up till now, when talking about productivity I did not get into details about where the production happened. When analyzing trade, it is no longer possible to ignore that issue. When one talks of trade one is clearly talking about production potentially happening in at least two different locations, i.e., two different countries and so it becomes of central importance to analyze the difference in productivity in one location versus another because productivity is a key factor in determining price, and therefore in determining where the production is more likely to occur. One can do this analysis for one item, multiple items, or whole economies.

One could also develop a model that would allow comparisons of productivity **within** countries, but that is not the purpose of this chapter. This chapter will only focus on trade, meaning it only focuses on cost comparisons **between** countries.

I want to introduce a concept that I think might make it a little easier to understand trade. First, recall Keynes' concept of a labor unit. A labor unit is usually imagined to be the lowest paid worker, the base worker, the least skilled. This person is paid the wage unit. That means one can define the base worker as one who is paid the wage unit. Other workers who may be more valuable are defined in terms of labor units by how much they are paid. Their pay may be multiples of the wage unit and therefore they are considered multiple labor units. For example, if they are paid 3 times the wage unit they are considered 3 labor units, if they are paid 10 wage units then they are considered 10 labor units. One could even imagine a worker who is paid ½ the wage unit being considered ½ a labor unit. A ½ labor unit worker could perhaps be a part time worker, or perhaps a worker in a different country where workers earn lower wages than the domestic country or "index" country where the wage unit is defined, (that being the wage paid to the base worker in that "index" country).

Let me say here, that in this model I am defining, once the wage unit is established, in the beginning of the time period under analysis, its value will stay the same. That value of the wage unit will remain a constant value, even if the pay of the chosen "index" base worker changes. This is necessary to give us a fixed reference point for comparison. One can refer to this value of the chosen wage unit as W_0. This model requires that when the pay of any worker changes, including the pay of those workers in the index country one has used to establish W_0, the amount of labor units those workers count as, will also change. For example, if during the time period under analysis, the pay of the base worker in the index country is cut in half, that worker, which formerly counted as one labor unit, would now only count as ½ a labor unit.

I want to combine this idea of the labor unit and wage unit, as I have defined them in the previous paragraph, with the concept of productivity. Productivity is usually considered production per worker, or production per capita. I want to modify this concept a little and look at production per labor unit. Call it "labor unit productivity". This measure, labor unit productivity, one could cause to increase, by increasing the production of a given amount of labor units. You could also cause it to increase by decreasing the number of labor units for the same amount of production. One way to reduce the number of labor units is to have fewer workers. Another way to reduce the number of labor units, once the value of the wage unit has been established, is to reduce the worker's pay. If that happened, if the total pay of all the workers decreased, then the total amount of "index" wage units (W_0) paid to workers would decrease and therefore the total amount of labor units those workers count as would decrease.

This isn't exactly the way Keynes used the wage unit and labor unit. He always considered the wage unit to adjust to match whatever the base worker is paid. I modify this so that I only consider the initial value of the wage the base worker is paid, the "index" wage unit, (W_0) and I keep that value fixed during the period of analysis.

I start by defining the base worker, and then determine the wage of the base worker. This becomes the established wage unit, W_0, which must remain fixed. The only way one would change this rule is if one were to factor in inflation. Since we generally look at trade from the position of one country, which I refer to as the domestic country, one should not only define the initial wage unit to base it on the wage paid to one labor unit in the domestic country, but if one adjusts it to inflation, the value of W_0 should change based solely on the amount of inflation that occurs after the value of W_0 is determined in that domestic country. If one includes inflation, the wage being paid to base workers in a foreign country would have to be compared to the inflation adjusted index (domestic) country's wage unit (after accounting for the exchange rate), to determine the number of labor units employed in the foreign country. However, one need not include inflation and W_0 will still give a point of reference that is useful in this model, perhaps even more useful because the values of inflation in all countries will have a fixed point of reference for comparison.

So, the base worker is defined by the value of the wage unit (W_0), and if, at any time in the period under analysis, you are able to find someone to work for less, that person would count as less than one labor unit. That's the idea.

Suppose country A has establish wage W_A as the wage unit for a base worker, suppose in country B the wage of their base worker is 1/4 of W_A or $W_A/4$. That means that each base worker in country B counts as 1/4 of a labor unit, whereas country A's base workers count as one labor unit. If the workers in country B produced at the same rate as the workers in Country A, on the average, then the labor unit productivity in country B will be 4 times the labor unit productivity of country A

We show this formally:

Country A's base worker counts as 1 labor unit, and country B's base worker counts as 1/4 of a labor unit.

Assume average production per base worker is the same for country A and B.

Let the amount of production of each labor unit in country A equal P_0. This also means that production in country A per base worker is $P_0/1 = P_0$. So, both production per base worker and labor unit productivity in country A is P_0.

Production per base worker for country B is also P_0. But that means when calculating labor unit productivity, the amount of production for every labor unit is P_0 per each ¼ of a labor unit. This is because each base worker in country B counts as ¼ labor unit. In that case the labor unit productivity for country B is P_0 per ¼ labor unit. That is, labor unit production in country B is $P_0/[1/4] = 4P_0$. That means labor unit productivity in country B ($4P_0$) is 4 times the labor unit productivity in country A (P_0).

At the start of the period under analysis paying a certain amount to base workers in Country B will get you 4 times as much product as paying the same amount to base workers in Country A. That factor favors locating production in country B

Now if, at the beginning of the time period, country A's base worker, who counts as one labor unit, was twice as productive as country B's base worker who counts as ¼ of a labor unit then country B's labor unit productivity would only be 2 times as much as country A.

I show this formally:

If production of base workers in country B is P_0 but the production of base workers in country A is $2P_0$, labor unit productivity for country A, at the beginning of the time period, where each base worker counts as 1 labor unit, is calculated to be $2P_0/1 = 2P_0$.

The production of each worker in country B at the beginning of the time period, is only P_0, so the initial labor unit productivity for country B is P_0 for every ¼ labor unit which equals $P_0/[1/4] = 4P_0$.

Country B is now only twice as productive per labor unit ($4P_0$) as country A ($2P_0$). And cost of labor per unit of production in Country A is twice as much as that for country B. This still has labor costs favoring production in country B but not by as much.

Let us say initially country A's base worker could be 16 times more productive than country B's. That will mean each of country A's base workers produce product in the amount of $16P_0$. Initial labor unit productivity for country A will be $16P_0/1 = 16P_0$.

And if production per base worker in country B is still P_0 then initial labor unit productivity for country B is $P_0/[1/4] = 4P_0$. In this last scenario, labor unit productivity in country A ($16P_0$) would be 4 times that of country B ($4P_0$). In this case, mostly because of the large productivity in country A, cost of labor for production in country B is 4 times more expensive that country A. So in that scenario, labor costs favor locating production in country A.

༺༻

We, of course, use the exchange rate to compare the actual value of wages in different countries. If the exchange rate is one dollar equals 100 yen, then a wage of one dollar in America is the same amount of money as a wage of 100 yen in Japan.

༺༻

What the concept of labor unit productivity gives us is a measure of the total labor cost of producing an item in a given country. And the important point is, that cost of labor can be reduced either by increasing productivity, or by reducing the amount of wages paid. The amount paid for labor is not the total cost and therefore not the only determining factor of price, but it is an important factor, and the one that is going to impact employment levels in each country the most. At any rate, this allows a comparison of labor costs and production between countries whose overall wage level differs and whose production per worker differs.

There is the concept used in studying trade which is called "the law of one price". This concept represents that trade tends towards an equilibrium where the price of a good would be the same, once one accounts for the exchange rate, no matter who is selling it, or where they are from. If, initially country A can produce, and deliver to a specific market, more of item 1 per unit of a designated currency than country B, then country A can sell item 1 for cheaper and they will get all the sales. That is, until country A can no longer produce and deliver item 1 more cheaply than country B. This could occur due to diminishing returns in country A reducing its labor unit productivity, or decreased unemployment in country A causing increased wages (also reducing labor unit productivity), or improved efficiency in country B increasing country B's labor unit productivity, or increased unemployment in country B causing reduced wages, also increasing their labor unit productivity. Or prices could be affected by other factors such as changes in shipping costs, etc.

Relative values of the total price can be further changed if the exchange rates change. If a change in the exchange rate for country A in the designated market causes an appreciation of country A's currency relative to country B's currency, that increases the price for the item produced in country A as compared to the price when the item is produced in country B.

Prices and exchange rates can move around, but in a perfectly competitive market they will tend towards an equilibrium where the one price rule works. That is, where the price of an item in a given market is the same no matter where it was produced. That does not mean that, at that point, the labor unit productivity is equal in all countries, nor does it mean that the total quantity of product sold in that market, coming from a specific country is equal to the total amount of product coming from any other country. What it means is that the price of a given item equalizes, the price becomes the same no matter where it came from. The law of one price says that not only **can** prices equalize, but that given enough time, in a perfectly competitive market, they **do** equalize, or rather they are always tending towards being equal. If you think of it, unless the purchasers of an item are restricted as to who they can purchase from, the law of one price is a fairly realistic idea. Markets for an item will tend towards one price, no matter where the item was produced. And if a given country (or entities from that country) cannot match the price in that market its exports will not be sold there.

There are a lot of factors involved in determining prices, the amount of product produced and sold, where the products are produced, where they are likely to be sold, whether a product is likely to exported from or imported to a given country, and what the trade balance between the domestic and foreign countries will be. I will try to look a little deeper into some of those factors.

Since I have mentioned that in current times economic policy makers are averse to allowing deflation to occur, one must realize that when referring to demand increasing or decreasing, one is really talking about it increasing or decreasing relative to a baseline inflation rate.

From an economic perspective, one generally assumes the motivation for trade is to maximize production of wealth so as to maximize the standard of living, with wealth being defined in the very general terms I have used in previous chapters. However, this model must be capable of accounting for other possible motivations as well if it is going to be generally applicable.

Supply Costs and Demand

When looking at what happens to items involved in trade, what will be produced, where it will be produced, how much will be produced, where it will be sold, when it will be sold domestically, or when it will be exported or when it will be obtained as an import, ….. one needs to look at both the supply side (cost to produce and deliver the item or items to market) and the demand side (amount of spending that will occur to purchase the item or items).

Total cost of production includes paying for more things than just labor. Factors that contribute to the cost of producing an item in a given country include:

Labor (Profits that are not considered excessive count as labor).

Shipping costs

Cost of raw materials or "intermediate products" or capital equipment needed for manufacture (The cost of importing these items is simply an expense added to the cost of production, but paying for raw materials of intermediate products produced domestically, in the macroeconomy, if one is including all transactions occurring in that economy, is basically paying for the **labor** to extract or produce, sell and deliver these items to the manufacturer).

Tariffs, and other taxes, fees, or even bribes. If business in a country allows for or requires bribes as a part of business, it is like an illicit tax, and it is a reason that works against businesses locating in such countries, because it makes business costs more uncertain.

And, of course, don't forget excess profits aka economic rents. The degree to which this last one can occur is related to the degree of monopoly power over the production and sale of the given item.

As for the demand side, understanding the demand for products on the international market is no different than the demand for products in a domestic market. Type 1 direct spending, that is, spending to obtain product that will be acquired for personal use of the purchaser or purchasers, will be the most important factor that drives the level of spending overall. And such spending is more likely to be done by the masses, meaning that distributions of income that short change median income earners, is likely to reduce overall demand, and also likely to be associated with reduced amount of production, as compared to that which would or could occur otherwise. This would generally mean a reduction in what the standard of living actually becomes, compared to what it could otherwise be.

Some Ramblings about Demand, Net Production, Employment Levels, NAIRU, Exchange Rates and Trade

Does trade always cause total wealth production to increase? The effect of trade on total wealth will depend on what effect trade has on total income, i.e., total demand, and also how much production occurs as a result of that demand. In addition, one needs to include what effect the trade has on preservation of existing wealth, and what effect is has on depletion of wealth. That is, the effect of trade on wealth is determined by the effect of trade on net production.

Suppose there is a situation where the decision to trade does not lead to any change in spending or demand, but due to the trading country having a higher labor unit productivity, the same spending leads to increased production. That describes a situation where one has reduced prices. If that were occurring overall for the whole international economy, that would describe a deflation (or at least a reduction in the inflation rate from the baseline) caused by **supply side factors**, i.e., increased production. If shifting employment and production from one country's economy to the other kept total income (or at least inflation adjusted income) the same, one could have a situation where, overall in the world, a higher standard of living is achieved for the same overall income. As long as the fruits of the increased production are shared, this situation could benefit the world at large.

Actually, since economists consider production and income to be the same thing, some of them may actually describe this as being a situation where increased production is itself increased income, and there is no such thing as having increased production for the same level of income. Obviously, those who have read this book know that I disagree with the notion that income and production are the same thing.

The fact is, if income shifted to another country due to trade, it is quite likely that overall income, added together from all the countries involved (after accounting for exchange rates), would not remain the same. If that shift of production to a different country led to a shift in distribution of income, so that the richer factions got a larger percentage of the income, and the poorer factions a lower percentage, then the multiplier effect would probably be smaller, and the total income and total demand could be decreased compared to what it might otherwise be. (We are talking about direct spending income, i.e., direct spending demand). Of course, even with the lower demand, there could still be increased total net wealth production, due to the labor unit productivity of the country the income is shifting to, being higher than the labor unit productivity of country the income is taken away from. If that were the case, moving jobs to another country could still increase overall standard of living even if total income were decreased (or at least decreasing relative to inflation), provided the increased wealth does not just become owned by a small minority of people.

Shifting jobs to a different country could mean that new jobs will cause people in the new country to leave their current jobs, causing job vacancies there, in which case total employment would not increase in that country. Or it could be that there were involuntarily unemployed people there, ready, willing, and able to step into the newly available jobs, in which case total employment in that country will increase.

Similarly, the country losing the jobs could have the disenfranchised workers becoming involuntarily unemployed, or see them moving into currently unfilled job vacancies in that country.

If one is considering the involuntary unemployment rate as it is related to NAIRU, then one knows that it is not practical to have involuntary unemployment get so low that total unemployment is lower than NAIRU, or excess inflation would result in the country where that occurs. That would not be a favorable occurrence in a country wishing to export, as the excess inflation would increase the price of that country's exports.

If one was attempting to make the country a viable trade partner, then one must be cognizant of the level of unemployment as it related to NAIRU. When deciding where to locate jobs, employers must be aware that too much employment in a given country could end up increasing wages in that country decreasing labor unit productivity, thereby reducing or eliminating the advantages of trade for that country. On the other hand, if, due to the balance of trade, a certain country's involuntary unemployment increases, that could cause a reduction in wages, and an increase in labor unit productivity, in that country. That could allow that country to sell their items cheaper, making them more competitive in trade.

This brings into play all those factors that affect NAIRU. For example, a completely totalitarian country, which is equivalent to an absolute monopoly, would be able to avoid excess inflation because the workers have no bargaining power, and workers having increased bargaining power is one ingredient of excess inflation. This would mean that there would be no worry about having full employment in that country, in terms of wages getting too high. This might make some employers desirous of locating their production processes in such a country, figuring their labor unit productivity would more likely be preserved there. On the other hand, such countries generally do poorly in terms of productivity because often, in authoritarian countries, hard work and innovation are not rewarded. Corruption, however, often is rewarded, and that has the disadvantage of introducing more uncertainty into the outcome of one's investment. Corruption also can increase the cost of business due to the corrupt officials expecting their share of the excess profits.

It could be that a business with a lot of monopoly power would locate their business to a lower wage country, not so much to increase production, but as a way to maximize their excess profits. It could be that locating their business in a lower wage country would increase labor unit productivity, that is, increase the amount of product they get from a given amount of spending, so that they could actually spend less for the same amount of product and sell it for the same price, increasing their excess profits, that is, increasing their economic rent. This may not only increase excess profits of monopolists, but it could also decrease workers bargaining power in the country that lost the jobs, by increasing unemployment. This could decrease wages in the country losing the jobs. One could see how this could decrease overall demand because the shifting of jobs to another country with lower wages is a redistribution of income to wealthier individuals from poorer individuals. Although this might increase the standard of living for some, the decreased income of the workers could cause a reduction in the standard of living for workers in both countries. In such a case, due to the adverse effect on total demand, the effect on production is uncertain, and trade may actually cause a reduction in wealth production for the world as a whole.

So, I have described at least two motivations for trade. One is to maximize production, and two is to control wages to maximize economic rents, i.e., excess profits.

If two countries had a significant amount of involuntary unemployment such that the unemployment level was greater than NAIRU in both countries, if trade led to increased employment and production in each country, then provided there were not significant negative externalities associated with the production, that would describe the ideal outcome for trade, that being more employment and more production, more net production, and if the increased wealth is shared, increased standard of living in general.

Let us say that the exchange rate changes for country A such that country A's currency loses some value in terms of other currencies. That is equivalent to reducing the wages in country A, relative to the other countries. That will effectively reduce the prices other countries have to pay for country A's exports, in terms of their own currencies. This would mean, compared to the other countries, the labor unit productivity has increased in country A, giving them an increased advantage in trade.

It is a different thing when talking about labor unit productivity versus worker productivity. With labor unit productivity the production per labor unit of country A could be increased relative to country B if the pay gets reduced in country A. In this model, the total amount of labor units is determined by the total amount of pay. Reduce the total amount of pay and you reduce the total amount of labor units the workers count as, by the same fraction as the reduction in pay.

Assuming that reducing a worker's pay in country A does not decrease the worker's productivity, this would result in the same amount of production by less labor units, causing an increase in the labor unit productivity in country A. This model is showing the possibility of increasing labor unit productivity by decreasing pay. This is equivalent to increasing the amount of product one can produce for a given amount of spending.

Let take as an example where we have country A at NAIRU and country B where unemployment is much greater than NAIRU. That factor will tend to favor jobs moving to country B, since they have higher involuntary unemployment. Since country B has more involuntary unemployment, workers there have less bargaining power and it will be easier to lower their wages, until country B gets to the point where they can start to take some of the jobs away from country A. Since country A has less involuntary unemployment, those workers are in a better bargaining position, and it is harder to reduce the pay of those workers in country A. These will be factors that allows country B to be more competitive in trade.

All that can occur provided the reduction in country B's wages can decrease prices for country B's products below what country A is able to charge, accounting for all the other costs including shipping, raw materials and equipment, taxes and tariffs, bribes etc.

This shifting of employment could lead to increased production and overall wealth, due to increased labor unit productivity. This presumably could increase the buying power of whatever the total income adjusts to. But it is also true that the effect of decreasing worker's wages by, in effect, shifting jobs to a lower wage country can have the effect of lowering total income and total direct spending demand.

If shifting jobs to a lower wage country causes involuntary unemployment to increase in the higher wage country, then that would decrease overall demand just because less people are working for the higher wage. Add to that the possibility that increased involuntary employment in the higher wage country hurts workers bargaining power, and wages of those that remain working could be lowered, decreasing overall demand even further. Those effects will reduce some of the advantages trade has on total employment and production. If the effect of lowering demand were great enough, it is possible that the advantages of trade in terms of increased production could be nullified altogether. Ignoring what trade does to overall demand is not something that can be done if we are going to get an accurate accounting of the effects of trade.

Comparative and Absolute Advantage

Suppose both countries are at full employment or rather, at NAIRU. That means that neither country would want more employment. Then it becomes a situation where the goal would become to maximize production and efficiency with the employment levels you have. One way they do this is looking at something called comparative advantage[33], originally introduced by David Ricardo in 1817. For a simplistic explanation of comparative advantage, suppose that country A is more efficient at everything, but can maximize overall wealth much more by putting all its resources into producing items 1, 2 and 3 only, rather than using up some of its labor and other resources to produce items 4 and 5 as well. If country A produced items 4 and 5 as well as 1, 2, and 3 then they would still produce wealth, but not as much total wealth as they would if they put all their resources into solely producing items 1, 2, and 3. Suppose country B could produce all 5 items but much less efficiently and would produce much lower amounts of all of them. Then it would be an advantage to let country B focus on producing as much of items 4 and 5 as they could, so that country A could put as much of its resources into producing items 1, 2 and 3. This would maximize country A's wealth production and they could provide any amount of items 1, 2 and 3 that country B requires, in return for a share of the Items 4 and 5 that country B produced. Obviously, since country B has put more of its resources into producing items 4 and 5, they will be able to provide a decent proportion of that production to country A, and to the extent that they can, they have allowed country A to produce more of items 1, 2 and 3.

---

33   https://en.wikipedia.org/wiki/Comparative_advantage

Even though country A could produce 4 and 5 more efficiently than country B country A having to produce 4 and 5 keeps them from producing the maximum amount of total wealth they would create by being able to focus on products 1 ,2 and 3. Country A has an absolute advantage in its ability to produce any of the items. But if country A produces all its own items with no trade and country B produces all its own items with no trade, they will produce less combined total wealth compared to letting country A focus as much as it can of its resources on producing items 1, 2, and 3 and country B focuses all its resources on items 4 and 5. This is called comparative advantage. Compared to each country producing all its own product, properly designed trade allows total wealth production to be greater than not trading.

It's not only comparative advantage that causes a shift in production location. Absolute advantage also occurs as well. Suppose country A is more efficient at producing item 1 and country B is more efficient at producing item 2. Then after considering all other expenses it is probable that wealth production will be maximized by having country A produce more of item 1 and country B produce more of item 2.

Now I would like to look at the effect of certain factors we must consider when determining the benefits and drawbacks of decisions to trade with certain countries or for certain items.

Externalities

If a country pollutes, violates human rights and behaves in other ways that destroy quality of life and overall level of wealth on the planet then these are called negative externalities. Free speech, human rights, personal safety, clean water, clean air, preservation of nature are all forms of wealth that can potentially be reduced as a consequence of business practices. Countries that do not pay a living wage or care for their citizens properly can directly damage those who suffer from the consequences, and diminish that wealth called human capital. That can also harm a sense of community and good will that people value, therefore harming these other things people value and that enhance life, these other forms of wealth.

If the negative externalities of a country's ventures significantly negatively impact overall wealth for the world, then it is appropriate to make that country have consequences for the purpose of attempting to modify their behavior. A couple of ways to create consequences could be by 1) totally or partially denying trade with a given country, or 2) instituting tariffs on certain goods, which is a tax on imports. That will increase the price of those goods from that country and reduce the amount they are likely to be able to sell as exports. Trade organizations, formed by treaties between multiple countries may be involved in imposing various penalties.

Monopoly Power and Trade

There is always some monopoly power, we will never be able to totally get rid of it. Worldwide trade is one factor that can actually make it more difficult to maintain monopoly power. Like anyone, monopolist will always try to maximize their profits. The difference is monopolist have the option of including the cost of excess profits in the final price of an item. Or to put it more accurately, since every economy always has some degree of monopoly power involved, the extent to which producers have monopoly power will strongly influence producers' ability to increase prices to maximize excess profits.

One of the ways producers maximize profits is to minimize essential costs including the cost of labor. They minimize labor costs by maximizing labor unit productivity. I discussed previously in this chapter how employers could use trade to decrease wages, by keeping employment levels from getting too high in any given country. That is, by keeping involuntary unemployment levels from getting so low that total unemployment levels are lower than NAIRU. The extent that a company has monopoly power in the world will increase the control they have over where jobs are located. To the extent their monopoly power allows, they will be able to locate jobs where they can maximize excess profits. This monopoly power, and ability to locate jobs may allow them to further decrease costs by being able to undercut rules and regulations intended to decrease and minimize negative externalities associated with their production processes.

We have already discussed how if a country was completely authoritarian, where workers had no bargaining power, then there would never be any "demand caused" accelerating inflation in that country, and this would be equivalent to having the level of NAIRU occurring at true full employment (no involuntary unemployment). One also knows that if we had a perfectly competitive market there would be no accelerating or excess inflation. Therefore, one could have NAIRU occur at true full employment if we have a perfectly competitive market, where there is no monopoly power, or one could have NAIRU occur at true full employment if there was one absolute monopoly over all production.

Even if authoritarian countries could be shown to increase production for some products for certain periods of time, one could consider that authoritarian governments are associated with significant negative externalities, affecting both its own citizens and the world as a whole.

Negative externalities are additional costs in that they reduce overall wealth. According to the model I use in this book, wealth is defined in the most general way possible, as being anything of value. It is total wealth, defined in this way, that affects the standard of living and quality of life. One could see how the reduction of wealth caused by the negative externalities of producing items for worldwide trade in an authoritarian country could overwhelm any advantages gained in terms of increased production of wealth, if there were such an advantage.

It is not just overall net wealth production being reduced by the reduction in in wealth and quality of life associated with totalitarian governments. The problem of reduced reward for effort and reduced motivation may cause a reduction in production, not just net production, and therefore increase cost of producing in the authoritarian country, since reducing production and productivity is a main way to reduce labor unit productivity in that country. And that factor may not only reduce current productivity but also productivity gains over time as well. The decreased motivation, that lack of rewards for innovation and hard work can actually slow the development of innovation and advances in technology and technique. Also affecting price will be the expectation by politically powerful interests in the authoritarian countries to receive a share of the excess profits.

In general, the profit per item and the total number of items produced and sold will determine the profits. But that is only for the manufacturers of the one item. The impact of trade is more complicated and will include the effect of the trade decisions on total direct spending demand for all the items in all the economies of all the countries involved. If there is enough monopoly power and they are able to take a significant amount of excess profits, leading to a lower share of income for poorer factions, this could significantly lower the overall direct spending demand across all the economies. This could adversely affect the sales and profits of even the monopolists.

Another situation where cost of production may be reduced in a country will be when factors allow for lower costs of items necessary in the production process, for example, certain raw materials may be more readily available in some countries than others. That will give those countries an advantage in terms of total cost for those items. The suppliers of those materials could be said to have a certain amount of monopoly power. This is a type of a natural monopoly. That will favor employment happening in the country where the raw material is available. They will need employees to collect and process the raw materials. Additionally, this situation will favor locating production of the final product in that same country, due to reduced shipping costs of those raw materials. Of course, one must consider cost and availability of all items necessary for production, but you get the idea.

Another interesting thing involving trade that monopoly power can affect is what I'll call differential pricing. To the extent that sales of certain products are monopolized in certain countries, those monopolies can exploit that, by charging more in higher income countries and less in poorer countries for the same or similar products. This could be called the law of multiple prices. The law of one price does not necessarily apply when there is monopoly power over the production and sales of the given item. Example, the new novel is published and under copyright. In America it might be sold for 25 dollars and in a poorer country the paperback is immediately released and sells for the equivalent of 7 dollars.

Tariffs

Tariffs may have a legitimate application if it is used to punish countries who cause a significant amount of negative externalities, as mentioned above.

If monopolists are moving jobs to a foreign country just to increase their excess profits or economic rents and the advantages to domestic country are not clear, that domestic country might consider Tariffs. For example, suppose jobs are moved to a foreign country and despite that prices do not fall in the domestic country significantly. One can assume that, in terms of supplying the domestic economy, the only reason for moving jobs to the foreign country is to increase economic rents. Tariffs might be considered by the domestic country in that situation, but in reality a better way to deal with that situation is to focus on decreasing monopoly power. If the goal is to decrease monopoly power, that will be more likely to occur, and more easily accomplished, by facilitating more trade, not by obstructing it with tariffs.

Tariffs add costs to imports but since they are generally not implemented across the board, there is plenty of room for favoritism and corruption, that is, tariffs can have the effect of decreasing true competition by helping special interests and political allies.

Even when tariffs might be legitimately called for, such as when dealing with significant negative externalities that are occurring as a result of the behaviors of a certain country, as discussed above, the implementation of tariffs can still be manipulated to favor certain industries. Those special interests could be domestic or foreign. In general, tariffs have a negative impact on trade, wealth production and standard of living. A well-known example, frequently cited as proof of how damaging tariffs can be, was the implementation of the Smoot–Hawley Tariff Act signed into law by President Herbert Hoover on June 17, 1930 as a response to the economic depression related to the stock market crash. The general consensus of the economics profession is that this act did not help, but instead significantly worsened the "Great Depression".

"The Act and tariffs imposed by America's trading partners in retaliation were major factors of the reduction of American exports and imports by 67% during the Depression. Economists and economic historians have a consensus view that the passage of the Smoot-Hawley Tariff exacerbated the Great Depression."[34]

DISTRIBUTION OF INCOME AND HOW IT AFFECTS TOTAL DEMAND AND PRODUCTION

Let us say that one consequence of trade is to increase inequality which causes a slowing of the direct spending velocity of money and reduces aggregate demand. It is possible that the effect of increased labor unit productivity on buying power may mitigate the effect of that decreased demand on net wealth production, to some extent. It is even possible that increased labor unit productivity will totally compensate for the loss of demand and even with decreased spending (relative to baseline inflation), buying power will not change as much. That would be a situation where increased production would cause a slowing of inflation due to supply side factors. Still distribution of income, and its effect on demand is a factor that must be considered.

It is also possible that, related to trade, distribution of income could change to favor wealthier people and yet, due to increased production, standard of living could still grow some for everyone, (just significantly more for the wealthy). Some believe this is the natural order and increasing inequality leads to increased standard of living for everyone, "a rising tide lifts all boats" they might say. Or they might allege that would at least be proof that increasing inequality does not harm people's standard of living. I do not think that this proves either of those things. Is it not possible, that in a situation where production was significantly

---

34 https://en.wikipedia.org/wiki/Smoot%E2%80%93Hawley_Tariff_Act#:~:text=The%20Act%20and%20 tariffs%20imposed,Tariff%20exacerbated%20the%20Great%20Depression.

increasing, that increasing inequality of income could actually be keeping most people's standard of living from rising as fast as it might otherwise?, or could the increased inequality of income be keeping a significant proportion of the population unnecessarily in poverty?

Currency Manipulation

In Chapter 49 it was shown how over time, if country A consistently has a trade deficit with country B, how Country B would come to own more and more of country A's currency or at least assets that give some country B associated entity control over the spending of an amount of country's A's currency. I have also shown in Chapter 50 how, due to country A's demand for country B's exports, and therefore Country B's currency, that the exchange rate may change to cause an appreciation of the value of B. That is, it will require more of Country A's currency to be able to acquire the same amount of Country B's currency in exchange. Over time, the depreciation of Country A's currency would cause their exports to be cheaper and may begin to reduce Country B's trade advantage.

One wonders, though, is there way for Country A to recover some of that Country A currency and those Country A denominated assets that Country B owns, and have it come back to be owned by Country A people or entities?

Yes if country A owned some Country B money it could use that foreign Country B money to purchase some of its own domestic Country A money. This would increase demand for Country A money and cause it to appreciate, making country A exports more expensive possibly. Of course if Country A were able to sell more exports to Country B. that would shift the balance so that Country A owned more of its own domestic Currency or financial assets. That would, at the same time, also increase demand for Country A currency and cause it to appreciate.

Anyway, which direction trade goes depends on the price of the items of trade when it comes to market. I have discussed several factors that influence in which direction trade goes. I have just explained how just in the process of trade, currency exchange rates can be affected, mostly in the direction of reducing the trade imbalance. I have talked previously about how currency speculation can have a stabilizing effect on the exchange rate, but I have not discussed in any detail another way exchange rates can be affected.

It is possible that governments or private entities (and sometimes private entities on behalf of governments) can simply initiate currency exchanges, with no motivation other than to increase demand for the other country's currency, causing it to appreciate and its own currency to depreciate. This is a purposeful attempt to weaken its own currency relative to the other country so as to reduce the cost of its exports to entities in that other country, in terms of that other countries own currency. This will allow them to increase or maintain a trade surplus or possibly reduce a trade deficit. This tactic is generally referred to as currency manipulation.

The idea is that since a country which has its own currency can just create as much of that money as it wants, it can just continue to create money and use it, or cause it to be used, to purchase that other country's currency.

Ideally this tactic would only be used by countries whose economies are weak. Who have significant unemployment, whose productivity is low, and whose wages are very low. It may be that such a country had been able to carve out a niche where they were able to cost effectively create certain products where the production process was very labor intensive and where cheap labor could really cut costs. It may be that without such products their economy would be much worse. But one assumes the goal of such a country would be to improve their economy, not just stay stagnant.

If we are looking at one country only, if a country's economy is low on demand, expanding the money supply can cause interest rates to be low and lead to more spending, i.e., demand. That is a situation where increasing the money supply can help the economy, when that strategy is properly applied. The effect of such an intervention could even be more dramatic for a poor country. In the General Theory, Keynes' explained how due to poor people having an increased propensity to consume, that a given amount of increased spending has a much greater multiplier effect. However, we know from the NAIRU model that once employment levels reach or approach NAIRU excess inflation becomes a risk and attempts to keep increasing demand further will not be helpful and will probably be harmful.

Analogously, economists also have an intervention that can be used in international trade that utilizes increasing the money supply to increase demand. This creation of money and using it to exchange with other currencies as a way to weaken ones on currency, can lead to cheaper import prices for their trade partners and help expand or preserve the amount of exports by the "currency manipulating country" and expand or preserve total income and demand in that country.

Keynes believed that stimulus techniques are intended to get the economy moving, i.e., to get as many un or underused resources activated as possible, to the point where the economy has enough economic activity and spending that there is no further need for that extra stimulus; no further need for interventions that will increase spending and demand. At that point stimulus measures should be stopped.

Keynes would no doubt believe the same thing about stimulus caused by so called currency manipulation. That is, once full employment is achieved (or rather as economist would look at it today, the unemployment rate approaches NAIRU), further attempts to stimulate the economy will not be helpful and probably actually be harmful. That would mean that attempts to use the currency exchange market to weaken once's own currency should only be a temporary measure at most.

In order to most benefit from the strategy the currency manipulating country must take the opportunity to activate those un or underused resources, increase employment and increase production and productivity. If they do so, they will find themselves in a much better economic situation, and hopefully they will be more competitive, as a result of increased productivity, and be in a situation that they can maintain some or all its gains.

To achieve that state, it is important for supply to match demand. Meaning that what is available for purchase will be things that people or entities want to obtain, or cause to happen with their spending. In trade that means the people or entities with funds to spend will value what their spending causes or contributes to causing to occur. It could be a good, a service, some labor or any other desired outcome. I leave very open and broad the possibilities for what one can call "the product". But I will say, that enticing the increased spending by advertisement or education, i.e., creating a market, is part of the process. Enticing people to spend on charitable contributions giving increased income to the poor, can be part of the process. So it is not so simple a process as deciding that a certain limited categories of products count as production, as if it was predetermined and genetically encoded exactly what people will be willing to spend to acquire or make happen. There are many different ways that transfers of ownership of money for a purpose can occur and all of this spending counts as income and can be important in maximizing employment and production and standard of living.

At any rate, it is important for the country who receives the stimulus to find ways to increase the amount of spending in their country. To work hard to increase production and productivity, and increase labor unit productivity in that way, so as to allow them to compete better in trade. And it is important that they understand that, when they get to the point where unemployment has decreased, so as to approach NAIRU, they are at a point where any further attempts to increase demand will have no further benefit, and may lead to excess inflation, at which point they should stop any such "currency manipulation".

Such economies, where the level of unemployment equals NAIRU, are nowadays referred to as full employment economies. When one has a full employment economy, the trick is no longer to find ways to increase employment, but instead be to find ways to increase the **net production** of wealth created by the employment one has. That is, increase production of wealth while minimizing destruction or depletion of wealth. (note perishable items are an important part of the production because they mostly help the economy by helping to preserve wealth, for example food helps preserve that form of wealth known as human capital). I would also suggest that an enlightened country might also want to have the goal of trying to reduce monopoly power in order to have NAIRU occur at a lower unemployment level.

If employers or investors in a country, say for reasons of greed, fail to use the extra income to support employment and production, then currency manipulation could be continued and perhaps it might lead to some more time where the exports will remain cheaper and will continue. But eventually the extra production of their money will backfire. Even excluding trade, looking at one country, it is possible for a central bank to increase money supplies to provide stimulus for a time, even in large amounts, without causing excess inflation (usually after which time the Central Bank will decrease the money supply). But if one just continues to create more and more and more money, as an attempt to create more demand, without production and productivity gains occurring and keeping pace, eventually the currency's value will begin to fall and probably dramatically, possibly leading to hyperinflation, which is a disaster for whatever country experiences it. That is a potential consequence from using a strategy of attempting to prop up an economy by just increasing the money supply, with inadequate attention to production and productivity.

So unless the country that uses "currency manipulation" uses the temporary benefits gained to strengthen its economy by increasing employment, production and productivity, the long run consequences of continuing that strategy will likely be negative and possibly severely so.

⁂

I believe the highest goals for international trade involve trying to maximize net production of wealth so as to produce the highest standard of living and the best quality of life for all. This requires that not only does one need to focus on what is produced, but that one needs to understand that incomes, and especially median incomes, need to be adequate to pay for the goods, services, labor[35] or other desired outcomes, so that the production of, or at least the existence of, these desired outcomes, all of which are forms of wealth, will be supported by the spending that occurs.

Anything that interferes with maximizing the net production of wealth puts us further from that stated goal. Those things that serve as barriers to achieving such goals are pretty much the same things whether looking at one country's economy or the economy of the whole world. Things that qualify as barriers include all that one might expect: greed, ignorance, arrogance, corruption, war, destruction of the environment, laziness, violence in many forms, prejudice, intolerance, and so on.

Unfortunately, sometimes justifications for the existence of some of these barriers can become incorporated into economic models, theories and policy recommendations. (Even if this occurs despite the best intentions of the theorist, who may not even be aware this is occurring.) Such theories can become widely known, even widely accepted, and even be considered mainstream economic theory. That this is the case in modern macroeconomic theory, I have no doubt. A large part of the motivation behind this book was the hope of being able to address and correct some of what I believe are erroneous conclusions and the harmful policy recommendations supported by such models and theories.

Going back to the idea of labor unit productivity, the definition tells us it can be increased by either decreasing wages or increasing productivity. But these are not equivalent measures. Decreasing wages ultimately decreases demand, and may actually lead to decreased production in both the short and the long run, due to its effect on demand but also on the supply side by its effect on the motivation and mental and physical well-being of the workers. The best way to stay competitive is by increasing productivity and net production of wealth. Net production of

---

35 [For those inclined to think labor is not a form of wealth, one must understand that without labor to build, improve or maintain items of wealth, and without labor having the knowledge and skills to create and maintain whatever it is hired to produce, those items will not be produced. Without spending, the labor will not exist in the form it does. The labor force will never have developed the necessary knowledge and skills to produce what we can produce. And, as such, could never be activated when such production is desired or demanded. Can you imagine a car existing as a useful form of transportation without engineers to design them, or labor to build them or mechanics to maintain and repair them? Spending does pay for the existence of and activation of labor and labor, whether actively occurring or in between jobs, is a form of wealth. Perhaps the most important form of wealth.]

wealth, Wealth produced minus Wealth depleted. Efforts by employers to take on the challenges of being honorable in the way they conduct business may be a little extra work, but can pay off, in the long run, by causing increased productivity. Practices like treating workers well, being ethical in business practices, providing safe working conditions, trying to avoid polluting and destroying the environment, practicing wise stewardship of natural resources, recycling….. all of those practices and the effort needed to implement them, help the world in general by helping prevent or reduce negative externalities and by helping preserve wealth and increase net production. But it also pays off by helping one get more from their employees because they are happier at work, have more job satisfaction, have more belief in their mission, have increased self-esteem, improved confidence, all of which energizes them, and improves their performance and productivity. Keynes might say that by increasing workers enthusiasm it would increase their "animal spirits" (drive and energy).

Opposite to that are people or entities who will use the opportunities of an international economy to focus efforts on reducing costs and increase labor unit productivity by wage suppression, or by other short sighted "cost reduction strategies". These might include such things as allowing or resorting to practices that lead to destruction of the environment, or allowing unregulated and unwise depletion of natural resources, or promoting business practices that increase global warming. They may resort to human rights violations including allowing unsafe labor practices. Such practices are short cuts and may be attractive to those who have a lazy mindset or who are just greedy, and these practices can (for a time) be rewarded. But there are prices to be paid in the long run. Unfortunately, the cost of the negative externalities caused by allowing or resorting to such practices must be borne by all of us.

Along those lines, businesses with monopoly power or who may be seeking to develop or increase monopoly power, or who simply want to keep wages low to maximize economic rent may choose to locate their production in countries which allow or support such poor business practices, including, and perhaps especially, ones that use methods to suppress wages. Such businesses may support political leaders in those countries who will support and allow the continuation of such practices. Not only do businesses and countries that utilize and allow such practices create all these negative externalities, and, as mentioned slow advances in productivity, but suppression of income for those peoples whose average income clusters around the median, will serve to have a negative effect on spending, and especially type one spending, and lead to a relative reduction in worldwide demand as whole, reducing employment, production, and standard of living for the international community as a whole compared to what otherwise might be achieved.

Generally the solution for such situations where the country has become hopelessly corrupt, will be having other countries who support environment regulations and human rights to band together to make such countries and business pay a price for allowing or promoting such business practices. Sanctions can involve tariffs, trade restrictions, fines etc.

You have probably heard or even wondered yourself that if the United States was running a trade deficit of 600 billion dollars wouldn't the country be 600 Billion ahead of the game if they just didn't trade at all? This might be true if the only thing that counts as wealth is the number of dollars we have in our pocket, but this 600 billion dollars is not a measure of wealth in this instance. This 600 billion dollars is a measure of the **difference** in the amount of SPENDING targeted at foreign entities versus the amount of spending targeted at domestic entities. The total amount of spending can be and is far greater than that 600 billion and all of that spending on imports and exports, promotes the production of wealth. You might remember this is what is measured on what is called the Current Account, and that the Current Account is a measure of "direct spending" (which I defined earlier in this book). Therefore, stopping all international trade, stopping all the spending done to pay for imports and exports, would stop all this wealth production spending promotes. The consequences of suddenly and completely stopping all international trade would be unimaginable. This is especially true given how integrated our economies are. Every aspect of our economy would be disrupted. This would not just lead to unemployment and anxiety about the future, but shortages of all things we depend on for our existence, leading ultimately to starvation, riots, disease and death on a mass scale. Many, perhaps most, would not survive it.

So people who think stopping all trade is a good idea, would quickly change their mind if they ever got their way. All that being said, it is of course true that a country would normally rather run a trade surplus, and not want to be a debtor nation, but there is no advantage to achieving that if it is done in a way that cripples the world economy. It is by measuring wealth production and quality of life, overall, for all people in whichever economy or economies one is looking at, by which the implementation of policy recommendations inspired by any economic theory must be judged. For international trade that ultimately means looking at the whole world's economy.

Epilogue

YOU CAN CRYSTALIZE knowledge by getting it right. In other words, if a concept sounds right, has some basis for believing it to be true, but is not fully developed, or has some contradictions and inconsistencies, then it can lead to confusion, and possibly never be fully understood. Such concepts may be more easily disregarded, and the glimpses of understanding, temporarily gained, can be lost or obscured and not lead to a stable foundation for development of further understanding.

Concepts that are more fully developed, that are more objectively true and reflect a more accurate understanding of reality, stand on firmer ground. In such a case our knowledge can be more durable. It is my hope that the understanding of macroeconomics portrayed in this book falls into that category. It is my hope that the material presented in this book can lead to a crystalized objective understanding of the basic tenets of macroeconomics.

APPENDIX A
The Employment Multiplier

THIS IS ADDED to show how to relate the Employment Multiplier Keynes mentioned in "The General Theory" to Keynes' Investment Multiplier. This analysis uses the more restrictive definitions where investment spending is only considered that which is paying for investment goods workers and where consumption spending is directed to the pay of consumption goods workers, like in the chapter titled "Capital Goods". Additionally, similar to the chapter on Keynes' Investment Multiplier, all spending is considered direct spending and the effects of loans are not considered. Consistent with Keynes' theories, this multiplier effect will only occur if the economy is at less than true full employment, that is, there still exists some amount of involuntary unemployment. This the same as recognizing that the economy is in a state where there is inadequate aggregate demand.

Richard Ferdinand Kahn, (1905-1989) who did work on the employment multiplier concept, was a student of, and a collaborator with, Keynes. I take as my starting point the equation from Keynes for the employment multiplier in 'The General Theory':

"$\Delta N = k' \Delta N2$"[36]

I utilize Keynes' wage units and labor units in the analysis. The employment multiplier of Kahn is as follows:

---

36 Keynes, John Maynard. The General Theory of Employment, Interest and Money (Illustrated) (p. 93). Green World Publication. Kindle Edition.

The Employment Multiplier

With Kahn total employment **N = N1+N2**

N is the total employment

N2 is the investment employment, i.e., **N2** would be that amount of employment which is paid directly from the investment spending

N1 is the component of employment paid for by spending other than investment spending, i.e., by consumption spending

For example, if it was a government program that created additional jobs, and all the additional investment went to the wage earners, then that would be the investment employment **N2**, i.e., those particular wage earners.

But usually it is not so simple, so think of **N2** as any employment, wage earners or otherwise that results directly from the investment, whether it be that the investment pays for a worker's entire income or just part of it, that amount of employment which investment pays for is **N2**.

And same with **N1**, any employment paid for by consumption spending is **N1**.

We define the employment multiplier **k'** by this expression

$\Delta N = k' \Delta N2$.

$\Delta N1$ then would be all that **extra** employment that occurred because of consumption spending and would be equal to $\Delta N - \Delta N2$.

$\Delta N1$ is all the extra employment created because of the multiplier effect.

If most of the investment goes places where it creates a lot of high wage employment like say the "financial industry" then the multiplier will be less, because the average income per worker will be greater.

If most of the investment goes to ventures where a lot of lower pay people get employed then the multiplier will be greater, since the average income per employee will be much less. Why? Because people who make a whole lot of money, spend a lower percentage of it on consumption. And people who make less money spend a higher percentage of it on consumption.

Already described was Keynes' investment multiplier **k**, where you increase "investment" and total income increases by the multiplier times investment, i.e., $\Delta Y = k \Delta I$.

The Employment Multiplier

Here you have the employment multiplier where you measure the amount of increased employment caused by investment and determine the total increase in employment as a result, that is, $\Delta N = k' \Delta N2$.

⚜

Another way to analyze this is to try to relate the employment multiplier to the investment multiplier. One can put the quantities **N, N1,** and **N2** used for the employment multiple in terms of quantities used for the investment multiplier if one uses Keynes' definitions:

In Keynes' terms the **N** is not the actual number of employees. It is the number of labor units. The most basic worker is the labor unit and other more skilled workers can be 2 labor units or 4 labor units or 10 labor units. **N, N1 and N2** defined this way become clear.

For those, whose income is paid partially directly from investment and partially from consumption, it is that portion that comes directly from investment that contributes to **N2**, in terms of labor units, and the rest contributes to **N1**, in terms of labor units.

If I hire one basic worker who counts as one labor unit, and half of his pay comes from investment spending, like a government program, and half his pay comes from sales of consumption goods, all paid for by current income, then **N2** increases by 0.5 and **N1** increases by 0.5. In that case total **N** increases by 1.

Two scenarios regarding that **N2** employment:

If they are highly paid investors then that **N2** portion of their income might be worth a thousand labor units since their pay is that much more than a basic work unit, employment might increase by 1000 labor units for just one person... Or the investment might go instead to increasing the employment of regular workers, meaning I could actually hire 1000 people.

In the first case where the effect on **N1** would be less, because the pay of labor units in **N1** comes from spending out of current income, and that rich investor is going to spend a lower fraction of their current income, on the average, than a basic employee. Meaning the multiplier effect, the effect on **N1** will be less when a lot of income goes to that rich investor.

The Employment Multiplier

Whereas, if the investment income goes to 1000 basic labor units, the multiplier effect will be much greater because the propensity to consume of the basic workers will be much greater.

Even though **N2** increases the same in either case, **N1** will increase much more in the second scenario, where the investment money pays for 1000 basic workers.

And total income **N = N1 + N2** will increase more in the second scenario, and with all that extra spending it is much more likely that production will be much greater in the second scenario as well. If production is greater it is likely that net production is greater as well, meaning it is in the second scenario that the total wealth of the society is likely to grow more.

These are the types of analyses one can do by using Keynes' labor unit and wage unit concept. I believe it is rational to assume that in the real world, in the short run, there tends to be a fairly stable distribution of wages. This means using the Keynesian idea of the labor unit to determine total employment levels over the whole economy is also rational, meaning as **N**, the number of labor units employed, increases, the actual number of people employed is also likely to increase, and probably in similar proportions, as regards to income groups.

Let us define **N, N2,** and **N1** as: **N** is total labor units, **N2** as the number of labor units whose pay comes from investment, and **N1** as the rest of labor units, who gain their income from sales paid for by current income.

If **W** is the wage unit corresponding to the wage of a labor unit. then increased investment ΔI is calculated as W times $\Delta N2$. That is, the Wage of each labor unit times the number of labor units will equal the amount of investment spending that caused the income of those particular labor units. In the most universal sense, what one has to mean by a labor unit is any person or fraction of a person (or persons) who are paid the equivalent of one wage unit. The recipients of that spending include anyone given income in the economy during that time period, even if their labor is just being available to be a recipient of a charitable givers' spending, allowing the charitable investment spender to have purchased a good feeling in his heart.

So, using the labor unit and wage one can relate investment spending to $\Delta N2$ by the expression

$\Delta I = W\Delta N2$ Or $\Delta I/W = \Delta N2$

Meaning I have now introduced Keynes' Investment into the employment multiplier formula.

Then one has total **N** related to investment as follows

$$\Delta N = k'\Delta N2 = k'\Delta I/W = k''\Delta I$$

Where **k'** is the employment multiplier. And where $k'' = k'/W$,

This gives a formula for change in employment as it relates to change in investment $\Delta N = k''\Delta I$. And comparing this Keynes' investment multiplier equation $\Delta Y = k\Delta I$, you have the employment (Kahn) multiplier working very much like the investment (Keynes) multiplier.

And in terms of the marginal propensity to consume.

Change in income $\Delta Y =$ (wage unit times $\Delta N) = W\Delta N$. Therefore, the marginal propensity to consume $= \Delta C/\Delta Y = \Delta C/W\Delta N$.

Which fraction is less than 1 because $\Delta C < \Delta Y$. This means that $\Delta C < W\Delta N$ or $\Delta C/W < \Delta N$. This, in essence is saying, the fraction of the income of the newly employed labor unit spent on consumption is less than the amount of the newly employed labor units' total income.

Now the above assumes that the wage unit is to a first approximation not changing significantly compared to amount of employment, which is a short run estimate. If the government spent money on public works, then $\Delta N2$ would equal the labor units directly paid by and employed as a result of the government investment.

And the total increase of employment would be $\Delta N = k'\Delta N2$ would include the labor units in government jobs $\Delta N2$ and the additional labor units in private sector jobs $\Delta N1$ (private sector jobs created as a result of the new government jobs).

APPENDIX B
Spending Directed at Causing Income for an Entity Versus Causing Income for a Human

SPENDING CAN BE directed at and cause income to a human or any entity able to participate in transactions and still count in the total for gross income.

In examining the macroeconomy, one is following the spending of money and its effect. Both individuals and entities owned and run by individuals or groups of individuals are capable of being spenders and recipients of spending, i.e., income earners as a result of that spending. The gross income one is looking at includes all spending. The gross spending that is the total direct spending, includes all direct spending, including spending where they spender and/or recipient is an entity other than an individual.

APPENDIX C
Should the Expression for Savings Be:

"Savings = Net Production"?

IF, IN MACROECONOMICS, savings refers to an increase in wealth, and if, as I have shown, the only part of savings that can increase wealth is net production, then why should I continue to include the preservation of investment money as a component of our definition for savings in the formula Savings equals investment plus net production.

The reason it is important for me to leave in the investment as part of "savings equals investment plus net production" is because many modern economists, going back at least as far as Keynes have accepted the "savings equals investment identity" as fact. Sometimes they say it is always true. Sometimes they like to say that it is an equilibrium point towards which the economy always moves, but always it is believed that, at least eventually, savings will equal investment.

And not only that, but many modern macroeconomists believe that the savings that equals investment is the only savings there is, and that any increase in wealth is accounted for by all or some portion of this savings that is the preservation of investment money.

They are, in essence, saying that the only way wealth increases during a given period of economic activity is that the quantity of money being used for investment spending grows without reducing the amount of the money supply in storage, i.e., the part of the money supply not being used for spending, in the given time period. This could only be true if somehow the current economic activity is causing an increase in the total money supply. This means that all wealth production results from an increase in the money supply caused, not by actions of the Central Bank, but the economic activity itself.

In my model, which I believe gives a true representation of what the variables in Keynes' $Y = I + C$ mean, the savings that equals investment is simply a preservation of the money that was originally put into spending as investment. It is not an increase in wealth. Any increase in wealth comes from net production. This savings that equals investment is not an increase in wealth, nor will it cause an increase in wealth over time.

The question remains, why don't I just make my definition for savings be "Savings = Net Production". Part of me would like to, but the current teaching in economics courses is that 'savings equals investment', with no accounting for net production. As such, I feel if I do not leave the 'savings that is the preservation of investment money' as part of the total accounting of the 'savings that comes out of the given period of economic activity', I will not be able to clearly explain the true place of that part of the savings. I will not be able to explain what it does represent and what it does not represent.

By including investment as part of the expression for total saving, I get to acknowledge that the money used for spending in the given time, will continue to exist at the end of that time period as part of the total wealth, but explain how it is not NEW wealth, and therefore does not in any way change the level of wealth. I get to show how it is only net production that causes any increase or decrease in the level of wealth. This is an important point since many of the "proofs" of various economic concepts rely on the absolute identity of any savings with the amount of investment spending, meaning they do not include any savings that increases wealth, i.e., they do not include net production as part of savings. That belief has led to the formation of many economic models that I believe are incorrect, which have led to policy recommendations that I consider misguided. Perhaps someday macroeconomists will be ready to have the savings formula be "Savings equals Net Production", but today is not that day.

APPENDIX D

KEYNES STATED "INTEREST has been usually regarded as the reward of not-spending, whereas in fact it is, **the reward of not-hoarding**"[37]

This means that he understood at some level what I have stated repeatedly in this book, that putting money in a bank account is spending, not saving. Hoarding in the sense he meant it in this quote is just that, holding onto cash and not even putting it in the bank to draw interest. Not tying up one's money. But in this book, while I have used the word hoarding in several sections, it cannot mean exactly the same thing.

Hoarding in the sense of how Keynes meant it in that quote is literally the stopping of spending, the keeping of ownership of money with one person or entity. Like holding piles of cash somewhere.

But people don't really do that , if they have a lot of cash they usually put it in a bank deposit. When I am referring to hoarding then, I must account for the fact money in the bank has switched ownership and can be further spent. By hoarding what I mean is the propensity to not spend, the tendency or mindset that slows spending **for irrational reasons**, like greed. That means things like not hiring people for a task or a venture, even though one wants the outcome and can afford it. Or not paying people a fair wage for their labor when you do hire someone. Or not taking advantage of promising socially beneficial business opportunities due to miserliness. Not giving to charity.

---

[37] The General Theory of Employment, Interest and Money by John Maynard Keynes, Chapter 13, Section V, Paragraph 1

APPENDIX D

What all this reduced spending does is slow the velocity of money, and, considering it is the poor and middle class who get the short end of the stick when we have reduced demand, the tendency to hoard leads to deficits in the type one direct spending described in chapter 36.

Hoarding tendencies, based on irrational repression of desires, work to slow the velocity of money, even if people put their money into the bank. One could even imagine a situation where demand and incomes got so low that banks would find it difficult or impossible to find any borrowers. In such a case, the interest they could pay on deposits would be so low that for the depositors there was not much difference in holding cash or keeping money in a bank. The money would then have close to a zero velocity.

If there are ways to speed up the spending of those people who have a "propensity to hoard", especially if that spending leads to increased direct spending, especially type one direct spending, that increased speed of spending will increase aggregate direct spending demand and stimulate the economy.

APPENDIX E

NOW I HAVE no doubt that there are people out there who don't like my definition of direct spending. Not that I have described the concept as being that part of spending that works to directly cause wealth production. The problem they would have with this is how many things I describe as wealth. They probably don't like that I include things like many forms of charity, or government transfers as part of the direct spending. This is, I assume, because they think that, even though it may be nice to have those outcomes that spending causes, they should not really be considered wealth.

Actually there is a very easy way to fix this "flaw" and allow my model to stand unaltered and still not upset those people's sensibilities. People should select those things they do not wish to be considered wealth and just assume the (what I would still call) direct spending that caused those things to exist does not directly cause any increase in total wealth. If the example is charitable spending or government transfers, the recipients of that spending would still have that money to be used for further spending, and that further spending may cause the creation of things those people **would** consider as adding to total wealth. But the actual transfer of ownership of money that we call the charitable spending or government transfers would not be considered to have caused any change in the total wealth of the economy directly. In other words, that spending has led to outcomes, but these outcomes would not have to be considered as adding to (or subtracting from) total wealth.

APPENDIX E

Please contact me at danbrightec@gmail.com with any questions, comments or criticism

I look forward to engaging in dialogue about this material with anyone who desires to, to the extent that life circumstances allow

12/1/20

www.ingramcontent.com/pod-product-compliance
Lightning Source LLC
Chambersburg PA
CBHW060417300426
44111CB00018B/2875